# AN ENCOUNTER OF PERIPHERIES

# An Encounter of Peripheries

*Santals, Missionaries, and their Changing Worlds, 1867–1900*

MARINE CARRIN
HARALD TAMBS-LYCHE

MANOHAR
2008

First published 2008



ISBN 81-7304-755-3

*Published by*
Ajay Kumar Jain for
Manohar Publishers & Distributors
4753/23 Ansari Road, Daryaganj
New Delhi 110002

*Typeset by*
Ajay Arts
Delhi 110006

*Printed at*
Lordson Publishers Pvt. Ltd.
Delhi 110007

# Contents

# Acknowledgements

This book is the product of a marriage. It was through our meeting at the South Asia Conference in Leyden that Marine decided to come to Norway to have a look at the vast collection of Santal texts, collected by the missionary Olaf Bodding, that is kept in the Oslo University library. This was in 1976. She had done fieldwork on the Santals, and was working on her thesis. Harald, too, was working on India, having begun a twenty-year stint of research in Gujarat in 1973.

By 1987 Marine came to Norway again, and by 1992 we were living together in France. It was about this time that the idea of the book was conceived. The vast amount of cultural research done by Bodding on the Santals and the role of the Santal Mission in the history of that people fascinated Marine. Her meeting with Olaf Hodne, himself a missionary of the Santal mission but also a writer and an intellectual, inspired her further to explore the Mission's history. Harald had never thought of working on missionaries. From a typical intellectual background, growing up on a research station, and from an atheist family, he had no links at all to Christian organizations. But he went to school in a rural area, and the Mission loomed large in the local world view. Skrefsrud, the founder of the Santal Mission, 'the apostle to the Santals', was a central figure in the picture painted of Norwegian history and identity. For Harald, then, working on the Santal Mission was a voyage of discovery into a country recognized but largely unknown.

While Marine's work among the Santals provided the necessary background to the book, the specific research we did together mainly concerned archival sources. Staff at the Manuscript Collection of the Oslo University library, at the University libraries of Gothenburg and Uppsala, at the Stadsbiblioteket, Aarhus, and at the British library (formerly the Indian Office Library), and at the library of SOAS, all helped us at different times, and we thank them all. The same applies to the library of the Centre d'Etudes de l'Inde et de l'Asie du Sud in Paris, where Sylvie Adamo has been particularly helpful.

Discussion with a large number of colleagues—too many to mention individually over a period of some fifteen years—have helped us greatly, and, as the book grew into shape, several colleagues helped us by commenting on chapters or getting to grips with particular problems. Jan Hultin's invitation to give a seminar at Gothenburg and the particularly warm welcome we received there, crucially helped in getting the work off the ground. Important, too, were invitations from Jarle Simensen in Trondheim and Örnulf Gulbrandsen in Bergen. Hans Hadder has been a constant aide, getting references and photocopying material for us, while Harald's long discussions with his brother-in-law Knut Odner has been extremely seminal for the perspectives on Norway. Knut Ramberg kindly gave us his excellent history of Lillehammer's main newspaper, the importance of which will be evident from the account we have given. In Denmark, Peter Andersen and Santosh Soren have been of great help.

In France, we are greatly indebted to our colleagues at the Centre d'Anthropologie, Toulouse: Daniel Fabre, Jean-Pierre Albert, Marlène Albert-Llorca, Dominique Blanc, Agnes Fine, and Djallal Heuzé, among others. Hinnerk Brühns, responsible for the Franco-German Research Agreement helped us finance our first voyage to the various Scandinavian archives. Among other French colleagues, Catherine Clementine-Ojha has been a great help. Her invitation to participate in a special number of the Archives des Sciences Sociales des Religions made us draw the strands together and greatly advanced the work. Gérard Toffin and Gisèle Krausskopff invited Marine to show our work at Nanterre, again providing valuable criticism.

Peter Robb helped us navigate colonial history, read some chapters, and provided constructive criticism. Among other British scholars, we should like to mention Avril Powell and David Hardiman. In India, David Oommen helped us in Bangalore, while discussions with Geoff Oddie in Sydney and Robert Frykenberg in Madison have been a great help and inspiration. To all these, and to the large number of people not mentioned who have shared generously their time and ideas, our most heartfelt thanks.

Anybody writing in this line is in evident debt to Jean and John Comaroff's pioneering work, a debt we would like to acknowledge here.

A special thanks to Ramesh Jain of Manohar, who, when several publishers had considered and rejected the book as either too specialized or too general, simply said: 'We will publish it'. Thanks, too, for the professional and very agreeable contribution of the Manohar editorial team.

None of all these, of course, share any responsibility for the shortcomings of the book. We have tried to cover a vast field, and we hope that the perspectives gained by this approach will compensate for the inevitable inaccuracies.

MARINE CARRIN
HARALD TAMBS-LYCHE

# 1

# Rethinking the World from Two Peripheries

In the nineteenth century links were forged between people living very different lives in various parts of the world. What brought them together was colonialism, a term that implies a distinction between an active, colonizing Western world and its colonized, passive subjects. New perspectives on the colonial encounter (Brimnes 1999) modify this perspective, stressing the active role of the subjects in the construction of a new order.

We deal here with a colonial frontier, a tribal people—the Santals—beyond the direct control of British India, and their encounter with missionaries from Scandinavia, on the periphery of Europe. Thus we describe a meeting not between centre and periphery, but between two peripheries. Skrefsrud, the founder of the Santal Mission, came from the Norwegian countryside, a peasant milieu barely touched by modernizing forces: his desire to convert the heathen may indeed be seen as a product of these influences. In some ways, the Santals were as close to modernity as he was: both worked as the first generation in modern industry. The railway, symbolically significant here, came to Bengal and to Norway in the same year—1854.

Yet Skrefsrud and his associates were part of the colonial set-up, and the power dimension of implanting a mission in Santal country is obvious. In this colonial encounter, the missionaries saw themselves as representatives of progress, of civilization—a cornerstone of the missionary myth. We deal here with the construction of this myth. Our story centres on a mission, but is not meant to be missionary history. As a narrative genre, such histories necessarily focus on conversion and—in some cases—the lack of success. Like the Comaroffs (1991, 1992) we use missionary history as a vantage point to study a cultural encounter framed by the colonial situation, with the missionary central to the meeting of cultures, rather than an agent for Christianity. Missionaries represent here the nodes of a series of cultural influences that act on them and through them, consciously or unconsciously, so that the question of agency cannot be reduced to their actions alone. But our story is different from that of the Comaroffs, and our missionaries do not appear simply as the conscience of the colonial enterprise.

The Santal Mission was independent, not bound to a missionary society, a particular country or Church. Its missionaries tried to create a Santal National Church combining Christianity with what was seen as the best in Santal culture, implying a conscious, if ultimately unsuccessful effort to provide some agency to the Santals themselves.

This may be why the Mission created a veritable storehouse of texts on Santal folklore. They are found not only in Bodding's voluminous production (esp. 1925-9) but also, unpublished and in even greater numbers, in the manuscript archives of the Oslo University Library. Written by Santal collaborators, these texts offer more than a glimpse into Santal views of the missionaries and of the Christian and colonial influence. This and other sources, added to Marine Carrin's fieldwork among Santals (Christians but especially non-Christians in different regions) enable us to explore the Santal response to the encounter and construct the Santals as subjects. Carrin's knowledge of Santali is crucial here. Unlike O'Hanlon (1988) we feel that the work of recovering the subject is both worthwhile and feasible whenever sources can be found. We think, like Ingold (1996), that individualism characterizes many pre-modern societies and is not an eighteenth-century European invention: that position, once held by Dumont (1966), seems to us to confuse the history of Western philosophy with anthropological theory. On the missionary side, Harald Tambs-Lyche's Scandinavian background provides a reading of the correspondence between the missionaries and the converted and their main supporters in Scandinavia, as well as literature on the mission and its founders. The missionaries became legendary figures in their lifetime and remained so well into the twentieth century.

The exchange of ideas that constitutes the main thread of our account is not confined to the Santals and the missionaries' homelands. The missionaries were trained in Berlin and set out from there; they developed links with the Baptist mission in Bengal, and other British Evangelicals; their first support came from this British Indian milieu, which extended to England and Scotland; later, they developed a network of supporters in the three Scandinavian countries which, in the 1890s, spread to Norwegian migrants in America. An extensive exchange of letters documents the network, as the missionaries travelled to these countries and received visits from them in the Mission Field. Such links are retrievable, but there are also other influences and events that must have been important. What exactly did Skrefsrud discuss with co-members of his Masonic lodge in Calcutta? He only states, later, that the contacts were useful. Clearly, though mail and travel was slower then than now, this did not prevent our actors from maintaining widespread networks.

The picture emerging from this mesh of contacts and ideologies leads us to agree with the critics of Orientalism (Said 1978). Said's view, that Orientalist discourse produces the East as the inferior Other of the West, conflates a number of discordant discourses and masks the contradictions between them (Moore-Gilbert 1997: 40-53). To view all Westerners in the East as involved in creating a specific view of the 'Orient' is too simple (Oddie 1999). There were different Orients, different kinds of knowledge, and different agendas: and these different agendas wrought contradictions among colonizers and colonized, as well as between them. A persistent trend in contemporary Indian historiography is to show Indian agency in the colonial encounter (Zastoupil and Moir 1999: 1-72; Brimnes 1999, Viswanathan Peterson 2003; Fox Young 2003); another is to stress the active role of subalterns as well as elites (Guha 1983; P. Chatterjee 1993; Haynes and Prakash 1991, Dube 1998). One element in our work is precisely to stress the agency of the Santals, in their encounter with the missionaries.

Our missionaries, like many others, made themselves 'advocates' of the culture they encountered, in which others saw little value. Our missionaries clearly partook of a 'civilizing mission' (Comaroff and Comaroff 1991, 1992), yet were also drawn to the ideal of innocence, making the noble savage a better candidate for salvation than his civilized counterpart. Oddie's view, that missionaries saw the main dichotomy not as 'Europe versus the Orient but the saved versus the damned' is, however, too simple (1999: 180-1). Our missionaries' respect for their converts' culture is framed by their own precepts, which again are not simply 'Western' but a particular variant of European values.

Pointing to the parallel between the home and overseas missions, Oddie states: 'The proclamation of the Gospel was necessary in Europe as well as in the Orient' (1999: 181). Our missionaries would have agreed with this view, current among Evangelicals at the time, which must be seen in the context of the new class structure the nineteenth century had created. The industrial working class was then a recent phenomenon, moulded into shape in Britain in the first half of the century, but the heterogeneous middle classes were equally new and filling a new place. A relationship fundamental to our theme was emerging between the two classes, where middle class and evangelical ideas merged in an effort to integrate the working class into a new kind of moral community. A tripartite class structure emerged in Britain, with the aristocracy, the middle class and the 'popular classes' forming the shifting alliances that, for Bédarida, explains the relative stability of Britain in the nineteenth century (1990: 117-19). For the missionaries in this study, fighting against promiscuity or alcoholism was part of the same crusade against sin, whether in Norway or Santal country.

What is often forgotten when missionary activity is conflated with colonialism, as Said (1978) does, is that many missionaries came from the lower classes and shared the reservations of subalterns with regard to those in power, at home or abroad. They were a 'dominated fraction' of the colonizers (Comaroff and Comaroff 1992: 203). A recurring theme in this study is the efforts missionaries made to escape that domination. Becoming a missionary was also a career. Missionary activity is part of the colonial experience, but the colonial world was as rich in contrasts and contradictions as any other period. As the Comaroffs put it: 'colonialism did (and does) not exist in the singular, but in a plurality of forms and forces' (1992: 211).

A dimension that stands out is the legendary character of many of the events narrated here. Missionary careers lend themselves to emplotment into hagiographical texts: their lives become legendary;[1] the subjects themselves were clearly aware of this. Skrefsrud, for one, was one who succeeded in tailoring much of his activity to suit the myth. But as we get to know other characters, he becomes less exceptional than we may think. In the late nineteenth century adventure was eminently possible and sometimes, perhaps, unavoidable. The idea of social mobility, the scope for advancing in society, is extremely strong during our period, as reflected by writers as different as Samuel Smiles and John Stuart Mill (Bédarida 1990: 85-9)—or, indeed, Charles Dickens. Though the statistical significance of such mobility cannot be established, the number of individual cases is great, and missionary careers are prominent among them.

For many, the colonial experience was indeed an adventure. The Raj was an opening of India to European influences and ideas; and though there were influences in the opposite direction, most were incarnate in Western personalities. For the British, the 'imagined community' (Anderson 1983) was an England seen in relation to its empire (Stoler and Cooper 1997: 22; Burton 1994: 33-41); for Scandinavians, this was less true. The empire, to them, was a foreign country: the few Danish colonies had not forged an imperial consciousness comparable to that of Britain or even France. Yet, and not least through their maritime activity, Scandinavians were not strangers to the colonial world. The empire was not their possession, but they freely moved in it and took it for granted as part of their life world.[2]

Santals also moved widely in the empire, emigrating to such far-off places as Mauritius. Yet few were in a position to enact their own myth, more so as the 'creation of difference' (Metcalfe 1995) transformed the colonial encounter in the second half of the nineteenth century. Between Scandinavians and Santals too, difference increased. The idea of a 'Santal National Church' may have been optimistic by 1877, when we first hear of it: twenty years later it had become impossible—as the missionaries were no longer trusting the Santals with even a limited degree of autonomous authority.

Skrefsrud viewed the Santals as a nation with a distinct culture to be respected, a view that derives ultimately from Herder. His view of the language, which he worked to develop and give a written form, clearly forms part of his Norwegian heritage. Both differ from the way Evangelical missionaries in southern Africa saw their peoples (Comaroff and Comaroff 1992), and which comes much closer to the trope Spurr calls negation (1993). The recognition of Santal culture modifies the opposition between barbarianism and civilization, as if the Norwegian was only too aware of coming from a nation itself struggling to have its culture and language recognized. There is, certainly, a strain of imperial rhetoric in the way our missionaries describe the Santals, but there is also an undercurrent stressing the similarity of the European and the Asian periphery in relation to Empire. At least in the early phase of the Mission, this parallel influences their work.

Our mission was certainly, like that of the London Missionary Society (LMS) among the southern Tswana, part of 'dominant, world-transforming processes' (Comaroff 1992: 33). But if both were part of imperialism, they were differently situated in relation to the 'grand imperial design'. 'Colonial evangelism' was not a single phenomenon, as missionary enterprises sprung from different strains of Christian policy in their countries of origin. As Oddie notes for Bengal, the various 'evangelical' missions—whether low-church Anglican or non conformist—tended to see themselves in opposition to the LMS, the Society for the Propagation of the Gospel in Foreign Parts (SPG), and other 'high-church' organizations (1999). This was not just a theological distinction, but also a matter of social and cultural difference, not unrelated to class or the stake each group had in the overall power scheme. Some organizations were effectively the missionary arm of the national orthodox church, as the LMS and the SPG largely were in England. Others represented highly controversial positions in their own country. In the colonial scheme, they had different roles to play.

As Kipling shows so well, colonial expansion was not simply a machine grinding its way into virgin territory. Rather, the various colonial frontiers were, like Santal country, the domain of adventurers who were busy with their own designs though they paved the way for more orderly expansive policies. Not all missionaries in British India played such a role: ours did for several years—until the colonial order caught up with them. That point is roughly where our story ends.

We shall deal more fully with these strategies. What we wish to underline is the complexity of their links to the colonial enterprise. And this enterprise itself was very different, in India, from what it was in Africa. India could never become a colony in the full sense of the term; from the start the British were aware of the necessity to govern India with the use of local institutions of governance. Thus the colonial system could not be reduced to two opposing sides, the colonists and the colonized. Tribal populations, such as the Santals, and evangelical missionaries united in opposition to the Hindu majority. At times, they sought the support of the colonial government against the common enemy, a constellation which is important in explaining whatever success the Mission had.

The missionaries were not trying to recreate 'the British yeomanry of yore' (Comaroff and Comaroff 1992: 37), but rather the kind of low-church community they knew from their own background. Unlike the Tswana, the Santals were a subaltern group suffering the intrusion and domination of others. The structural position of our missionaries, then, is like that of the mission to the interior in Western countries: the missionaries defend 'their' people without challenging the overall system. This theme is persistent in efforts at juridical reform, and struggles against alcohol and usury, prostitution and other forms of integration into the new economic system at the lowest level. To say as the Comaroffs do about the LMS in Southern Africa, that their 'tools and tropes' (1992: 37) make the missionary activities metonymic expressions of advancing capitalism, would be too simple in our case. But then, others were responsible for these economic and technical changes in Colonial Bengal. There is a parallel to the efforts of Verrier Elwin in later years, to isolate tribal groups from the impact of a degenerate civilization. The showcase for this was to have been the colony that the missionaries founded in Assam. To alleviate land hunger, they leased large tracts of land for cultivation and led the migration of thousands of converts. This represented an effort to help the Santals, but also to delimit and isolate a Christian community which would be impermeable to heathen as well as capitalist influence. In the long run, however, the colony became more and more like the neighbouring tea gardens. In the end, then, the example underwrites the Comaroffs' view that the motivation of social practice, and the pulse of collective forces, are different matters, and that the second tend to prevail (1992: 36). Yet the dialectics of the situation are clearly different from the African case.

These may be seen as differing fragments in the complex totality that is the colonial encounter. Viewed from India, the encounter is particularly complex, and the inequality of the parties perhaps less marked than in most parts of the colonial world. The most striking difference between the colonial experience of India and southern Africa is that the cultural impact of the West is much more limited in India. Settler colonialism, central to the South African situation, remains a secondary element in India—even in Bengal, where the 'planters' did have an influence. The Government of Bengal, throughout the period, saw itself as ruling on behalf of its Indian as well as its British subjects, even if the concern for Indians remained paternalist. To an important extent, the building of the colonial system in India is as much a matter of internal colonization by dominant Indian groups as of British colonization of the latter. In the end it was Hinduism and caste society, as much as colonial forces, that became the major external influence on Santal culture and society.

Looking at Santal history over the last hundred and fifty years, one realizes that it has been determined by oppositions within India rather than between India and the West. These oppositions are however complex, for the Santals themselves distinguish between the *maran diku (big foreigner)*—rajas, brahmins, dominant castes, moneylenders and others seen as exploiting the Santals—and the *hurin diku (small foreigners)* who, while part of Hindu society, are exploited like themselves. For the Santals, then, the colonial encounter is one with multiple opponents, all tending to impinge on Santal cultural, economic, and social autonomy. The role that the missionaries play as a fragment of Santal history is different from the role of missions in the global context. Sometimes the missionary impact sides with Santal autonomy, while at other times it represents foreign domination.

Thus we need to review the role of missionaries in the colonial period and also to question that totality itself. Colonial expansion was one of the main processes of the late nineteenth century world, but not the only one. Subalternist historians and literary critics have tended to represent colonialism through Foucaultian perspectives of power and discourse, combined with a Saidian reading of them, to create a disappointing analysis for the anthropology of colonialism, since it tends to mask the multiple voices of the colonial encounter. We must be wary of this tendency to concentrate on one master narrative (Sivaramakrishnan 1999: 78). If we wish to build a viable ethnography of that period, we must be open to multiple totalities and to various possible emplotments for the historical events. Thus for the Santals the main event of that period is the rebellion of 1855. It may well be seen as framed by the colonialism against which it fought, but we must also ask what happened in Santal society to make mass mobilization possible. Thus Guha (1983) tends to see the rebellion in reactive terms, as an emotive and ritualized assertion of identity, but he does not really ask what dynamic factors were active among the Santals themselves. Migration, expansion, and containment in relation to land were some of these factors, accounting for important events in Santal history.

As for the evangelical missionaries, it is not obvious that the religious revival which produced them, can most readily be accounted for by colonial expansion. Other revolutionary changes occurred: for instance, it is difficult to overestimate the importance of popular literacy. Santal land hunger and popular hunger for knowledge in Europe are just examples of central themes, each in their own context, which have considerable autonomy in relation to the colonial encounter. More generally, colonial knowledge did not develop according to a single scheme. 'European ideas about nature, for example, were caught up in the rivalry between the Cartesian fascination with classificatory science and the romantic sensibility' (Sivaramakrishnan 1999: 78), and this was even more true with regard to religious ideas. As for colonial knowledge, we must account for its own historicity: it was constantly transformed to serve in changing political contexts.

Our point here is methodological rather than empirical: the chosen context for our events largely determine our interpretation of them, and, inversely, we must be prepared to change the context when another interpretation imposes itself. History does not exist prior to interpretation, it is the interpretations that make history (de Certeau 1975).

The particularity of ethnography, in history as well as in contemporary fieldwork, is the endeavour to understand different people's life world in their own terms. In order to understand in equal measure, the lived-in worlds of Santal and Norwegian peasants, converts to the Hinduized Kherwar sect among the former as well as Evangelicals among the latter, as well as Scottish freechurchmen, Norwegian Lutherans in America, or the enigmatic Grundtvigian movement in Denmark each in their own context, we must start by putting them on equal terms. It makes no sense to regard one such life world as more real than another. From that point of view, the striking fact of the late nineteenth century is the mobility of ideas, the geographical extent of networks, the number of encounters between people whose ancestors never met. To grasp what emerging colonial power relationships do and mean to all these people, we must see them in the subject's own terms.[3]

Dealing with multiple situations and numerous individuals in this way, one is confronted with fragments looking for a plot. Weber, in his essay on the Protestant ethic, did the opposite: he looked for typical fragments to incarnate his plot, the plot being the ideal type. Weber's method suits a particular approach to history; our approach is a loan from anthropology used to relativize historical generalizations. This is what is done in micro-history (Revel (ed.)

1996, Robb 2000). As anthropologists we do ethnography first and then emplot the findings historically: we do not read the ethnographic material as an expression of history.

We start with a small number of people limited in space and time, with three pioneer missionaries and their converts. They took part in an encounter that was eminently colonial, but was not *the* colonial encounter. It was constituted by social situations[4] that brought together various strains contributing to the production of meaning. Such meetings are to be seen simultaneously as events that link multiple pasts with the described present. In social space as well as in time, they are the fragments that must be ordered with reference to a totality, while the links point outward to the multiple totalities which invest the fragments with sense.

In principle, the fragments chosen for any plot are as arbitrary as the plots chosen to give sense to the fragments. The anthropologist—and the historian—must make a methodological choice here, to avoid producing something like the 'new novels' of modernist French literature—rather than the historical anthropology we set out to write. Our choice, then, has been to start with the fragments, then sift them while searching for specific types of links. The links we have chosen are those that form networks[5] constituted by social relationships. The totality that frames our narrative reaches its limits where the links fade into insignificance. This is why our story takes us from the highlands of Central India and Calcutta to Scandinavia, Britain, Germany and the American Midwest—a veritable global network.

Networks are meaningless unless something is communicated across the links, and here we have privileged the flow of ideas. Many of these ideas fit an overall perspective which we may identify with evangelicalism: but this is itself a fuzzy entity, formed by loyalties and friendships that may cross the boundaries of faith and confession, while serious splits develop between people who share the same theological foundation.

But relationships only make sense in opposition to non-relations, and ideas to their opposites. Often, people in our story get together because they share the need to distance themselves from a third party, or merge their ideas—which may later prove incompatible—to oppose other views. Thus a network with its flow of ideas cannot be the whole story: there are also boundary markers, though their role here is as background rather than as plot.

Missionaries were, of course, not the only individuals to be highly mobile at the time: it was an age of migration, abounding in cosmopolitan settings. Missionaries in Calcutta came from different countries and social classes: so did the people one would meet in the seamen's quarters of the world's ports, or in most of the places to which large-scale migration took place.

Yet missionaries also differed over doctrine. The splintered nature of Protestantism implies that Protestants, at no time or place, speak with one voice or share one common world view. The theological debates, to which we shall return, are not relegated to a closed universe of religious specialists, apart from the 'real' world. They reflect or express social oppositions, of class, ethnicity, or nationality, of debates concerning moral and political issues. Protestant missionaries, then, do not form a group but only a category of personnel sometimes working at cross-purposes though sharing a common project of evangelizing the world.

In all the Protestant countries, theological debate was grounded in the class structure. In eighteenth-century Britain, there is the image of the 'sandwich', in which official Anglicanism unites high and low, situating the dissenters in the middle—an image upheld by the number of dissenters among the industrial entrepreneurs that formed the new middle class. This pattern grows more complicated in the nineteenth century, as Methodism—especially the Primitive Methodists—recruited mainly from the new working class, while the Evangelical revival within Anglicanism gives it a solid, low-church, base in the new middle classes (Bédarida 1990: 133). In Germany and Scandinavia, too, the situation is complex even though a basic tendency relates High Church tendencies to an elite and to older middle-class elements while Low Church and Evangelical movements tend to be associated with upward mobility within the working and new middle classes. The changes in class structure and the intense religious activity that characterize the nineteenth century imply, however, a high degree of religious and social mobility for many of the individuals we describe, and certainly for our main persona, Skrefsrud and the Börresens.

While congregations differed widely in their views on salvation and other theological tropes, however, Evangelicals had a lot in common. One main theme transcends the division between colonizer and colonized. Work among the 'dark' masses at home and that among the equally dark heathen were seen as part of the same global enterprise (Thorne 1997). It is typical that Börresen was shocked, on his return to Denmark, to find that trains were running on sundays, and that many would be Christians accepted this 'heathen' practice. His reaction was immediately recognized and classified, in Denmark, as the view of the Home Mission, as opposed to the liberals who also supported the Mission. Here, as elsewhere, we find our missionaries caught between several competing rhetorical tropes.

At the same time, the links between home and colony are stronger than these divisions, for the Mission's supporters also engaged, albeit in different ways, in propagating Christianity at home. The difference between liberals and the Mission of the Interior was largely one of class. The liberals were particularly effective among the middle classes, urban and rural: the Mission of the Interior worked among the labouring poor. As Thorne puts it, in Britain 'the missionaries deployed by organizations like the Lancashire itinerant society were arguably the most visible bourgeois presence in the working-class community for most of the first half of the nineteenth century' (1997: 239-40), while in Norway and Denmark this remained true at least till socialism became an issue, in the last decades of the century. In Scandinavia as in Britain the discursive practices and organizational structures of the Evangelicals 'comprised the principal occasions . . . on which the respectable classes in Britain came into contact with the poor' (Thorne 1997: 240).

John Stuart Mill, who was no evangelical, drew a parallel between the savage and the lower classes: both were unable to subordinate nature to culture, or primal desires to rational and moral thought (Spurr 1993: 159). The power to sacrifice present desire to a distant object is equally absent in 'savages, in soldiers and sailors, and in a somewhat less degree in nearly the whole of the poorer classes in this and many other countries', he said (Mill 1874: 50). This theme will emerge in our missionaries' comments on the Santals.

Yet the proselytizing activities at home also brought the heathen to the gaze of the masses. Literature on foreign missions became popular reading, in Scandinavia as in Britain, though with a certain time lag which generally fits the lag in industrialization. In the 1860s, when missionary ardour was diminishing in Britain, it increased strongly in Denmark and Norway. 'The attractions of foreign missionary intelligence', says Thorne, 'were considerable in an age before alternative means of enlightenment, entertainment, and even assembly were widely available. This was particularly true of public missionary meetings at which audiences were treated to a foreign missionary's eyewitness account of travels and battles among the heathen' (Thorne 1997: 239). This was a genre in which Skrefsrud excelled and his meetings drew the masses wherever he went. The enthusiasm he raised was fuelling the home efforts of his colleagues, as well as raising funds for the mission.

What of the Santals? They certainly were not a 'people without history'. In 1855 they had risen in rebellion against the British—the most important resistance to colonial domination, in fact, before the 1857 'mutiny'. Though they were crushed, the rebellion proved conclusively their capacity for organized resistance. They rebelled against Hindu landlords and moneylenders as well as the British, and were not naïve about the realities of colonial exploitation. Their culture attests to long-term contact with Hindu civilization, though their distinctiveness makes it impossible to see these influences as instances of assimilation. We know, too, that their presence in the Santal Parganas, where our missionaries met them, was recent: they had settled there around 1830, encouraged by the British, who admired their capacity for clearing the forests. The depopulation of Bengal after the 1770 famine had opened large tracts of the plains to tribal populations from the foothills to the west. The repopulation of the plains led to a double movement, tribal people either becoming landless labour or retreating to the hills (Bose 1993). This may explain the desire for new land that led to Santal colonization of the Santal Parganas, and which is only one link in a long chain of migratory movements. It is not easy to reconstruct a coherent narrative of migrations from Santal tradition, but the importance of the migration in shaping Santal identity is clear.

Though much of this history is necessarily sketchy, we know enough to realize that the Santals, like other tribes, were not simply hidden in the jungle until discovered by colonialism, but that contact and conflict between tribes and plains Hindus had a long history. Thus Santal distinctiveness as it exists today is not a colonial creation; Santals must have been concerned with maintaining a distinct identity for centuries.

Santals share important elements of this identity, however, with other groups speaking languages of the Northern Munda family. Thus Santal people are, and must long have been, conscious of their cultural links to the Munda, the Ho, the Kharia, the Bhumij and the Birhor, though modern political links between these populations only began to take form around 1910. Thus neither the identities of these groups, nor the distinction between 'tribe' and 'caste',[6] are colonial creations, as Bates (1995) would have it—though colonial developments may have reified or strengthened existing cultural contrasts (Bayly 1995).

There is indeed a danger of fetishizing cultural difference, though this, persistently in our case, is what the actors themselves tend to do. Skrefsrud's interest in the Santal language and culture induced him to isolate 'his' people from other tribal groups as well as from caste society. He seems to have aimed at mapping exhaustively a mental territory, an enterprise resembling what the compilers of the numerous 'catalogues' of 'Tribes and Castes' set out to do. The similarity of these two approaches emerges clearly from Skrefsrud's answers to Risley's ethnological questionnaire, intended precisely for the production of such a catalogue.[7] Here we see the missionary ethnographer stereotyping culture to a general classificatory scheme, while in his correspondence he underlines the unique character of the Santals, and deploys this specificity in context: honest, brave and hard-working, the Santals are the stuff of which good evangelical Christians are made.

Both missionaries and Santals speak with many voices in different contexts, and their dialogue dissolves into several distinct discourses. This dialogic perspective (Bakhtin 1981) is real enough, as shown by the Santal texts in the archives, and by the *Mare Hapram ko Reak Katha*,[8] a compilation of Santal customs written by Skrefsrud as an interview with Kolean Guru.

What does the encounter between missionaries and tribal groups in the hill tracts of Bihar in the late nineteenth century tell us about cultural processes at the time? As indicated, what fascinates us is how the analysis takes us across a large part of the globe. In terms of current anthropological debate, then, globalization is nothing new, and 'culture' is not easily cut into bounded, national or regional 'cultures', though boundaries were integral to the constructions of our protagonists.

We see our work as more than the story of a particular encounter between missionaries and an indigenous people. Foreign missions were a major element of popular culture in Europe at the time, and part of the spirit of an age heavily inspired by Evangelical ideals (Bebbington 1989, Thorne 1997). Their interest in the missionary enterprise brought the masses of the colonizing countries close to the colonial encounter itself. Missionaries may not always have acted as the 'conscience' of colonialism, but they certainly played a part in legitimizing the colonial enterprise among those who did not themselves profit from it directly. This was perhaps even more true in countries that played a secondary role in colonial conquest. Yet the nineteenth century was not only the apogee of colonialism, but also of emergent nationalism in Europe, and the discourses wrought by this process profoundly influenced our missionaries, producing a respect for indigenous culture unusual in such encounters.

This respect does not, however, affect the unequal relation between the missionary as colonizer and the Santals as colonized, for the latter remain the object of a foreign project. At the same time the missionary enterprise entered directly into the complex relations between the colonized: there was an endeavour to support the Santals against economic, political and cultural encroachment from the Hindu majority. While this defence of the Santals was linked to the missionaries' efforts to isolate their field of conversion from competing influences, the result was a strengthening of Santal ethnic identity and a sense of separateness from the Hindu fold. The missionaries tried hard to drive a wedge between 'their' tribals and the majority population, but they did not create the difference. The Santals were already, as their rebellion in 1855 shows, contesting intrusion and exploitation from outsiders. The relative success of the missionary enterprise, was partly due to the way many Santals saw the missionaries as fitting their own designs for the future. This does not mean that the Christian Santals were to realize the dreams of a better Santal future. Like other players on the colonial scene, they were caught in the webs of a consciousness that was partial.

As anthropologists, we are aware of a double emplotment. As Weber wrote, an event only becomes action through the interpretation of its actor. Life worlds cannot be observed, they must be inferred. Skrefsrud creates his own myth, and so do his Santal counterparts. As anthropologists, we enter at a second level, to emplot the actors' myth into a wider perspective of cultural exchange, taking care not to lose the specificity of the actor's view: it is the understanding we gain of the several actors who constitute, as it were, the archive of the historical anthropologist (Comaroff and Comaroff 1992: 34) and not the sources themselves. The latter are trapped in their own modalities,[9] whether administrative rhetoric or missionary hagiography. We need to disentangle motives from modalities and to re-emplot the reconstructed subjectivity within the larger context. Missionary letters constitute a particular genre. One is defined by being destined for publication in the missionary journals. Here, the intentional subjectivity of the letter form merges with the need to inform, entertain, and influence the journal readership. Other letters enter into the project of network-building: convincing the other in order to make him a true ally. The letters provide us with the closest access to the life-world of the missionaries. On the Santal side, the only comparable window to their life-world is found, on and between the lines, in the archive of Santal texts in Oslo University library. Though they aim at informing the missionaries about Santal custom and folklore, close reading reveals an effort at responding to missionary influence, saying, in effect, that Santals have their own culture—an affirmation that also implies a reformulation of Santal culture.

In the various life worlds of our persona, fiction is as important as fact. 'Historical situations', says Hayden White, 'do not have built into them intrinsic meaning in the way that literary texts do' (1978: 85) and, he continues, 'they are rendered comprehensible by being subsumed under the categories of the plot structure in which they are encoded as a story of a particular kind' (White 1978: 86). Or, as the Comaroffs put it, events are constructed fragments of a totality. These totalities are themselves constructed, not just from the elements that enter into them, but equally from 'the construct from which the silence and spaces between events are filled, through which disjointed stories are cast into master narratives' (1997: 17). This, then, is the historical imagination. In our story, events taking place in Norway, Denmark, Britain, or America, are deployed to lend meaning to the encounter between missionaries and Santals. Skrefsrud, in his correspondence, uses emblematic signs of the jungle to render the Mission attractive to Western supporters. Santal converts are invited to participate in this process, writing to Western correspondents, more insidiously making them participate in the highly motivated discourse of the missionaries. Power, in this semantic space, is defined by the ability to include the others' story in one's own plot. Here lies one source of inequality in the colonial encounter, for the missionaries have access to plots that range much wider than those known to the Santals.

This is also true of the historian who remains the author of his plot. Our story might be constructed, through the figure of Skrefsrud, from the history of Evangelicalism in Norway. It might equally be a fragment of the social and political history of a particular part of India. We might frame our story by the Evangelical missionaries' social reform work in India. Or we might discuss ideological and economic changes in the Santal country as part of the relation of Evangelical protestantism to capitalist expansion—were the missionaries vanguards of the market economy? We have chosen all these and some others to weave a web of interpretative contexts that correspond to the various life worlds of the people we discuss. In choosing our plots, we use our imagination to construct, in anthropological terms, the cosmopolitan dimension of our missionary encounter, quite conscious that the emplotment is our own subjective choice.

## NOTES

1. Or, as the Comaroffs put it, missionary lives have a particularly epic character (1992: 238).
2. The term life world is used, here, basically in the sense of Schütz (1962).
3. Simmel and Weber were the pioneers here: for a more recent statement see Barth (1995).
4. In the sense Gluckman (1940) gave to the term.
5. In the sense given to the term by Barnes (1954).
6. The words 'tribe' and 'caste' are colonial terms. What we say here is that the differences between the cultures then classified as 'tribal' and the various communities called 'castes' are older than these terms.
7. See, e.g. Bates (1995), Bayly (1995).
8. 'The story of our ancestors'.
9. It is through a study of these modalities that Cohn (1996) reconstructs colonialism's forms of knowledge.

# 2

# From European Reformation to Bengal Renaissance

Since the reform, the Church no longer hedged between the individual and the divine: the vernacular Bible and new-found literacy made religious knowledge accessible to all. Rethinking from below came to characterize the Protestant world, leading to a plethora of different churches and sects.

Weber's analysis of protestant ideas (1930) implied a conception of modernity, wrought not in the philosophies of the Enlightenment but in the religious speculation of the reform which grew, during the seventeenth century, into rational systems of ethical practice. Thus rationalism was not opposed to religion but developed as a form of it. This idea makes a difference: the makers of modernity were not the elite, but artisans and simple folk, the strata from which most missionaries were later recruited.

This rational ethic developed through several stages. With Luther, the devotee's work became a calling, a duty to fill the place in which God had placed the individual. But he must also believe, for only faith can earn God's grace. Then, there is Calvin's doctrine of predestination—the individual can do nothing to influence his destiny in the other world. He is effectively cut off from communication with God, who alone knows his fate. This creates a new solitude, isolating friends from friends, since nobody can know if they are damned or saved. The main thrust of Calvin's work, according to Weber, is to found a new kind of individualism.

Yet the reformed individual tended to question his fate, at any rate in the seventeenth century. There are signs: those marked for damnation receive a heart of stone, making them unfit to do good. Those to be saved, God through his Grace renders capable of a pure life. Blatant sinners, then, are destined for damnation: others may still hope. But the Lutheran, too, is steeped in doubt, since none can be sure to really have faith. The assurance of salvation thus poses a problem to all protestants, and becomes a central trope in protestant discourse.

Along this axis, the different protestant sects and churches spread out. To German Pietists, faith implies assurance. Methodism starts from a Calvinist base, but those who live a saintly life can earn the certitude of salvation. Sects descended from the Baptist tradition stress communication with God; the inner voice gives rise to the Western idea of conscience, most typically among the Quakers (Weber 1930). Gradually a single universe of discourse was formed, a continuous debate within churches and sects as well as between them.

Protestants differ in their view of the Church. When Luther posted his ninety-five theses in 1517, the support of Prince Friederich and the learned Melanchton, as well as his fellow priests, helped him resist the ban the Church issued in 1520. But his views soon sparked off a popular movement, whose radical ideas were not Luther's. He soon had to counter extremism by introducing conservative elements in the organization of the new Church. The peasant rebellion of 1524-5, inspired by the utopian radicalism of Münzer and Karlstadt, was a threat to the Lutheran establishment, saved only by the intervention of the State. Thus from the start, Lutheranism, like Anglicanism later, was divided with one wing linked to the takeover of religion by the early modern state, another to popular religion. Is the Church, as British Dissenters[1] and German Pietists held from the seventeenth century onward, a community of believers independent of the state, or is the latter, as Anglicans and orthodox Lutherans believe, part of God's ordering of this world? Dissenters divided into Congregationalists and Presbyterians, differing as to the central authority they accepted for the Christian community. The Baptists stressed individual will more than their rivals: assurance of salvation rests on individual conscience, and is potentially available to heathens and Christians alike. This view led logically to the development of foreign mission by the end of the eighteenth century.

From the eighteenth century there was a veritable battle for souls in England, between High Church, Low Church, and Dissenters. The schism repeats itself across the Protestant world. The result is a continuing struggle between official churches and the orthodox on the one hand, and low-church dissenting movements on the other. Where the correct interpretation of scripture was privileged, such questions were left to trained theologians. For the Pietists, however, religion was a matter of the heart, leaving little room for theological sophistry. In such groups, lay preachers led the worship. Between these extremes, there were efforts to create an Evangelical priesthood, its personal experience backed by a theological stance that would not estrange it from the congregation, but make for leadership within it.

For orthodox Lutherans, the only true church was the one correctly interpreting the scriptures and Luther's writings, and outsiders had no hope of salvation. For many Pietists, too, the only true church was their own group. Others, between the pietist and the orthodox poles, distinguished the Church in a broad sense, from the many different churches. It might well be that God had willed such plurality so that different aspects of truth be known.[2]

For the orthodox, God's word sufficed to save the sinner; only his resistance could keep him away. The missionary, then, had just to proclaim the Word; God would, if He willed, effect a conversion. This explains the popularity of itinerating, preaching in public, whenever possible, as a missionary strategy. Liberals and Evangelicals, however, felt they must convince the individual: most powerfully by the example of Christian love. Missionaries must lead exemplary lives: heathens would realize the value of their example.

Who could be saved? Opposed to strict Calvinism was the Universalist or more moderate Arminian view that every human or, at least, every Christian, might be saved. To most non-calvinist Evangelicals, the conversion of a heathen was certainly a miracle of God's grace, but they were conscious of having to work themselves to effect it.

The Pietists were the first among the lasting popular movements in the Lutheran world. From 1670 Spener held private meetings: *Pia Desideria*, the 'manifesto' of the pietists was published in 1675. They opposed an individualist, subjectivist[3] religion to the doctrine of the State Churches, without challenging the theological foundations of the Church. They were soon taken to task by the Orthodox, yet Pietism spread rapidly, and soon came to dominate the courts and universities of Northern Europe. Its centre was Halle, the Saxon university from where the Danish king Frederik III[4] recruited Ziegenbalg, the first protestant missionary to India. Established at Tranquebar,[5] this first example of a foreign mission supported by the state was active until the early nineteenth century. Under Frederik IV,[6] the Danish court turned pietist, and Denmark plays an important role in this phase of Protestant history.

Even so, radical pietists opposed the official Churches. Denmark-Norway, like other Lutheran states, tried to enforce the preaching monopoly of priests. But good Christians were supposed to read the Bible in family circles, and it sufficed to invite friends to make a revival meeting. By 1741, monopoly of the State Church on preaching became Law,[7] and pietism declined, as Enlightenment ideas gained influence (Skard 1976: 139-40). By the end of the century, the typical priest was a rationalist, often seeing himself as a missionary of the Enlightenment faced with popular superstition.[8] But Pietism retrenched in a number of sects, of which the Moravians were, perhaps, most important. Persecuted in their homeland ruled by Catholic Austria, they migrated to Saxony, forming small, utopian communities. The best known, Herrnhut[9] was founded in 1722. A tight organization, led by a council of elders on the model of the apostolic church, made these communities survive the Enlightenment to become nodes of revival as the eighteenth century closed. Their centre was moved to Schleswig-Holstein, within the domains of the Danish King, in 1772. Above all, they distinguished themselves by missionary work.[10] The sect spread to Norway by 1737, Denmark in 1739, and later to Sweden and Finland.

Popular literacy was one of the seventeeth century's revolutions, with Protestant Germany leading the world. Five years of schooling was obligatory for all children in Denmark-Norway from 1737, though the law could not be fully enacted. Here, as in Germany and Britain, the Bible and catechism were the chief, and usually first, texts people read. Most other books were in practice reserved for the higher classes,[11] and while priests and schoolmasters tried to turn the masses towards rationalism, they themselves tended to interpret the scriptures literally. This largely explains the religious revival from the late eighteenth century, which brought Pietism back in force.

The revival began in Britain. Here, the Charity School Movement was started to counter the Academies of the Dissenters. Both had enormous effect on popular literacy, though they probably reached a smaller section of the population than in the Lutheran countries. There was much continuity between the old Dissenters and the revival,[12] and the Puritan traditions of the Civil War survived[13] in a number of religious societies, whose form inspired John Wesley's work. Active under William and Anne, they upheld the ideal of the Primitive Church (Bebbington 1989: 36; Trevelyan 1944: 326). In 1738, John and Charles Wesley[14] both had strong religious experiences and, through open-air meetings, founded the Methodist movement which became central to the revival. The pursuit of 'holiness' in daily life, Wesley's main aim, was influenced partly by High Church ideas and partly by mysticism, which had Catholic roots (Bebbington 1989: 37-8).

The Wesleys did not rate Luther highly, yet influence from Lutherans came to relativize the Calvinist elements in Methodism.[15] John Wesley visited Herrnhut to study Moravian doctrine and practice.[16] For two years, he was a member of a predominantly Moravian fellowship, and there were talks about possible union as late as 1785-6. But the Moravians insisted on salvation by faith alone, to the point, it seemed to the Methodists, of neglecting their Christian duties. Increasingly, the Methodists had come to value works as a sign of grace (Bebbington 1989: 44-6).[17] Moravian inspiration led Wesley to build a community of believers within the Church, rather than to form a separate sect, and the movement grew steadily during the century. But in 1784 John ordinated the first priests, founding the Methodist Church. The activism typical of Methodism spread to other denominations. Itinerancy was important, and contributed to refound religious dissent (Bebbington 1989: 38-42). Typical of the mid-century is the co-existence of official Latitudinarianism and low-church Methodism within a single Church, producing conflict but also an open field for debate. For the English-speaking world, the idea of foreign mission came as a novelty and led to the founding of the Baptist Missionary Society in 1792 and the London Missionary Society in 1795.

The Charity School movement depended on the local parish, and brought people into School management, which helped build the congregationalist spirit characteristic of Low Church activities.[18] A number of organizations provided them with a resilience in Britain, which as yet had no counterpart on the Continent. In continuity with these, and uniting Protestants of different denominations, the British and Foreign Bible Society was founded in 1804. It helped spread the revival to Germany, where similar societies were founded in Basel 1804 and in Berlin 1805, followed by others.[19] In the British empire, Auxiliary Bible Societies were formed, to deal with translation and propagation on a regional level.

The link between enlightenment and revival was not just a matter of literacy and institutional development. The opposition between religion and science developed gradually, becoming acute only by the last quarter of the nineteenth century. Even the Halle Pietists, under Francke's leadership, saw religion and science as one, since the latter demonstrated the perfect order of God's creation (Viswanathan Peterson 2003: 97-100). The Enlightenment brought a new stress on empiricism, inspired by Newton and Locke, which from about 1730 became the prevailing philosophical temper in Britain. Wesley was, above all, an empiricist (Bebbington 1989: 53-4). The key here was a new stress on observation and experience,[20] which were conflated: the assurance of being saved was as good an observation as any other.

In Scotland, the link between enlightenment and religion was particularly clear. Its thinkers of the eighteenth century were, above all, moral philosophers. If Hume was something of a free-thinker, others were close to the 'Moderate' party of the Kirk, replacing the hellfire sermonizing of the 'High-flyers' by an emphasis on social duties, as Berry puts it (1997: 13-14). Several writers have stressed the links between the theological heritage and the new social theory developed by the Scots (Chitnis 1976, Sher 1985, Allan 1993). The Scots were not rationalists in the philosophical sense, but empiricists, and one of the concepts forged – by Reid – was common sense, a term our missionaries, Skrefsrud and Börresen, were to use profusely. As the Scots opposed their common sense to the superstition and witchcraft of the Highlands, so our missionaries opposed theirs to similar phenomena among the Santals. Maybe this term, better than rationality or science, sums up the particularity of the Western mind in the later colonial period.

As the ideas of Hume and Berkeley became known, empiricism grew apart from the simple views which inspired Wesley (Bebbington 1989: 53). Still, the conflict was not between empiricist epistemology and religious experience, but rather opposed the subjective experience of truth to the sacraments and rites of the Church.

By the century's end, the term Evangelical was used for different protestant denominations having their roots in the revival (Bebbington 1989: 1). For British Evangelicals, the doctrine of assurance was central. Conversionism, the 'belief that lives need to be changed' (Bebbington 1989: 3), is crucial to Skrefsrud and Börresen, who both underwent conversion and stressed how the experience changed their lives. Activism, 'the expression of the gospel in effort' applies to most missionaries. Biblicism, the central importance of the Bible, is equally salient. Participation in a common Protestant discourse, rather than common doctrine, unites Evangelicals. Our missionaries move in this universe, taking surprising turns, as when Skrefsrud became a Baptist only to return to Lutheranism some ten years later. Such twists were legitimized by the individual quest for salvation. Evangelicals were ready to accept views quite different from their own, as long as the personal quest was beyond doubt. What characterizes the other—the non-Evangelical or the heathen—is the absence of such endeavour. Thus orthodox, apparently less fanatical Christians may be less open to other views, since they doubt the individual quest.

If the Enlightenment frames revival in Britain, the German revival was linked to the romantic movement, which in the early nineteenth century made Germany the cultural dynamo of Europe, as France had been earlier. Romantics and revivalists both opposed rationalism and materialism, stressing the spiritual dimension (Holmquist and Nörregaard 1939, I: 13-15, 24-5). From India, the first Orientalists, such as Jones, influenced the romantic movement, above all in Germany (Hulin 1979, Holmquist and Nörregaard 1939). Turning north, the movement took another generation to reach Norway, around 1830. There, the revival came first: in Calcutta, as we shall see, the elite movement preceded the popular one.

Romanticism gave a prestigious gloss to religiosity. Novalis came from a Moravian background, as did several other figures in the new wave of German thought (Holmquist and Nörregaard 1939: 26). A crucial link between romantics and revivalists was forged by Schleiermacher (1768-1834). His father, a Calvinist army chaplain, joined the Moravians, and Schleiermacher was greatly moved by their new faith. It took a conflict with his father to escape Moravian influence, but in 1787 he shifted from their seminary to the Halle University, dominated by Semler, the founder of Bible criticism. Schleiermacher tended towards an ethic humanism freed from metaphysical overtones. Yet he kept close to pietist devotion (Holmquist and Nörregaard, I: 33-4). In 1796, he moved to Berlin, moved in literary circles, and became a friend of Schlegel. He felt called to awaken these circles to religion, and in 1799 published his *Speeches on Religion for the Educated Among its Derogators*. The individual, he held, is fundamentally religious; ethics, arts and sciences are close to religion, which transcends sectarian differences. Yet the true

Church is a free union of believers — as found among Moravians. Forceful religion must have form and content, but is not exclusively Christian: variety enriches the adoration of God. Schleiermacher's ideas influenced German theology.[21] In 1810, as a founding father of Berlin's University, he became its professor of theology (Holmquist and Nörregaard 1939, I: 35-40).

Revival appeared among Catholics too. Johannes Gossner was born in Bavaria in 1773, studied in Augsburg, and became a priest in 1796. Influenced by mysticism, Gossner grew away from Catholicism to preach in a style inspired by the revival, until he was defrocked in 1817. He went north, working as a teacher, and gained a reputation. In 1820, the liberal Tsar Alexander I invited him to be a court preacher. Though bound by office to the Orthodox, Alexander had become head of a Lutheran Church when the Swedes ceded Finland in 1812. Gossner's sermons were appreciated by the liberals, but Orthodox priests opposed his protestant ideas. In 1825, the liberal decabrist insurrection was crushed, and the Tsar died. Nikolai II, his successor, was a reactionary, champion of the Orthodox Church. Gossner had to leave, and went to Altona, under Danish rule, where he met the Moravians. In 1826 he converted to Protestantism. From 1829 he was pastor at the Bethlehem Church in Berlin, which had become a centre of revival under Johannes Jänicke (1748-1827), who had links to the Moravians. He was among the founders of the Berlin Missionary Society (1823). Gossner, too, turned to missionary activity, founding the society for which Skrefsrud and Börresen began their work in India.

When Friedrich Wilhelm IV succeeded to the Prussian throne in 1840, the revival received royal protection. The king, an active Christian and a romantic, dreamt of restoring the medieval German empire. It had been Catholic however, and as king of Saxony,[22] he was the main protector of the protestants. His solution was to identify with the early Church and, implicitly, with the pietists. During the revolutionary years 1848-9, this alliance proved a bulwark against radicalism.

For Scandinavians, Berlin at this time was not just the centre of romanticism, but also of pietist religion. It was here that Skrefsrud and the Börresens prepared for their missionary life in India, and their constant references to the early Church may echo not just their own pietist links but also a dominant rhetoric of mid-century Prussian culture.

## A COLONIAL BOOMTOWN AND ITS HINTERLAND

In 1792, William Carey (1761-1834), cobbler and autodidact, had founded the Baptist Missionary Society. In his *Enquiry into the Obligations of Christians*, he stressed the duty of bringing the Gospel to all the world's peoples, and decided to go to India. He travelled on a Danish Indiaman, for the East India Company's territory was closed to missionaries. The Company feared Carey's universalist ideas,[23] and when he arrived at Calcutta in November, 1793, he was refused access. He continued to the Danish colony Serampore, where he was cordially received by the governor, and established himself as an indigo planter. He and his collaborators installed a press, publishing their paper *Friend of India*, and numerous Bible translations. They founded several schools,[24] which later became Serampore College, a centre of protestant education in India (Potts 1967; Forrester 1980). Carey brought revivalist Christianity to India, opening the field for our story.

Soon, missionaries were active not only among the Hindus of the plains, but also in the tribal hinterland. In 1826, T. Christian was sent to the Santals by the Society for the Propagation of the Gospel in Foreign Parts. He died within the year, however, from the jungle fever that was to become an emblem of missionary suffering in the jungle. The Baptist missionary E. Leslie worked in the Rajmahal Hills for seventeen years, from 1824 to 1841, before succumbing to the same ailment (Chaudhuri 1995: 245).

There was a feeling that the hills were without real religion, and thus free from the ideological opposition of brahmins and other Hindu leaders. Some missionaries preferred the egalitarian hill peoples to the caste-ridden society of the plains. Caste had a long history in the plains. Myth dates the ordering of Bengali caste society to king Prthvi, around the fifteenth century (Inden 1976). Yet, as Bayly notes, large peasant populations, as well as pastoralists and tribals, were still imperfectly integrated in an overall ranked caste pattern as the nineteenth century began. Nor was the ranking of castes as fixed as it would become later (Bayly 1999: 64-96). Caste, though present in embryonic form at an early date, is not the unchanging essence of Indian society, but has its own history. For Bayly, the eighteenth century after the disintegration of the Mughal empire is marked above all by brahmin ascendancy, since the Marathas and other Hindu successor states were eager to legitimate their status as real Hindu kingdoms. Administrative expansion and growing bureaucracy called for literate specialists, a role for which brahmins—and kayasthas in Bengal—were well suited. This was the admini-strative elite, fluent in Persian, that the Company inherited as it took over the Diwani of Bengal from 1757.

Calcutta was founded in the late seventeenth century, when the East India Company became zamindars of three villages. The English factory was in Gobindapur, where the Company built a fort and warehouses. Sutanuti was a centre of handloom weavers, while in all the villages the majority were fishermen and farmers (Banerjee 1989: 3). Trade goods were collected by agents, and interpreters played a crucial role which for some became highly lucrative, as did the Indian functionaries in the judiciary. The new rich were not all from the traditional elite (Banerjee 1989). Calcutta boomed, and by the end of the century it had attracted a sizable Bengali elite. The colonist elite were Company personnel, their lifestyle immortalized in Hickey's memoirs. Many were not British.[25] The surveyor of Roads was an Italian (Robb 2000), there was the Swedish pastor Kiernander. Then there were Eurasians, both Anglo-Indians and 'Portuguese'.[26] The White Town clustered by the Fort, while the Black Town grew around Sutanuti in the North. Indians were banned from settling in the White Town, but the wealthy among them, mediating between British and Bengalis, gave sumptuous dinner parties in the Black Town. Here, too, developed the bazaars and hutments of artisans and vendors, recruited from many castes and occupations (Banerjee 1989). In the early days, Company servants tended to accommodate to Indian society, and several married Indian women. Questions like how to tell the difference between a black mistress and an Indian wife indicates a fluid but ever present social barrier. The children of such unions were easily absorbed into Company service, and though most high posts were kept by Britons, there was little discrimination against Eurasians until about 1830 (Ballhatchett 1980: 96-7). Robb (2000) paints an amusing portrait of life in Calcutta in the 1790s. The life of many a resident of a 'middling kind' turned on the juggling of credit and the search for patronage, showing structural stress in an economy at once capitalistic and dominated by the Company's monopoly. Europeans and Indians alike were players in this game, and often the latter provided credit, the former social connections. At this time, wealthy Bengalis started to withdraw from business and invest in real estate, urban and rural (Banerjee 1989).

Calcutta became the node of a colonial economic system based on agriculture. Land tenure in early British Bengal is usually called 'zamindari', a term that covers 'a motley collection of rural overlords' (Bose 1993: 70). They were at least of four kinds: old princely families; landholders who paid a fixed land tax and behaved like feudatory chiefs; those who had collected land revenue for generations; and revenue-farmers established since the Company took over the Diwani in 1765.[27] The Permanent Settlement treated all equally, liquidating the princely states[28] and elevating grant holders and tax-farmers to zamindar status. Criticised by Burke, this put an end to the fortunes of many landed families, and produced a heterogeneous elite of businessmen, zamindars, and others, settled in Calcutta—the leisure class that made the Bengal Renaissance possible. They present a confused picture, with new families eager to establish rank and old ones defending precarious positions. This created a need to legitimate rank. Thus the new elite's imposing town and country houses, but also the growth in legitimating accounts of caste rank (Inden 1976).

By the early nineteenth century, the British traders were becoming administrators. Their increasing self-segregation reflected ideological change in England, marked by utilitarianism, liberalism, and evangelism (Banerjee 1989: 34-5). Greater race awareness coincided with the opening of India in 1813 to Europeans outside the Company's service. It was suggested that 'Indians objected to Eurasians because of their mixed birth' (Ballhatchett 1980: 97-8). The Company Charter of 1833 declared that 'neither religion, birthplace, descent or colour should be a bar to official employment' (ibid. : 99), but the trend was towards racial segregation, so that by 1857-8 mixed marriages were an exception at least among the elite. The Company employed Bengalis as trade and administration grew, but also to reduce costs, since British functionaries required high salaries (Banerjee 1989).

The 1770 famine was a low-water mark in Bengal's population (Bose 1993: 18). Hunter estimated that a third of a population of some thirty million succumbed (1975: 45).[29] Labour was scarce. For tribals on the Bengal frontiers, immigration to the plains became a real and interesting possibility. From 1770 to 1860, the population increased. More land was cultivated, and production rose (Bose 1993: 14). Landlords raised rents, particularly between 1830 and 1860. The system has been called *lathi raj* (rule by the stick) (Palit 1975, Bose

1993: 118). By 1860, there was no room any more for tribal peasants to settle in the plains.

In rural Bengal, four ecological zones relate to different systems of production. Most of West Bengal belongs to the moribund delta, extending eastwards into present-day Bangladesh, where the active delta takes over. But the parts most relevant for tribals lie beyond the delta. One is the Himalayan foothills, where the expansion of tea plantations from the late nineteenth century attracted tribal labour. South of this area, the clearing of land produced a structure of *jotedars*—small entrepreneur landowners—and tenants, among whom tribal people were prominent.[30] Beyond Bengal proper, the raised ground on its western fringes formed a transition towards the Chotanagpur plateau (Bose 1993: 12). This tract, including the Santal Parganas, was one of rice cultivation highly dependent on uncertain rains. In the nineteenth century this was still tribal land.

Birbhum, bordering the Santal Parganas, was among the areas worst hit by the 1770 famine. Vast tracts were deserted. Nadia, Murshidabad, Midnapur, Burdwan, Rajshahi, Dinajpur and adjoining districts of Bihar were similarly affected. Ten years later, the jungle had spread so far that the Company offered 'a reward for each tiger's head sufficient to meet a peasant family's subsistence needs for three months' (Hunter 1975: 41). The resettlement (1770-1820) was largely done by migratory ryots on temporary tenure. On the western fringes, they were often tribal. From about 1820, permanent ryots took over (Bose 1993: 21). In Rangpur and Dinajpur, clearing of the jungle took off by the second half of the nineteenth century. Santal, Oraon and Munda migrants from Bihar started to come after the Santal rebellion (Bose 1993: 23), and the migration reached its peak towards the end of the century. Tribal labour also predominated on the tea plantations in Jalpaiguri and Darjeeling from the 1880s.

It was in 1788 that the Company marked indigo as a profitable crop for export. It was a concern of the Company, but not its monopoly. Mainly a British capital venture, Indians played a subsidiary role. By 1810 indigo exports were firmly established[31] (Bose 1993: 45-6). It was a profitable cash crop at first, but by 1830, the Dhaka magistrate thought indigo reduced the peasant to 'little better than a bond-slave to the factory'.[32] The growers received an advance for the crop, which must be sold to the factory at a price fixed by the latter. They were continuously in debt, with no way to quit, especially after the crisis of the late 1820s and 1830s, when indigo prices slumped. Growers could buy much less rice than they could have grown. During the 1840s, many indigo concerns failed, especially in 1847-8. Planters squeezed the growers to get the crop at a price they could pay (Bose 1993: 48-51). This led to the 'blue mutiny' of 1859-60 and the end of indigo cultivation.

The 1847-8 crisis led to an increasingly colonial economy. From the eighteenth century, Indians had their part in Calcutta's growth. As elsewhere in India, they often furnished the capital for colonial expansion. Early in the century, as machinery became available, Bengalis as well as British took it up, leading to modest but significant industrialization.[33] The expansive atmosphere seems to have left little room for animosity. The Bengal Renaissance was a result of fortunes created in this expansive period (Kling 1975: 30).

Meanwhile, utilitarians and liberals replaced conservatives and orientalists, changing the ideological mood of Calcutta. The conservatives, like Burke, held that a just government must understand and preserve the culture of their subjects. Influenced by orientalists such as William Jones (1746-94), Burke saw the Indian political order as grown from an Indian variant of Natural Law. Jones had founded the Asiatic Society in 1784, and translated what became the Institutes of Hindu Law. The orientalists succeeded in making Hindu society comprehensible to an educated British opinion. They defended caste, and the policy of non-interference with Indian culture, even with such practices as *sati*, — widows burning on the pyre of their husbands—or the cult of Jagannath, whose devotees sometimes threw themselves in front of the god's chariot.

The liberals, like Bentinck, were influenced by the Utilitarianism of Bentham and James Mill.[34] They wanted to change India, following a Western model, and were joined by Evangelicals and missionaries. Both believed in the superiority of Western values seen as Universal, and disdained Hinduism, which, for James Mill, had caused the barbarian condition of India. Liberal influence was at its height in the 1830s and dominated the scene till the Mutiny.

The Bengal Renaissance flourished in the economic expansion of the early nineteenth century, in which both Bengalis and British participated (Kling 1975).[35] At the height of the Serampur Mission, the *Friend of India* urged the British to invite Indians to 'conversation parties', to interest them in art, culture, and politics, as seen by the British. The Hindu-Christian encounter was central to the Bengal

Renaissance. The Bengali elite's houses had Corinthian pillars in front and English furniture inside. Such signs of prosperity and cosmopolitan culture obviously asserted rank. Fluent in English, the elite participated in the rapidly developing exchange of ideas. Still, in 1855 they were barred from joining the British-dominated Bengal Club.

Derozio, appointed to the Hindu College in 1828, led his students to feel that India must be regenerated by Western culture, seeing Hinduism as the cause of Indian backwardness. They formed the Young Bengal movement, forging their dreams on ideals borrowed from British literature (Mukherjee 1978). Dressing in Western fashion, they declared they were eating beef. Orthodox Hindus reacted, forcing the suspension of Derozio's journal *Parthenon* when it came out in 1830 (Gray 1975: 113).

Rammohun Roy, whose father prospered in early colonial days, was the central figure of the Renaissance. Educated in Persian and Arabic, he studied Sanskrit in Benares, and became familiar with British culture. Roy was in his forties when he retired from business, this was in the early 1820s. Roy and other reformers were brahmins of established rank. The Hindu conservatives tended to be kayasthas or others of relatively inferior rank, needing to assert orthodoxy while demonstrating ability to take part in the debate. Typical here was Radhakanta Deb, who founded the Dharma Sabha in 1830 (Mukherjee 1978).

Roy's theology 'represented an attempt to synthesize the different traditions he had studied into a universal monotheism which resembled the Unitarianism of the West' (Gray 1975: 107). He saw it as a reaction to the degraded state of Hinduism, where women suffered from *sati* and infant marriage. Blaming the puranic scriptures, Rammohun hoped to reform Upanishadic philosophy through Western and Christian ideas. The Hindu College in Calcutta was founded in 1828 and Roy felt the Western education it provided was an important step towards social reform. But he opposed the foundation of the Sanskrit College in 1823.

Carey worked in Serampore, and Roy discussed religion and philosophy with the missionaries. Marshman criticised *A Guide to Peace and Happiness*, describing Jesus' teaching, which Roy intended as an introduction to Christianity for the Hindu elite. The Baptists felt it neglected the Lord's divine nature, reducing Christianity to moral precepts. Roy answered their critique in 1820 and 1821. Here, for the first time, Christian missionaries and indigenous intellectuals held discussions on equal terms. Roy allied himself with the Unitarian W. Adam, with whom he translated the Bible. They founded a Unitarian congregation in 1813; this being too liberal for British Unitarians in India, they turned to America.[36] The echoes of this contact is seen in Emerson's pantheism. But the congregation closed in 1823. Roy pondered whether India should follow Christ or look for some comparable figure in its own tradition. He founded the Atmiya Sabha and, in 1828, the Brahmo Samaj, based on the Vedantic tradition, and opposed to the cults of puranic Hinduism.

Roy also contacted the Presbyterians. Their dogma did not interest him, but Duff's and Grant's educational projects did. Duff (1806-78) represented a new, pragmatic and evangelical, generation of missionaries. Roy had urged the Presbyterians to send him, but Duff soon turned against the Brahmo Samaj. He did not reject all Hindu tradition, but in it he looked for an ancient, monotheistic God. Politically, Duff became Bentinck's ally, with important responsibilities for public education. Grant worked to introduce Western education, with, as a corollary, knowledge of Christianity – to him the religion of rationality as well as true ethics. We are at the height of the liberal age: from 1835, the Company decided, under Bentinck's and Macaulay's influence, to finance instruction in English only.

The liberal attempts at reforming Hinduism divided Bengali society. While the elite turned to the Upanishads, the people expressed their identity through various sects (Banerjee 1989: 71). Roy's criticism of caste and 'degenerate' Hindu customs allied him with the missionaries, and may have provoked the conservative response. The Brahmo Samaj stagnated. When Debendranath Tagore assumed its leadership in 1843 most members were practising a Puranic hinduism tinged with Tantrism. Debendranath had attended Hindu College, but put an end to the imitation of Western ideas. Literature on the Bengal Renaissance tends to privilege liberal views, yet liberals became a minority in the Bengali elite after 1858. As Bayly (1999) shows, the conservatives are at the roots of the later nationalist movement. The Bengali elite our missionaries face is dominated by them.

Inden (1990) and Metcalf (1995: 132-8) stress how the Orientalists constructed a coherent Hinduism, seen as a single though complex religion. Important here were the German romantics. The word

Hinduism—replacing the older term Brahmanism—is itself a product of the early nineteenth century. Now Indians from Roy to revivalists were busy constructing a reality to fit the image. Later, administrators like Lyall and orientalists like Monier-Williams started to stress the 'entangled confusion' or 'confused tangle' of Hindu ideas.[37] 'It suited the British', says Metcalfe, 'not to press forward too vigorously with the consolidation of Hinduism' (1995: 137), now that Indians were using the concept to nurse a budding nationalism.

The fertile encounter between British and Bengali ideas is followed by Bengali retrenchment and the reinvention of Hindu tradition. Tribal people on the Bengal frontier had been influenced by their Hindu neighbours for centuries. But the Hinduism they confronted was changing in the second half of the nineteenth century. It became more conscious of itself as a social force than the motley Hindu sects and castes had been, acquiring a vision of its own civilizing mission which it retains today, and which may be one example of the continuity Robb (1997) sees between colonial and nationalist influences.

Yet missionary accounts bypass this influence and Calcutta, its centre. One exception is Skrefsrud's wife, Anne Onsum (Hodne 1950), who describes her awe of the magnificent temples and the richness of Hindu culture in the city. Skrefsrud never wrote of the city's splendour, nor did Börresen. Yet they stayed there two years, kept in touch with Christian circles, and went there for supplies. Here Skrefsrud was rebaptized, and joined the Masonic lodge. In spite of its absence from missionary narratives, Calcutta is very much part of our story. Some two hundred kilometres away, the Santal country was still the frontier, in social and cultural terms. Here, our missionaries engage in their cultural encounter. The confrontation is triangular: the Santals are faced with Indian society and Hinduism, as well as the missionary enterprise. Their rebellion is still fresh in the minds not just of the Santals, but of Indians and Europeans in the area.

## PROTESTANTISM IN SAINT OLAF'S KINGDOM

Europeans tend to construct the colonial other in terms not used when looking at themselves. We try to show, here, the otherness of our European subjects, looking at their background in ethnographic terms.[38] We do not suggest that the Norwegians are like Santals, but we do want to see the two peoples in the same perspective.

Unlike the mythical santal kings the old Norwegian kings are historically documented. But five hundred years of Danish rule separates the eclipse of the medieval Norwegian kingdom (1319) from the birth of the modern state (1814). There is a an underlying cultural continuity (Odner 2000), yet the construction of the modern nation depended on reinventing tradition. Norwegian myths lean heavily on Saint Olav, who ruled from 1014 to 1028, then, trying to regain power, fell at Stiklestad in 1030. He is credited with miracles, and seen as having christianized Norway.[39] Soon he was recognized as a saint, and Stiklestad became a centre of pilgrimage. The cathedral of Nidaros,[40] thirty kilometres away, remains the centre of Norwegian Christianity. The legend of Saint Olav is at the root of a conception of royalty and Norwegianness (Odner 2000), which may be compared, in symbolic terms, with the myth of a Santal kingdom.

Through the efforts of Archbishop Eystein, Olav became Norway's eternal ruler. From 1162 to 1319 its kings were said to hold their kingdom in fief from Saint Olav, becoming sacred kings.[41] The laws made by the various assemblies of chiefs, were from around 1250 said to derive from 'Saint Olav's law'. Olav probably made no laws, but served as the ultimate source of their legitimation till late Danish times. For Norwegian peasants, the Danish king was still the guardian of 'Saint Olav's law', which explains their confidence in the king's justice. Repeatedly, they sent delegations to Copenhagen to plead, only to find the members arrested by officials on their return. The important idea here is that of divine justice transcending the state.[42] The king's symbolic role has survived changes leaving him no power in the state (Odner 2000: 6-12). Since the sole function of kingship was symbolic, sacredness survived modernity.

In Norway, the reform was brutally proclaimed by the Danish king in 1536. Troops pillaged the churches: silver and gold were melted for coinage, and Church property was confiscated and sold. These events probably made a stronger impression than the religious changes accompanying them. The Catholic archbishop mounted an insurrection, which failed dismally (1537). Still, cults of the Virgin and Saint Olav persisted in remote areas into the early nineteenth century. This must have strengthened the idea that the official Church is a worldly institution, without real religious legitimacy. The official and religious role of the priest conflict in all state churches, as do peasantry and officialdom in Scandinavia. In Norway, where the priest was often a foreigner, the distance between him and his flock was even greater than elsewhere. In the eighteenth century he is typically a rationalist, modernizing agriculture, fighting superstition, and viewing Catholic survivals and belief in spirits (trolls, gremlins) in much the same way.

Priests had prestige, since the class of officials had few rivals in colonial Norway. The older nobility was gone, and Danish kings were reluctant to grant feudal tenure in Norway. From 1660 they were absolute monarchs. The few immigrant merchants were concentrated in Bergen, which into the nineteenth century remained a colonial entrepôt for a hinterland stretching north to the Russian border. The eighteenth century brought exports of timber from the small ports in the south, equally colonial in character, even if the merchants were local men. While the trading houses grew fast in the eighteenth century, many were bankrupted by the English blockade of 1807. The crisis provides the plot for the novel *Captain Worse* by Alexander Kielland, a favourite of Thomas Mann. Here, the house of Garman is saved by the captain, who, personifying the rising petty bourgeoisie, becomes a Moravian by marriage. With the fall of the merchant aristocracy, officials came to dominate the elite.

The dynamic force among peasants and petty bourgeoisie was the Haugean movement. Born in southeastern Norway, Hans Nielsen Hauge (1771-1824) grew up in an atmosphere of revival, led by a pastor influenced by the Moravians (Bang 1924, Molland 1969a, Kullerud 1996). To Hauge, the pietists' mystic stress on faith is too sentimental. He wants religious thinking to be rigorous: he reads Luther, and the great authors of the Danish church. He is contemporary with the German revival, but timber exports linked southeastern Norway mostly to Britain. Religious ideas were probably transmitted by seamen, forming a link at a popular level, bypassing the elite.

Hauge says he was torn, in his youth, between his religious calling and the desire to get rich by commerce. On 5 April 1796, he was working in the fields when suddenly he felt an indescribable joy, certain that God had called him to convert people to Christ. That year, he published his first two books, *The Rules of Evangelical Life* and *Deliberations on the Misery of the World*. The next year he began his travels all over Norway, preaching as a layman at innumerable meetings. More books followed, and were widely read. But the State Church defended its monopoly on preaching, and Hauge was imprisoned several times. His teaching is puritan rather than pietist, representing the capitalist spirit as well as the protestant ethic (Weber 1930). Much of it recalls Methodist views. The 'Norwegian apostle' saw idleness as the greatest of sins: he always knitted as he walked from one meeting to another. God must be celebrated by works, by economic success in His name. Like his disciples, Hauge engaged in trade, and in 1801 started a large firm in Bergen, exporting fish and other products of the Norwegian north. It was a religious co-operative, though Hauge was the legal owner. He was accused of enriching himself at others' expense. In the summer of 1804, the authorities ordered officials to report on his activities. By October he was again in jail, to await the deliberations of a commission of inquiry.

In 1801 the British shelled Copenhagen, uncertain of Danish neutrality. In 1807, they launched a blockade and Nelson attacked Copenhagen again to destroy the Danish navy. Denmark-Norway became Napoleon's ally, but without the fleet, communication with Norway was impossible. For the Norwegians, this meant famine, since they depended on Danish grain. Hauge, at first, languished in prison, but in 1809 was suddenly freed and ordered to organize the extraction of salt from the sea. Traditionally imported from Scotland, salt was scarce. Hauge, with his practical bent and technical interests, seemed to be the only man capable of such an enterprise. For his services to the nation, he was freed in 1811, until the decision of the commission was to be known. By 1813, he was found guilty of preaching illegally, but acquitted of all allegations of fraud. Even so, he was sentenced to two years of forced labour. Following an appeal, the sentence was commuted to a fine, extremely heavy for the period. Hauge was now a broken man, passing his last years in retirement, and dying in 1824.

While criticizing the Church, Haugeans saw themselves as orthodox Lutherans and, like the early Methodists, did not break with the Church. They founded the low-church movement which later came to dominate the Norwegian Church. At the time, their main rivals for popular devotion were the Moravians. The novelist Kielland respects the latter's piety, but caricatures the Haugeans as puritans *par excellence*, country bumpkins whose economic success baffled established merchants. In the countryside, they were known as enterprising farmers. Hauge may be the most important influence on the Norwegian Church since Luther. His movement faded by the 1850s, but it had changed the religious and social climate of the country. The colonial elite was challenged, on all fronts, by new men whose puritan values helped build new businesses and a strong, anti-elitist cultural identity.

A regional movement existed among Norwegian intellectuals in the eighteenth century.[43] National feeling at the popular level is less evident, though Norwegians opposed themselves to Swedes, with whom they were often at war, and were conscious of Danish dominance. The American War of Independence, in which quite a few Norwegians were involved, inspired more concrete ideas of nationhood. The British Navigation Acts were the main obstacle to the growth of Norwegian shipping and Americans were natural allies for the Bergen merchants (Skard 1976: 32).[44] Washington and Franklin became popular heroes with the Norwegian elite. When the French revolution turned into a bloodbath, they tended to contrast this 'madness' to the order and dignity of the American one (Skard 1976: 37-46).

The real impetus for independence came from the blockade: the colony was forced into actual independence by isolation from its motherland. Led by the Danish prince Christian Frederik, Norway repulsed Swedish attacks. In January 1814, at the peace conference in Kiel, Denmark was forced to capitulate. Sweden would cede Finland to Russia, but get Norway in return. Norwegians were bitter. There was a desire to resist Swedish takeover, merged with loyalty to Denmark, and they wanted Christian Frederik, heir to the Danish throne, as their king. The latter wanted to be enthroned at Nidaros, linking Saint Olav's kingdom to his dynastic claims. Logically, this would lead to reunification once he succeeded to the Danish throne. This is how European powers saw his plans, a clear break of the Kiel compromise.

The Prince played the gamble, hoping that Russia and Britain would withdraw their support to the turncoat king of Sweden. But the Norwegian elite refused absolute monarchy.[45] They wanted to choose their king. Christian Frederik, knowing he was the obvious candidate, agreed. There was no time to lose: four days later Stockholm was to celebrate the conquest of Norway (Jensen 1963: 12-13). So Christian Frederik announced the election of a constitutional assembly and asked all Norwegians to swear by Norwegian independence. The Swedish army was still spread out, and the constitution must be voted before the Swedes would be ready to attack Norway. The constitution was signed and the king elected on 17 May. These events constitute the birth of the Norwegian nation-state in myth and in fact, though the parliament of 1814 was dominated by the officials, largely of foreign origin.[46] Full independence could not be maintained, but through British pressure, the Swedish king accepted the Norwegian constitution on taking over the throne of Norway.

Norway and Sweden were thus united under a single king. The constitution made Norwegians more independent of the royal will than Swedes, and until 1905, Norwegian politics turned on the struggle between the parliament and the Swedish king. For Norwegians, democracy and nationalism become two sides of the same coin, since the opposition was both conservative and Swedish.[47] The nation, then, relates to ethnicity rather than the state, and is seen as the realization of a natural quest for freedom, ideas we may trace to Herder. Herder's writings were still recent in 1814, and a rendering in Norwegian, *The Result of History* by Henrik Wergeland, only came out in 1843-4. Wergeland's work, however, appears as the peasants, strongly influenced by the Haugean movement, were making their presence felt in Norwegian politics. Herder's ideas were relevant to a situation in which elite and peasant elements were looking for a common, national platform.

Norway was a state in need of nation-building [Eisenstadt and Rokkan (eds) 1973]. Its radical constitution, idiosyncratic in Europe under the holy alliance, was entrusted to a class who saw itself as a thin layer of civilization over a population lacking culture and rationality. Its situation was akin to the elites of modern third world states, for the country's colonial structure was still evident.[48] Roads were bad, and there were no navigable waterways. To other Europeans, the interior was largely seen as tribal.

Between 1814 and 1858, Norwegian perceptions of cultural and national identity changed. Three elements stand out: the development of schooling and communications, the political emancipation of the peasantry, and the construction, in a peculiarly romantic idiom, of the idea of the nation. By Skrefsrud's time, Norwegians felt they belonged to a nation, though struggling for independence. Freedom was seen as a right to be oneself, a self inherently Norwegian. Skrefsrud's ideas of the Santals as a nation in need of a national church, reflect this heritage. Gradually, Norway became less the colonial other than a subaltern among European nations. Hauge and his followers had contributed greatly to these transitions. But all over northern and western Europe Evangelical Christianity had made its mark on society, so much so that the mid-century may be seen as the apogee of Christian activity and influence.

## CHRISTIANITY AT ITS APOGEE

The main Christian tradition Skrefsrud and Börresen met in India was British Evangelism, which had come a long way since Carey's time. By the 1850s Evangelical attitudes had become characteristic of the times (Bebbington 1989: 105). 'Evangelism had imposed on society', wrote G.M. Young, 'even on classes which were indifferent to its religious basis and unaffected by its economic appeal, its code of Sabbath observance, responsibility, and philanthropy; of discipline in the home, regularity in affairs; it had created a most effective technique of agitation, of private persuasion and social persecution' (1936: 5). Yet everyone did not share in the spirit of the age. J.S. Mill, whose utilitarian liberalism was no longer the fashion, describes the strict Calvinists and Methodists as 'intrusively pious members of society' who, in their eagerness to improve morals, tried to be their brother's keeper (1863). By 1853 a third of the clergy in the Church of England was thought to be Evangelical. In Scotland and Wales their position was even stronger (Bebbington 1989: 106).

Christianity was at its apogee. The results of the 1851 religious census shows that about half the population over ten years of age was attending church, a degree of religious activity never equalled, certainly not in the eighteenth or twentieth centuries. Yet the contemporary reaction was that the number of churchgoers was deceptively low (ibid.: 107-9). As in the eighteenth century, artisans and an upper crust of the working class were active, while religion was much weaker with unskilled industrial labour.[49] Poverty was important: many working families did not have clothes good enough for church display. The real strength of Evangelism was among the expanding middle classes. 'It may well be', says Bebbington, that

> a stronger influence on the lower classes was a folk religion heavily indebted to paganism. The survival of rural witchcraft is vividly illustrated in the novels of Hardy, but there is also a growing body of evidence suggesting widespread belief in esoteric remedies for misfortune, the sacredness of

nature and the importance of ritual observances at turning points in personal life and the annual cycle. Such notions were not confined to the countryside. City churches, as in Lambeth, were thronged with working-class attenders at harvest festival and on New Year's Eve, the two occasions when church services regularly marked events in nature rather than in Christian story (1989: 113-14).

Our view of Western society in the mid-nineteenth century must thus account for the survival of significant pre-Christian elements in popular culture. Evangelization and Home Missions reflect this situation, and there is a parallel incorporation of pre-Christian customs in Catholic countries like Italy. The perspective certainly fits Norway. Starting from the eighteenth century, when only a small minority were active churchgoers, the evangelical movements had accomplished in some hundred years the conversion of large sectors of the people to Christianity as a social practice. Later, Christian dominance was challenged by new doctrines. But that is from 1870 onwards, when our missionaries were in the field.

Spontaneous, local outbursts of revival were typical of the expansive Christianity of the early nineteenth century. Organized revivalist campaigns, current later, were still in their beginning in the 1850s. But the strongest impact was through regular methods of mission. Evangelical services were usually better attended than conventional ones, drawing audiences from subaltern groups such as domestic servants and agricultural labour. There were prayer meetings, where conversions were frequent. Here, laymen might take a lead. Bible classes were aimed at groups such as 'female servants, mothers from the working classes, working men, ladies, young men, candidates for confirmation or church membership and children' (Bebbington 1989: 118).

Evangelicals engaged in house-to-house visiting from the 1780s. In 1825, the Nonconformists started their own visiting society in London (Bebbington 1989: 114-18). Anglican churches too were active in the effort to reach the poor and religiously indifferent. The term Home Mission came to be used for such organizations, which were soon copied in other countries. It was the city slums and poor working class areas which were their main targets, in a counter-strategy to emergent socialism.[50] In the latter half of the century, three quarters of the charitable organizations, according to one estimate, were evangelical (Bebbington 1989: 120). Charity was mixed with liberalist ideas, stressing the danger that those helped would no longer be willing or able to help themselves.[51] Help should be freely given: government relief was rejected, as was any kind of compulsion towards charity.

The foreign Missions were also important in this culture of philanthropy, a salient feature of nineteenth-century British society. Popular education was largely the work of the Church and other denominations, in contrast to the state education of Lutheran countries. Even by the mid-eighteenth century, the religiously active had been literate. Literacy declined in the early nineteenth century, due to industrialization and urbanization. The Sunday school movement, from the 1780s onwards, worked to counter this decline, reaching children who worked during the week. During the nineteenth century it became more religious, as secular schooling grew. Still, half of the children in Britain went to religious schools in 1850. Only in 1870, with the Education Act, did schooling become a responsibility of the local authorities. It must have seemed quite natural to missionaries to use education to reach the natives.

By the mid-1850s Norway was still poor, but there now began an economic expansion lasting till the early 1870s. The class of officials was tying the country together, improving communications in physical and cultural terms. Timber exports rose again after the British blockade, as France for a while replaced Britain as the main market (Jensen 1963: 48). Fish exports rose sharply, and by 1880 the Norwegian merchant fleet was the third largest in the world. Still, Norwegians emigrated to America in ever increasing numbers, culminating in 29,000 emigrants in 1882 (ibid. 147). Many were poor, but there was also a brain drain, notably of engineers—incomes were low, though the standard of education was relatively high. In politics, the years from 1814 to 1830 saw the rise of the peasantry. By 1833 the peasant opposition held 45 of 96 parliament seats, and, with support from liberal sections of the bourgeoisie, effectively formed the majority. They stood for frugality, limiting state expense. But more important is the democratic affirmation their power implied. Unlike the officials, they were not of foreign origin: though well off, they were men of the people. Their participation served to cement the political community into a nation.

The Haugean movement was central to the spread of literacy. Hauge's own writings sold in large numbers: the catechism and Bible were commonly read. Outlying districts were still served by ambulatory schools, moving from one farm to another, a practice introduced in 1739, when attendance became compulsory. Though the quality of education left much to be desired, most people had reached a degree of literacy by the early decades of the nineteenth century.[52] In 1827 permanent schools were established in the main parishes; By 1860, they became the rule. Skrefsrud, however, went to an ambulatory school.

If Hauge was the 'prophet' of a specific, Norwegian Lutheranism, the architect of the modern Norwegian Church was Gisle Johnson, Professor of Theology at the University of Christiania from 1849. Orthodox, he mainly fought the vestiges of rationalism in the Church. From his time, liberals remained a minority in the Norwegian Church. He was Low Church, and sided with the Puritan tradition from Hauge except for the priestly monopoly of preaching, which he saw as fixed by the Augsburg Confession (Hämre 1986: 13-17). The Norwegian Church became a state-sponsored Low Church movement, lacking the High Church element of its Swedish counterpart and the latitudinarian and liberal tendencies of the Danish Church.

By the time of Skrefsrud's youth, Johnson's doctrines were the ruling ideology of the Church. Skrefsrud, however, was far from orthodox, becoming a baptist for a while. Even after his return to Lutheranism, Skrefsrud remained close to the Free Church movement. Börresen shared with Skrefsrud a view of the church as a community of believers, which inspired their work among the Santals.

The ambiguous position of the pastor is clear from Asbjörnsen and Moe's Folk Tales, collected in the 1830s and 1840s. In *The Companion*, a farmer's son finds, in front of the church door, a large block of ice with a corpse in it. When the priest comes, he tells the boy the corpse is that of a vintner who added water to the wine. As the guilty has paid with his life, the boy feels they might still bury him in Christian soil, and sets out to pay for the burial. He is joined by the 'companion', who serves him at no charge, procuring for his master the princess, the kingdom, and great fortune. In the end, the companion reveals his identity: he is the spirit of the frozen corpse (Asbjörnsen and Moe 1982, I: 415-29). Clearly, God's justice is less harsh than that of the Church.

The late eighteenth-century Norwegian priest is mainly an official, and often a rationalist. Even so, some priests were thought to have miraculous power, to drive out ghosts or the devil (Hjellestad 1933,

II: 76). Belief in 'subterraneans'[53] was still common. They are like humans, but are not Christians: they are powerful, rich, and control fate. Typically, we hear of a fisherman leaving his catch to the spirits and receiving silver in return: his fate is sealed, however, when he yearns for their hoard of silver and throws a cross on them. 'There shall be vengeance, for you broke the leg of my son!' shouts the spirit wife. But the man's animals fall sick, he breaks his leg: in the end he becomes a poor man (Hjellestad 1933, II: 74-5). These spirits seem to have served as a model for Bodding, when he later attempted to transform the *bongas* of the Santal religion into folklore.

## THE MAKING OF A MISSIONARY

Lars Olaf Skrefsrud was born in 1840, on a small tenant farm in the hills near Lillehammer.[54] In eastern Norway, the rich farmers formed the peasant aristocracy of a heavily stratified society, where labour was typically provided by the 'husmann'[55] system of tenancies. The husmann was, above all, an 'agricultural labourer for the farmer from whom he rented his tenant farm. Usually his work duties were unlimited, so that he had to appear for work . . . whenever the farmer needed him. The rent . . . was calculated in terms of money, but was almost always settled by work . . . the duty to work applied to the whole year. Still, there was but little cash entering into the reckoning, since the husmann usually got grains and other victuals from the farmer' (Bull 1985: 84-5). The market economy had not yet fully penetrated the countryside.

Usually, tenant production was insufficient, and the husmann was constantly in debt to his master. The debt made for complete dependency: many tenancies were for life, but a tenant could be evicted if he failed in his duties—or if the master wanted to realize his credit. The husmann was less dependent if he had a cash income to pay the rent. This was the case of the artisan-husmann class, to which Skrefsrud's father, a carpenter, belonged. Poor but independent, they comprised a number of exceptional personalities (Odner 1996).[56] Some were attracted by the new technology, and many went to America. Thus Skrefsrud was a mechanic, as was Börresen. These links to technology were typical of an age when progressive politics, technological improvements, and religious activism merged in an optimistic belief in the capacity of rational man to solve the problems of humanity. This belief was in many ways a legacy of the Scottish enlightenment. For Skrefsrud and Börresen, the conversion of the heathen was an important part of universal progress. The opposition between science and religion was yet to come. Though Skrefsrud came from a poor family, he probably had better schooling than his contemporaries from similar backgrounds in Britain and on the continent.

The development of a national culture in Norway is contemporary to the Bengal Renaissance. Both forged links to a third nascent nation, the United States, represented by the New England School. We may compare, then, cultural life at Calcutta, Boston, and Christiania, even if the latter was yet but a small town. The New England School was an elite movement, like the Bengal renaissance, in spite of enigmatic figures such as Thoreau and Walt Whitman from New York. In all three cities, the building of national culture was an elite endeavour. There was a contrast with life in the countryside and among the lower classes, where Evangelical Christianity or popular Hinduism were respectively important. In this period of parallel nation-building, however, links between the people and the elite were forged in different ways in India, America, and Norway. In India, one has to distinguish not only several Indian intellectual and cultural milieux, but also the colonists from the colonized. This duality, still present in Norway, had disappeared in America. In all three cases, the distinction between the people and the elite was more fundamental than that between foreign and indigenous elites. Thus the differences between East and West were less central than the cross-cutting ties of cultural influence.

In Norway, the integration of the peasantry served to unite interests, while the educated strove to define Norwegianness. Emblematic here is the poet Henrik Wergeland, who 'norwegianized' his language by using Norwegian symbols and idioms, much as Whitman did in America.[57] Wergeland united the ideals of the French enlightenment and revolution with a love of British ideals of freedom and early elements of national romanticism. More than anybody else, he forged a link between nationalism and political freedom, which set a tone of political rhetoric for the future.

Romantic influences from Germany were translated by other writers. Skrefsrud read Novalis (Hodne 1966), whose idea that art is part of nature (Todorov 1977: 201) echoes with Wergeland and other Norwegian romantics. Important are Asbjörnsen and Moe's collections of folk tales serving, more than anything else, to define

Norwegian culture. For the officials of 1814, culture was an elite monopoly: the folk tales taught Norwegians that culture is present in the humblest of its representatives. Here, indeed, was Herder's 'spirit of the nation'. This conception of folk culture inspired Skrefsrud and Bodding among the Santals.

In 1849-51 Marcus Thrane, Norway's first socialist agitator, formed labourers' associations all over eastern Norway. The movement grew fast: between 20 and 30 per cent of all adult men, in the district where Skrefsrud grew up, may have taken part in it. The main strength were tenant farmers (Bull 1985: 72, 75-113). Thrane was active at Lillehammer, where for some years he ran a private school. Still Skrefsrud never mentions him nor his agitation. Thrane, indeed, was later to criticize Skrefsrud's mission when he went to America and wrote in the Norwegian-language Chicago press.

The Thrane movement shows a mixture of modern and archaic features. It had the millenarian overtones of the peasant risings of an earlier day. It was said that once the poor were properly organized, the *Bondklubbo*[58] would come and turn everything upside down: husmenn would get their own farms and farmers would be forced to give up their 'stolen' land. Others talked of the 'Northern Power', large flocks of workers from the north and west of the country, who would sweep through the land to restore justice. These traditions had ancient roots, and we should be wary of seeing the Thrane movement as modern (Bull 1985: 102-3). Like the Santal Rebellion, it affirms the rights of subalterns in a changing world over which they had no control. In Norway activists turned up in force to prevent the sale of a husmann's land for debt. Both movements drew on myth and tradition to legitimize their opposition to dominant groups.

Thrane incited workers to emigrate. In these years, emigration increased: in 1861, when Skrefsrud came out of prison, 9,000 Norwegians went to America. It was still the poor who left, largely husmann; officials and merchants wanted to keep them in their place. The State Church became a centre of anti-emigration propaganda, stressing the godlessness of America. But popular religion was another matter, and the first Norwegian church in America was a branch of the Haugean movement. Thrane's movement was crushed, but wrought real fear among those in power. After Thrane's arrest in 1852,[59] efforts increased to influence the working classes through Christian propaganda. Honoratius Halling, a priest, started a number of Christian Working Men's Clubs, and was, with Gisle Johnsson among others, a founder of the Norwegian Home Mission in 1855. The years 1852-71 were marked, for the Norwegian working class, by religious agitation. Only in the 1870s did the Union movement begin; only in the 1890s did socialism become a common word (Bull 1985: 375, 475-501).

Socialism was not the only enemy: there was also alcohol and immorality. We have excellent sociological studies of lower-class culture in Norway in Skrefsrud's time. This is the work of Ejlert Sundt, a priest and reformer. *Moral Standards in Norway* (1857/1968) deals with the husmann class, close to Skrefsrud's home. Sundt's problem here is the large number of children born out of wedlock, which he explains by the high marriage age. Farm hands had no resources to marry. After years of service one of them might be offered a tenancy—the only way to finance married life. In the years that had passed since puberty and confirmation, many had children, who were not necessarily unwanted, and if the couple remained together it was considered normal to have two or three children before marriage could be formalized. Pre-marital sex was not thought immoral.

Sundt accepts that given the workings of the system, there was little to be gained by preaching. Yet, he was shocked at the laxity of sexual morals. Most poor families had only one room, and often sister and brother slept together, even approaching adulthood. Though servants had quarters separated according to sex, it was common—at harvest and other busy times—that both sexes slept side by side in the barn. Sundt's reformist tendency turned against these economic and physical conditions, and against the lack of sexual morality.

This is a general theme in traditional Scandinavian culture, not restricted to the lower classes. The custom of *nattefriing*, where boys visited girls in bed on Saturday evening, was common in the poorer or hillier tracts (Löfgren 1980). For Skrefsrud, then, promiscuity among the Santals must have resembled the liberal sexual mores of his own youth. But these were sinful practices the Christian must fight. Rather than a civilized European confronted with the sexual life of savages, Skrefsrud confronted his own sinful past. Alcohol provides a similar story. Impulses for the teetotaller movement came from America and Britain. It was not yet active when Skrefsrud left Norway, but temperance was tied to the revival. All sources agree that drink was a serious problem among the lower classes. The vehemence of the Norwegian revival, as regards alcohol and sex, must be seen in this context.

Skrefsrud is typical of his times. His mother took him to revival meetings, while his father, who drank heavily, frowned on such things. The mother came from a Haugean family, and Skrefsrud has described his first revival meeting, where the child felt a religious happiness he later lost. Skrefsrud despised his father but loved his mother dearly. As an adult, he was deeply devoted to the mother figure of Caroline Börresen, while his own marriage was, by all indications, a failure. We are told that his mother tried—in vain—to raise a loan, so that Lars could continue his schooling. Instead, he was apprenticed to a coppersmith at Lillehammer (Saeter 1940: 22-4). He read religious literature, but also drank and went dancing. From about 1856 he worked at Brumunddal, and was confronted with evangelical religion at the meetings of one Martin Fremstad (Döhl 1944: 9). Lars longed to leave for the capital, to work at Nylands Verksted,[60] in the forefront of technological modernization. But at his father's burial, his friends pushed him to drink. They went on for days: finally, he broke into a shop in Lillehammer, with his brother and another companion, and went to jail in 1858.

Skefsrud was sentenced to four years, but freed after two years and four months, partly for good conduct, but also since he had served part of his sentence in solitary confinement. In that year Nyland finished their first steamship. In prison, Skrefsrud had the vision which decided his calling. He wanted to kill himself, when Christ appeared, saying: 'I have annihilated your sins: go away in peace.' Liberated, he talked of the miracle to other prisoners, and was helped by the prison director, who became a close friend. Gradually, he realized his calling: he must become a missionary (Nyhagen 1990, I: 100-1). Skrefsrud read voraciously, soon finishing whatever interested him in the prison library, and the director procured more books. He read Novalis, Kierkegaard, Swedenborg, and conventional religious authors. He taught himself German, English, and Latin, as well as some French and Greek. His exceptional gift for languages was evident. One visitor is important: Anne Onsum, his future wife. Earlier, he had loved a seamstress, intensively courted by the Lillehammer youth: but she had no intention to become a missionary's wife (Hodne 1966, Nyhagen 1990, I).

Out of prison, Skrefsrud went to Stavanger, where the Norwegian

Missionary Society had founded its seminary in 1842. He had recommendations from the prison director among others. But the School would not admit an ex-convict. Due, a leading Moravian who had contacts in Germany, urged Skrefsrud to go to Berlin. He gave him a letter of recommendation to Börresen, a Dane, who had helped many Norwegian students from pietist circles.

Born in Copenhagen in 1825, Hans Peter Börresen grew up in the old navy quarter, Christianshavn, then a depressed area. His father was a naval carpenter, but they were poor, and the father died when Hans Peter was six years old.[61] They lived on public charity, and the boy went to a charity school. He never liked reading, but had an excellent head for practical matters. The maritime milieu brought an interest in foreign countries, and he was fascinated by the coloured people he met in the port. Even though his mother made fun of the revivalists he dreamt of becoming a missionary. Börresen was impressed by the religious instruction at school. After trying cobblery he was apprenticed as a blacksmith, becoming a mechanic. A handsome boy, with a good voice, he sang in the best choir in Copenhagen. At one time he wanted to become an actor. Hans Peter wanted to get along in the world. By the war of 1848,[62] his applications for a job rejected, he wanted to join the army, then planned to emigrate to England. But Börresen's sister had married a German, and lived in Berlin. In 1852, he joined her there (Birkeland 1902; Gjesing 1961).

Börresen was now a master mechanic, and got work with a firm of locomotive builders. Soon, he calls himself an engineer.[63] He certainly became a technician and trusted employee, with a respectable salary, and was able to help his mother. But he was lonely in Berlin. In 1853, he took his New Testament and sat down in the Tiergarten to read. His eyes fell on the story of the prodigal son. He felt that he, too, was lost, and knelt down: 'You must take mercy on me, for I have been baptized in Your Name!' An inner voice answered: 'Stand, your sins have been forgiven'. A friend from Copenhagen thought he'd gone mad, 'praying, singing, and going to Church' (Nyhagen I: 82-3). His mother, says Börresen, laughed at him. He interested himself in mission among the Jews, then thought of going to Africa (Skrefsrud 1897: 21-2). At this time he met J.F.C. Hempel, an Evangelical from Wittstock in Brandenburg, where he had his own factory. Bankrupt, he now worked for the company in Berlin, as Börresen's superior. The Hempels frequented the Bethlehem Church, founded by refugees from Prague and named after the chapel where Jan Hus had preached. A centre of pietist activity in Berlin, it had been Gossner's church. The priest was Gustav Knak, a powerful preacher, enthusiastic of the mission. Börresen married Caroline, Hempel's daughter born in 1832, two years later (Nyhagen I: 84-5). Their home became a link between Prussian pietists and visitors from Scandinavia, who sometimes lodged with them.

Skrefsrud arrived in Berlin in 1862, and was well received by the Börresens. He worked in a mechanical workshop, and entered the Gossnerian Mission School. In the evenings, he lodged with the Börresens, feeling like a son of the family. He finished his exams in a single year, as one of the best students, some of whom had taken four years (Döhl 1944: 18). Börresen went to Sweden to build a branch factory for his employers, and was offered a managerial post there. But then J.D. Prochnow, the leader of the Gossner Missionary Society,[64] visited the Börresens. He urged them to go to India, where missionaries were needed. Skrefsrud, says Börresen, was like 'oil thrown on to the fire' of this plan.

Before leaving for India, Skrefsrud returned to Norway, where he married Anne Onsum. The marriage established, for Skrefsrud, close relations with the leading families in Lillehammer, which were to stand him in good stead later. Clearly, his conversion and will to become a missionary earned him the goodwill of the best local circles. Anne was an earnest Christian who shared his enthusiasm for missionary work.

The organization of Gossner's missionary society was characterized by a lack of bureaucracy. Prochnow directed the whole operation. In the field, missionaries organized themselves to make a living: there were no funds from home. India was among the first of the Mission's fields. In 1839, nineteen missionaries were sent to the Gangetic plains, and in 1841, we find six among the Gonds. In 1844, Gossner sent four missionaries to Burma, but in Calcutta they met the widow of a German doctor who had dedicated his modest fortune to the mission. The missionaries accept her support, and after several abortive attempts (Tibet, Simla) decided to work among the Kol. They had seen Kol men working as coolies on the Hooghly. They went to Chotanagpur, where they were well received by the officials, and received some land from the Raja, whose family, it seems, was impressed by the pamphlets they had brought. Still, they were unable to convert a single tribal in the first five years. Then, in 1850, four Oraons, followers of the Kabir Panth,[65] want to hear about Jesus. When they demanded the *darshan*—vision—of Christ, the missionaries could not satisfy them. Still, they do convert, and by 1857 there are seven hundred converts. Then the mutiny breaks out. The local zamindar puts a price on the missionaries' heads, to procure them for sacrifice to the Goddess Durga. Many converts were killed, and the missionaries took flight. But the Gossnerians returned to Chotanagpur, and from their work descends the largest Protestant Church in northern India. It is here that we find Skrefsrud and the Börresens, as missionaries for the Gossner Society, from 1863.

## NOTES

1. The term Dissenter was used in Britain at least from the time of Elizabeth (Miegge 1995: 423).
2. As Georg Sverdrup believed (Hamre 1986).
3. The term 'subjectivist' does not reflect Pietist views. For Pietists individual inspiration came from God and so represented truth. To critics from the established church, individuals were limited in their appreciation of truth.
4. Ruled 1699–1730.
5. The Danish colony south of Pondicherry.
6. Ruled 1730-46.
7. In Norway, the law was recalled officially only in 1842 (Skard 1976).
8. In Scotland, several central Enlightenment figures were priests. This synthesis between rationality and religion is less evident in Scandinavia, however.
9. Also known as the community of Brethren, or Herrnhutists, after their first settlement Herrnhut, 'fear of God'. Among their odd practices was marriage by drawing lots, to gurantee that God's will was done.
10. They opened missions to the Danish Caribbean (1,732), Greenland (1,733), the North American Indians and insular South-East Asia (1,735), South Africa (1,736) and Labrador (1,771). By the 1960s there were 25,000 in Europe and 46,000 in the United States, but 2,10,000 in the third or the fourth world (Molland 1969a, b).
11. E.g. Trevelyan 1944, Bebbington 1989.
12. Puritanism remained a strong influence on Methodism, while 'Puritan' and 'Calvinist' were terms of abuse in the Church of England (Bebbington 1989: 35-8).
13. 'The religious revival arose from the conflicts under James II', but did

not 'wholly subside with the crisis that gave it birth' (Trevelyan 1944: 325-6).

14. Born in 1703 and 1707 they both went to America as missionaries, but returned in 1737 and 1736.
15. John sailed to America with Lutheran refugees from Austria. Their ministers, like the Danish missionaries to Tranquebar, were trained at Halle. A Herrnhutist, Peter Böhler, became his 'chief guide' towards conversion.
16. At Herrnhut, there were different views: Wesley concluded that assurance was a gift from God, not intrinsic to conversion, but usually possessed by the believer.
17. This is what Weber associates with worldly asceticism.
18. Manifest in societies such as 'The Society for Promoting Christian Knowledge' (1698), of which the 'Society for the Propagation of the Gospel in Foreign Parts' (SPG) was an offshoot (Bebbington 1989: 327-8).
19. Württemberg in 1812, Sweden in 1813. Denmark 1814, and Norway 1816. Still, Hamburg was the port of entry for the British Bible Society, and it was from there the revival spread.
20. Several religious figures such as Thomas Scott and Henry Venn talk of experience or observation as an authority for religion, along with the scriptures (Bebbington 1989: 57).
21. His defence of Schlegel's novel 'Lucinde' — advocating free love — forced him to leave Berlin. After a professorship at Halle, lost by Napoleon's invasion in 1806, he returned to Berlin in 1809.
22. Most of Saxony was annexed to Prussia in 1815.
23. 'Universalist' implies potential salvation for all: non-Christians should be converted to save their souls. These ideas stem from the sixteenth century debates on whether American Indians had souls. Universalists also constituted a small but well-known sect of dissenters.
24. Chartered as the 'Royal University of Fredericksnagore', the first European-style university in India.
25. 'an indiscriminate migration to Bengal during the eighteenth century of Europeans of all kinds', as Marshall puts it (1976: 21).
26. This term included descendants of Portuguese adventurers on the Bengal and Arakan coasts, but was also used rather extensively for those who were neither native nor British.
27. Bose 1993: 70, citing Hunter 1894: 31-4.
28. A policy which contrasts with later efforts at bolstering them, as in Rajasthan.
29. Other estimates talk of a fifth.
30. Similar structures existed in the Sundarbans, but here Muslims and Namasudras furnished the labour.
31. From 1800 to 1815 production rose from 40,000 to 120,000 maunds.

32. Chowdhury 1975: 133. In 1829, Rammohan Roy wrote that indigo growers looked better off than their neighbours, but Bose feels he must be referring to an even earlier state of affairs.
33. Bengal's first steam engine came in 1818. By 1845 there were 150, generating 6,000 horsepower.
34. Bentinck (1748-1832) is remembered, among other things, for his reform of the Criminal Code.
35. The literature on the Bengal renaissance is vast. See Borthwick 1984, Crawford 1987, Gray 1975, Hannerz 1992, Kling 1975, Kopf 1969, 1975, 1979. Majumdar 1960, 1963, Mukherjee 1978, Mukhopadhyay 1979, Poddar 1970, Zastoupil and Moir 1999, and for the missionary role Forrester 1980, Howells 1927, Laird 1972, Oddie 1994, 1999, Potts 1967.
36. Roy corresponds with J. Sparks of Baltimore, a friend of de Tocqueville and of Thomas Jefferson, the president.
37. See Metcalf 1995: 136.
38. Kramer, a South African anthropologist settled in Norway, writes of Norwegian culture as 'tribal' (1984).
39. Norway is said to have been united by Harald Fairhair, around AD 900.
40. Present-day Trondheim.
41. One Indian parallel was Mewar, held in fief from the god Eklingji (Stern 1976).
42. This notion of kingship may have survived till the death of Olav V in 1991, when people spontaneously lighted tens of thousands of candles in the snow outside the palace to mourn him.
43. Thus the *Norwegian Society* in Copenhagen from 1772, recruited from students, officials, and merchants.
44. Norwegian tonnage doubled during the war. L.H. Fisker, admiral of the Norwegian navy 1807-14, had served in the War of Independence under French flag.
45. Their view, inspired by French ideas of the sovereignty of the people, was stated by Georg Sverdrup in a meeting at Eidsrold on 16 February. We meet some other members of his family later.
46. Of 112 representatives, 59 were officials, 37 came from the rich peasants, and 16 were merchants. By their numbers and knowledge of constitutional ideas the officials dominated the proceedings (Jensen 1963, 15-16).
47. The world freedom, in Norway, conflates nationalism with democracy, as was evident when Norwegians debated their relation to Europe.
48. Almost all towns were on the coast. The two exceptions were mining communities run by a state monopoly.
49. Apart from Irish Catholic immigrants.
50. Among organizations directed at specific groups were the YMCA (1844), initially aimed at 'shop assistants and their peers', and the

Missions to Seamen (1856). They often received financial aid from rich Christians.

51. Chalmers, for example, insisted that 'in no circumstances, high unemployment included, should the able-bodied poor have a right to relief' (Bebbington 1989: 121).
52. Indications from sources such as literacy tests of soldiers, are matched by reading as a common practice. Peasants and members of the nascent urban population read and wrote.
53. 'Underjordiskc', also called 'haugfolk' (hill-men). They are like men, but are not Christians and iron will hurt them.
54. The house is preserved, in the midst of the recent Olympic installations, as Skrefsrud became a national hero.
55. 'house-man'.
56. Such as the sociologist Thorstein Veblen and Ole Evenrud, inventor of the outboard engine.
57. Like Whitman. Wergeland wrote poetry without rhyme or metre.
58. The club or mace of farmers. In the sixteenth century rebellious peasants referred to the 'army of the huns' which would kill the nobles and restore the manor to the people. They carried a mace (Bull 1985: 103).
59. With 143 of his collaborators.
60. Founded 1854.
61. Döhl, eager to construct the Santal Mission as Norwegian, affirms that Börresen's family was of Norwegian origin (1944: 17). We have found no such mention elsewhere.
62. The war with the German empire, which Denmark won, resulted from the conflict over Schleswig-Holstein.
63. The title was not yet protected. Yet Börresen, boasting, let out that he had been 'Principal of the Royal Engineering College for sons of noblemen in Berlin' (Sherring 1875) which was nonsense. But it seems he did teach at a technical college (Gjesing 1961: 25-6; Nyhagen 1990, I: 82).
64. Founded 1836.
65. The Kabir Panthis are the followers of the poet-saint Kabir, who lived in the fifteenth century. In the *bhakti* tradition, he was devoted to a single God and denounced caste difference and the cult of images.

# 3

# Santal Memory and Identity

## THE HISTORIC DEPTH OF SANTAL IDENTITY

The Santal today number some five million, and are spread out over a large area mainly in the states of Jharkhand, Bengal, and Orissa. Many have migrated further afield, to Assam, the Nepal foothills, and northern Bangladesh. They are usually described as a tribe, once a salient category in colonial ethnography. Several scholars contest the use of the term claiming that the distinction between tribe and caste is a colonial invention.[1] Others, like Bayly (1995) admit that the various compendia of 'tribes and castes' encouraged a consolidation of ethnic ascriptions, but do not imply that social boundaries were absent earlier. We can hardly assume that there were no ethnic groups before the colonial period. Moreover, older Indian sources tended to distinguish the Savaras[2] from the people of the plains (Kosambi 1975).

Several factors belie a wholesale invention of ethnicity for Santals and other tribes. First, most tribal groups speak languages radically different from the surrounding peoples, which cannot be the result of colonial discourse. Nor is it obvious how radically different gender relations, kinship structures, or religious ideas could have emerged in colonial times. These differences are as striking now as they were in the nineteenth century. If tribal culture was created by a short moment of colonial influence, then it remains to explain how it has changed so little in spite of the radical transformations of more recent times. We must assume, then, that the central elements of Santal cultural specificity were present before colonialism moulded the place that tribes were to occupy in its schemes. That process is central to the modern history of the Santals.

Kaviraj (1993) holds that in India there has been a shift from fuzzy group identities in the premodern period to distinct, modern communities. Individuals did hold group identities, but they were not relevant to all dimensions of selfhood, and enumeration and classification was not yet of central importance (Chatterjee 1993: 223, Karlsson 2000: 234). Fuzzy identities may apply in many cases, but we doubt whether they do to the Santals.

Dumont (1966: 106) identified peripheral populations with the margins of society. But the Santals feel they do not belong to the caste system. To see tribes as defined by their marginality denies cultural specificity to them, taking for granted that they will ultimately join the national mainstream. Fortunately, historical analysis does not always conceal tribal identity, as Samaddar shows (1998). He urges us not to legitimize the *memocide* which deprives tribal people of their identity.[3]

The debate between Ghurye (1943)—who denied cultural specificity to tribes—and Elwin who defended their cultural difference (1944), is central to Indian discussion of the problem. Ghurye was partial to an assimilationist policy, while Elwin, keen to protect tribes from exploitation and cultural degradation, wanted to shelter them in their own territories. The sanskritization model (Srinivas 1952, 1962, 1967) ascribes to lower groups a mere imitation of higher caste behaviour and values, though Bailey (1959) used it to analyse low-caste strategies on their own terms. Hinduization (Ghurye 1943) relates to Hindu influence pervading tribal cultures to move them along an implicit scale of cultural evolution. This mode of acculturation tinged with paternalism still prevails. By 'progress' or 'uplift' Vidyarthi (1964) for instance implies that tribal people should develop high-caste ways, sanskritization and hinduization being perspectives that serve assimilationist policies. For our part, however, we see exchanges between the great tradition—identified with brahmanic elements—and the little tradition, which corresponds to local knowledge and belief (Marriott ed. 1955).

The Santals resisted dominance in various ways, and the Santal rebellion is well known. Yet few scholars have paid sufficient attention to the semantic of Santal identity. Their resistance is marked not just by the construction of ethnic boundaries (Barth 1969a,b), nor the mere preservation of custom, but also by the capacity to symbolically inscribe elements borrowed from others. The Santals consider themselves as a people speaking a particular language, and are aware of sharing life styles and values that are different from those of the Hindus. We use the term ethnicity here to imply that the distinctiveness of the group and a conscious identity have developed historically, through contact with others.[4]

Santals call themselves *hor hopon ko,* children of men, as opposed to *diku,* outsiders and foreigners. They distinguish *maran diku,* upper caste Hindus seen as oppressors, from *hurin diku*, low caste Hindus regarded as neighbours.[5] The custom of *bitlaha* or banishment of those who did not respect endogamy, current until the late 1950s, shows clearly how Santals defined an ethnic boundary by punishing with the same rigor the incestuous and the exogamous (Carrin-Bouez 1986, 1991).[6] They see themselves as members of the Santal *samaj* (society) and the formulation of Santal ethnicity is rooted in the consciousness of a distinctive past. It is on this basis that Santals act, in different social and political contexts, as members of a 'scheduled tribe', or as *adivasis*[7] 'first settlers' or *jharkhandis.*[8] They are not, thus, an isolated tribe, even if our missionaries tended to see them as such. Missionary discourse—as that of the Catholics among the Munda—stresses the ethnic barrier between the tribes and surrounding peoples. To them, the pristine tribal culture has been flawed by intrusions from the lowlands.

For contemporary Santals and Mundas, to be an *adivasi*—means to descend from a group of ancestors who cleared the land. If first occupancy cannot be proved, it still grounds a feeling of belonging which gives form to ethnicity. For Sivaramakrishnan, however, the people who first settled in what he calls the anomalous zones of the Jungle Mahals were people of mixed origin in search of new lands. 'Becoming native to a place', he notes, 'was always preceded by a movement into that place, voluntary or forced . . . sometimes being characterized (as) the original migration' (1999: 88). The Santal case epitomizes such recent migration whereas the Munda have undergone a long process of sedentarization followed by stratification. Sivaramakrishnan seems to suppose that Santals had no identity when migrating. For the anthropologist, this is problematic. Yet sedentarization has certainly contributed to the development of certain aspects of Santal culture such as chiefs and priests.

Colonial discourse redefined the ties of the Santal to the forest that they cleared, eradicating wild animals. The embeddedness of the forest in Santal symbolism, we feel, is too deep to stem from colonial developments. Even though the British constructed tribal territory, they could not have created tribal culture. What historians have analysed are developments in colonial policy and control, which certainly helped recast identies, but also provoked resistance that later crystallized in ethnic claims.

Santal myths consistently stress identity in relation to neighbouring peoples. Some narrate how the ancestors left Chotanagpur in protest against Munda chiefs who were getting hinduized—those who stayed became dependent on the Mundas. This is said to have happened some five hundred years ago. The Santal creation myth tells us how the god Maran Buru taught Pilcu Haram and Pilcu Budhi, brother and sister, to brew rice-beer. Drinking, they forgot they were siblings and commited incest. From this union twelve children are born, forming twelve clans. The boys and girls start to question their kinship relations. But through *maya* (illusion), Maran Buru made them forget the rules of kinship, and he married one to the other. He then gave land to each of the first seven clans: the Hansdas (elders), Murmu (priests), Kisku (kings), Hembrom (noblemen), Marandi (land-owners), Soren (soldiers), and Tudu (musicians). Maran Buru then created five inferior clans: the Baske (those who ate the leftovers), Besra (the libidinous), the Core (toads), the Pauria (whose name has no obvious meaning) and the Bedea (those who were left apart). The clan organization reflects the dual opposition of the Kisku and Murmu, and alludes to a functional division. Later, due to migrations, the clans segmented into 160 sub-clans (*khunt*).[9] In sub-clan myths the split is often attributed to an ancestor eating forbidden food, or forgetting how to sacrifice properly; his kin are then reduced to inferior status. Such mistakes qualify junior groups in most sub-clans. The elders, who committed no transgression, are called *nij,* seniors, and considered superior. The unity of a sub-clan is maintained by commensality and common ritual performance.

Other traditions, such as Santal poetry, link the Santals to Champa, identified by some early writers with the kingdom in northern Cambodia.[10] More probably, Champa was in the Ganges valley, or in Hazaribagh north of Chotanagpur. Chattopadhyay (1944) thinks the Santals entered Hazaribagh by the pass known as *Campa duar*, and continued into the Chotanagpur plateau. Waddell (1893) felt that place names in Santal tales refer to the central Gangetic valley, and that they came to Hazaribagh as a result of the Aryan onslaught. Intensive cultivation and political subjection may well have driven the Santals into the hills, but no evidence identifies the Santals or other Austro-Asiatic peoples with the inhabitants of the northern plains before the forests were cleared.

The contiguity of Santal culture with that of its Austro-asiatic speaking neighbours is clear. Santali is very close to the language of the Birhor of Hazaribagh,[11] and clan names are similar (Roy 1925). We do not know if the Santals were once hunters and gatherers, like the Birhor, but their tradition claims they subsisted on game and forest produce when on the move. Neither do we know when the Santals began to cultivate; in their creation myth, Maran Buru teaches them to sow. But Hunter (1975: 214) thought 'that the Santal was from no distant period an agriculturist . . . and that his language and festivals clearly proves it'.[12] The Santals themselves say they became settled agriculturists in the eighteenth century—seven generations back in 1970.

The Western Jungle Mahals[13] were ruled by chiefs never reduced to submission by the Mughals (Thapar and Siddiqi 2003). The Santals were then practising slash and burn cultivation (Hamilton 1828) such as was still found in remote parts of Singhbhum in 1970. Fields must lie fallow some two years so one must clear new land, for which Santals competed with others like the Malers who farmed in a similar way. They seem to have hunted and gathered in the rainy season,[14] as did the Paharias who depended more exclusively on this activity. Santals used to collect *sabai* grass with which they thatched their roofs. The Paharias grew maize as their staple food on the hills, while Santals grew rice on the slopes. They developed a mythology of rice centered on agricultural operations. While they were sought by *zamindars* for clearing land they were not seen as ideal tenants.

According to tradition, the headman (*manjhi*) led migration to new lands. When founding a village, he brandished a branch of the *sal* tree,[15] symbol of the ancestors, and consulted oracles. The first settlers often belonged to a single clan, but later arrivals were accepted and adopted through fictive kinship. The communal task of clearing forest led to a sense of community, and settlers shared the land, which the *manjhi* distributed. Chosen by the villagers to dispense justice, the latter enjoyed a share for his services. He conducted negotiations with outsiders, while the *naike* led the seasonal rituals.

## THE FOREST DWELLERS IN MODERN HISTORY

Historians of the Muslim period speak of the Jharkhand, including Chotanagpur, Birbhum, and Western Burdwan (Mukherji 1975), as a forest region with insular tribal populations. Since accession to the Diwani, the East India Company tried to increase revenue from the Jungle Mahals. As they were fixing the revenue there in 1793, large tracts were uncultivated, but Santals were clearing waste lands to plant rice (Sen 1984). The famine was one reason they came: three years after the famine, so much land lay unused that the Council tried to attract subjects of princely states to these territories. In 1776, the scarcity of labour was still a problem for landlords and the price of land was low.

In eighteenth century Bengal, the main type of insurrection were bands of armed sadhus or fakirs, sometimes joined by demobilized soldiers. Poverty-stricken peasants swelled their ranks following the 1770 famine, as they attacked mofussil factories, revenue offices, and the kachharis and granaries of landlords. Tribals, too, were involved: in the wake of the famine, highlanders plundered the Rajmahal hills and the British had to intervene (Bose 1993: 144, citing Ghose 1901). In 1786, there was massive protest in Birbhum against the increased revenue (Bose 1993: 146). The insurgents were beaten. It is likely that Santals were among them, as in the more succesful no-rent campaign in the district in 1789. Thousands of peasants had been on the march, and were joined by disbanded soldiers of the old Birbhum state (Bose 1993: 146, citing R.K.Gupta 1977).

By the early colonial period, Santals were found in Birbhum, Midnapur, and Singhbhum (Duyker 1987, Blochmann 1968). The first mention of them is in Shore's account (1795) of three 'Soontars' accused of murdering five witches in Birbhum. Hamilton (1828) describes the western half of the district, where the forest was broken by small patches of cultivation 'occupied by a poor miserable proscribed race of men called Santals'. Forest clearing was part of a migration which continued to gather Santals in the Jungle Mahals in the first quarter of the nineteenth century, along with Paharias and the Bhumij peasantry.

After the Permanent Settlement of 1793, zamindars and chiefs found it hard to collect the revenue since the assessment was too high (Sen 1984: 44). They had no right to remission, even for calamities such as drought, and the indebted zamindars lost their forts between 1780 and 1800. But they resisted the transfer of their estates to outsiders (Jha 1967, Sivaramakrishnan 1999). It was difficult to collect rent from Santals, however: if they found the demand too high they left to take land elsewhere (O'Malley 1911: 59). In the Jungle Mahals, the Chuar rebelled several times between 1799 and 1832. They were mostly Bhumij, the original inhabitants of the hills between Ghatsila and Barabhum. They owned their land

and claimed Kshatriya status (Sen 1997). Probably there were Santals among the rebels and in Midnapur and neighbouring areas they knew about the rebellion. The 1799 rebellion wrought great instability in the region, causing hardship among the peasants (Sen 1997: 37). In Manbhum, the ryots rose against the zamindar. Here, Santals and other tenants had to withdraw to the forest when sepoys burnt their villages.

The tribal fringes of Bengal were characterized by the *mandali* system in which the village headman was responsible for revenue and the maintenance of order. Santal land was often tilled in common, but the British preferred to deal with recognized leaders. The British saw a potential for development in the Jungle Mahals. Wood and Metal ore were abundant, but the zamindars did not invest in communications. Minerals and forest products were left unexploited, and agriculture was stagnant, as the zamindars were often unable to pay even for a dam (Hunter 1975). The Permanent Settlement wrought the area open, and started an infringement on the right of *adivasis* over the forest. The forest was leased to Europeans. Santals were not allowed to cut trees or collect forest produce without paying. As the Company introduced laws from the 1810s onward to protect landlords, the latters' interests came to coincide with those of the colonial regime, while their efforts to increase rent deepened conflict with tenants. Tribal people of the Jungle Mahals were reluctant to go to the courts, and preferred to flee into the forest, the most common strategy of resistance as long as there was space for it (Bose 1993: 147). This left no trace in the documents of administrators, so that the movement was ignored by the authorities. Instead, the Chuar revolt of 1799 and the Bhumij rebellion of 1832 were held responsible for the migration of Santals to the Damin-i-Koh. There were some reforms in the early nineteenth century, such as a draft to exempt the forest tracts of Midnapur, Burdwan, and Ramgarh from existing regulations. The government blocked land purchase in the Jungle Mahals as no buyer could enter the troubled areas. In 1805, a Magistrate was appointed to administer the area. Some Santals—mostly headmen—were given permanent leases by zamindars.

The 1809 Chuar revolt was followed by other popular revolts in several parts of the Jungle Mahals. After the revolt, which had impoverished the country, new regulations caused much discontent as the land passed to new zamindars like the raja of Burdwan. The

British responded by establishing indirect rule. From the 1820s, in Bengal as a whole, 'the balance of forces was clearly tilted against the peasantry'. They responded, and the two worldwide depressions of the early 1830s and late 1840s saw more than usual unrest (Bose 1993: 147-8). In 1831, the inhabitants of four Ho villages in Chotanagpur raided the surrounding country. The spoils were distributed and whatever was indivisible held in common by the insurgents. The violence of such raids, however, often remained symbolic since there was no killing.

A personal feud for the succession of Barabhum turned into the Kol insurrection of 1832 (Jha 1964). The rebels maintained solidarity with neighbouring tribal groups: the Kols of Singhbhum, for example, supported the Dhangar Kols. The government had to protect the frontier of the Jungle Mahals from the Kols. Finally the raja of Singhbhum, instead of suppressing the rebellion, gave villages to a Kol leader. Following the Bhumij revolt of 1833 the district of the Jungle Mahals was broken up.

The mandali system was still the backbone of the Santal economy in these regions. Tribal labour was better off in districts such as Midnapur and Bankura, where 'the communitarian forms of their social organization had remained substantially intact' (Bose 1993: 78). Tribal leaders negotiated rent and contracts on behalf of the community, and up to 1810-20 the scarcity of labour got them easy terms, which were permanent, heritable, and transferable. Zamindars did not interfere in the relations between a mandal and his community. By 1830, with increasing population, Zamindars exerted pressure to impose 'more rigid rental contracts based on accurate measurement'. In 1839, British officials in Midnapur ruled in favour of the zamindars; mandals had only ryoti rights with no proceeds from their rent-collecting function (see also Sen 1984: 42-3). Still, 'intra-tribal relations under the mandali system were able to stand external pressures until the 1860s' (Bose 1993: 78). Later, mahajans assumed the power of a tenure holder and enhanced the rent. Among the Mundas of Chotanagpur, Thapar and Siddiqi feel, there had long existed a structural conflict between class solidarity and chiefly claims (2003: 35-6).

Bose feels that the main conflict was between zamindars and peasants, indicating the 'absence of kin-based vertical ties' (1993: 146-7).[16] But Sivaramakrishnan cites the solidarity of zamindars and tenants during the Chuar rebellions (1999: 50-1; also Devalle 1992:

114). The class and ethnic solidarities created through these and later movements were to have important consequences later (Devalle 1992, Carrin 2002).

## THE SANTALS IN THE DAMIN-I-KOH

Jungle zamindars were 'lords of transition' in a zone between forest tribes and regional states, subsisting on barter and raids. In or around the Rajmahal hills, zamindars used to recruit Maler and Paharia auxiliaries to raid their enemies. In 1772, Captain Barker was commissioned to establish peace. In 1770 Augustus Cleveland, appointed collector of Bhagalpur, took the first steps to place the region under British authority. He exempted the Hill people from revenue, gained the confidence of the Paharias, and proposed a form of rule which recognized aspects of their customary law.

In 1809-1810 Buchanan Hamilton visited Bhagalpur, which then included Mongyr and the north-eastern part of the future Santal Parganas. He found 500 Santal families established in the area called Damin-i-Koh; their settlement at Dumka was recent. They had come to escape the zamindars.[17] According to Bradley-Birt (1905), the Paharias were then in control of the Rajmahal hills, in the northern part of the Damin.

In 1823, the Government declared the 'tract occupied by the hill people . . . (and) the level of the lands skirting the hills outside zamindaris and estates the property of the Government' (O'Malley 1910: 43). In 1824, J.P. Ward was appointed to define the limits of the government estate. He took nine years to complete his survey. Ward proposed that *pattas* be granted to 49 Santal headmen. Cleveland had died in 1784 but his policy was taken up by H.C. Sutherland, and the territory of Damin-i-Koh was created in 1833 (O'Malley 1910: 37).

However, Ward's survey led to endless litigation (Rottger-Hogan 1982: 84) as the zamindars protested. Around 1827, the Hill people seemed content though efforts to civilize the Paharias had failed. In the late 1840s, however, the British had to intervene in the Rajmahal hills to pacify the Paharias (Bradley-Birt 1905). In 1837 the Board of Revenue approved Ward's proposals.

The Santals had come to the Damin to escape the zamindar oppression in Birbhum and Singhbhum. They had heard of virgin lands, but were also incited by contractors and administrators to clear the jungle, in which they excelled (McPherson 1909: 35). They served as a link between highlanders such as the Paharias and the lowlanders. They moved from the south of the Jungle Mahals towards the north, reaching Dumka towards 1810. During 1815–1830, Sutherland, magistrate in Bhagalpur, noted that Santals were clearing the forest in Godda sub-division. Ward, too, found Santals in the northern part of Godda, where they had thirty villages and in Barkop where they had more than twenty-five. Much later, they were still moving into the Santal Parganas from Singhbhum and Dhalbhum (O'Malley 1910).

Soon, however, most zamindars and landowners were Hindus. Bengali merchants were attracted by the new opportunities, buying rice and mustard from Santals and shipping it to Britain by Calcutta. The Santals received money, salt, and tobacco but at less than market rate. They were soon in debt to the moneylenders.[18] They were opposed to assessment, finding it unjust to pay rent for land they had themselves cleared, and, since large areas lay fallow every year, to pay for land not cropped. This created conflict with zamindars and the government. Tensions were mounting in a system which put local power in the hands of Hindus and Muslims. Different police systems were competing to control a situation where bribery was common. Tribal groups clashed with the bureaucracy, since they thought in terms of the customary authority of tribal chiefs. The courts were far away in Bhagalpur, and the *daroga* (police inspector) often prevented the Santals from raising their complaints.

The Damin-i-Koh was a protected area where the laws of Bengal did not apply. Ward had proposed to allot land to non-tribal people in order to 'set the hillmen an example' (McPherson 1909: 34), but the government wanted to reserve the land to encourage 'the hill race' in its agricultural pursuits. Yet Santal settlements were useful to control the Paharias. The Damin was transformed to render habitable those regions infested by wild beasts (Hunter 1975: 311). The main object of the government in settling the Santals was to gain revenue. But there was also talk of encouraging missionary activity. 'These people have no definite religious system to guide them . . . it is not too much to suppose that the labour of a devout missionary would make rapid progress and extend . . . to the Hills where in reference to the character and religion of the Hill race the facilities for propagating the Gospel would be equally great'.[19] Christianity, besides, might serve to pacify the region.

In 1837, J. Pontet became superintendent of the Damin-i-Koh, responsible for revenue. He was briefed to protect the Santal. From his 1839 report we learn that their land was encroached on by plains people with the connivance of amins and naib sejwals. These cases were judged by munsiffs, and the mahajan invariably won[20] (Man 1867: 113). Santals were evicted whilst zamindars and traders grabbed their land, and darogas were eager to keep the Santals from complaining in court. The dishonesty of the mahajan and the increasing poverty caused by hereditary debt bondage, embittered the Santals. Pontet had no right, however, to intervene in disputes (Sen 1997: 123). 'All that could be done in the limit of powers at his disposal Mr. Pontet did. Disobeyed and harassed by the police who had no respect for a magistrate with neither assessment nor civil powers, his opinion and advices were obstentatiously neglected' (Bradley-Birt 1905: 164-5).

By then the scattered clearings Shore and Hamilton described had given way to larger Santal villages, as Captain Sherwill noted in his survey of the Damin-i-Koh in 1851. Looking for coal and iron deposits, he describes the economic conditions in the countryside. The villages are still surrounded by dense jungle, but large sheets of cultivation cover the tops of the hills. The standard Santal dwelling houses about ten family members. Among implements, he notes a wooden press for extracting mustard oil, while domestic animals such as buffalos, cows, and poultry are abundant. Sherwill notes that the Santal population had risen from 3,000 at the time of Buchanan's visit to more than 80,000, while the number of villages had risen from 40 to 473.[21] But already, the extension of indigo farming[22] was competing for fertile land.

At the heart of the Damin was the town of Burhait, where fifty families of Bengali traders lived, with a good bazar and two weekly markets. Sherwill found 'the amount of grain, the produce of the valley exposed for sale was very great: numerous carts from Jangipur on the Bhagiratti were in attendance to convey it towards Murshedabad, and eventually to Calcutta from whence much of the mustard . . . is exported to England' (Sherwill 1851: 566-74). Rottger-Hogan remarks: 'so rapidly had the Santals been plugged into the world economy . . . it was not the Santals who moved by stages to the complexities of modern economic relationships, but rather the market economy that engulfed the Santals' (1982: 81).[23]

The earlier protectionist attitude was gradually changing. Hunter notes the high proportion, 47.5 per cent, of children in the population (Hunter 1976: 279). No statistics, notes Rottger-Hogan, allow us to compare the demographic explosion with grain production. But the latter seems to have reached a limit by 1850, as further clearings were limited by outcrops of basaltic rock (Hunter 1976: 341). It is difficult to know to what extent conditions were getting worse. Hunter feels that 20 to 25 acres would be a comfortable holding for a family (ibid.), but the Santal average was just about 10 acres (Rottger-Hogan 1982: 85). Zamindars had to cope with bad crops and yet fulfil their contracts; they shifted the burden to the peasants. Santals generally held annual leases and paid in kind.[24] They became ever more dependent on the mahajan and the rate of interest reached a hundred per cent. They could not generate surplus, and had practically no hope of recovery. Still, Santals clung to their mahajan, whose penetration created new demands but also social tension. In times of hardship they lived on forest produce.

The monetary expressions of concepts such as rent and property were alien to the Santals, who used to think in terms of festive consumption. Surplus or not, Santals had to spend on traditional festivals, or face anger and resentment. The mahajan's graft was bad enough but even worse were cattle lifting by his men and the rape of Santal women by mahajan and daroga.[25] These changes contributed to the breakdown of the older mode of production. From around the middle of the century, the Santals began to labour on railways and roads. Such works had created a demand for labour, with a rise in wages as well as prices. A tribal proletariat emerged and the exploitation it suffered certainly explains several later revolts (Singh 1978), but was a factor even in the Santal rebellion of 1855.

It was in 1854 that the railway came to India.[26] At first Santals were not conscious of what 'the iron horse' would be, as they laboured to lay tracks north and south of the Damin. But 'their services were in great demand and their wages high. Those who were free to go hurried to this new field of labour' (Bradley-Birt 1905: 182). This did not prevent Santals from rebelling against engineers and foremen. It seems they were not protesting only against work conditions but, rather, understood that the iron horse was one of the most efficient means of their enemy, the merchants, to greater profit. Tribals were also getting involved in the clearing and settlement of the north Bengal districts of Rangpur and Dinajpur, which gained momentum in the later part of the century. Here, labour was severely exploited, and we may suppose that the supply of workers exceeded the demand (Bose 1993: 77-8).

It was in 1854, too, that the CMS missionary E. Droese started work among the Santals of the Rajmahal hills. Work among the Paharias had started in 1850. The CMS were also the first missionaries to re-enter the hills after the uprising of 1857, in 1861, and to demand a grant for Santal education. It may not be entirely arbitrary that modern technology and missionary activity coincided: a possible link is the demand Droese found for education and literacy. The Santals, unlike the Paharias, struck Droese as 'being of a peculiarly teachable disposition'. Droese also claimed that 'in the villages where education had spread, there was no insurrection' during the Hul of 1855 (Chaudhuri 1995: 248).

## REBELLION AGAINST THE *DIKU*

Central to Santals were the two concepts *hor hopon,* children of men, and *hor disum*, the Santal country. The oppressors—zamindars, moneylenders, tax collectors, and planters—were all known by the term *diku*, 'foreigner'.[27] The contrast between *hor* and *diku* acquired this sense gradually, as Santals realized the oppressive nature of the colonial regime. By 1854, the term *diku* epitomized exploitation. Resistance was mainly aimed at moneylenders and merchants, but there was no question of refusing to pay rent; the Santals would simply ask for a reassessment and petition the government.[28] They also complained of the indigo planters, who had set up factories in the Damin and forced Santals to grow indigo. On the eve of the rebellion, they wrote a pamphlet against the planters in Hindi and in Santali.[29]

The Santal elite found itself increasingly excluded from the revenue system. By creating individual property and responsibility for revenue, the colonial system worsened the lot of the tribal cultivator. Debts were now inherited. Private property was an idea foreign to Santals. Traditionally, the village chief controls the distribution of land, but neither he nor his clan have property rights. Unlike Munda lineages,[30] the Santal lineages had no monopoly on land. Any Santal might have access to it.

According to Man (1867) the origins of the Santal rebellion can be traced to the 1830s. Land tilled by Santals had been transferred to plains people, and it was impossible to obtain redress. This fuelled the resentment felt by tribal and low caste groups, victims of the same exploitation. Moreover, Santals did not agree to the principles on which the rent was based. Sidhu, one of the leaders of the rebellion, wanted to tax each bullock which would do justice to the nature of Santal farming, where much land was left fallow. The Santal insurrection was an expression of economic and social demands, which have much in common with other examples of peasant insurgency (Guha 1983: 137), or even with the Thrane movement in Norway. But it also had its own symbolic character, expressing ethnic identity through the charismatic hero, fighting injustice.

By 1854, three generations of Santals were working to repay family debts (Hodne 1966: 21). Important, too, was the discrimination the Santals suffered from their Hindu neighbours, who saw them as outside the pale, below the untouchable Dom or Chamar. The Santals in turn assigned a low place to the Hindus in their own hierarchy (Bradley-Birt 1905: 162). Yet they could not ignore them. Land pressure had made retreat into the jungle impossible. That year, strange rumours were heard. Some cosmic disturbance was at hand: a she-buffalo ran all over the country and wherever she stopped, people were threatened by death. The Santals wondered whether to wait for the catastrophe. Another rumour ran that they were going to kill the *dikus*. At the entrance to every village three domestic tools were placed: a 'worn-out winnowing fan, a wooden cow bell, and an old broom; that they may know you are Santal' (Archer and Culshaw 1945: 220). These symbols of Santal identity marked the transition, during the last fifty years, from shifting to settled agriculture.

In 1855 Bir Singh, a traditional chief, declared that Chando Bonga, the Sun deity, had ordered him to fight injustice. Following the command, he and a few companions went to the market where they plundered some Bengali shops. Bir Singh was killed on the spot by the police. Even so, it is said he had powers to put his victims to sleep so that he could rob them. His action was legimate to the Santals, avenging the injustice mahajans had done to them. In the beginning of 1855, more than 7,000 Santals assembled to revenge Bir Singh's death.

On 30 June, insurgents from the Damin were joined at Bhagnadihi by Santals from other regions—Hazaribagh, Birbhum, and Bankura: eight or ten thousand had answered the call of the two brothers, Sidhu and Kanhu (Datta 1940: 14). They announced their vision:

they evoked a lost kingdom in which every clan had its fort. One night, a sheaf of paper fell on Sidhu's head and they saw Thakur, a white man with ten fingers on each hand, a symbol of power indeed. Accounts differ in detail: some say the man held a Bible, to others it was the Gospel of Saint John.[31]

Sidhu and Kanhu claimed that Thakur had ordered them to deliver the Santals from oppression. They ordered petitions to be sent to various administrators and zamindars, stating their intention to take over the Damin and found a Santal raj.[32] The text as dictated by Siddhu accuses the judges of extortion, and affirms that the country does not belong to the British: 'This is the sin of the Sahibs. And it is from this that Thakur has commanded me that the land does not belong to the Sahibs' (Bidwell 1856). The declaration ends in threats which were reiterated in a second petition the Santals planned to take to Calcutta, a plan they had to drop so as not to scatter their forces. The missives state that certain castes, such as the oil-pressers, potters, and blacksmiths, who had good relations with the Santals, would be spared the vengeance directed against the high castes (Datta 1940: 57).

Thakur continues to appear in various forms: a tongue of fire, a mountain, a *sal* tree,[33] and then a chariot wheel, a royal symbol that incited them to restore the lost kingdom. On the strength of that vision the brothers declared their intention to kill the district administrator and obtain justice. They took the title of Thakur, wore turbans, another royal symbol, let themselves be carried in palanquins, rode horses, and mounted an elephant during parades. But they always maintained that it was Thakur, the god, who would bring plenty and help them found the Santal raj. Sidhu and Kanhu stated they would not fight: Thakur would fight for them. They declared themselves masters of the movement inspired by the god 'coming from heaven' to free the Santals. Thakur had told them that the land belonged neither to Sahibs nor Hindus. From that point on, Thakur's attributes ceased to be essential. The brothers organized seances of possession where they made inspired speeches—the Thakur *parwanah*[34]—sent to surrounding villages with a sal branch, the traditional invitation to join a mass meeting or a hunt. They soon drew to themselves the rest of the tribe.

It is in the wake of their vision that Sidhu and Kanhu, helped by their two brothers, decided to take the Santals along with them and march to Bhagalpur. Thakur's order was to kill Pontet, so that the

Santals might obtain justice, and find their kingdom again. The first bloody encounters took place on 7 July 1855. Kanhu and his escort killed a police inspector who had acted against the Santal during some of the first incidents, and several Hindus in the marketplace at Litipara (Pakaur subdivision). The *hul* then spread from Taldonga south-west of Birbhum and Sainthia south-east of Bhagalpur. The government named a new District Administrator, A.C. Bidwell, who on 17 August issued a proclamation inviting the Santals to give themselves up, promising amnesty. The Santals, however, retreated to the hills. From the Damin, the insurgency spread to Birbhum, Midnapur and Bankura (Sen 1997: 67). By November the British realized that the movement had turned into rebellion, and they then declared martial law in Birbhum and Murshidabad. They chased the rebels into the hills. The British were impressed by Santal valour: They 'stood whenever their drum was beating' and seemed to ignore the danger of firearms as their leaders had assured them that the British weapons could not harm them: they were protected by Thakur and the *bongas*, (tribal deities) (Sen 1997: 127-8).

By 15 July 1856 the Santals are beaten. Civilians, landowners, merchants, higher caste Hindus and Muslims, had been assisting the army with elephants, boats, and supplies. On 2 September there was a resurgence. The Santals, still led by Sidhu and Kanhu, attacked thirty villages and an indigo factory. In February 1857, Kanhu was captured by the police with the help of a Santal informer, and executed. His brothers were killed during the last confrontation. The rebellion ended in bloody repression. It is hard to know the number killed: while Sen (1997: 61) stresses that twelve to fourteen thousand Santals were weakened and decimated by hunger and illness, Macphail (1922: 61) feels the rebellion has cost some ten thousand Santal lives.

The movement was led in an autocratic manner by Sidhu, Kanhu, and their two younger brothers, who played a subordinate role. The brothers were landless farmers with no traditional position. The followers were mainly Santal, but eyewitnesses noted the participation of agricultural or artisan castes, such as the Mahto and Kurmi. During the rebellion, notes Guha (1983), low-caste people were repeatedly found to have hidden the loot of the Santals. Moreover, in their texts[35] they claim their rebellion was a struggle against the mahajan, equally benefiting low-caste people, though the Santals and their leaders had shown the way. The revolt saw 'a complex convergence . . . of tribalism, religious communitarianism and class consciousness', evident in the 'cooperation achieved among various Santal sub-groups and a deliberate decision not to attack the non-tribal poor' (Bose 1993: 152).

## THE SYMBOLISM OF THE SANTAL REBELLION

Thakur appears in the creation myth after Maran Buru who created the world, and causes a rain of fire to destroy humanity. But he then saves a human couple born from the eggs of sea-birds. Thakur appoints Maran Buru as their guardian. But while the latter is a tolerant grandfather who teaches humans to brew rice-beer and induces them to incest, Thakur is a punitive, authoritarian figure who brings labour, death, and property into the world. When Thakur first appears to Sidhu and Kanhu, it is in the image of the oppressor: Thakur is also the term for a landlord. In the context of the rebellion, the myth of Thakur is remodelled by Sidhu and Kanhu to provide ultimate authority, utterly foreign to Santal thought: the traditional chief's power forms part of a hierarchy of divided rights.

Since God speaks through them, they speak truth, and Thakur becomes a myth in his own right. His authority, a cultural loan from the colonial order, allows the leaders, through possession, to transmit the 'orders from Thakur' in their own voice. The content of Sidhu and Kanhu's prophecies stem from an identification with the dominant where their destruction can be imagined only in a religious idiom. Their legitimizing discourse is framed by two figures: one is the sacred book, the other the royal chariot wheel and umbrella appearing in the sky. Scholars (Fuchs 1965, Datta 1940) note seven apparitions of Thakur. When Kanhu, the younger brother, was arrested, a book on railway technology which probably belonged to an engineer was found in his pocket. This book may symbolize European prestige, but a Santal narrative[36] written near the end of the century claims that Sidhu and Kanhu, who were sent to school by their stepfather—a well-to-do farmer—wanted to learn writing in order to run their kingdom. Here, writing is vested with symbolic efficacy.

A Santal who converted to protestantism, Chotrae Desmanjhi, fifteen years old at the time, alludes to these events in his autobiography (1938). He affirms that the book was the Bible, an interpretation also found in official letters. 'A shrine was erected', says O'Malley, 'consisting of a mound of mud crowned by a cart wheel, at which the villagers were instructed to present offerings of grain and milk, and to sacrifice kids and buffaloes. Here the worshippers were shown the slips of paper and the book (which proved to be none other than the Gospel according to St. John), and were told that in them were written the orders of the god' (cited by Ray 1983: 86). The reference to writing shows how Santals imagine the link between writing and power. Its internalization may have inspired the petition, translated into Hindi, addressed as a last recourse to the government.[37]

The revolt of the Santals began with an attack on moneylenders and during the rebellion the Santals wrought vengeance on them, attacking them repeatedly (Guha 1983). They were cut into pieces and each mutilation was compared to the fullfilment of part of the debt: as the head fell, the full amount was acquitted (Bradley-Birt 1905, Guha 1983). The Santals considered moneylenders and middlemen to be a kind of *diku* pollution, so that the streets of the village must be swept. There was some ambiguity in the fact that Santal ideology appropriated royal symbols for Santal leaders, while the rajas of Pakaur and Maheshaur, who granted leases to non-Santals, were detested. The palace of Pakaur was one of the insurgents' targets, where they decided to establish the residence of the *subah*.[38]

Possession rituals were used to legitimize the killing of Hindu oppressors. To kill a Hindu was not, for the Santal, a simple elimination of the enemy: British reports are unanimous in stressing that victims were tied to trees and sacrificed to Thakur. Vengeance killings needed to be ritualized. But are we really talking of sacrifice? When the moneylender Dindayal was killed, they cut his head and placed it in a niche in the temple, which they painted with his blood. (Datta 1940: 37) Such cases evoke a parody of Hindu sacrifice rather than the sacrificial act itself. Parody of the dominant is of course a recurrent practice in subaltern strategy.

## THE IMPACT OF THE *HUL*

It took almost two years to crush the rebellion. In the Damin, as in the Jungle Mahals, however, the rebellion failed to attain its objectives. 'The same kamiotee system and zamindari oppression continued unabated. This was applicable to all the Santals of Bengal as a whole' (Sen 1997: 128). Still, from 1855, the 'non-regulated' district of Santal Parganas, measuring some 14,000 square kilometres, was created from the Damin territory. The Santals were placed under a form of indirect rule where their chiefs kept some traditional powers, such as the right to administer justice in certain civil and criminal cases (Archer 1984). They enjoyed *man* land free of rent.[39] A Deputy Commissioner acted as the government's middleman towards the tribal chiefs.

The 'Rules for Civil Procedure' that Yule, now in charge of the Santal Parganas, established in 1858 start with the phrase: 'All claims to be preferred viva voce', clearly to remove inequality between literate and illiterate parties. Statements were taken in English only, to guard against implicit understanding between Bengali protagonists and court officials.[40] Decisions, recorded in English, were explained verbally to the parties in their own language. A copy in English was available to the parties; any translation was to be procured by them. The British administration wanted no Hindus meddling in its dealings with tribals.

A creditor's claim on the crops must be made at least fifteen days before they ripened. The grain might then be held by the headman until the case was settled. If the cultivator objected, claim and counter-claim were treated as a single case. All debts must be registered in the presence of the *manji*, and no further claims could be made. Land might be sold to pay debt, but no tools. Indebted Santals who lost their land, should be able to continue farming rented land or offer themselves as labourers.

The ideology here is explicit, 'to cause speedy and just decisions with no more of form than is necessary to secure justice' (Yule 1858: 14). It is hard to deny Yule's good intentions. Yet it is striking how the colonial administrator is seen as neutral, so that his control of the proceedings, to the exclusion of non-Santal Indian interests, becomes a guarantee of justice.

Two years earlier Yule had introduced special 'Sonthal Police Rules'. They abolished the various categories of Indian police,[41] replaced 'by the people themselves, and the Sub-Assistant, Assistant, and Deputy-Commissioners'. Again, no Bengali babu was allowed to come between the Santals and their colonial masters. What was good for the Santal was not, it is clear, necessarily so for India's emergent elite. Administrators were to deal directly with traditional authority in the tribal area,[42] by creating offices controlled by villagers—at the will of the administration—to oppose the zamindar's men (Yule 1856: 16). The abolishment of the *amlahs* and other indigenous officers of inferior rank, was meant to break down what was seen, by Santals and by Yule, as a nest of corruption.

The Santals attempted to rise again in 1857 and allied with the Bhumij, joined the rebel forces. Yet this revolt fizzled out quickly, for they were weakened by their losses. The government, fearing a new rebellion, offered concessions which did not solve the economic problems. It only guaranteed some judicial rights. The Santals, led by Sundar Majhi, rose again in 1861 but the government again granted concessions, such as a ban on the felling of *sal* trees, which helped appease the situation (Sen 1997: 78). But in 1863 Beadon, then Lieutenant-Governor, reinstated the Bengali courts; customary law was no longer recognized. This was the situation when our missionaries arrived in 1867, but Campbell, Lieutenant-Governor from 1870, was again ready to take cultural specificity into account.

When Johnson, Skrefsrud, and the Börresens established their Mission in 1867, the Santals were getting poorer. Land was scarce, even if they turned increasingly to wet-rice cultivation, and labour migration had become important. Still under the shock of their rebellion, they felt the religious powers had failed their leaders. Accusing the bongas of letting themselves be corrupted by enemy sorcerers or alien gods, they also suspected the whites of tricking their leaders to believe that guns could not hurt the rebels.

The rebellion crushed Santal hopes of improvement under British rule. In its wake, they neither recovered their lands, nor did they get compensation for their loss, though the authorities had become aware of their problems. Their Rebellion made Santals discover, in their own past, the point where history and myth meet. Foreign domination became a point of reference in their quest for identity. The repression that followed made them rethink their origins in terms of the Golden Age, when each clan had its own territory. A Santal identity emerged, capable of enduring later conflicts.

## HISTORY, MYTH AND TIME

The Santal were thus not without a sense of history. The historicity of their life-world must be set in their conceptions of time, which differ from nineteenth-century European concepts. Famine and plenty rhythms autobiographic time; years were not counted but related to remembered famines. Santals talk about *sukal*, a good season, in opposition to *akal*. Whenever a Santal meets kin or a friend from another village he asks about *suk* and *duk,* good and bad news. These terms evoke such meetings, exchanging news, and smoking together. They stand for sociability or getting around.

Two meals are served each day, the first made of left–overs from the previous day. The housewife cooks a more complete meal in the evening with rice and vegetable curry, as well as fish or meat if she can afford it. When rice is plentiful, an additional meal may be eaten around three o'clock in the afternoon, and brought by the women to their husbands in the fields.

To time rhythmed by work is opposed another time that reveals the bongas' activities. Evening is the time when cattle return to the cowshed, and children are put to bed, with grandmother singing lullabies. Crows and bats make noise in the trees and bongas follow humans into the village street. It is getting dark, but we still hear the voices of women coming home from work, carrying their tools on the head. Widows whisper accusations against the young girls of following lovers in order to get 'gifts'. Men talk about village affairs and the evening meal is eaten before going to sleep. On full-moon nights boys and girls meet at the dancing-ground, singing till late in the night. Midnight is the time when witches roam, darting arrows at the doors of their victims' houses. They leave in their beds a human form while they themselves go to the witches' meet.

Just before dawn is the time when bongas try to attract victims into the other world. A man gets up to urinate behind his house, where a female deity takes the seductive form of a girl and makes love to him.[43] But this may end tragically with the deity attracting her lover to a pond, where he will lose his shadow if his image is reflected in the water.

The Santal year is marked by a number of festivals. *Baha* is a fertility ritual but also the time when possessed oracles go to fetch *mahua* flowers in the forest, and it is taboo to pluck wild fruit and flowers in the preceding weeks. *Raban din*, cold days, last from *Aghar* (November-December) to *Phagun* (February-March). The first crop is ripe by the end of *pus,* January, just before the new year. Now is the time to arrange marriages, to be celebrated a month later. After the winter crop, people repair their tools and visit friends.

In the construction of the Santal world, time and space merge, and the forest is of central importance. Santals identify themselves with trees and particularly value the branches of *sal* trees.[44] These are used to indicate the time until an auspicious event, such as a hunt-meeting, or until a *bitlaha* is performed. The number of leaves fits the number of days.

The forest abounds with fruit trees, such as *mahua*, *mango*, *imli*[45] *khajoor*, as well as mushrooms and tubers that women dig out. *Sal* leaves provide fodder for animals while the bark, roots, shots and plants are collected by the *ojha* or medicine-man. They include animal products like bear fat or tiger teeth, sold by ojhas in the markets. *Neem* twigs are used to clean the teeth. Most forest products are collected during the summer, when the Santals are free from work in the fields. The women gather flowers and fruits of the *mahua* tree which symbolizes fertility (Carrin-Bouez 1986). The fruits are cooked and served with cereals while the flower juice is used to prepare a liquor offered to the bongas and drunk by villagers. The *ojha* drinks it before praying to the bongas. Oil is pressed from the kernel for a cosmetic used in women's hair. Bamboo is used for housebuilding and fences. House beams and rafters are made of *sal,* which symbolizes the patriline. Household instruments such as the husking pole, pestle, and mortar, too, are of *sal*. Winnowing fans, hats, rain coats, mats, flutes, fish traps and cages for keeping birds are made from bamboo. Also, the Santals use several earth colours to decorate their houses.

In 1851, Captain Sherwill noted that the Santal were expert hunters and that they kept skull trophies of the best hunts. Like other Munda groups, they hold ritual hunts in the spring,[46] before which nobody is allowed to reap the paddy. Hunting expeditions unite a number of villages. They are highly ritualized with sacrifices and sexually explicit songs dedicated to the hunting deity Rongo Ruji (burnt vagina) who provides the game but also stands for the burnt forest. The hunters form two groups, beaters and drummers. The men may shoot their arrows only when ordered to do so by the *dihuri*, the hunting priest, who is mostly an ojha (it is the medicine-men who know the forest). Sharing the game was by strict rules. First, the name of the killer's village was called, and its chief got a foreleg; the second foreleg went to the hunter who hit the game. During the hunt, women observe several taboos, such as not combing their hair,[47] and the *dihuri era*, the hunting priest's wife, keeps watching a pot of water: when the water becomes red the blood of animals will flow.

Santal narratives insist on the strict discipline hunters should observe and on the ritual obscenity which marks the night they sleep in the forest. During that night, the *pargana*,[48] assisted by other dignitaries, holds court and hears the complaints of villagers.[49] Though this court has never enjoyed official recognition, it remained important in colonial times and still serves to assert identity in a context of reinvented tradition (Archer 1985). Court decisions were often respected by colonial administrators, and Skrefsrud used the assembly extensively.

Men talk of the good old days of their youth, of the hunt, where they learnt how to behave towards elders and experienced both friendship and rivalry. Women keep the memory of going with a friend to pluck flowers and dig tubers in the forest. For both, the forest is the place of pleasant memories, such as illicit love, before it is tinged with fear of the bongas.

## THE WORLD OF THE BONGAS

The bonga world is *parom nel*, behind the senses. It is hierarchical: benevolent bongas are the deities of the creation myth, who reside in the sacred grove, provide protection, and are propitiated during agricultural rituals, while the most malevolent bongas inhabit the wilderness. But bongas pervade social space and the forest, permeating Santal life. To be a Santal is to be under the bonga's eye, though bongas do not look at men directly. They do not speak clearly to humans, but give laconic warnings in dreams or visions or show their wishes through possession. Malevolent bongas constantly invade the social world, and their number is infinite. They live in the forest, in stagnant waters or uncultivated fields, and are associated with natural calamities such as storm or rain. If a pregnant woman goes near a bonga, the deity is enraged, and the child will be born prematurely. *Jugunis*—the spirits of women who died in childbirth—rape and kill young men who become their slaves (Carrin 1996b). Male bongas rape women and take them to the other world. But while men may get spiritual powers from bongas and return to become ojhas, female victims meet a violent death. The bonga lover is a favourite theme with the Santals. To be seduced by them is exciting but dangerous since it means entering another world, signaled by inauspicious time. Dreaming of the bongas' world is seen as living a second emotional life. To an extent, bongas are said to have *shakti*—the ubiquitous Hindu term for power. Some even have matted hair, like the shaivite ascetics and many Santal ojhas.

The bongas' power is destructive, though ojhas who master the relationship describe it as emotionally positive (Carrin-Bouez 1986).[50] Classifying the bongas allows him to manipulate them during exorcism.

In narratives the *bonga* world is described as similar to the world of men. Bongas eat like men, and wear clothes but males and females both have long hair. Bongas, boys and girls, bathe in tanks and pools. But their feet are turned backwards, and they sit on snakes. You enter their land by a crack in the earth. They react quickly as if their mind was made of fire. Bongas are particularly eager to trap humans who transgress rules or forget promises. They appear as threatening, invisible forces generally identified too late by humans (Carrin 1995). Thus a woman is walking in the forest at night when she meets a bonga and asks him for tobacco, a rather improper gesture for a woman at night. The bonga answers, 'you will soon dance' three days later, the woman vomits blood and dies.

Disruption of the clan was held to cause sickness, and Baha songs tell us how epilepsy came into the world when clans were fighting. The Santals, deeply egalitarian in spirit, resent the split into sub-clans which produces difference in rank. Equality among Santals does not imply a general equality of men. They are patrilineal and patrilocal: clan names follow the male line and the eldest son receives the main share of the inheritance.[51] It is rare that property is divided in the father's lifetime. If so, division is equal among brothers: the father may keep some immovable goods, especially if he has remarried and quarelled with his sons. Daughters have no rights in land when there are male heirs, but are given a cow and some articles as dowry. Still, at marriage the daughter receives from her brothers a small plot which is her property. If there are no sons, the daughter may inherit and transmit land to her children.

The property a man acquires at inheritance is his own. The *ghar jawae*, the resident son-in-law, and his children may inherit half the property of a father-in-law, sometimes more. The *kirin jawae*, the social father found for an illegitimate child, marries the mother and transfers his bongas to the child. He gets money and sometimes cattle in compensation and considers the child as his. Adoption is frequent but generally does not affect inheritance. An unmarried girl is under her father's authority, and a wife depends on her husband. The culprit of a rape must pay a fine to the victim's father or husband, and feast the village.

In Santal regions which are still traditional, one finds two kinds of land ownership: that of the original founder of a settlement, and that of a later settler, invited to work the fields of others. Among the founders there are often two clans, that of the *manjhi* and that of the *naeke* or village priest. In every village, there is a *manjhi than* (shrine) in front of the headman's house, dedicated to his ancestors. It is a platform covered by a thatched roof, where two stones represent the founder manjhi and his wife. There is a central pillar of *sal* and a second pillar supporting a pot of water. The other public shrine is the *jaher than* or sacred grove, consisting of four *sal* trees and a *mahua*. They are dedicated to the *jaher bonga ko,* Maran Buru, his wife Jaher Era, the Monreko Turui Ko, and Pargana bonga, a deity associated with territory and the control of witches. The *mohua* is for Gosaen Era, the common wife of the five brothers, the Monreko. The grove and its deities stand for Santal identity.

Clans are exogamous.[52] Although clan rank is fluid, Santals generally regard Kisku, Murmu, and Hansda as superior, with Conre, Besra, and Beda inferior. Some divide the clans in three groups: high, middle and low. Most Santals consider the first seven clans to be higher than the remaining five who 'came later'. The distinction seems to be more semantic than functional. Superiority implies prestige but hardly influences marriage alliances. The Kisku and Marandi, who quarelled in old times, still avoid intermarriage. Villagers avoid uttering their *khunt* (sub-clan) names which relate to the *abge bongas*, tutelary deities of the 'original place' of the sub-clan. The house bongas and ancestors reside in the *bhitar*, the ancestor's enclosure, where they receive regular offerings. Offerings to the *abge bongas* are made in uncultivated fields. *Khunt* members observe totemic food prohibitions. *Khunt* rituals are observed only by male members since women retain natal ties after marriage (though they cannot enter the *bhitar* of their father's house since the ancestors might follow them). Women cannot sacrifice animals, but prepare other offerings for the ancestors.

Quarrels during the hunt may cause accidents, but do not necessarily involve human responsibility, for 'who can be sure of the path taken by the arrow?' It may be influenced by evil forces, as the body is invaded by evil agents causing sickness. Witches are seen as females eating their victims, in passion as when a man is said to 'eat' his sexual partner. Such intrusion involves the transfer of substance: witches invade their victim's body by manipulating menstrual blood, and malevolent bongas cover victims with their shadows. The victims of witches get emaciated, vomit blood and die slowly, while bongas provoke sudden death. Evil thought attributed to bongas evokes malice towards kin. In one story, a woman tries to push her husband into a well, but in the evening he returns from the field as if nothing has happened. She says to herself: 'If it is him, if he is not dead, O Sin Bonga, I will die myself!'. The husband understands, but says nothing. Later, when a grandfather, he tells the story to his grandchildren. The woman, sitting under a cotton-tree, screams: *riri!* as the possessed do, evoking the witch taking vengeance on her kin. She dies, and the husband thinks: 'by telling the story I made the oath come true.' Women should not be possessed by bongas as they may then become witches.

The supernatural qualities of witches and malevolent bongas are often described as physical features: both have feet turned backwards and indulge in cannibalism. They rape their victims but cannot procreate. Both are excessive beings, who get no rest and roam from place to place. The Scandinavian missionaries saw bonga worship as a demon cult. They felt Santals propitiated them to avert disaster, and reduced the faith in tribal deities to mere superstition (Skrefsrud 1876). In stories from the Oslo archives, some male victims become mad and must convert to escape their bonga lovers. Here, the bonga world of cannibalistic deities, lust and disorder is opposed to the Mission compound, where order and rationality prevail.

In all the Munda groups, each village is a ritual unit whose members share sacrificial food and avoid intermarriage. Most village dignitaries are selected by the clans, but the priest is chosen through possession indicating the bonga's choice. The *manjhi* is the hereditary secular head of the village, responsible for the observance of custom and the solution of conflicts. He presides over a council of five[53] which deals with conflicts and sanction offences. He is responsible for the *manjhi than*, and organizes the *kulhi durup*,[54] the village assembly, where all may speak. Arbiter of the right to speak, he represents equity in terms of discourse. Perhaps for this reason, Santals say that the *manjhi era*, the chief's wife, is never a witch.

The *jog-manjhi* collects sacrificial animals for festivals. He is the guardian of morals, especially of the young. In the case of an illegitimate birth, he must find a father for the child.[55] His role is particularly important during the *sohrae* or cattle festival, when he looks after the youth sleeping at his house. He is the master of ceremonies at name–giving, initiation, and marriage. The *naeke* is in charge of religious ceremonies to the bongas. As sacred head, he and his wife symbolically represent the ancestor couple. He is responsible for maintaining patrilinearity and exogamy; if they are violated the *jaher bonga* will be polluted and take revenge on the community. Each of these functionaries have assistants: the *paranik* is assistant to the *manjhi*, the *jog-paranik* to the *jog-manjhi* and the *kudam-naeke* to the *naeke*. While the first two mainly have social functions, the priest's assistant is in charge of removing impurity. In case of epidemics he offers some drops of his own blood to the malevolent deities.

Another religious figure is the *jan guru* who 'teaches knowledge'. He is feared, since he is the witch-finder. For ordinary ailments, people prefer to call the ojha, who, possessed by tribal and sometimes Hindu deities, practices divination and exorcism. The ojhas are also shamans who may marry bonga to receive spiritual power. They often have tutelary Hindu goddesses whom they invoke to fight minor bonga or Hindu *bhuts*. Thus the ojha is at the border of Hindu and tribal society, and his 'pantheon' reflects the opposition between them. His magical powers include the ability to fly and restore the dead to life. But unlike witches and *yogis*, the ojha uses his powers positively. He gets his powers from his female bonga. He is invested with feminine sensitivity and wears matted hair (*joto*) evoking *shakti*, fire, and the ascetic heat of Siva. Thus mystical powers are linked to physical characteristics which transform the ojha, giving him a fantastic appearance.

During the nineteenth century, most offences were regulated by customary law and oaths. Conflicts were settled by the five village elders or by the judgement of the burnt forest, during the annual hunt, where the council of five manjhi includes village headmen drawn from the vicinity.[56] The pargana area includes a maximum of twelve villages: its chief, also called pargana, is elected or inherits the function. In the north of Orissa, he is enthroned wearing a turban and receives a *tika* on his forehead like a king. His duty is to preside over the hunt council and judge conflicts or transgressions. A messenger transmits his instructions to villagers. The British recognized the *parganas panch* in 1856 in the Santal Parganas, and the pargana took care of police functions.[57]

The community is strict with offences such as incest, adultery, and witchcraft. Justice is administered by kin groups linked by marriage, in matters of inheritance, land, witchcraft, and divorce. The sanction for breach of endogamy or incest is *bitlaha*, where offenders are exiled, sometimes killed. The ceremony was extremely violent and forbidden by the British.[58] It involved a hunt in which the offenders were the quarry symbolizing their 'bestial' nature.[59] The culprits' houses were destroyed and their ancestral altars defiled. Readmission might be possible, especially in case of incest between classificatory kin, if a fine was paid to the pargana council. An affair with a *diku* equals incest, so the *bitlaha* also marks the ethnic boundary.

No Santal may eat with non-Santals, and a Santal woman may not eat food cooked by non-Santals. She would be punished as for having sexual relations with them. Men are less strict but generally avoid eating food cooked by Muslims, Paharias, Doms, Chamars, Muchis, Hadis, and Bauris. Some relatives are banned from eating from the same plate: the maternal uncle and aunt with nephews and nieces, a girl's husband with her elder brother, or a younger brother's wife with his elder brother. These rules apply to affines such as daughter-in-law and father-in-law, girl's father and husband's father, or husband and wife. If a husband eats the leftovers from his wife's meal he cannot sacrifice to the bongas. As a general rule, younger relatives may consume the leftovers of their elders. Those who belong to the same *khunt* share sacrificial food when they propitiate the clan deities in the forest. They belong to the same *kond* or unit of commensality.

When offenders want to make amends, they generally take an oath, pay a fine and feast the village dignitaries. The meal implies eating the offence in order to forget it.

## THE CONCEPTION OF PERSONHOOD

When a Santal is born, the village becomes impure and the deities of the sacred grove are polluted. Purification starts with the shaving of both *naeke* and *manjhi*, followed by parents, midwife and child. Then the men, led by the *naeke,* bathe in the river. Meanwhile, the midwife takes the two arrows she has used to cut the umbilical cord and goes to bathe. At the ghat, she 'plants' the arrow in the water. She 'buys' the ghat, obtaining for the child its place in the world, as its bones will return to the river after death. Later, she purifies the mother with cow dung water and *atnak*[60] leaves, marking the child's bond with the vegetal world. The child is then named in the clan of his father, who makes an offering to introduce the child to the bonga world, the family, and the tribe.[61] Two names are given: the first is the village name by which the child is known, while the second is chosen by elaborate rules, by which the grandfather is reborn in the grandson, stressing the importance of alternate generations.[62] The same principle is observed in the female line for a daughter. Some days later, the child eats his first rice ceremonially and is presented to the village. The piercing of the ears is done when the child is about eight to make it observe clan and village taboos. When a boy is ten, his maternal uncle confers full identity by burning his forearms five times in the name of the bongas. A ceremonial tonsure should be done before a male child is married.

Some Santal think the soul returns in the third generation and that it cries until the child is named. Baptism and Christian names have muddled the notions connected with the destiny of the soul after death, related to reincarnation on the one hand, and becoming a bonga on the other. Naming links the individual to the bonga world.

The kinship system shows the importance of alternate generations, an Austro-Asiatic feature found in most Munda groups. There is a joking relationship between grandparents and grandchildren. In the Santal Parganas, there may have been a tendency to matrilateral cross-cousin marriage in the nineteenth century (Gautam 1977),[63] while today alliances are between second-degree cross-cousins (MMBSD and FFZDS). The rules now exclude first degree cousins while second-degree marriage is valued.[64] Basing himself on material from northern Orissa, Bouez (1985) identifies both symmetric and asymmetric principles in Santal alliance.

A Santal family consists of parents and their unmarried children. Some households include old parents and some are joint, with brothers and their families sharing one hearth. Divorced or widowed siblings may also live in the house. If a man has no son, he may invite a youth to stay as a *ghar-jawae* and work for him; later to marry the daughter of the house. The young man loses status, but his children will inherit the land.

Birth rituals and name-giving confer status on the individual, but it takes marriage to become a full member of society. A Santal woman never fully joins her husband's descent group,[65] and retains ritual and inheritance rights in her natal family. Her flesh and bone symbolically pass to her husband's line, but the blood of the ear, which alludes to agnation, stays with her father's family. Still, a married daughter never worships her father's bongas.

The child's position is determined by that of his father's clan. Marriage, especially one's first, involves the whole village. Unlike other Munda groups, the Santal had no youth dormitories, but communal dancing favoured premarital relations, and virginity was not particularly appreciated, as Skrefsrud puts it in his report to Risley. The go-between asks the girl's parents if they have a new pot, thus alluding to the procreative powers of the girl.

Most Munda groups demand a bride-price, but the Santals generally agree that theirs was reduced to a symbolic amount before the missionaries came. Still, prestigious marriages imply a higher bride-price. If a couple elopes, the bride-price is increased. It is given to the bride's relatives in cash or as gifts, and may be followed by a feast for the bridegroom's party. Generally there is no dowry, and marriage expenses are shared by the two families. On the whole, equal prestations stress the equal status of bride's and bridegroom's parties. Seven forms of marriage are found among the Santal: regular exchange, elopement, capture, intrusion marriage, widow remarriage, marriage of a co-wife and *ghar jawae* marriage. The regular marriage involves the maternal uncle,[66] who takes the boy to see the bride. The parents take omens: a bad omen means that villagers must sacrifice a goat and several chicken to counter its effects. At marriage, the bridegroom puts the mark of vermillion on the bride's forehead, while the father' sister's husband ties the couple's clothes together. The mark of vermillion changes a girl's bongas. Marriage, then, is an event when the relationship with the bongas becomes particularly close. To protect herself from the wrath of her father's bongas, the bride kicks a pot of clay with burning coals from her natal hearth. When the bride's party arrives at the husband's house, the mother-in-law ties a bracelet of *sal* leaves on the young wife, marking her inclusion in her husband's lineage. Still, suspicions of witchcraft turn on the wife's ambiguous status. Again, the repetition of the ritual sequences in bride's and bridegroom's houses indicate equality between the families.

Elopements take place during inter-village dancing when an agnatic group from the host village seize the partners and celebrate their marriage immediately by putting a mark of *sindur* on the bride's forehead. Sometimes, the girl is taken at the market or in the forest, never in her own village. The girl and her family are expected to accept the union even if they dislike it. But often the young couple agree to this form of marriage to evade resistance from the girl's father. Polygynous marriages were more common after the *hul* than now, since most Santals are unable to keep more than one wife. The first wife's acceptance is needed.

In case of impotence or other difficulty, the spouses may divorce.[67] Still, if a girl has been married in the most prestigious way and received *sindur* in her hair, she will join her first husband in the other world. Otherwise, the divorcee no longer belongs to her husband's line and bongas. She lives in her parents's house but is generally eager to find another partner. Divorce never occurs if the woman is suspected of witchcraft.

Boys and girls are eager for marriage and try to adjust, even when marriage implies parting from one's village lover. Lovers may, however, meet again during Sohrae, the cattle festival celebrated in autumn when the crops are ripe. Clandestine engagements during Sohrae lead to lasting relations, accepted by Santals as a way of adding excitement to marital life. Missionaries were scandalized by these Sohrae 'bacchanals'.

At marriage, the spouses are sprinkled with *tulsi* water to bestow fertility. It strengthens the bones, which symbolize continuity in time, since the life principle resides in the skull. A child is made when Thakur gives life to a bone and the flesh that grows around it. In metaphors, bone is likened to stone and symbolizes male body parts such as the chest. Still, the feminine part, the flower (*baha*–uterus) is associated with menstruation and reproduction (Carrin-Bouez 1986).

To ensure children the major bongas must be honoured and the main occasion for this is the Baha or feast of flowers held in March. There is another, private, ceremony *jivet karam* which complements the Baha and ensures women's fertility.[68] It turns on the magical properties of the *karam* tree; a guru sings different myths of two heroes, Karmu and Dharmu, who grant wealth and prosperity to devotees. The names derive from the Hindu *dharma* and *karma*, relating to religious duty and personal destiny.[69] The Karam ritual shows how Santals reinterpret a Hindu model.

## DEATH AND THE DEAD

There are several souls in the body. Only the skeleton is immortal, thanks to the 'big breath' or life principle, which dwells in the bones of the skull. The other 'little breath' dwells in the stomach and shelters the soft soul, which leaves the body after death and enters a plant or an animal. Then there is the shade which leaves the body in sleep. The deceased become ancestors, then, after three generations, turn into bongas. It is the big breath who becomes a bonga[70] while the little breath is ephemeral.

Santal funerals have six stages: cremation, first purification, possession, cult of the domestic deity, immersion of the bones, and final purification. Relatives and other villagers assemble at the mortuary house with bows and arrows, digging sticks and flutes. The body is smeared with turmeric and oil and exposed with his or her ornaments in the courtyard. At the foot of the bed the weapons and other objects of the deceased are displayed, then carried away by the funeral party. Four men of the deceased's lineage carry the corpse to the river where cremation is done. Women are not allowed on the cremation ground. The procession is led by the ojha. Service castes such as Mahali attend and the potter provides the pot or winnowing fan used for divination. At a cross-roads, they stop as the deceased takes leave of the villagers and village bongas. The ojha worships the clan bongas of the deceased, the village bongas and Maran Buru. The body is placed with the head facing south, covered with *sal* branches. The ojha waves a fowl thrice around the corpse and sacrifices it.[71] The eldest son lights the pyre. The mourners take a bath but are still impure. On the bank of the river, the eldest son is shaved, followed by the other agnates. Later, they drink rice-beer and evoke the life of the deceased. The *jadu patua* paints the destiny of the deceased while possessed by his shadow.[72] Relatives want to provide a good painting and recitation from the *jadu patua* who knows the road to the other world.

The pollution period varies from nine to five days, less in the case of the poor. On the tenth day, a barber shaves the male agnates. They offer beer to Maran Buru and take a bath. Two men are possessed in the deceased's courtyard, by the deceased and by Maran Buru. Now the deceased is an ancestor and they offer him a meal placed on the rafter of the house. The final ceremony is important, for no male of the village can marry or take part in a festival till the ashes and the flower-bones of the deceased have been immersed in the Damodar River. A cow is presented by the wife's brother and sacrificed later, as a symbolic farewell to the deceased by the wife's relatives. Finally, the eldest son dives in the river with the pot containing the ashes: the dead person has been united with the ancestors. This custom, once difficult to observe due to Hindu pressure (Gautam 1977: 144) was reinstated during the 1970s.[73] Death is seen as a victory for the malevolent bongas. The deceased has failed in his duty 'to belong to the living', like the branch of a tree.

Death is expressed through spatial metaphors. The departed has gone 'to fetch salt', evoking a long voyage. The deceased becomes a bonga after three generations but this may be shortened by hastening the funeral cycle. After washing the flower bones, the soul leaves its temporary shell,[74] and goes to Hana Puri,[75] the other world, where it may suffer from past mistakes. We may read Christian influence into these punishments, but we also find stories describing Hana Puri as a labour camp, evoking colonial labour (Carrin-Bouez 1993). Even the idea of becoming a bonga is forgotten, and as humans are limited in number, the inmates must make new ones from the bones of the dead. Time has no place here: nobody knows who decides about new births. This seems to be an innovation in Santal eschatology, which generally asserts that Thakur is granting each individual a life span. Thakur's intervention represents Hindu intrusion, and it is said that Thakur invented death and boundaries. Before Thakur there was a golden age, while his name (landlord) evokes the Kaliyuga when Santals work for Sahibs and their Hindu middlemen. Kaliyuga is the time of debt,[76] loss of land, and wage labour. Thus Hanapuri is associated with servitude. In other stories, Jom Raja, a Santal version of the Hindu god Yama, appears with his messengers; a witch or a thief receives retribution, but the idea of several lives, as in Hindu karma, is generally not present.

These situations, where time and space are entangled, suggest that Santals locate inner time in different places: Hana Puri, the world of the bongas, and the land of Kamru the magician. These three worlds may be seen as modalities of time. Hana Puri is a looking-glass world where the dead reap the result of their actions just as the bonga world is a world that mirrors human life. In eschatological terms, Hana Puri is a stage that souls pass through before becoming bongas. The living do not pass these boundaries, except witches who have a foot in the bonga world, and ojhas who mediate between the bonga world, the land of Kamru guru, and this world. While a succession of worlds is offered the ordinary human after death, the individual may find his own way by accessing supernatural powers.

## NEIGHBOURS AND OTHERS

As is clear from Sherwill's account, other groups were and are present in the Santal Parganas, some having close links with the Santals, while others figure in their folk tales.

Brahmans are few. The Rahri and Maithil Brahmans are landowners letting their lands to Santals, Mundas or low castes. Inferior only to them are the Kayastha landowners. The Vaishya merchants include moneylenders, sweetsellers and others. The Sunris distil and sell alcohol as well as opium. The Sadgop farmers are among the largest Hindu groups in the tribal area, and claim equal status with the Kayasthas, but this is seldom acknowledged by others. The Kurmis, also farmers, see themselves as superior to Santals, with whom they have close relations and may eat.

The Paharia highlanders are the second largest group in the Santal Parganas. Their speech is close to Kurukh, the Dravidian language of the Oraon. They used to raid the lowlands, and were classed as a criminal tribe. After the arrival of the Santals they adopted terrace cultivation. The Bhuiyas or Bhumiyas claim to be Rajput,[77] but speak a Munda dialect. In the nineteenth century, they were employed as ghatwals (guardians of mountain passes). Now they are farmers and field labour.

The Lohars are Blacksmiths but rank below the Kamars who do similar work. Both come from Bihar, are shaktists and venerate goddesses, especially Kali. In times of crisis, however, they often go to the Santal ojha. Kamars may act as sacrificers for higher castes. The Kumhar potters who also make clay images are very active in the local goddess cults. The Pal potters are known as Thakur Pandits by other Hindus as they serve in Shiva shrines in the Santal Parganas. Some castes participate with Santals in the same Hindu cults. Thus the Tantis, weavers who supply clothes to them, are often devotees of the god Dharmo, a popular form of Shiva.

The Jadupatuas are Hindu, Muslim, or a mixture of both. They go from house to house among the Santals, showing scroll images of the dead. The paintings are immersed with the bones of the deceased. The *jadu patuas* also serve as mediums in the houses of mourning. Other clean castes are the Napit barbers, the Goala herdsmen, the Mistri carpenters, and the Jogis who work as low-caste priests (Bhowmick 1963). The Bagdis, a low caste, are among the largest non-tribal communities in the region. They used to be soldiers. Now, they often do construction work alongside the Santals. The Bauris were once palanquin-bearers but most now work as day labourers. In the plains they are seen as untouchables. The Mahalis were palanquin bearers in British times: now they are basketmakers and also work as day labour. They speak Mahali, a dialect of Santali, but are Hinduized and seen as untouchables. The Turis are an offshoot of the Munda and speak a Munda dialect. They, too, make baskets and work in the fields. The Santals keep their distance and do not eat with them.

The Doms served as soldiers with rajas or zamindars, remunerated with rent-free land. They have frequent contact with the Santals and carry out the cremation of the dead. In Santal folktales they appear with the ogres and the Asuras; they possess magical powers and take advantage of Santal credulity. The most impure Doms are considered untouchable. Dom musicians have risen considerably in the hierarchy, becoming priests of Dharmo Thakur in the plains. They are often gurus of the low castes. The Muchis and the Hadis are among the lowest of untouchables, and fervent devotees of Kali. The Muchis are tanners and shoemakers and some are musicians. The majority, however, labour in the fields. The Hadis are scavengers and removers of nightsoil. They are also musicians, and Hadi women are midwives like the Ghasis, a caste of small farmers and labourers.

Thus the Santal Parganas, like the whole western fringe of Bengal, is not a 'uni-ethnic' region as opposed to 'multi-ethnic' caste society (Bailey 1961). As poor peasants, Santals have fewer relations to specialist groups than many lowland populations. But the specificity of their region lies in the particularity of their own culture rather than in territorial monopoly. This implies much less stress on hierarchy in dealing with other groups than is the case for Hindu peasants.

If the Santals do not now Sanskritize themselves it seems they did so in the past, as in the Kherwar movement. But they resist Hinduization whenever Hindu influence implies domination. They do not hesitate to criticize the Brahmans and the high castes of landowners.

As we have seen, Santal religion, custom, and ritual differ considerably from that of the Hindus. They clearly form a distinct group with an ethnic consciousness which cannot be simply a reaction to colonial developments. Looking at Santal conception of time, we have stressed that the Santals linked past with truth and the evocation of the ancestors. Ordinary men talk of the good old days as the memory of their youth. Does this process apply to history? A close reading of Santal myths and narratives show that the Santal sense of history is focussed first on myths and second on the nineteenth century as Sahlins (1985) notes for Hawaii. The transformations imposed by colonialism were different to the changes that the Santals had experienced in the past. This does not imply for us as for P. Banerjee (2002: 246) that the sense of historical past and the sense of the Santali past conflict. Both are expressed in Santal narratives and merge in the interpretation of the Santal rebellion. Sidhu and Kanhu embodied the myth of a lost kingdom whose reality was proved by royal symbols as well as by their inspired speech. They represented a dream of autonomy, a Santal raj. Santals often take for granted that their History starts in 1855. For us, the *hul* marks a break between myth and history but does not produce 'a conflicting articulation of the past-present relationship' (ibid.), rather the break opens an historical consciousness, to build a Santal identity able to inspire resistance. The memory of the lost past was mobilized to imagine how the future could bring back a cyclical time, a time of truth.

## NOTES

1. Cohn 1987a, Bates 1995b, Béteille 1986, Sivaramakrishnan 1999, and others.
2. 'Forest-dwellers'.
3. Samaddar notes that Mahtos and Santals are often conflated in nineteenth century judicial records of the Jungle Mahals, which implies solidarity between these groups, as during the Santal rebellion (Guha 1983), but not necessarily identification.
4. We define ethnicity as an aspect of social relations in which members of a group see themselves as culturally distinctive from others (Barth 1969b).
5. Low caste Hindus often appear as 'ceremonial friends' or fictive kin in Santal folktales (Bodding 1925-9).
6. Today the Santals perform mock funerals of those who have transgressed the rules of tribal endogamy (Carrin 1997).
7. In 1915 Munda and Oraon students formed the Adivasi Mahasabha in Ranchi to fight discrimination.
8. The word *Jharkhand* is constructed from *jhar*-grove and *khand*-country.
9. The Santal archives contain many stories relating the split into sub-clans. Gausdal (1960) has translated a sample of these.

10. This region is inhabited by Mon-Khmer speaking tribes, whose Austro-asiatic language is related to Santali.
11. Carrin visited Birhor settlements in Hazaribagh in 1974. They had few contacts with Hindus and still lived as hunters and gatherers. They understood Santali.
12. Von Fürer-Haimendorf, however, classes the Santal as one of the 'advanced farming societies' among Indian tribes, and notes their dependence on land ownership (1985: 111). Gautam, noting that their traditional cultivation may support twenty or thirty people per acre, stresses that this density depends on hunting and the collection of edible roots and fruits. As the forest diminished, the Santals had to migrate or to change their method of cultivation (1977: 57).
13. The term Jungle Mahals was used in the late eighteenth and early nineteenth centuries for the country extending from the hilly parts of Birbhum to Ranchi, characterized by forest and red laterite soils. These areas were united as the district of Jungle Mahals in 1805, which was dissolved in 1833 (Samaddar 1998: 59n).
14. This is clear from their rich vocabulary of natural species (Carrin-Bouez 1985, Carrin *forthcoming a*).
15. *Shorea robusta* L.
16. This would make a clear contrast to the Rajput states of Western India. The question is whether, in Bengal, zamindars had traditional legitimacy among their people, or were essentially tax-collectors imposed from above.
17. Buchanan Hamilton's unpublished manuscripts, cited by Roy Chaudhuri 1965: 73.
18. Interest rates in grain was 100 per cent on very short terms (Sen 1997: 29).
19. S. Sen (1984: 123), quoting a letter from Dunbar.
20. Amins and naib sejwals are police officers. A munsiff is a court scribe, and mahajan is the term used for a merchant or moneylender.
21. In 1850, Sherwill found that the Santals cultivated 1,62,560 acres or 4,91,744 bighas.
22. In Ilambazar there was an indigo factory occupying 20,000 bighas of land.
23. McPherson (1909: 36) notes that grain prices were still very low in 1843: Rs 2.5 a maund in the interior, and Rs 1.5 a maund on the Ganga.
24. The rent varied greatly from one region to another, with important differences between the southern and western Jungle Mahals where land had been measured and the Damin-i-Koh where the Santals objected to assessment. In Manbhum, rent increased sharply whereas it was protected in the Damin. As late as 1888 the Commissioner of Burdwan remarked that the Santals and other tenants were not used to receiving money.

25. The *Calcutta Review* (1856:24) mentions the rape of Santal women by non-Santals, implying defilement for the entire tribe. Roy (1961: 63) notes that domestic animals were taken away by *dikus* without payment.
26. The first railway in Norway opened the same year. Both were owned by British interests and built by Robert Stephenson & Co. In India, work started simultaneously at Bombay and Calcutta, but went faster in the east.
27. Bodding (1932-6) stresses that *diku* means a Hindu of 'good caste', and that the service castes, themselves subject to exploitation, were never called *diku*. But even in the Santal Archives they are called *hurin dikus*, small *dikus*. The latter are not oppressors.
28. Their trust in the Company's justice recalls similar petitions of Norwegian peasants during Danish rule, as well as the Thrane movement's petition to the king.
29. J. Pontet, letter, 25.07.1855.
30. Among the Mundas, the *khuntkatti*, descendants of the founding ancestors, hold the best village land. Villages often have one clan only but may be divided in chief's and priest's moieties. Santal villages have several clans, including those of the chief and the priest.
31. Other versions allege that Thakur either gives five plain leaves of paper to the boy, or the God himself is writing the message. Santal accounts, from people who lived during the rebellion, are fragmentary on this point. See O'Malley 1910: 48-9, Hunter in Ray 1983: 72, etc.
32. In 1856 Bidwell, in his inquiry into the causes of the Rebellion, mentions a petition in English, no doubt written for the Santals by literate but low-caste Hindus, as stated by Guha (1983: 187).
33. The ancestors reside in *sal* trees (Shorea robusta), a symbol of Santal identity.
34. *Thakur Parwanah*—the orders of Thakur—implied that Santals should join the *Hul*.
35. *Hul reak' katha*, 8vo 1448-0. See also Andersen, Carrin and Soren (forthcoming), for the archive material on the rebellion.
36. *Hul reak' katha*.
37. Between April and August 1854, the Santals sent several petitions to the magistrates at Bhagalpur and Birbhum. They accused the moneylenders of using false measures and weights and describe themselves as the Jungly Sonthals. Letter from Bidwell, 10.12.1855, inquiry into the reasons for the Santal rebellion, India Office Collections.
38. Sidhu and Kanhu use the title *subah*—governor of a province—in the sense of a supreme and inspired leader.
39. None of this was recognized in the Jungle Mahals where Santal headmen were still seen as ryots.
40. All false claims were punishable as criminal offences. Decisions are to

be made 'forthwith' whenever possible: if not, arbitrators may be appointed. Documents must be filed at the time of making a claim. If the defendant is absent, the case may be postponed, not so in the absence of the plaintiff. In case of arbitration, arbitators are to be nominated by each party and by the *hakim*. The decision is by majority, written out in each party's vernacular. It is final. Summons were by drumming. Village chiefs were responsible for summoning defendant and witnesses (Yule 1858: 5).

41. 'The Naib Sezawals, Darogahs, Mohurrirs and Jemadars and Burkundazes'.
42. 'Among the Sonthals and Paharyas, the Manjees, Pergunnytes, Desmanjees, and in the hills, the Sirdars, the Naibs, and other subordinates, with the Chowkeydars, Goraits, or whatever they may be called, will do the duty expected of them, each in their respective tracts or villages, and without reference to the race or tribe in which the occurrence may have taken place' (Yule 1856: 15).
43. *ado*–to pass water–also means to ejaculate, make love.
44. The symbolism of the branch conveys the idea of generation. During migrations, the Santal chief brandished the branch for men of his clan to follow him.
45. Respectively (*Bassia latifolia* L.) (*Mangefero Indica* L.) (*Tamarinus Indica* L.) (*Phoenix dactileferas*, L.)
46. Game is disappearing in much of the Santal country, but the collective hunt is still practised in many places, such as the north of Orissa.
47. The hair stands for the forest and the comb the progress of hunters, which should not be interfered with.
48. A chief traditionally having authority over twelve villages. Historians often use the term *parganait* for the chief and *pargana* for his territory, but most Santals today use *pargana* for both. The term is of Muslim origin, probably from the Mughal period.
49. Even when game is absent the court is held: the hunt must be simulated by dance where men play the roles of game and hunter. The court seems even more important than the hunt.
50. Similar ideas are found among the Saora (Vitebsky 1993).
51. *Hatin*—sharing, inheritance, also used to indicate that one's part is 'equitable'.
52. Nowadays exogamy is observed only at sub-clan level; transgressions are severely punished.
53. This council was called Monre Hor Ko, 'five old men', though the term panchayat may be used now.
54. Lit. 'sitting in the street'.
55. *Bonga tala*, to place the child among the bongas.
56. 'Its function is to settle extra village disputes, to adjucate in all matters

which the villagers themselves fail to decide and to act as an appellate court for village decisions' (Archer 1984: 15).

57. Today, they are elected by *manjhis* and elders in Mayurbhanj and the Santal parganas. In Keonjhar, the office is hereditary.
58. More than ten *bitlahas*, each involving thousands of Santals were held from the beginning of the century to 1950 (Archer 1984).
59. It was, as Archer (1984) puts it, a mock marriage where villagers degraded the culprits using obscene symbols.
60. *Terminalia tomentosa*, W. & A.
61. Illegitimate children are easily absorbed since a step-father is found who transmits his own bongas to the child (Archer 1984: 82-92).
62. The eldest boy is named after father's father, then mother's father, father's next youngest brother, mother's eldest brother, and father's younger brothers (Archer 1984: 373; Bodding 1919).
63. This view is not shared by S. Bouez (1985) nor by Parkin (1992).
64. In some regions such as Keonjhar, there is now a tendency to hypergamy while in neighbouring Mayurbhanj they prefer symmetrical alliance. Bouez sees the asymmetry as a result of rank difference between clans, but also finds evidence of generalized exchange between them (1985).
65. Marriage enables her to assist her husband in domestic rituals, where she offers cakes to his ancestors. She can also worship the village bongas with other women in the sacred grove of her husband's village, separated from the men but at the same time.
66. Santals say that he has already given a wife to the boy's lineage. They presuppose, here, an alliance which is not uncommon, but by no means general.
67. Lit. 'the tearing of *sal* leaves'.
68. The *karam* is a whole class of rituals. *Mak 'More karam* marks the end of an illness. *Janam Karam* is held when a *karam* seedling has appeared in a man's plot. At the installation of a *pargana* the start of an ojha's practice or to honour the memory of a deceased chief or priest, *karam* may be performed. The *karam* tree is Adina cordifolia, Hook.
69. Carrin 1986, Andersen 1992. Variants of the myth are shared by the Bhumij (Sinha 1957) and other Munda groups.
70. Gautam (1977), basing his argument on the child being named after his grandfather, says the dead return on earth in the third generation.
71. In some areas, the *ojha* pierces the eyes of the fowl to make the deceased see in the other world.
72. Hadders (2001) describes and analyses the Jadupatias and their role among the Santals.
73. The cow sacrifice was celebrated in Mayurbhanj in 1970 in the context of re-Santalization. In Santal Parganas, they sometimes offer some drops of the cow's blood on the ashes.

74. The Santals do not have megaliths like the Mundas or the Hos. Traditions seem to imply that they once used to bury their dead under slab-stones. The chest of the elder son is called 'maran buru' big stone, which also alludes to the name of the creation god.
75. *Hana Puri* is located 'beyond human regard', *parom nel*.
76. *Rin*, a long term debt, implies high interest. *Panca* is a short-time loan of grain at a more moderate rate.
77. They trace their ancestry to the Surabansi raja of Manihari (Gautam 1977: 32).

# 4

# A New Colonial Order: Bengal in the 1860s

## INDIA AFTER 1858

If the *hul* changed the Santals, the Mutiny changed Bengal. India became a Crown Colony. The age of liberalism and reform ends, the liberals become a minority, and the general feeling among the new rulers is that excessive reform contributed to the rebellion. 'Almost all of Dalhousie's reform measures were subjected to severe criticism during and after the Mutiny' (Metcalfe 1990: 93). The Widow Remarriage Act, said Disraeli, had 'seriously disquieted the religious feeling of the Hindus'.[1] Yet the ideology of non-involvement does not prevent the state from increasingly engaging with Indian society and transforming it, through a steady expansion of its administration.

Three main elite agencies competed for power and influence in post-mutiny Bengal: the government, the settlers, and the Bengali elite. The government, though British, showed the will to rule on behalf of Bengal and India, and its interests did not coincide with those of the British settlers. The conflict came to a head over indigo, and exploded again with reactions to the Ilbert bill, which allowed Indian judges to decide cases involving Europeans. But while the indigo planters largely defended their economic interests, opposition to the Ilbert Bill came from all sections of Europeans, from businessmen to railway employees. Significantly, this now included most Civil Servants. What united them was a need to distance themselves from Indians, with increasingly blunt expressions of racism from 1860 to 1880. The settlers were, for their part, conscious of forming a cultural community, commonly described as Anglo-Indian.[2] This is is clear from their literature (Moore-Gilbert 1986), which reaches an apogee in Kipling's early work.

Planter interests never recovered from the indigo crash, in spite of the growing importance of tea. Indigo planters dominated the

Calcutta scene in the early years, as tea planters were never to do. Jute, too, produced a different elite structure. The export trade was at first controlled largely from Dundee, and British capital continued to be important: power never centered on Calcutta as was the case with indigo. Jute growers were largely financed locally, often by Indians settled in the countryside, who did not form part of the Calcutta elite.

The third elite group, growing fast in this period was the Bengali Bhadralok. At the time of the Bengal Renaissance, they were close to the colonial establishment. Liberals of the two elites were united by indigo, and both suffered from the indigo crash, while the Hindu revival gained ground among the Bengali elite. In an increasingly colonial economy, there was a growing cultural distance between Anglo-Indians and Bengalis, including a new affirmation of Indianness, which moved steadily towards the nationalism of the next century. Racism among Europeans was matched by cultural retrenchment among Indians, who now took a secondary role in the economy. This exclusion must be seen in relative terms, however, for in spite of it the Bengali bourgeoisie were strengthening their influence, now opposed both to government and to Anglo-Indians.

More and more, the question rose of creating and maintaining the superiority of an elite of officials who, though mainly from middle-class backgrounds, saw themselves and lived as an aristocracy. Indian princes, lower-class Europeans, Anglo-Indians, and missionaries who associated directly with natives, muddled the racial hierarchy (Ballhatchett 1980: 160-7). The Mariscano scandal of 1866 involved an Italian described as a 'musician' and a 'loafer', who had killed a German Jew (former owner of a grog-shop in Egypt) in a quarrel over the latter's mistress, a Jewish girl of Polish descent who said the German 'had brought her from Odessa as a slave'. The *Friend of India*, finding the incident typical, thought 'the civilizing power' had 'reason for shame'. There was official fear that drinking and whoring westerners would 'degrade our race in the eyes of all who see them' (ibid.: 124-5). The 1864 Bill to control prostitution suggested a distinction between prostitutes 'frequented by Europeans' and those not so frequented (Ballhatchett 1980: 40-2).

'Nowhere', said Fabre-Tonnerre, Calcutta's health officer, 'are the lower classes of Christians and Natives more debased, and unclean than in the metropolis of India. Everything about them bears the stamp of a total absence of every moral, religious and social feeling.

Hence the great number of prostitutes . . . who, by their indecent conduct, scandalize the morals of the population'. His remarks are typical of a new puritanical public spirit which grew through the rest of the century, in India but also in Britain, Scandinavia, and America. Missionaries and Evangelicals were its vanguard in India, but were joined by sections of the Indian bourgeoisie.

Government policy vacillated, but a significant trend was to seek popular support through the paternalist protection of subaltern groups, peasant and tribal. Here, too, the indigo controversy marks a watershed. The reforms that resulted were different from those of the earlier, liberal period. Paternalism is marked in education, which increasingly aimed at the people as well as the elite, sometimes against elite opposition.

## THE INDIGO CONTROVERSY

As long as indigo was profitable and seen to benefit growers as well as planters, its cultivation presented no political problem. But indigo prices fell drastically around 1830. As payment for the crop was in advance, peasants had to grow an unprofitable crop. The planters used force to make them sow indigo. In the 1850s food prices rose, and the situation got worse.

Many missionaries worked in the indigo districts, and became deeply concerned with the problem. From 1855 onwards, they campaigned to reform the indigo system, and the next year the Calcutta Missionary Conference appointed a sub-committee which criticised it severely.[3] Twenty-five missionaries petitioned Canning, the Governor-General, through Halliday, the lieutenant-governor, for an official inquiry. Halliday refused, claiming that various measures were under way: an inquiry would 'raise extravagant expectations' among the people. The missionaries then petitioned the British parliament, which debated the question in June 1857 without immediate results, though the debate brought the problem to the attention of the informed public in Britain (Oddie 1999: 101-10). The Mutiny averted official attention from indigo, but consumer prices rose sharply.

Indigo growers demonstrated in large numbers and a Commission of Inquiry was appointed by the new Lieutenant-Governor, J.P. Grant. It heard 134 witnesses; the planters were attacked by ryots and missionaries. The report was highly critical of the indigo system, and the missionaries' stand greatly increased their popularity with the Indian public and press (Oddie 1999: 110-17).

Among the missionary witnesses was James Long, an Evangelical born in Ireland and working for the CMS. He had told Seton-Karr, the president of the Indigo Commission, of the *Nil Darpan*,[4] a popular Bengali play by Dinabandhu Mitra, which criticized conditions in the indigo-growing areas. Seton-Karr mentioned it to Grant, who thought an English translation would be a useful indication of popular feeling. Long was asked to arrange for the translation. Scandal erupted when Seton-Karr had 500 copies distributed at the Government's expense to officials and others. The secretary of the planters' organization,[5] W.F. Fergusson, asked for an explanation, then sued for libel. The printer got a nominal fine, but it was Long who had instructed him, and so the missionary stood accused in a criminal case. He was found guilty, jailed for a month, and fined Rs. 1,000, immediately paid by the Bengali writer, Kaliprasanna Sinha, indicating the support for Long among the Bengali elite. The missionaries saw him as a martyr, and sympathy was widespread in government circles. But planters and colonists were furious. The case did wonders for the missionaries' popularity among the Bengali population (Oddie 1999: 118-42), but widened the gap between the races (ibid.: 147). *The Englishman*—representative of the planters' view—denounced the evil resulting when missionaries 'deviate from their religious duties',[6] hinting that this was what happened in the West Indies when missionaries campaigned for the emancipation of slaves.

Missionaries were the main European activists against racism (ibid.: 148). Long lectured to natives on secular subjects, which he felt gained influence for missionaries and lessened the prejudice against them.[7] In April 1866, some CMS missionaries invited Europeans and Indians to a soirée at the house of the Rev. J. Barton, Principal of the mission's college. It was 'something of an experiment' but went off well, and other such evenings followed. The *Indian Mirror* felt it was up to Missionaries 'to remove the spirit of bitter antipathy and rancour which so violently rages between the two races'.[8]

Yet anti-racist missionaries were caught in the web of racism and were not above prejudice in dealing with their Indian co-workers. Underhill, the BMS secretary, who came to Bengal in 1855, asked why so many eminent natives were evangelists, not pastors.[9] Others

contractors divested the managers of responsibility for the workers, and safety precautions were minimal (Tomlinson 1993: 123-5: Rothermund and Wadhwa 1978).

In the nineteenth century several factories were started by Europeans in the Santal homeland. Summer and Helathy manufactured iron in Pachet in Birbhum. Mackey and Co. started the Birbhum Iron Works. D. Erskine ran several collieries. Motte and Farquhar were in mining and cast shots and shells (Roy 1961: 61-2). These industries, primitive and labour intensive, built a solid system of exploitation of labour.

The indigo crash of 1830, and the crisis in 1847, when the locally based Union Bank collapsed, led to the decline of Indian capital in the modern sector. There was a spirit of retrenchment among the Indian elite, manifest as resistance to the increasingly colonial character of the economy. Indian and European elites grew apart, ending the open-minded encounter of the Bengali Renaissance (Kling 1975).

## THE CHANGING BHADRALOK

By the second half of the century it was 'only too clear that many Indians had acquired a more than adequate understanding of Western ideas and were apt not only to discuss but also to criticize British policies', while 'most of them had unaccountably failed to recognize the superiority of Christianity to Hinduism' (Ballhatchett 1980: 123).

The Bengal British India Society—a Bengali association—was founded in 1843, the Indian League in 1875, and the Indian Association in 1876. Elite culture in Calcutta had been a mixture of Mughal court culture, Sanskrit classics, and rural folk culture: now the Bhadralok were a 'generation of Banians and absentee landlords' (Banerjee 1989: 79-80). Poets such as Ramprasad and Bharat Chandra praised Kali and other symbols of popular religion. The new rich had been patrons of music and dance, but by the mid-century, the ties linking patrons to clients were breaking down. A new generation of Bhadralok grew apart from the traditional folk culture (Banerjee 1989: 83). By the 1870s, their cultural expression had developed stylistic unity. In the nineteenth century, poets developed new genres, such as the folk theatre (*jatra*), which, like Kalighat painting, targeted the hypocrisy and dandyism of the Babus (1989: 131-3). From the mid-century, popular opinion lost its respect for religious myth, and became 'sarcastic towards the surrounding present'. But conflict was not as clearly expressed as in 'songs of rebellion of the Santal peasants (1855-7) or the revolt of the Mundas under Birsa in 1895' (1989: 200-1).

The Bhadralok were poised between their accommodation to Western life styles and values increasingly seen as traditional and Hindu. An early response to universalist views of Bengalis as civilized but underdeveloped had been a desire for 'improvement' (Chakrabarty 1997: 375-6). Ever since the debate on *sati* they saw themselves as reformers of Indian morality. The gender aspect is salient, the remarriage of widows and the ban on child marriage emblematic of the pressure to conform to Victorian morality. The British looked askance at the *nautch*—dancing girl—as a form of entertainment: she went out of fashion with educated Bengalis. A new moral climate was developing now. There was a feeling that India's men 'did not properly order their household' (Metcalfe 1995: 94), and educated Indians tended to accept the British insistence that linked the 'status of women and that of the country in general'.[14] The new middle-class morality appeared as a defensive response to such criticism, and the stress on female education and the wife as a 'companion' were obvious borrowings from the West. But the response to the 'modern' demand to split the domestic from the public domain was an effort to isolate an Indian domestic sphere from the public one, tainted with Western concepts[15] by stressing the englobement of the latter by the larger concerns of *dharma*. The response was firmly anchored in Indian ideas (Chakrabarty 1997: 387-9).

Order and discipline were seen as typical of the English home.[16] Yet the ideal, educated Hindu woman was contrasted to the memsahib's assertive behaviour, efforts to beautify herself and distancing from housework (Borthwick 1984). The Hindu wife's education should mainly be devoted to household tasks (Chakrabarty 1997: 381-2).[17] She must be able to subordinate herself 'to others and to dharma . . . (and) free the soul from the slavery of the senses'.[18] The early discourse on female education merged with traditional ideas of Indian womanhood, stressing modesty, self-sacrifice and devotion to home and husband. To the Bengali bourgeoisie, this differed from what they saw as Western norms. Yet the parallels to Evangelical norms are strong. Both were patriarchically oriented norm systems, opposed to emergent feminism. Bengali and British Victorian discourses on home and womanhood developed in parallel, competing for the respectability that was a paradigm of Victorian middle-class discourses, European or Indian, and their respective civilizing missions. In the ensuing rivalry, the Indian family could outdo the British.

The development of the Brahmo Samaj from Roy's syncretism to reformed Hinduism is symptomatic. As late as 1850, its leading members were still trying to integrate Hindu and Western tradition. Brahmin members had been required to give up their caste privileges, and the Brahmo had campaigned to allow the remarriage of widows, to stop child marriage, and to promote female education. But Hindu conservatives had been active at least since Radhakantha Deb founded the Dharma Sabha in 1830. Towards the uprising they grew stronger, and from 1860 Hindu revival dominated the Bengali cultural scene. Then, in 1866, Keshub Chandra Sen, Roy's intellectual heir, gave a talk on Jesus, Europe and Asia. Christian Bengalis such as Kumar Dutt were pleased, so too the missionaries. But Debendranath Tagore and other members of the Brahmo Samaj were shocked. The talk became the final straw that broke the movement. Tagore defended caste and protested against the remarriage of widows. Others, too, opposed the 'Keshubists' who espoused Roy's universalist ideas.

'A great interest in caste affairs', notes Inden, 'arose among English-educated brahmins and Kayasthas around 1850 and lasted until about 1935. Numerous caste associations were founded, and many Bengalis, scholars and otherwise, spent their time collecting *kulajis*[19] and publishing histories of their caste, often claiming ranks higher than those traditionally accorded them' (1976: 4). Such texts had existed since at least the fifteenth century, but now were being written in large numbers, while others were revised. The new interest in rank reflects the increasing importance of caste as society settled after the shocks of the preceding century. It also relates to British efforts to catalogue rank (Inden 1976: 4). Yet the endeavours to assert rank predate British efforts, and cannot be reduced to an indigenous response to colonial administration.

Hindu revival and conservatism, slowly merging, became nationalist. Sen felt its force and lost his influence when pressure was brought on him to marry his daughter, aged seven, in traditional Hindu fashion to the Prince of Cooch Behar. The pressure came not only from his conservative opponents in the Brahmo Samaj, but also from the British. By the 1870s, the influence of the Samaj was extinguished.

If the Brahmo Samaj had been a vanguard of liberal criticism, the Arya Samaj, founded in 1875 by Swami Dayanand Saraswati, was important to the Hindu revival. Dayanand Saraswati, a Gujarati, influenced the intellectual climate all over India.[20] The Arya Samaj opposed caste barriers, but its values were brahmanical. It constructed an all-embracing Hinduism under the influence of Western orientalists, the confrontation with Christianity, and the debates of the Bengal Renaissance. Hinduism was not yet a current term at the beginning of the century, but now it became standard usage, and was recognized as a 'world religion'. The only values capable of integrating 'Hinduism' were those of the brahmans, with some ideas from the ascetic sects. This implied hierarchy, and as the Hindu centre affirmed itself, regional and low-caste variants were becoming peripheral and subordinate to it.

The spread of ideas from centre to periphery that Srinivas termed 'sanskritization' has a long history in India. But the developments of the nineteenth century gave the process an integrated form, an all-India consensus as to what 'sanskritic' religion *was*, and this spread quickly from centres such as Calcutta to peripheral representatives of the elite. These now became the vanguard of Hinduism at its frontier, with an implicit mission to 'improve' or 'purify' the practices of the populations they were able to dominate.

## MISSIONARIES AND EVANGELICALS

The early Baptist missionaries had played an important part in the Bengal renaissance, struggling to create a Christian vernacular literature which wrought dialogue with the Hindu elite (Copley 1997: 14). Among those who continued the work was Long, who campaigned for vernacular education to spread knowledge among the masses (Oddie 1999). 'The Government will do little, the zamindars and the Bengali elite even less. Missionaries must do it', for 'how can we expect Christianity to pervade the masses in this country, when they are utterly unable to read God's word ? (ibid.: 43-4). Education, then, would have to precede proselytization.

Not all missionaries shared Long's view, and he had few conversions to his credit. At the first of a series of missionary conferences in Calcutta, September 1855, Wenger conceded that

English educated youth was more able to understand the Bible, yet its command was to 'preach the gospel to every creature and not only to educated young men'.[21] The Conference voted that those fluent in the vernacular 'should devote all their time to preaching', while educators and others should 'give it as much time and effort as they can' (Copley 1997: 16). The next conference, in Ootacamund in 1858, came to similar conclusions. The note was optimistic in the wake of rebellion: 'This great country is speedily destined to become one of the richest of the Redeemer's many crowns'.[22]

The Missions were eager to recover from the damage they had suffered during the Mutiny. But after 1860 popular enthusiasm for foreign missions declined in Britain; the membership and annual income of the CMS was stagnant from 1850 to 1871 (Metcalf 1990: 95). It became difficult to recruit missionaries, and their number declined.[23] By the time of the Lahore conference (December 1862 to January 1863) doubts began to be felt. Missionaries must be careful not to irritate their public and avoid 'bazar controversies'. Conflict between the men on circuit and the educationists was less of an issue (Copley 1997: 20-1). This was the position when Skrefsrud and Börresen arrived, but we should note Wenger's view, since he became one of their mentors.

Missionaries had lost the position they had held under the liberals. But they gained new allies among the Evangelicals of the administration (Metcalf 1990: 92-121, Oddie 1995). Both opposed the nationalist sentiments of the Hindu elite. The most prestigious of these men was Sir John Lawrence, Viceroy from 1865 to 1869, 'the man Long most admired and who seems to have confided in him to the greatest extent' (Oddie 1999: 158).

In Punjab, Evangelical influence continued, due to personalities such as the Lieutenant Governors Lawrence, Robert Montgomery, and Donald MacLeod. Most ardent was Herbert B. Edwardes,[24] to whom Christian policy implied the teaching of the Bible in schools all over India. MacLeod supported Edwardes ideologically, but refused a measure which might be seen as discriminating against Hindus, and warned his friends against using the state as an instrument of conversion. Lawrence, too, was aware of the danger of banning Hindu customs like polygamy or child marriage, 'very objectionable from a moral point of view, but to which Hindus were very attached and for which they seemed ready to shed their blood'.

Punjab's director of Public Instruction, W. D. Arnold, challenged the advocates of proselytism. The British ruled India as trustees for Hindus and Muslims and had no right to use its resources for Christian proselytism. The Evangelicals replied that the British had gained power by their moral superiority. Yet evangelical zeal found little favour with Government, even though the latter 'did not on that account abandon the high ground of moral idealism' (Metcalf 1990: 93-107).

## DEVELOPMENTS IN EDUCATION

The East India Company had taken an early interest in higher education, but in 1836, under liberal and utilitarian influence, primary schooling was taken up. Following a recommendation from Adam, Macaulay proposed a small addition to the 'present emoluments of a village schoolmaster', whenever he could 'satisfy an examiner appointed by us of his fitness to teach elementary knowledge well'. In this way, 'three or four thousand schoolmasters' might be brought to improve their teaching. The implementation of these ideas, however, was limited, until 1855, to parts of East and Central Bengal. That year saw the start of 'the circle system' of improving existing, indigenous schools.[25] Like policies that were to follow, it avoided the cost of public schools. Pandits paid by the state each supervised about three village schools, and taught in them for a limited time each week.[26] The results were promising, and the Lieutenant-Governor increased funds for 1862, introducing a scheme to train teachers. Village schools identified[27] by the Inspector of Schools were invited to send their teacher to a 'normal school' on a stipend.[28] Baboo Bhudeb Mookerjea, who became Inspector of Schools, was to play a central role in public education in Bengal for many years (Croft 1881: 1-2).

The *pathshala* system led to considerable expansion in indigenous education. By 1866–7, the 3,037 schools under this system had 29,666 pupils.[29] Mookerjea was working on two new measures: to bring girls into the *pathshala*, and to open night schools. He brought up several questions. The *pathshala* tended 'to rise above their level', as Croft puts it later. Their expansion and qualitative improvement seemed to prove their success, but they reached mainly the upper and middle classes. Rewards and scholarships should be used to enable pathshala students to study at higher levels. But the *pathshalas* 'never were, and are not now, pure mass schools', so that education for the masses must be taken up separately (Croft 1881: 4).

The next year brought 2,129 girls into the pathshalas, subsidized by the grant of a rupee to the guru for every four girls recruited: total attendance now stood at 44,722. Mookerjea showed that 67 per cent of the pupils of Burdwan came from the labouring classes, as against 39 per cent in Agra district, whose schools were praised as a model. He saw that system as the best strategy for future mass education. But Clark, inspector of the South Eastern Division, felt that 'downward filtration of education' had reached its limit. He wanted an education tax and compulsory attendance—radical measures, which were to be introduced the next year in Britain.[30] An effort was made in the statistics of 1869-70 to document the class distribution of pupils, showing that about half the children then came from a lower-class background (Croft 1881: 5-6).

After 1857, grants-in-aid to missionary schools were cut, as the government felt they brought it 'more openly into conflict with Indian religion' than even radical legal reform had done (Metcalfe 1990: 94).[31] But missionaries like Duff felt that the uprising was a blow from God: the Government had neglected its duty to christianize India. While Duff campaigned for a Christian policy, others felt missionaries should work quietly for reform. Bishop Cotton took issue wih the missionary demand for Bible teaching in government schools: the scarcity of Christian teachers made this impossible. But the circle system helped the growth of missionary vernacular schools.[32] The Christian Vernacular Education Society, dominated by the CMS and active since 1858, also helped considerably. Yet the CMS closed its vernacular boarding schools in 1865, while establishing a college in Calcutta. 'It was felt that Christian parents avoided normal parental responsibilities' by sending their children into the Mission's care (Oddie 1999: 152-4).

In 1838 Adam had pledged for education among the tribes of Bengal.[33] There were then no schools among Santals. J. Phillips[34] in Midnapur was the first to open such schools, while Droese had started in Bhagalpur before the Santal Rebellion. After the suppression of the latter Droese stressed how the 'extreme ignorance' and 'absurd religious beliefs' of the Santals was a major cause of rebellion, whereas Christian education had kept other villagers away from it. Chapman, Bihar's evangelically minded inspector of education, shared this view. So did Yule, another Evangelical, and Commissioner of the Santal Parganas (Chaudhuri 1995: 248-9). Such considerations led the CMS to apply for a grant for schools among the Santals, which the Bengal government refused (Metcalf 1990:

94-5). Yule regretted the refusal of 'the noblest scheme of education ever to my knowledge set afoot in India', but felt 'convinced the contraction would not last long'.[35] He saved the scheme. The CMS grant set the scene for the support the Santal Mission was to enjoy.

The negative attitude of the government had caused a setback to missionary activity, since education grants had become an important way to finance the work. The CMS was generally positive towards grants-in-aid by government. The BMS and the LMS were hostile at first: as dissenters, the BMS felt education to be the task of voluntary organizations. Ultimately they accepted grants, however (Oddie 1999: 53-4).

Droese had begun by recruiting six pathshala teachers to teach the Paharias. He soon found them incompetent, however: according to him, only one of them could read. The other five hardly aspired to more than 'bazar-accounts and a capacity of writing their names' or at the most a letter in Kaithi Nagari – the Bihari variant of Hindi. He found it necessary to educate the teachers. But neither they nor the parents were enthusiastic about the new and 'useless' forms of knowledge – 'reading books does not fill the belly'. The teachers objected to what Droese wanted them to teach, especially the Bible and geography, which were 'contrary to the ideas of Shastras'. Yet three of Droese's ten schools worked to his satisfaction, and here he introduced more advanced courses in Persian and English, as well as grammar, geography, history and the Bible in Hindi. These schools were intended to train teachers for the schools Droese wanted to open in the future (Chaudhuri 1995: 248).

It was the Bengal government who finally asked the CMS to prepare a plan for Santal education. Their plan provided for ordinary village schools as well as vocational schools teaching various crafts. There was even a modest advocacy of female education (ibid.: 249). The debate on Santal education also concerned their place in Hindu society. In turning down the proposal, the government held that the Santals lived 'in close vicinity with . . . towns and villages, mixed with general population' and were 'employed freely by zemindars and speculators of land of all classes'.[36] Yule, however, argued that Santals were 'utterly distinct' from Hindus and Muslims.[37] In other words, were the Santals to be seen as a tribe or a low caste? Government favoured the latter view, even though Santals were as 'debased in ignorance and devoid of rational religion' as were most tribes.[38] Clearly, the conversion of low-caste labour was seen as more dangerous than that of distant hillmen – a view possibly inspired by experience from southern India, and which still has echoes today. In 1861, the CMS opened a training school for Santal teachers in Bhagalpur, and ten village schools in the Santal area. The grant covered half of their expenses. By 1881 there were 57 schools with 982 students.

## GEORGE CAMPBELL: A NEW EDUCATION POLICY

In 1870-1 the Government of India inquired into the educational achievements of the three Presidencies, no doubt inspired by the 1870 Education Act in Britain. In Bengal, the result was a Resolution from the new Lieutenant-Governor, Sir George Campbell, in 1872. The object of the government was, he declared, 'to extend primary education among the masses of the people'. He set aside Rs. 4,00,000 for education, a sum unheard of till then, to encourage 'in rural villages proper indigenous education, that is, reading, writing, arithmetic, in the real indigenous language and character of each province'. This was to be done by grants-in-aid, and inducing the village, landlord or 'other party' to cover part of the cost. 'But of all things', he states 'must be avoided a grant which may be used to turn out clerks and attorneys; education of that kind is separately provided for . . . What is wanted is to teach ordinary village boys enough to enable them to take care of their own interests in their own station of life. . . . It is beyond all things desirable not to impart at village schools that kind of teaching which, in a transition state of society, might induce boys to think themselves above manual labour or ordinary village work' (Croft 1881: 7-8).[39] This educational philosophy is close to what Skrefsrud and Börresen were to practice. This was no coincidence: they built their schools within the frameworks defined by Campbell. There was tremendous expansion in government-aided schools under the new scheme. From 1872-3 to 1876-7 the number of pupils rose from 2,05,939 to 3,60,513.

George Campbell was the Lieutenant-Governor ideally suited to support Skrefsrud and Börresen's enterprise. Born in 1824, in a moderate landholding family in Fife, he had one session at St. Andrew's University, yet his formal education totalled 5 years. His father campaigned for the 1832 Reform Bill. 'I was born a Radical', comments Campbell (1893, I: 6-7). He was destined for an Indian career, and went to Haileybury, the college of the East India Company.

The Indian languages taught were useful; so was political economy, which 'had not then been sent to Saturn'. The liberal heritage of the Scottish Enlightenment is evident here. His remarks on religion marks him as a moderate Evangelical.

Campbell arrived in Calcutta in 1842. In 1843, he came to the North-West Provinces[40] (1893, I: 13-17). Here, he imbibed the spirit of the Punjab School of administrators, trying to get close to the locals.[41] Campbell served through the Sikh war, and was then posted near Benares. Apprehensive of the terror of magistrates in Bengal,[42] he was relieved to find 'a good deal of room for patriarchal rule'. Still, he feels, the north-west system is 'the most perfect that exists in the world'. (1893, I: 147-61). After 1857 he went to Oudh, working under Lawrence. He retained the ryotwari ideas of the North-West,[43] criticizing Lawrence's efforts to appease the zamindars (1893, II: 52-8, Metcalfe 1990). In 1862, against his wishes, he became a judge of the Bengal High Court (1893, II: 95-6), rejoining Lawrence who was now Lieutenant-Governor (1893, II: 110-11). It is probably Lawrence who wanted Campbell to succeed him.

Like several other administrators, Campbell was something of an ethnologist. He ridiculed Risley's racial classification by measurement of skulls. Long and short skulls are commonly found in the same race, he asserted: 'There is a remarkable example of that in my own family. My own head is so long and narrow that no hat will fit me without stretching; while on the other hand my next brother has a head so broad and round that he cannot be fitted without stretching the hat the other way to make it broader. If our skulls should be found in proximity, and an ethnologist is led to class them as belonging to widely different races, he will be very much mistaken' (1893; II: 127).

But Campbell saw language as a 'very persistent feature' (1865, 1886). He reified culture, rejecting race as a criterion of classification. His main ethnological interest was in the tribes of Central India, and he writes of the Santals and Mundas: 'The Kolarian tribes of Bengal are a very excellent and sturdy people, very prolific, good cultivators and excellent colonists. . . . Their only fault, if fault it be, is to rebel in a very uncompromising way when they think that they have been subjugated to tyranny. The Santal rebellions were not without much provocation' (1893, II: 130). In the Central Provinces, he interested himself in the Gonds, Khonds, and Baigas, and noted he had ruled over 'nine-tenths of the unconverted aborigines of India'

(1893, II: 170). He took their interests seriously, criticizing his predecessors who sent in soldiers to impose an unpopular chief. 'In my time, a poor man, chief of a wild hill tribe, had the decision of the Indian Courts in his favour, but his Bengalee opponent appealed to the Privy Council in England. The wild man of the hills had not the means to follow him and fee lawyers there, so he took measures according to his lights, caught an idiot beggar, carried him to the top of a hill, and there formally sacrified him to propitiate the gods that rule the Privy Council' (1893, II: 200-1).[44] When the Government of India, says Mason, would not let Campbell have his way with the Santal, he 'replied that in that case he must have soldiers to shoot them' (1985: 296). The government gave in, and Campbell's proposals—partly influenced by Skrefsrud's ideas — were accepted.

## ENTERING THE FIELD: FROM THE GOSSNER MISSION TO THE BAPTISTS.

Skrefsrud arrived in Ranchi in 1863. Since 1850, the Gossner Mission had been working among the Oraon, a large Dravidian-speaking tribe in Chotanagpur. In the field, they tried to make a living, without financial aid from home. Skrefsrud, with his German colleague Krüger, was put in charge of a new station at Purulia. The leader of the mission, Batsch, said it was ready, but on arrival they found the bungalow half finished, with no roof, windows, or doors. Skrefsrud was sent to a closed copper mine in the woods, where they might have doors for free. But the trip, in the midst of the rainy season, was strenuous, and he came down with jungle fever.

Early in 1864, the Prussians invaded South Jutland. For the Germans, the war was an important step towards unification, and a vengeance for the Danish victory of 1848. It rudely tested the Scandinavist movement, working for federation. Swedish and Norwegian volunteers came to the Danes' aid, but they had already surrendered. Skrefsrud could not hide his Danish sympathies, and Batsch wrote to Berlin that they should avoid recruiting Scandinavians.

In early 1865, the Börresens arrived with Anne. We do not know whether Berlin intended Börresen and Skrefsrud to work together: Batsch would have none of it. But the Scandinavians refused to be separated. With the conflict, another argument came up: Batsch alluded to the close lien between Caroline Börresen and Skrefsrud, and provoked a scandal. The Scandinavians left the Mission, and found themselves in Calcutta, subsisting on Börresen's savings.

Calcutta was a dirty city, but the difference from European cities was only just becoming noticeable[45] by the 1860s. It was still some decades before Kipling was to write of Calcutta as the 'City of Dreadful Night'. Bombay and Calcutta had become metropoles attracting immigrants and fortune-seekers from all over the Western world. Thus we should not be surprised that Skrefsrud and Börresen should find refuge with a Norwegian, Fritz Petersen, a platelayer with the East Indian Railway. Petersen 'supplied them with all their needs, and helped them in every respect' (Hodne 1966: 68, 69n). They appreciated his aid, though they later found he lived in a most ungodly manner. Then they were offered a furnished villa by the Bengali Christian Dutt family, who were to assist the Mission later. In the hardening racial climate we may wonder at white missionaries being aided by a Bengali family. But James Long shared a house with the Rev. K.M. Banerjea for some time from 1867, the year both men lost their wives (Oddie 1999: 144-6).

Skrefsrud and Börresen were in Calcutta when the Brahmo Samaj split, though they seem to have ignored these events. But they had many links to the Calcutta Evangelical circles where missionaries from several congregations met. Some administrators frequented the same milieu. Central here was the Bible Auxiliary Society. In 1876, Skrefsrud joined the Freemason's lodge in Calcutta, where he was active at least until he left for Europe in 1882. He later stated it was the place to meet men of influence. It has been said that nowhere was freemasonry more important than in European circles in India. Kipling, another Freemason, told how he met Muslims, Hindus, members of the Brahmo and Arya Samaj, and Sikhs in his Lahore lodge. The guardian was a Jew. There is little doubt that Skrefsrud's Calcutta lodge was equally cosmopolitan.

The Dutts were Baptists, and Skrefsrud and Börresen got close to that congregation, which had already worked among the Santals. One of their missionaries, R. Leslie, toured the Santal country in 1834, and J. Phillips had published a Santali grammar, while starting to evangelize among them. The Scandinavians met R. Johnson, a recent convert to Baptism, who was starting a mission to the Santals at Suri. He wanted their help. Skrefsrud visited him there, and they became friends. It is less clear what Börresen thought of Johnson. Several later remarks show that their relation may have been more ambiguous. The Scandinavians were then waiting for an answer to their application to the Danish Missionary Society. In May 1866 they wrote again to Kalkar of the DMS, saying they now had both a mission field and economic support.[46] They wanted a connection with the DMS, so their new mission may not be 'like an orphan'.[47] But Kalkar doubts their assurance, stressing that the DMS has limited funds. To his collaborators he mentioned other doubts, and rumours from the Gossner mission probably influenced his answer (Nyhagen 1990, I: 136-7). But before it could reach them, Skrefsrud and Börresen decided to take up Johnson's offer.

What the Scandinavians later said about this period shows their wish to distance themselves from the Baptists. Skrefsrud (1877: 2) implied they only got advice from Johnson on starting their own, independent mission, while Börresen tells how Johnson had asked them for help several times.[48] Johnson had money of his own, and the Dutt family helped him pay his assistants (Nyhagen 1990, I: 139). The BMS did not pay them directly at first, but did so later (ibid.: 144), probably incited by Wenger. That Lutherans were accepted by the Baptists may show Evangelical solidarity, but why did they not join the CMS or the LMS, both active in Bengal (Thorne 1997)? Lutherans such as Droese worked for the CMS, and Lewis (1878) says Storrs had offered Skrefsrud full missionary status with them, but that the latter refused. When Wenger asked the BMS in London to recruit the Scandinavians, he stressed this refusal. He thought the Norwegian might have joined the more liberal LMS if they had been active among the Santal, but more importantly, he felt that Skrefsrud might soon become a Baptist.[49] The official reaction from the Anglicans is clear from a leading article in *The Southern Cross*, criticizing eccentric missionaries who started work on their own, outside the recognized societies.[50]

In 1867, Johnson and the Scandinavians arrived at Rampur Hat on the frontier of the Santal Parganas. Together they found Ebenezer, their first mission station, some twelve miles from Rampur Hat. On 19 December 1869, their first congregation of Christian Santals was formed with fifteen members, of whom they had baptized seven; the rest came from other Christian missions (Nyhagen 1990, I: 171). A year later, they were 22 (Jörgensen 1920: 78-9). From the start Skrefsrud, who learnt the language very quickly, and Börresen, an eminently practical man, took a large share of the responsibilities.

Johnson had recruited Skrefsrud and Börresen as his assistants, but they were never BMS missionaries. The main support for the mission came from various Baptist congregations. There were then fifteen Baptist chapels in India, the most important being the one in Allahabad, whose pastor R.J. Ellis collected money for them. He was followed by Th. Evans, who visited Ebenezer in February 1868. The idea of a mission financed by Christians in India probably emerged from discussions between Johnson and Evans.[51] Thus an 'independent, indigenous Indian Home Mission to the Santals' was founded at Ebenezer on 10 November 1868. Evans, Wenger, Carr—a businessman of Allahabad—and Parsons, a respected missionary, formed a council of Directing Elders; all were Baptists known to or active in the BMS.

On 5 April 1868, Skrefsrud was rebaptized by Wenger (Hodne 1966: 146). Was it a strategic move? He worked for a Baptist mission where many thought highly of him, yet he did not have the security of a salary. Johnson wrote to Underhill, the BMS' secretary in London, that they must take Skrefsrud 'by the hand and lead him gently. He longs to join our Society permanently, but his conscience tells him that, were he to be baptized *now*, it would be chiefly to obtain relief from his temporal difficulties'.[52] Skrefsrud must have felt that rebaptism was the way to full acceptance by the BMS. Wenger, a Swiss, was a linguist and translator, whose Bengali Bible won universal praise. He had himself been rebaptized as an adult, when he worked as a tutor in England.[53] He was something of an intellectual among missionaries and his views may well have influenced Skrefsrud (Hodne 1966: 143).

In July, 1869, Johnson went home. By the time he handed over the accounts to Skrefsrud, the mission had a capable leader who was now himself a Baptist (Hodne 1966: 90-2). Yet the situation cannot have been clear, for in September Skrefsrud wrote to C.B. Lewis of the BMS, asking what authority he had to act for the Mission. Lewis confirmed that the BMS subsidy would continue, and otherwise referred Skrefsrud to Evans.[54] It was not clear whether the IHM was an independent Mission or a separately funded part of the BMS' activity.[55] The BMS changed the Council of Elders to a Managing Committee, with the same members (Hodne 1966: 93-5). Skrefsrud seems to have wondered what the new set-up would imply for him. He had no formal recognition as leader of the mission he was expected to run. Funds largely depended on what Börresen could collect[56] on his annual tours of northern India, until he left for Europe in 1876. It was laborious and time-consuming, but it worked,[57] and the IHM granted Börresen and Skrefsrud some independence in running the mission, which became known among members of the British colonial elite.[58]

Their next missionary was a Lutheran, born in 1839 in Härnösand in Sweden as Olof Edward Tynelius. His father was a tanner. At fifteen the boy went to sea; a year later he came home, was confirmed, and trained for a Master's certificate. He sailed to Australia and China, and served in the Peruvian navy, where he took part in the war against Spain (1864-6). He seems to have thought about conversion several times, but as he returned from Peru in 1867 on a ship bound for Glasgow, he read a tractate the skipper gave him, and one night 'knelt down on deck and submitted himself to God'. Next year, he boarded a ship for India, thinking to become a missionary. He wanted to leave ship in Bombay, but the skipper refused, so from there to Calcutta he kept''witnessing' and singing hymns. They thought him mad, and the captain finally let him go. He left his belongings with a Swedish engineer in Calcutta and set off for the interior. At Rampur Hat he met Skrefsrud, whose mission he had heard of, and came to Ebenezer. Bodding later characterized him as a 'big handsome man with a childlike soul',[59] but Skrefsrud liked him, and he turned out to be good at languages. In less than two years he learnt Santali, and later became proficient in Hindi and Bengali as well.

Cornelius, as he was now called, soon set off on long evangelizing tours, partly from missionary zeal and partly to get away from Börresen's domineering ways. In 1870 he was posted at Dudhiani, well to the west of Ebenezer. Then he was moved to Sultanabad: the house he was building there was burnt down by lightning, but this did not stop him. He was incessantly active and became very popular among the Santals.

In 1873 they were joined by Hägert, who was born in Pommerania 1844, worked as a maître d'hotel in Paris, and then joined his brother catering in Calcutta. His brother had become an Evangelical, influenced by the missionary Bomwetsch. Hägert went to Allahabad, where Th. Evans influenced him to become a Baptist. He visited Ebenezer in 1872 and became an assistant missionary in 1873. He was responsible for the schools, but Skrefsrud, back from Europe, accused him of dishonesty and of using the teacher's services for his own good. Then, in 1875, Hägert was sent to build a new station. Skrefsrud was to arrange for land with the raja, but before he could do so, Hägert obtained land from a local chief. He also planned to collect money himself. This was too much for Skrefsrud. A BMS meeting led by Lewis supported Skrefsrud, and Hägert left. He started his own mission in the western part of the Santal Parganas (Nyhagen 1990, I: 217-20), which was taken over by the Scandinavians after Hägert's death.

Evans was Corresponding Secretary for the mission till 1873, printed the annual reports, and always acted as if the IHM was independent of the BMS. This was also how it was seen by the Christian public in India (Hodne 1966: 96-7). But it was also seen, by Evans, the BMS, and others, as a Baptist Mission. In the early 1870s, three of their five missionaries were Baptists (Skrefsrud, Simmonds,[60] Haegert) while two were Lutherans (Börresen, Cornelius). The Managing Committee was Baptist, and until 1874 effectively led the Mission (Hodne 1966: 101). It was they who hired new missionaries, or occasionally fired them. Yet Baptist control did not prevent the mission from receiving contributions from wider evangelical circles in India.

## PROGRESS AND RESISTANCE

It was not easy for the missionaries to win Santal confidence. In the autumn of 1869, they found the simple building used as a church in flames. Apparently, the 'heathens' had wanted to scare the missionaries (Jörgensen 1920: 73). We also hear of rumours indicating everyday resistance (Scott 1987). Around 1870, it is said that the missionaries are there for their own profit, that they get 'such and such a sum for every Santal baptized'. At the liquor shops there is talk of 'unheard shameless things' occurring at baptism, so no decent woman should have anything to do with Christianity (Jörgensen 1920: 79). In the autumn of 1871, there were large meetings among the Santals with speeches which made the missionaries fear open revolt. Skrefsrud listened to the grievances and presented them to government, which earned him the confidence of many Santals (ibid.: 84). He participated in preparing proposals for land reform, working with McPherson to formulate the *Regulation Land Settlement* (1872), which became law through Campbell's support.

Converting the chiefs was one of Skrefsrud's strategies.[61] He identified with them and tried, with some success, to imitate their oratory. In the *Fifth Annual Report* (1872-3), he mentions two assemblies of chiefs he had organized, where it was declared that Santal converts should lose none of their rights as members of the tribe. Yet there was still resistance. Matru pargana, an influential chief of some thirty-six villages, led the opposition, with his brother Naran who was pargana of the Benagaria area.[62] He called the chiefs and they decided to expel the missionaries, declaring the converts excluded from Santal society. It is not clear whether Matru was calling for violent action. He was arrested—probably at the missionaries instigation—but released in january 1873, after eight months in jail. Matru is ill and very feeble when Skrefsrud succeeds in curing him—not without converting and baptizing his adversary. The story as told by the missionaries fits an established scenario.[63] Matru's conversion marks a step forward for missionary influence in the district.

In their account of these early years, the missionaries made much of their individual converts. A certain scenario repeats itself: the individual is transformed, immediately or gradually, by conversion and goes on to proselytize and to convert others. The snowball metaphor is apt here: the missionaries clearly believed that this process could and would continue untill all Santals had become Christians.

One of the first Santal girls to be baptized was Lacho, who had a serious skin disease. The Börresens accepted her, though she was 'lazy' and 'without any goodwill'. Gradually, say the missionaries, she changed under their influence, and was baptized in 1869. From then on she was 'an untiring worker among the women, going around to the villages to spread the Christian message' (Jörgensen 1920: 90). She died in 1874, the year of famine.

Another early convert, Hatia, was often called the dreamer, as he had 'remarkable dreams, which were fulfilled, and it was one of them that led to his conversion. The Devil cult of the Heathen was never able to satisfy him, so he had let go of it a long time before he became a Christian. In his longing for the unknown God, he dreamt one night that a man came to tell him to go out into the fields, where a message would be brought to him. This he should take to the white men who had settled nearby'.[64] What Hatia found was a leaf from a hymn book: he was soon converted. Soon after, Hatia went to his village, and returned with a whole flock of the inhabitants. When the missionaries, surprised, asked why they came, Hatia simply said they wanted to become Christians. But we did not even preach to them, said the missionaries. 'No, but I did', said Hatia (Jörgensen 1920: 91).

Hatia went around preaching

> like the disciples and the original Christians in the days after Pentacost. Starting by announcing in his own village what the Lord had done for him, he then went to others further abroad, and became, if we remember rightly, the instrument of converting 16 families. He... left his property to the care of his brother, while he now spent all his time and effort in preaching.... He was continually travelling and became Börresen's companion on all the latter's voyages, and in this way he became well acquainted with the Gospel. . . When we were walking across hills and dales... he often broke into laughter from pure joy and expressed his burning desire soon to be taken home to Jesus. In the year of famine he was one of our most energetic preachers.

In 1878 Hatia was put at the head of the colony of migrants to Murshidabad district, where he stayed till 1881. Then he returned to Ebenezer, preaching for Hindus and Muslims of the area. He was always welcome, says Börresen: 'Whereas the European Missionary, when preaching to Hindus and Muslims, tries in the most philosophic language . . . Hatia came to them with the simple Gospel . . . but was himself living and true proof of everything he said; and as fellow Indians they realised more fully the power of his words'.[65] Hatia was hardly a typical convert, but already engaged in his own religious quest. Such a man might otherwise have turned to one of the Vaishnavite sects.

Hinduma was a widow and about sixty when baptized. She was the first of several widows evangelizing among the women and looking after the sick. Skrefsrud called her 'the prophetess' (Jörgensen 1920: 90). Widows seem to have found a new social role in the mission. Traditionally, they were often the targets of witchcraft accusations.

The first Santal catechists, Siram and Hindu (Hinduma's son),[66] were recruited in 1870.[67] Siram was to become a central personality in the mission. The general idea is clear: Santals are to be converted by Santals. In 1873, there were 275 converts organized in seven small congregations. The chiefs feared that the new faith would destroy the distinctive Santal identity.

From the start, however, Skrefsrud and Börresen's work is characterized by their wish to respect tribal culture. Gradually, their goal became the building of an independent Santal church. That church must one day be controlled by the Santals. It should serve a 'primitive' people without formal education. The model was the original or apostolic church, terms the missionaries used interchangeably and never defined precisely.[68] 'We did not start', says Skrefsrud during a visit to Sweden, 'to teach them Luther's or any other catechism, but sought to get them on their knees, praying. . . . When they had experienced spiritual life in their hearts, then we started to instruct them'.[69] The lack of dogmatism implies independence from other congregations: such a church has little use for theologians. 'I am convinced', writes Börresen in 1883, 'that the practice of preaching, of running the Church, and the ability to mix with Christians as well as Heathens, in letting oneself be guided by the Holy Spirit, are far more important than an exam, dry and rigid, from a University'. In the same letter Börresen declares there is no shortage of young Santals ready to assume the responsabilities of priesthood.[70]

In 1872 Cornelius left the mission. The reason was a certain Mrs. Body. She had come with her husband, W. S. Body, to India in 1870, when the latter was recruited as a missionary by Johnson. But the IHM had refused to accept Body as his wife was judged unfit for a missionary's life. When her husband died in 1872, however, Cornelius lost little time in announcing his engagement to her. Börresen and Skrefsrud immediately sacked him. Cornelius and his new wife were rebaptized, and were supported, as independent missionaries, by the BMS. Later, they joined the Plymouth Brethren.

Some converts tell their own story, though it is still cast in a missionary scenario. One of the first girls in the school Mrs. Börresen founded was Anpi. In a long letter of 1883, to an unknown correspondent she relates the story of her conversion.

One day, when I was a little girl, I went to a rice field . . . I sat down and I looked around me and thought: who has been creating the world? And as I thought back and forth, I said to myself: surely, these things have been created by the Lord. . . . I would say to my parents: let us go to the land of my mother's brother in the jungle. But my parents did not agree. . . . About one year later, my grandfather came to us from that country longing for me to come there. I again said to my parents: Let us go to the land of my mother's brother and his family . . . my parents said to each other: 'We have only two children to take. Let us go to the forest country'. We left our land, to visit our friends and relatives. But neither my parents nor I understood why I wanted so much to go to that country. After staying for sometime, my parents said: 'We should go back to our forefathers' land'. Siram came to us to talk about God, and I went off with my little sister to listen to Siram. . . . My mother said it was not for a little girl. She did not understand its significance. And the Heathens around us were very much opposed to the idea that we become Christian. Still, I took my little sister on my arm and went there daily to hear Siram. Sometimes, my father also came. I told my parents what I heard. And even if they did not like to listen, I continued to tell them . . . I don't remember how many weeks after this I said to my parents: 'Let us go and be baptized'. But my father would not agree to that. In the meantime, my little sister died. One day, as my parents were talking about that, my mother said to my father. 'Don't you understand now, (it must be) the Bonga (God). Let us go and get baptized'. When I heard my parents talk in this way, I went to Siram without asking their leave . . . . And at last my parents also began to attend Siram's preaching. But after sometime, they started to fall away. 'We don't want to get baptized. Let us go to the land of our forefathers'. Next day, I said laughing to my mother: 'Here is my little sister: let us go to school!' Next day, I realized my intention. I took my smallest sister and went to school in Ebenezer. My parents were very angry.

After sometime, they listened to God's Word . . . and one day, we were baptized by Papa.[71] This is what I remember about my conversion. This is what I remember from my childhood. As for later events of my life, I want to tell you something. The first time that Mama went to your country, in 1872, I was growing up and studying in school. After Mama's return and the marriage of . . . .[72] Mama called me daily after school to help in her work and look after the other girls. And so I worked.

When Mama prepared to go to your country in 1881, she left her work to me, and I worked for a long time but then I got sick and was very sad not to be able to do my work . . . .

## SONA: THE CHILDHOOD OF A MODEL CONVERT

We know Sona's life better than that of any other convert, since Bodding wrote her biography, which helps us envisage the Santal subject at the time. Though Bodding uses Sona's life to show a succesful conversion, the book is the most complete biography we have of any Santal woman at the time. Sona herself wrote some reminiscences of her childhood. 'Much of what is told below is rendered directly', says Bodding. 'When the story is in the first person, the translation is always literal'.[73]

The Santal concept of time frames the beginning of Bodding's story. We do not know when Sona was born, Bodding says. The mother will remember her 'day of sitting'. It rained that day, or it was the time when the *mahua* flowers were falling, while ploughing, planting rice, harvesting . . . 'One is not able to proceed much beyond the season' (Bodding 1919: 5). Otherwise, one refers to an important event: the 1855 rebellion, or 1866, which was a famine year. Sona's mother told her that she was just strong enough to 'run about' then, so Bodding assumes she was born around 1863. She was born at Ghat Haripur 2 miles north-east of Benegaria. Her parents lived where the Benegaria Road, built later, branches from the Rampur Hat to Dumka Road. There was still a jack-tree there in Bodding's time, planted by Sona's father (ibid.: 6).

Sona had little to say about her father's parents, who may have died before she could remember them. She was given her father's mother's name, as was the custom: her paternal grandfather was probably Mangat, since the son of Sona's youngest paternal uncle bore that name. The uncle lived in Chitragaria, just north of Benagaria, and studied Santal tradition with Skrefsrud under Kolean Guru. He never converted. His son Mangat did, but was 'a weak and probably fallen man'. Budhan, the elder brother of Sona's father was one of the Mission's earliest converts: his daughter married a cathechist (Bodding 1919: 7).

Sona soon had to help with the work, looking after the animals. While doing so she saw some of the missionaries' effects transported on carts. The overseer called for help. 'He was not a Santal', says Bodding, 'or the people of the neighbourhood would not have acted as they did'. He asked several Santals for assistance, but they could not or would not leave their work. Then Sona saw a man hiding behind the ditch of a rice field. What struck her was that the man was afraid. There were rumours, at the time, that the missionaries abducted people to sell them to terrible monsters called *Gormukha* or *Ekaguria*.[74] 'They eat people, cook them in oil in a large vessel and hang the body at the door of the house, so they can take a bite when they jump out or come in. And they pay a basketful of silver money for each human being they can get. These days we hear no more of such things', comments Bodding, 'but it was a very real fear some decades back' (Bodding 1919: 9). Sona adds that there were other, similar stories about the missionaries at the time, which Bodding places at 1869-70.

Sona's maternal grandparents lived in Ghotokpur, east of the Mission's outpost, Belbuni, and were among the first converts during the early years.[75] Bodding stresses that 'Mother and child are easily drawn to the home of her parents' (1919: 10). Sona must have been about nine then. She often visited her grandparents, and learnt basic Christian knowledge from them, as they were instructed for baptism. Sona liked what she learnt, which pleased her mother: but the father got angry. In Ghotokpur, a child was bitten by a serpent, but the

Christians prayed, and the child was saved. Then a young boy fell sick with high fever. Again the Christians prayed, and before they finished, the boy rose from his bed. 'I thought to myself' says Sona, 'it is a magnificent bonga that they have'. Does Sona's remark imply that some Santals saw Christ as a new and more powerful bonga? Possibly, for the bongas do not form a closed pantheon, and some Hindu gods and goddesses were already seen as bongas. Even the train was sometimes called the *relgadi-bonga*.[76]

## THE 1874 FAMINE AND MASS CONVERSION

In 1874 there was a famine. Börresen was authorized by the Deputy Commissioner to supervise irrigation work, to prevent a recurrence of the drought. He took the opportunity to preach to thousands of Santal workers, baptizing a large number. The critical situation allowed Santal converts to preach to non-Christians eager to know more. Thanks to theirs and Börresen's activity, the mission counted some 1,600 conversions in 1874.

Sona's family took part in the work, and listened to Börresen preach. His Santali was still rudimentary, and Sona did not understand what he was trying to say. But at the end he said 'Come on, come on to heaven!' Everybody knelt down. Sona thought, 'He says: come up to heaven! Why, then, don't they rise to the heavens? Why do they kneel?' (Bodding 1919: 11). Yet she kept coming to the services, and Bodding feels she did so on her own initiative. One day, as people in Ghotokpur lined up for baptism, Sona joined the line. Börresen was examining the candidates. An elder spotted Sona, saying: 'Your parents are not baptized. Are you going to?' Sona, embarassed, left the line. Yet she picked up whatever she could about Christianity, and told it to her parents. On 26 August 1874, they were baptized. Sona could not join them because the missionaries did not baptize children at the time.

Sona's mother died four months later. The father became a postman. He started to drink, and his daughters were sent away: Sona to the girl's school in Benagaria, her sisters to their mother's brother. It was Budhan, her Christian uncle, who brought Sona to Benagaria (Bodding 1919: 12). After about a year, Sona's father married again.[77] But the morning Sona's stepmother arrived, she was bitten by a snake and died. Sona got Mrs. Börresen's permission to visit her father, and went there with Anpi. She scolded her father for having 'taken a stranger into his house'. This was a difficult moment for her father. Since he was a Christian, the heathens would have nothing to do with him, and since he remarried a heathen woman, the Christians would not help either, even to take the body away. He begged Skrefsrud to send someone to help. Skrefsrud would hear nothing of it. The father then asked Sona to act as go-between. Skrefsrud did give in, and the body was buried, but the father was a broken man, moving from one village to another, until he left his children, his rice ripe in the field. Later—probably in 1894—he came to Assam, going from one plantation to another till he arrived at the mission colony. There he found another wife, with whom he had two girls. Muston, who remembered him, took him on, but he stayed only a year. He returned to Chitragaria, dying soon after. Though Sona remembered her father with nostalgia, she says no more of him after he left (Bodding 1919: 14).

The famine conversions provoked negative reactions. Several journals,[78] and the Catholic Church, criticized the missionaries for taking advantage of the distressed. Later, Bodding explains[79] that the Santals blamed the famine on God's wrath, and wanted to convert, conscious of their error of ignoring Him. By 1874, the congregation numbered 2,000 adults and 4,000 children, an influential community within its restricted territory.

## SCHOOLS AND THE POLITICS OF LANGUAGE

Skrefsrud, Börresen and Johnson had established a boys' boarding school at Benagaria in 1867 and, a year later, a school for girls. Lack of funds kept them from opening the thirty schools they had planned. Their view differed from that of Droese, who felt, in 1857, that the real problem was to find competent teachers (Chaudhuri 1995: 251). The standards were not as high as in the Santal schools the CMS had been developing from 1859 onwards. Here, the first optimistic phase under J.E. Hallet had been replaced by a more concentrated effort under E.L. Puxley's leadership from 1861. These efforts were to produce a very different educational policy: that of the Scandinavians was much closer to Hallet's early work. The teaching was oriented towards practical matters. Religious instruction was important, but there were plans to train pastors, evangelists, and religious workers. Christian Santals taught adults to read and write in ambulatory schools. At first, Bengali was the medium of instruction. Later, Skrefsrud advised the Inspector of Schools that with the introduction of Santali the students improved and took to the Roman alphabet more readily than to the Bengali (Hodne 1966: 304).

Meanwhile, the missionary conference in Allahabad, 1872, was disappointed with the rate of conversions. The Free Church missionary Bhattacharja felt that Hinduism would not 'crumble to pieces [as] soon as many sanguine friends expect'.[80] Sherring pointed to rising attendance at Mission Schools,[81] in spite of the stagnating number of missionaries. Less stress should be put on conversion and more on educational work. This was a significant shift in perspective (Copley 1997: 21-2).

Skrefsrud wanted the Santals to accept the schoolteacher as part of the village system and to allow him free land.[82] This recalls Droese's report, in 1857, that the *manjhis* had offered him free land for his schools.[83] This is a recurrent theme, which seems to indicate an eagerness on the part of these Santal leaders to be seen as progressive while acting as patrons, rather than clients, in the educational scheme. The collector of Birbhum, too, felt that some villages were ready to meet the charges of the schoolmaster, but Phillips felt they were not ready for such a scheme. The result of an inquiry was negative (Hodne 1966: 308, 308n). The Inspector of Schools notes, as an exception to the backwardness of Bhagalpur division, the progress in the Santal Parganas, where missionaries have 'succeeded in establishing a considerable number of efficient village schools wherein Sonthali is taught'. After dealing with the CMS and their training school at Taljhari, the report turns to the Baptist Mission schools, Benagaria:

> The two training schools for boys and girls respectively are under the responsability of an able and earnest scholar and missionary, the Revd. Mr. Skrefsrud, assisted by Mr. and Mrs. Boersen. Mr. Skrefsrud's perfect command of Santali, combined with his general knowledge and the unselfish earnestness and simplicity of his character, have given him considerable influence over the Santal population. The unsuspecting confidence and perfect reliance of the Santals in the truthful words and pure intentions of the white man in their midst, who understands them and sympathizes with them, is very marked. In Mrs. Boersen the girls have a kind hearted and pleasant companion and friend. . . .[84]

Even more interesting is Skrefsrud's own report, attached to the main report, which states clearly his educational ideas:

> Although I was fortunate enough to learn to think for myself from my early youth, and also to teach others the same, still I have received a new impulse from you to do so in communicating knowledge to the Santals. My object is, therefore, to teach the

boys in the training school to think, thus giving them a few tools with which to work for themselves. Now, I must say, that the Santals in the training schools are on the way to learn to think, and I hope they will try to teach the village people to do so too. The cramming of facts, I think is the greatest curse in the Educational department, and shows a great misunderstanding of pedagogy.

We are now sending out our first class of boys to take the place of the less efficient village scoolmasters. We are going to send away all Hindu schoolmasters in Santal villages to replace them by Santal masters—Christians without distinction. We are going to pay the village schoolmasters for the first four to five years, after they will be incorporated in the Santal village system, and will receive *khet* (land) for their labour, which will consist in teaching the boys and girls in the village to read, write, and a little arithmetic, and keep accounts with the zemindars and *mahajans.* The schools will thus be permanent in the village system. It has been proposed to Government, and backed up by the Commissioner and Government of Burdwan, that Government should give Rs 6 per month for each village school for five years, and the Santals bind themselves to incorporate the masters into their village system after that, and pay them as they pay the *manjhi* of the village . . . . It is, in my opinion, an excellent plan, as it suits the Santals, and is according to their institutions, and would thus work well amongst them. We have seven village schools at present, but are paid by Government only for five. We have 63 boys in training-school, but are paid . . . only for 30. We might establish 30 village schools with Santal masters, at once, if we had funds. 4 of the village schools are conducted excellently, but the other three are not, wherefore the master will be replaced by first class boys from our training-schools.

Both the boys from the training-school and the village-school have a marked influence for the better upon the people of their own villages. All superstitions are giving way for true ideas. A desire for knowledge manifests itself amongst old and young, and the whole tone of the community is raised.

The Santals know me now from one end to the other of the Santal country under the name of Karp Sahip [sic], and I intend to use the influence, which I did not seek but which came by itself for their good. I do not intend anymore to work upon the individual, but upon the mass, to raise not the individual, but the mass mentally and socially, spiritually and morally . . . . Great changes have taken place since I saw you. A Santal will not lose caste now by becoming a Christian. No Santal will now have any objection to giving his daughter in marriage to a Christian. Two large meetings have already taken place amongst them for leaving the Bongoo altogether, and becoming Christians as a people; in fact, they were going to decide for it, if I had not hindered them, I not being prepared for the crisis just then. If they become nominal Christians as a people, and then put themselves under instruction, and if they incorporate the schoolmasters into their village system, a great and most promising step will have been taken.

The report shows Skrefsrud's original ideas about education and the missionary enterprise; his description of the teacher's task clearly fits—or was made to fit—Campbell's ideas. It shines with the bright optimism of the early days, and the sense of his own importance. Indeed, the official report goes on to state that there are 63 boys in the training school at Ebenezer, not 30 as officially assumed. But then the report adds, more soberly: 'This school has been in existence only four years, and is therefore considerably behind the other training school at Taljhari'.[85]

Stressing that they do not use education as a means to conversion, Skrefsrud underlines its value among Christians. 'Our aim is to get the people converted first . . . (then) give them the necessary education which their surrounding require; but we studiously avoid awakening aspiration in them which, in their social status, could only be doomed to disappointment: qualitative, not generic, superiority is the object of our educational efforts'.[86]

In a letter,[87] Skrefsrud tells about two Christians meeting some Bengali brahmins, who

> several times got something to think about from our simple Santals . . . There was one Maloti Raja who challenged the Santals come to pay their rent, to . . . speak to him about religion if they had the courage. One of our Santals said: 'I have the courage'. So the brahmin starts to quote a *sloka* from his sanskritic books and to praise Agni as a great God and everybody's ancestor. Our Santal asked what that was supposed to mean, to which the Brahmin retorted by laughing: 'If you can't even understand that, there is no point in talking'. 'Then I won't talk to you', the Christian answered, 'if you speak in a language I can understand and I cannot answer, then you can tell me this. I only have to answer you in Santali, to pay your compliment back'. Then the Brahmin taught that the fire was our god and forefather. The Christian answered: 'Then kiss your father who is burning in your pipe of tobacco, let us see how much filial love you have in you'. The Brahmin answered he would burn himself and so could not do it. Then the Christian laughed and said: 'Then I will advise you to come to my god where you shall not need to have such fear'. The Brahmins laughed and said (to their kin): 'The Santal is wiser than you are'.

This story presents itself as a parable of what Skrefsrud wanted to achieve, a new Santal conscience steeped in common sense and free from Hindu superstition. In the story, the Santal refuses inferiority and stigma, affirming the kind of equality that Skrefsrud himself—and his countrymen—had achieved in relation to national and European elites. Like the Santals in their folktales, Skrefsrud shows no respect for brahman erudition—common sense affirms the equality of man. But his story differs from the Santal tales in one respect: in their stories, the brahmans never admit their fault nor laugh at themselves. The paradigm of power, pervasive in Santal stories, is absent here. Today, in spite of subaltern affirmation of various kinds, one feels that the Santal narrators were more realistic than Skrefsrud was.

## SONA AT SCHOOL

School changed the life of many Santals, and Christianity became part of a new identity, expressed through a Christian idiom, which formed—but also limited—their sentiments. Sona entered the girls' school in the spring of 1875. Anpi told Bodding that when Sona's father left, he trusted his daughter to her care.[88] From that time on, says Anpi, they were close friends. Still Sona felt lonely, longing for her sister Randhan, who was with her uncle in Ghotokpur. Three times she ran away to see her[89] (Bodding 1919: 15). In the end Randhan came to the school, but got sick and died. 'I had not learnt much' then, says Sona, of 'where they go after death . . . if I should be able to see her again . . . I just cried and said: 'Where are you, Randhan ?'. At her mother's burial Doman—who later worked for Haegert—said her mother had gone to Jerusalem,[90] so Sona thought Randhan, too, had gone there, to a village far, far away. Bodding ascribes her deep religiosity to that experience (1919: 16). Sometime after Randhan's death Sona overheard a conversation between Christians. Jesus, they said, was killed for the sake of sinful men. 'I thought . . . how could such a thing happen? One human being sins, and another is punished. I could not get peace of mind, before I could be enlightened'. . . . Bodding comments that none of the sacred scripture was available at Benagaria then. Among the few books available, was a translation by the Scottish missionaries of an English textbook for children. Bodding muses that it was both 'encouraging and shameful' that this book—badly translated, he thought—should be of use. 'Why were there not more and better books?', he asks, blaming the early missionaries (Bodding 1919: 17). We also note how the reaction to injustice, here, is muted by a Christian schema, where suffering is marked positively as a step to true understanding and salvation. This is not a part of traditional Santal views.

As Sona received baptism,[91] she thought of the boy bitten by a snake, and the one who had cramps, in Ghotokpur while she was a child. 'He who saved these two, would heal me too, whenever I got sick. It was my childish mind', she adds, but then tells of the two or three times God saved her. Once 'after I had Joseph, I was lying ill for three months. I begged and prayed. . . . It made me so sad to see the children, and I felt as if I should never get well. But God heard my prayer and healed me'.

For Sona as for others, it was a hard time at school, says Bodding, criticizing the 'Prussian discipline with more punishment than reward' of Mrs. Börresen's regime. Sona got through it rather lightly. She was bright, and gave no reason for concern except when she ran away to see her sister. Anpi, now a 'house girl' with Mrs. Börresen, remained a close friend. She was some eight years Sona's senior, but their friendship lasted till Sona's death (Bodding 1919: 18).[92]

## CREATING DIFFERENCE

The missionaries were proud of their 'simple' Santals. But even at this early stage, they themselves did not live so simply. Two photographs from 1874 (Nyhagen 1990, I: 168, 193) show their bungalows. In front of Johnson's bungalow, a group of Santals is seated in a well-kept drive, in front of nicely arranged palms and small trees. Behind there is a wide lawn, with a semi-circular pathway and other decorative arrangements—and then, at a safe distance, the bungalow itself. It is magnificently colonial, with a large veranda and a thatched roof. Metcalfe comments on the genesis of such dwellings. From the start, he says, 'the British conceived of India as a land of dirt, disease, and sudden death' (1995: 171). Disease was seen as due to the environment. Britain itself had been a land of filth, poverty and disease until the mid-century brought sanitary reforms. Yet the 'fevers'—malaria, typhoid, cholera and others, were thought to be the product of India's 'tropical' climate (ibid.: 172). From the 1860s, dirt was perceived as part of the 'difference' that set India apart from Europe. Even as parasitology became established in Europe, the British in India clung to the climatic theories of disease (Arnold 1986: 138-41; Metcalf 1995: 175). One answer was to distance oneself from the Indian environment. The form this took can be imagined 'as a set of nested boxes, each walled off from the larger Indian world outside' (Metcalf 1995: 177). Metcalf cites the bungalow as an example, along with the cantonments, civil lines, and hill stations. The photos of the missionary bungalows show how they fit this picture. Though they lived among the Santals, the mission station was precisely the kind of enclave created by such distancing strategies.

These strategies involve objectification of the other, and in characterizing the Santals, intemperance becomes metonymic of indolence. In his 1871 report, Skrefsrud says: 'drunkenness, indolence and improvidence are the greatest enemies the Sonthals have, and these must be attacked and conquered before the Sonthals can be raised spiritually and socially'. In 1872, he turns to the authorities to complain about the problems of drink among the Santals. He wants the four liquor shops nearest to Ebenezer closed, which is done, introducing a campaign against drink that lasted for many years.[93]

At the time of the 1873-4 famine, Börresen revived the campaign. During Skrefsrud's absence, he reported to government that liquor shops flourished while people were starving.[94] His letter was published in the *Friend of India* and drew the attention of Campbell, who demanded a report from the Commissioner of Bhagalpur. The latter reported the number of shops, the system of excise, and the measures he intended to take. Campbell would not accept a policy that led to drunkenness. He asked the Commissioner to reduce the number of shops, even if the income from excise should suffer. Local authorities were sceptical: fewer shops would lead to an increased consumption of illicit liquor (Nyhagen 1990, I: 273). The authorities, finally, proposed to auction the licences to make them harder to obtain, and to reduce the number of shops.

In 1874 Richard Temple became Lieutenant-Governor. He, too, was an Evangelical and opposed to drink. Skrefsrud approached William Muir, who had visited Benagaria and the CMS mission. Temple made another inquiry, sent a questionnaire to the missions, and asked for the opinion of the Santal chiefs. Skrefsrud called a meeting of Santal women. About three thousand came, and he asked them to use their influence to stop drinking. Three hundred chiefs signed a petition to close the drink shops. He sent a report to government blaming the 1855 rebellion and most subsequent problems on drink, claiming that Santals drank little around 1820, but heavily after the rebellion.[95] He proposed a ban on liquor shops, restricting home brewing to two festival occasions. Only a few shops at Suri, Dumka, etc. should provide the Santals with rice beer for religious purposes. Similar moves were made by the CMS missionaries. The efforts to restrict liquor sales was the main theme of a Conference of the Santal missions at Ebenezer.[96] The CMS, the Scottish Free Church Mission, and the American Baptists were present. In a minute the Lieutenant-Governor[97] stated that the chiefs would be called and British officers explained that excessive drinking would not be tolerated. The virtue of sobriety was to be taught in school (Hodne 1966: 294-5).

The government's decision, in the spring of 1876, was moderate compared to missionary demands. The number of country spirit shops was reduced from 409 in 1875 to 221 in 1876. The licence became more costly, raising the price of liquor beyond the means of poor tribal people. The Catholic missionaries opposed these measures, and the Protestants felt they did not go far enough. Yet they seem to have had some effect, even if illicit distillation partly replaced the licenced shops (Nyhagen 1990, I: 275-6). Still, the Santals knew they were seen by their neighbours as victims of alcohol. This was one element in the Kherwar reform movement, which grew in the 1870s. Articles published in the *Friend of India* show that Skrefsrud struck hard when he found Christian Santals drinking with the heathens. He found the Government measures half-hearted. The Lieutenant-Governor's measures were ridiculed in an anonymous letter to the *Friend of India* on 10 July 1876: one of our missionaries may have been the author.

In the spring of 1874, Börresen dissolved the Managing Committee of the IHM. The *Times*, in a series which made the Mission known outside India, comments on Börresen's 'audacity to dismiss a committee which he thought useless—fancy a missionary dismissing a committee, and stating that he would act in his own way! They cost us 'from £30 to £40 a year, more or less, to come up here to talk about what few of them understood!'[98] Börresen was alone that year, with his wife and Skrefsrud in Europe. The year before, there were no signs that relations between the Scandinavians and the managing committee were particularly strained. What had happened?

When Evans went to England in March 1873, Börresen became secretary. Skrefsrud, who left for Europe in May, says they found several letters in the Committee's archives, which came as a shock to Börresen and himself. Thus Evans had written, before Johnson left: 'We will see that it will be a *Baptist* mission, and *only* Baptists can be allowed to manage it.[99] He mentioned other letters, but refrained from citing them; as they seem to be lost, we only have his word for it. Soon after, Skrefsrud wrote to Johnson, who wanted to return to the mission he had founded, that Börresen and himself 'had been received by Nobody, paid by Nobody, can be dismissed by Nobody'.[100] He suggested Johnson might join Cornelius, who was now independent, at Jamtara. Clearly, the Scandinavians wanted no meddling in their affairs, certainly not by the one who had invited them, paid them out of his own money, and knew very well how the IHM had started. Hodne felt that before Skrefsrud left, he and Börresen must have decided to get rid of the Managing Committee (1966: 104-5).

That year an older BMS man, Pearce, returned to India. Apparently, Evans had asked him to look after the IHM during his own absence. But he achieved very little. Börresen wrote to Carr,[101] the treasurer, complaining about having to get money from Allahabad, which cost 9 rupees a month.[102] He had already tried to obtain control of the funds in July 1873, when he visited Allahabad. Carr refused, and wrote to the BMS in Calcutta, proposing a closer relationship to the IHM. G.H. Rouse, then in Calcutta, wrote to Underhill in London, saying they now had on their hands 'something like the old Serampur controversy'.[103] 'The missionaries resent interference, and since Mr. Evans left, have become first their own secretaries, and now their own treasurers'.[104] Börresen met Rouse and Wenger, only to tell them he and Skrefsrud had decided to replace the Managing Committee with three Consulting Elders, Lazarus, Dear, and Wenger, who received letters asking them to stay in the new role. Wenger and Dear were both leaving for Britain. In fact the Elders only met once, in 1875; Lazarus did not come, while Wenger, still on home leave, was replaced by Lewis (Hodne 1966: 105-108).

The whole operation was a case of power politics.[105] It worked, partly since Evans was away, partly since Börresen used his diplomatic talent in silencing Wenger, Lazarus and Dear. Meanwhile, Skrefsrud calmed the BMS in London, affirming to Underhill the alliance between the two missions (Hodne 1966: 109). Skrefsrud and Börresen were now free of any outside control. It is from now on, that they begin to speak in terms of a 'Santal National Church'.

## NOTES

1. Speech of 27 July 1857, cited by Metcalfe: Only sixteen widows in all India—fifteen in Calcutta—had been remarried under the Act: yet it was seen by the 'higher classes of Hindus' as government interference in a matter of religion (Metcalfe 1990: 93).

2. Terms like Eurasian or Portuguese were used to describe those of 'mixed race'.
3. Among its members were the prominent missionaries Duff—known for his educational work—and Wenger who became a close friend of Skrefsrud.
4. 'Nil'—blue or indigo; 'darpan'—mirror or devil; thus the double meaning 'mirror of indigo' or 'blue devil'. For text and commentary, see Rao and Rao 1992. The translation was by Michael Datta.
5. The Landholders' and Commercial Organization.
6. *The Englishman*, 13.07.1860, cited by Oddie 1999: 96.
7. *Calcutta Christian Intelligencer*, August 1860, cited by Oddie 1999: 98.
8. Cutting attached to letter from Barton to Dawes, 21.04.1866: Of another meeting, the *Friend of India* (14.06.1866) wrote 'The Bishop of Calcutta has successfully attempted to revive the friendliness of thirty years ago' see Oddie 1999: 148.
9. *Calcutta Christian Observer*, November 1855: 535, see Oddie 1999: 73.
10. In 1854 the CMS ministered to 7,000 Christians in Bengal, but had no Indian capable of administering the sacraments. Church Missionary Record, December 1854: 273, Oddie 1999: 75.
11. 1,11,218 maunds were exported in 1839-40; the 1855-6 season saw exports grow to 11,94,470 maunds.
12. In 1872-3, a severe depression cut prices by half, but inland demands for sacking to transport grain during the famine helped recovery, and there was a period of prosperity which ended with an unexpected slump in western demand 1882-3. Another recovery, peaking in the late 1880s, ended with the crisis of 1890-1 which saw prices fall by nearly half. The market again flourished by the end of the century.
13. Population density fell from some 700 a square mile to 550, between the late 1850s and the late 1870s.
14. Britain's power and prosperity, said a Bengali newspaper, dated from 'the time when women were accorded a higher status than is implied in the present Hindu conception of women's privileges and rights' *The Hindu*, 15.09.1890, cited by Metcalf 1995: 106.
15. *Daivakarma*-duty related to the Gods—and *pitrikarma*, related to the lineage and its ancestors, were to be kept rigorously separate from *vishaykarma*, the pursuit of material interests. Chakrabarty here cites *Kalikata Kamalalaya*, published in 1823 by Bhabanicharan Bandyopadhyay, described as 'a guide to "good conduct" in the urban life of Calcutta' 1997: 387.
16. This demands a sense of time. It is essential, says Anakulchandra Datta, an early writer on 'domestic science', 'that there is a clock in every house and that . . . the women are taught to read it' (A. Datta, *Grihasiksha*, Calcutta, 1906, cited by Chakrabarty 1997: 378).

17. The ideal was the goddess Lakshmi (Chakrabarty, ibid.: 379), who bestows wealth and harmony on the household (Gupta 1999).
18. Deenanath Bandyopadhyay, *Nanabishayak prabandha,* Calcutta, 1887: 30, cited by Chakrabarty 1997: 383.
19. *Kulajis*, 'books of clan rank', were 'the corporately approved "charters" of subcastes' (Inden 1976: 2).
20. His goal was 'to endow the regenerated 'Aryan' nation with a scheme of purified varna classifications. Everyone was to read and know the sacred vedic scriptures', regardless of caste (Baily 1999: 170).
21. Proceedings of the General Conference, Calcutta: 43-53, cited by Copley 1997: 15-16.
22. Proceedings of the South Indian Missionary Conference, Editorial Committee's Statement and Appeal, Appendix, i-xv. Madras, 1858.
23. While the CMS had 107 missionaries in India by the end of the 1850s (as opposed to 54 around 1850) the number had barely risen to 109 by 1871. The number of LMS missionaries declined, from some 150 in 1847–56, to 140 a decade later (Metcalf 1990: 97, Stock 1899-1916: 336-7, 536, Lovett 1899: 690).
24. Commissioner of Peshawar 1853-9 in a Memorandum 'On the elimination of all Unchristian Principles from the Government of British India'.
25. According to Oddie, Halliday, then Lieutenant-Governor, was inspired by Long's work. Halliday asked Long to apply for a grant-in-aid and this was used by Halliday to propose such a scheme in the Council of Education (Oddie 1999: 45-52).
26. Each teacher was paid a sum 'equal to that gained by his pupils, every one of whom, on attaining a certain standard, was rewarded proportionally to his progress'. By 1860 the 172 schools under this system in Bengal, had 7,731 pupils.
27. Later Croft used the word 'discovered'.
28. Many older teachers refused, so villagers could nominate a successor, who would then receive the training and the stipend. A year later the three normal schools involved each had 75 gurus under training.
29. Schools supported by grants-in-aid are not included here. There were now 19 lower-class normal schools, more than half training teachers for the *pathshalas*.
30. In the Education Act of 1870.
31. Ellenborough, head of the India Office, wrote to the Company's Chairman in April 1858, that no measure could be more effective 'to tranquillize the mind of the Natives, and to restore to us their confidence, than that of withholding the aid of the government from schools with which missionaries are concerned'. Stanley for his part felt that teaching the Bible was unacceptable in such troubled times,

and curtailed grants while applications were refused for some years (Metcalfe 1990: 94). Still, the government was keen not to offend Evangelicals in England.

32. There were 5,396 pupils in these schools in 1861; by 1871 there were 15,013. English-language schools showed only a marginal increase.
33. He referred to a declaration of the Bengal government of 1784, that 'conquest over their minds was the most permanent and rational mode of dominion': 3rd Report on the State of Education in Bengal.
34. American Freewill Baptist Mission.
35. *Calcutta Christian Observer*, January 1860.
36. Ellenborough's dispatch, 22.07.1857, General Report on Public Instruction in the Lower Provinces of Bengal, 1857-8: cited by Chaudhuri 1995: 250.
37. General Report . . . (above): Appendix: Yule to Bengal Government 11.11.1857.
38. Ellenborough's dispatch, see n. 36.
39. Similarly, Robert Lowe, one of the fathers of the Education Act, stressed that popular education should not elevate pupils beyond 'their station and business in life': cited by Bédarida 1990: 222.
40. He praises the Revenue Settlement of Bird and Thompson.
41. A useful contact was Jimmy Saheb, son of a Colonel, who had gone into Mughal service and kept a native house for his wives, and another to receive Europeans (1893: 26-7). Such men were a throwback to an earlier period: they tended to disappear after 1857.
42. In Bengal he discovers an affair of arsenic poisoning of cows by the Chamars, eager to have hides for their business, and fights police corruption.
43. Campbell wrote the chapter on 'Tenure of Land in India' for a publication by the Cobden Club. He refers for some of his views to a memorandum by William Muir, later Vice-Chancellor of Edinburgh University, who became chairman of the support committee for the Santal Mission in London.
44. This is an ideology close to Kipling's views in the *Jungle Book*.
45. Municipal sanitation was recent even in Europe. By 1848 Britain got its first Public Health Act (Metcalfe 1995: 173), and much was done in London before the General Board of Health was dissolved by political opposition in 1854 (Rolt 1970: 139-44; Barker and Robbins 1975, 1: 71).
46. They are referring to the Dutt family (Hodne 1966: 68-9).
47. Skrefsrud to Kalkar, 02.05.1866.
48. *The Freeman* 19.07.1867; C.B. Lewis to F. Trestrail, 07.06.1867.
49. Wenger to the BMS Secretary, London, 28.02.1867.
50. *The Southern Cross* (from 1868 The Indian Church Gazette), 03.08.1867.

51. Evans thought the time ripe 'for India to commence an independent work for the evangelization of the country' (*The Friend of India* [Weekly], 19.01.1871, cited by Hodne 1966: 96). Skrefsrud later (letter to L.T. Gjendem, 18.02.1893) explained that by 'home mission' he and Börresen wanted to indicate that evangelization should be the work of the Santals themselves, not of foreign missionaries (Nyhagen 1990, I: 223-4).
52. Johnson to Underhill, 06.12.1867; quoted by Lewis 1878: 6.
53. Wenger was from Switzerland. He was rebaptized in 1839.
54. Reported in *The Missionary Herald*, September 1877: 200-2 (cited by Hodne 1966: 92). Skrefsrud seems to have interpreted the answer as an instruction to wait and see what Evans would be doing.
55. Things were not clear. In the Minutes of the BMS meeting in London, 6 April 1869, a decision is recorded to establish an independent Mission to the Santals, but then the word 'Mission' has been crossed out and replaced with 'Fund' (Hodne 1966: 93). Hodne feels this was done at the same meeting.
56. 'A letter of introduction signed by Th. Evans and Robert Carr on 21 December 1869, covered the first page of Börresen 's Collection Book, and it certainly opened the doors for him the first time' (Hodne 1966: 95).
57. In 1872 Evans reported that Rs. 35,000 had been collected (*The Christian Spectator*, March 1872: 340).
58. Nyhagen mentions John Lawrence, Viceroy; R.N. Cust, of Punjab and the North-West Provinces; D.F. McLeod, Governor of Punjab; George Campbell, Governor of Bengal, W. Muir, Governor of the North-West Provinces. (1990, I: 224).
59. Bodding to J.J. Ofstad, cited by Nyhagen 1990, I: 161.
60. Benjamin Simmonds, born 1848, grew up as a Primitive Methodist, but converted to Baptism in his youth. Johnson brought him to India, where he was invested as a missionary by Wenger and Pearce. He came to Benagaria at Christmas 1870, and was quite active untill he left the Mission in 1874 (Nyhagen, 1990, I: 162).
61. Later missionaries criticize this approach, claiming it led to 'superficial' conversions (Jörgensen 1920: 83, Bodding 1919, Nyhagen 1990: I, Hodne 1966).
62. Jörgensen tells us Matru was a 'rude drunkard' who exploited the population (1920: 79). Other sources do not allude to this, but all agree that Matru opposed the missionaries and wanted to get rid of them.
63. Jolly (1996: 247-9) writes of deathbed conversions as a recurrent strategy among Marist missionaries of Vanuatu.
64. Börresen in Hatia's obituary, written in 1881 and published in *Dahkwala*, no. 8, 1882: 6-7.

65. Börresen in Hatia's obituary, see no. 64.
66. Hindu, as a widow's son, may have had a weak starting point in traditional Santal society: mission work may have improved his prospects. If so, his mother too might have some reason to appreciate the mission.
67. *Fourth Annual Report (1870-71)*.
68. As the later missionary A. Malme puts it they wanted to establish 'a kind of Christian ecumenicalism of an indigenous character rather than a strict denominationalism' (Thesis, II, 266, cited by Hodne 1966: 195).
69. Göteborgs Weckoblad, 18 October 1883, cited by Hodne 1966: 193.
70. Börresen to Graham, 10.03.83, published in *Dahkwala*, no. 7, July 1883: 102.
71. The converts, as well as Skrefsrud, refer to the Börresens as 'Papa' and 'Mama'.
72. It has not been possible to identify the name from the handwriting.
73. We have followed the same practice here. In 1919, as Bodding was marrying his third wife and storms were gathering around him, he published Sona's biography. His wife may have inspired him to stress the role of women in the Santal Christian community. More probably, he wanted to disprove allegations that the early years had produced 'rice Christians', whose faith did not stand up to the exigencies of later missionaries.
74. 'horse's head' or 'one-legged'.
75. They were baptized, probably by Börresen, on 14 August 1872. Bodding says not many converts were left, due to the failure to baptize children then.
76. *rel* – from English rail; *gadi* – from Hindi and Bengali, 'cart, wagon'.
77. His wife was not a Christian, says Bodding, as there was no wedding; he uses this word to distinguish the Christian from the heathen marriage.
78. *Times*, *The Englishman*.
79. *Fifty-second Annual Report*.
80. The success of the Santal Mission during 1873-4 was sensational in this perspective.
81. The attendance stood at 75,475 in 1861 and 1,22,372 in 1871 (Copley 1997: 22).
82. *Santalen* (1898, 2: 22) Skrefsrud states that five hundred *manjhi* had agreed to the project.
83. Droese to Cuthbert, Secretary of CMS' Calcutta Committee, 04.05.1857.
84. General Report of the Director of Public Instruction, Bengal, for the year 1871-2: 23. (British Library, India Office Collection, V/24/975).
85. Ibid. : 369-71. We are grateful to Peter Andersen, who shared with us his notes from these records.

86. *Tenth Annual Report.*
87. Skrefsrud to Hertel, 10.03.1880
88. A typically Santal way of doing things, says Bodding, adding that the Santals are conscientious not to betray such trust.
89. Later Sona's son Benjamin was to do the same, when he was at school at Kaerabani. 'One should certainly not judge such behaviour too hastily', remarks Bodding, implicitly criticizing Mrs. Börresen's strict regime.
90. The reference, says Bodding, is probably to one of the first Psalms translated, 'Jerusalem, my happy home'.
91. Bodding thinks she was baptized on 1 April 1876. Another Sona was baptized in 1878, two in 1880. Sona did not remember the date, but the names of some other youth baptized the same day correspond with the 1876 register. It was Börresen who baptized her.
92. On Sona's death Anpi wrote to Bodding: 'I have some sorrow at heart. When I came to Dumka, I went with great joy. I felt as if I was going to a daughter's home. . . . I am weeping as I write to you. For she was my 'friend and child of justice' The word, remarks Bodding, 'that I have translated as justice, is used about religion and faith; she wants to say that Sona was bound to her by the same faith' (1919: 19).
93. J. Phillips, the author of the first *Santal Grammar*, wrote in 1873 in *The Friend of India*: 'Intemperance is the bane of that people. It breaks up the schools, and indisposes their minds to receive the divine message.'
94. The licensed shops sold country spirits distilled at government controlled distilleries, taxed by the strength of each gallon.
95. In his answers to Risley's ethnological questionnaire.
96. 13 October 1875.
97. *Restraint of Intemperance,* 27.05.1876.
98. The *Times*, 31.08.1874.
99. Cited by Skrefsrud in *The Indian Home Mission*: 19.
100. Letter cited by Hodne (1966: 105) from the Copybook at Dumka.
101. On 20.02.1874.
102. Letter cited by Hodne (1966: 105) from the Copybook at Dumka.
103. This refers to the conflict several years earlier between the Serampur missionaries and the BMS.
104. Rouse, in the Minutes of the Conference held in Calcutta from 24-9 November 1873. Cited by Hodne 1966: 106.
105. Hodne is more diplomatic: 'the whole procedure was a question of authority' (1966: 108).

# 5

# Evangelicalism, Cosmopolitanism, and Radical Roots

## FAME AND INTERNATIONAL CONNECTIONS

Before 1873 Scandinavians had heard little about their countrymen's work among the Santals. They had their own missionary societies, led by the respective Churches. In 1865 the journal of the Norwegian Mission Society mentions that a Norwegian, Skrefsrud, has gone to work for the Gossnerians in India. It says no more, perhaps since they had refused him—and rumours of Skrefsrud's dismissal from the Mission may have reached them, too. The 'Danish Missionary Journal', edited by Kalkar, in a survey of missionary activity for 1871 mentions Börresen and Skrefsrud's work briefly. In 1866 Kalkar had refused to support them when they wrote from Calcutta, but was now more positive, perhaps since Prochnow, in spite of their conflict with the Gossnerians, supported them warmly. In 1873 Kalkar proposed to recruit Börresen for the DMS Tamil Mission. Others opposed the move, fearing that Börresen might have Baptist or Methodist views.

Then came the famine of 1873-4. Börresen's mass conversions made the Santal Mission famous. Several British papers, notably the *Times*, wrote of them,[1] sparking off fund raising activity in Britain. Duff, who had returned home, wrote about the famine and appealed to the Scots for help. Archibald W. Graham, who knew about the IHM from a friend in India, wrote about it,[2] and advertised for contributions in two Edinburgh newspapers (Nyhagen 1990, I: 199, 225-6). In 1875, he published *The Gospel in Santhalistan, by an old Indian*—a potpourri of quotations from letters, Skrefsrud's speeches in Britain, and a book by a British official. He makes no mention of the Baptists, a point they did not miss. The book served as a source for Hertel (1877) and for the Gossnerian Jellinghaus, who published—anonymously—*Das Evangelium in Santalistan* in 1878 (Nyhagen 1990, I: 229-31).

Graham was born in 1799. He was a medical officer in India for many years.[3] On his retirement he settled in Edinburgh as an active freechurchman and elder of the Barclay Free Church, a centre of evangelical activity, which Moody and Sankey were to visit. Graham was an active supporter of foreign missions and became the node of the Santal Mission's support in the British Isles. Several Norwegian freechurchmen lodged with him from 1876 onwards, to study the organization of the Free Church of Scotland (ibid.: 226-7). Some of them were to play active parts in supporting the Santal Mission in Norway.

German missionaries, too, used to stay with Graham, and he had close contacts with the Swedish Home Mission.[4] At one time, he tried to recruit missionaries to the Santals from the Swedes. He corresponded with Hertel in Denmark, and Paulsen in Norway. Another project dear to him was the Assam and Cachar Missionary Society, founded by two Germans, Blaich and Roth. Graham was an enthusiast of practical education, who in 1868 tried to interest the Indian government in sending artisans and farmers from Britain to instruct their Indian colleagues—a 'Peace Corps' before its time. Such ideas must have been close to the views of Börresen and, to some extent, Skrefsrud.

From 1874 Graham was indefatigably collecting funds for the Santal Mission. He was particularly keen to develop commerce and industry in the Santal country: he also proposed to recruit Santals to build railways in Africa and to send Christian Santals as emissaries to Central Africa (ibid.: 226-8). Conversion should lead to good works and thus to prosperity. There are echoes, here, of the spirit of the Scottish Enlightenment. Graham was active in Free Church circles for about forty years until after 1890.[5]

## SKREFSRUD GOES HOME

In April 1873 Mrs. Börresen left for Europe with her children to arrange their schooling. But by May, Skrefsrud's attacks of malaria were getting serious. Dr. Lazarus, member of the Managing Committee,[6] told him to take a break in Europe (ibid.: 194-5), and this trip proved crucial for the mission's future.

Edinburgh was central to Skrefsrud's schedule. He visited it in April 1874 and again in the autumn, making a strong impression. It was Graham who arranged the visit, and Skrefsrud spoke on two different occasions at the Free Assembly Hall. The second time, Alexander Duff, the educator missionary, and George Campbell, ex-governor, also spoke. Duff found Skrefsrud's talk unforgettable, while Campbell and Skrefsrud strongly praised each other's work, the latter stressing that Santals were ever ready to fight for the Empire (ibid.: 229). Skrefsrud also spoke at the BMS annual meeting in London, at Exeter Hall. Again it was a great success—at least four thousand were present. The missionary was becoming the hero of the day.[7] At Birmingham, too, he spoke at the BMS annual meeting. It was well attended, as was his last speech in Newcastle, with more than one thousand present. These meetings also brought money.[8] The BMS acted as host to Skrefsrud in England, so no separate support structure was created; but Graham became the cornerstone of future support in Scotland (ibid.: 228-32).

The year before, Newcastle had seen the breakthrough of the American camp meeting in Europe, with Moody and Sankey. Moody had first come to Britain in 1872, speaking at the Mildmay meeting in north London. Established by William Pennefather, it was here the ideas of 'holiness', which transformed British Evangelicalism in the last quarter of the nineteenth century, first became popular.[9] Skrefsrud's success may be partly due to the spirit created by Moody: people were eager to listen to miracles. Skrefsrud often spoke of his own conversion, and shared with Moody—once a shoe salesman—the earthy vocabulary of the practical man. But Skrefsrud the mechanic does not seem to have dwelt on the holiness dear to the American preacher. Moody's theological position—'Calvinist if anything'[10]—certainly differed from Skrefsrud's, but was close to Pennefather and other Anglicans of a Calvinist tendency.

'Holiness' meant one might pass, through a second fundamental experience, to a state of grace not reached by simple conversion (Bebbington 1989: 151 ff). Skrefsrud probably held that his early conversion implied the necessary gift of grace, and like earlier British Evangelicals, he did not feel that the struggle to avoid sin ends with conversion. The 1870s revival in Britain was to lead to a more inward-looking and socially less active form of Evangelicalism. Its consequences for mission work were not, however, yet felt.

Perhaps Skrefsrud missed a chance when he visited Germany in the winter of 1873-4. His meetings in Berlin were modest compared to those in Britain. But he did establish contacts, notably with the Baptist leader Lehmann who had been contacted by Wenger a few years earlier when the IHM needed recruits. His daughter organized support, and from 1874 contributions from Berlin started to come in (Nyhagen 1990, I: 233-4).

Skrefsrud spent the winter of 1873-4 studying Sanskrit at the Humboldt University. He never registered, but says he was treated as a honorary student, and asked to collect ethnographica for the University.[11] He describes himself as the 'favourite student' of one of the professors. This was his only experience of academic study. Jellinghaus' book had probably little to do with Skrefsrud's visit, but its author was active in the Gemeinschaft movement, which spread among German Evangelicals in the 1870s. It was rooted in the old pietist milieu, but influenced from America through Robert Smith, a follower of Moody (Holmquist and Nörregaard 1939, II: 106-7). They tended—like Skrefsrud's friends in Scandinavia—to withdraw from the older, more bureaucratic mission societies, and either supported those which used laymen as missionaries,[12] or founded new ones on this model. The Santal Mission must have suited them perfectly.

Skrefsrud visited Norway twice. In the autumn of 1873 he mainly saw friends and relatives, but next year he was quite active. In Christiania he met the Pietists who helped him when he came out from jail. He spoke at Enerhaugens Samfund—the working man's association founded by Honoratius Halling—and visited his jail director. He saw his old cell, broke down and wept, and on his knees thanked God for the time he spent there (Nyhagen 1990, I: 234). Then he went to Gjövik, where the Norwegian Missionary Society held a regional meeting. On the banks of the lake, Skrefsrud spoke informally. In *Morgenbladet*, a leading Christiania newspaper, the Rev. J.J. Jansen wrote later:

> There stood Lars Skrefsrud with his dark lightning eyes and with glowing words on a hillock in the midst of a dense crowd that hung by his lips. None moved . . . so as not to miss a single word. He told of his life—from prisoner to God's messenger. He told of his work in Santalistan—wonder upon wonder of personal energy and the effects of the Gospel. My soul was taken in, as it seldom has been. I felt that I was in touch with the Spirit. I felt I was standing before one of those mighty personalities, that bend fate by their God-filled will.[13]

The way Skrefsrud carried an audience became part of his legend, but the language here is typical of the way religious personalities were constructed at this period. The appeal to sentiment was central, but this sentiment was also grounded in the manichaean view of progress in which Christianity emerges as light.

It was perhaps harder for Skrefsrud to return to Lillehammer, where people knew him from childhood and knew 'all' about his crime. But he found his wife's family and several old friends impressed by his conversion and accomplishments.

Lillehammer had come of age. The great changes of the 1850s and 1860s had made the town prosper. The question of a railway through the Gudbrandsdal valley was raised, and industry was growing. Mesna Brug, expanding since 1874, was to become a leader in agricultural machinery in the country (Ramberg 1994: 92-3). There was a cotton mill, a soap and a tobacco factory, a mechanical workshop, a distillery, and a brewery (ibid.: 79). Yet the 1860s had been a time of crisis. Cheap wheat from America and the Ukraine forced important changes in agriculture, from grains to husbandry, but the crisis was overcome.

The relative consensus of the years of progress were followed by a strengthening of the political left. Left-wing newspapers were started all over the country.[14] Politics was only one aspect of a broader cultural activity. In literature, romanticism was being replaced by realism. Ibsen's work, best known abroad, is only the tip of an iceberg. Literature, art, and music were all highly active, and intimately connected with politics. Societies for public debate grew up in a number of places. In the Lillehammer area, Gausdal Samlag organized meetings where hundreds of people gathered to discuss culture and politics. It was founded by the farmer Per Bö, who helped Chr. Bruun build the first Norwegian Folk High School.[15] The school, credited with having introduced the ideas of the Danish churchman N.F.W. Grundtvig to Norway, was called Vonheim – the home of hope (Ramberg 1994: 93-4).

Through his in-laws Karen[16] and Thorstein Lunde, Skrefsrud arrived at this Grundtvigian bridge-head, which became his main base in Norway, seconded by the pietists and the nascent Free Church groups. These three had little to do with each other: it was Skrefsrud's personality that bridged the gap between them. He made no attempt to contact the Baptists in Norway, in spite of his links with the British Brethren.

From the late 1860s, Lunde was central to almost everything in Lillehammer. He was born—a farmer's son—in 1832 in Gausdal, close to the farm that Björnson later bought, and the school that Bruun founded. He became a close friend of both, an active Grundtvigian, and Björnson often stayed with him. As a youth, Lunde worked in a shop at Lillehammer. He went to sea, then became a shop assistant in Christiania. Returning to Lillehammer, he set-up his own shop. Dealing in cloth and grocery, he became the most important merchant in town and, by local standards, a rich man. A political liberal, for a long time radical, he was Mayor of Lillehammer several times. With Fagstad and Fliflet (the head of the local police) he founded a committee in 1877 to support the Santal Mission (Nyhagen 1990, I: 318-19). Lunde was intelligent and never short of ideas, but could be temperamental and domineering (Ramberg 1994: 96). In 1870, he was accused of organizing a demonstration against a visiting merchant who undersold the local shops. He reacted with a sharp comment in the local newspaper, but when the accusation was withdrawn, he wrote again to excuse his anger (Ramberg 1994: 103). Skrefsrud, the tenant's son, now moved in the best circles at Lillehammer: very different from the pietist artisans who formed the supporting circle in Christiania.

## GRUNDTVIG AND BJÖRNSON: CHRISTIANITY, NATION, AND RADICALISM

Early in the nineteenth century, a radical Danish priest, N.F.W. Grundtvig, criticized both high church rationalism and low church pietism. Grundtvig became a kind of prophet in Denmark, and, later, for many Norwegians too. His ideas characterize the Danish State Church even today. It is hard to specify his doctrines: he opposes those who put the Bible at the centre, stressing the importance of the 'Living Word', which, he feels, has manifested in and through the Church since its beginning. His foremost example is the declaration made at baptism. What is transmitted, here, is the spirit of an ethical tradition rather than dogma, yet Grundtvig is not a moralist. For him, the beauty of the Creation and the joy of life are central values.

Influenced by Herder, Grundtvig stresses the national spirit as fundamental to man. No one can be free if this spirit cannot express itself. He asserts that its Scandinavian form is the old Nordic religion: far from a set of barbarian cults opposed to Christianity, it is a precursor of it, and points towards the same ethical principles. Grundtvig's poetry—many of his songs are still widely sung, especially in Denmark—made a synthesis between Christian ethics, the old Nordic pantheon, and the eulogy of Nature and Youth, producing the blend of liberal Christianity and democratic nationalism that characterizes Danish, and to an extent Norwegian, culture to this day. This makes Grundtvig the central figure in the construction of Danish nationalism. Since all national spirits are equally true, this in no way prevents Grundtvigianism from playing a similar role in Norway. Its ideas and followers are also important in Scandinavism, the movement to unite Norway, Sweden, and Denmark. Their role was important during the wars between Denmark and Prussia in 1848-51 and in 1864.

Most important for us is Grundtvig's conception of the National Church, which should be democratic and theologically broad-minded. While Grundtvigians did not go as far as the Free Church movement in opposing state control, or the ultra-liberals (Deists, Unitarians) in matters of faith, they saw the Pietists and the Orthodox as their main enemies.

But for Grundtvig, religion was not just a matter of the Church. The movement was what we would call today a counter-culture. The Folk High Schools were to teach practical subjects as well as national and religious tradition, avoiding the 'dead letters' of classical education. The anti-elitist spirit may be seen as compulsory in a teaching programme which was otherwise left remarkably free. There were no exams. It was such a school that Chr. Bruun had founded near Lillehammer.

Bruun soon engaged in debate, clashing head on with Pietists and the Orthodox. He was critical of state schools with their 'cramming', he was a nationalist, and a romantic idealizing the yeoman farmer. Yet—and this led to schism later—he was politically conservative, sceptical of the general vote, a royalist, and a supporter of the Union with Sweden (Ramberg 1994: 131-32). Björnson, the republican writer, shared Bruun's idealization of the peasantry and bought a farm close to Bruun's school. In the early 1870s, they formed an influential circle which not only took a leading part in cultural life around Lillehammer, but became a centre of gravity for the Norwegian Left. Thus Lillehammer acquired a cultural and political importance quite out of proportion to its size.

Bruun, like Grundtvig, held that the present was not a missionary age. But now he met Skrefsrud.[17] Here, Bruun found a missionary to his own liking: he felt that Skrefsrud's success was due to his respect for Santal culture.[18] The view that true culture and religion came from the people, that education should develop that culture rather than replace it with foreign elements, seems to have gone straight to the heart of the self-taught missionary, and led Skrefsrud to stress that schools should develop Santal culture rather than create an elite estranged from it. This influenced his vision of a 'national' Santal culture, and of a democratic constitution for the Santal church. Grundtvigians were fighting for local, congregational democracy in the Danish and Norwegian churches. Skrefsrud's enthusiasm for Neo-Norwegian,[19] which the Grundtvigians shared, seems to parallel that for Santali.

As a man of progress, Skrefsrud saw in it the work of God's will. His own experience, as he states in his sermons, was crucial: if God could use a convict sinner to spread light among the heathen, there was hope of a lighter future for all. He had himself been poor, and knew only too well that material progress can have a liberating effect on the soul. Börresen was no different in this. All this appealed to the Grundtvigians.

Bruun had fought as a volunteer in 1864, and his capacity to take a stand pleased Skrefsrud. He also liked the joyful Grundtvigian religion with its stress on grace rather than sin. They found each other, too, in their dislike of the Lutheran orthodoxy of the State Church at the time, which dominated the Norwegian Missionary Society.

The Grundtvigians staged large popular meetings annually at Lillehammer, the first in October, 1872.[20] Between 200 and 300 people would attend, a large number for a town of 1700 inhabitants. Johan Sverdrup, the liberal leader, spoke on the key issues of the day. So did Olaus Arvesen, Editor of *Oplandenes Avis*, the left-wing newspaper at Hamar. Skrefsrud made a great impression on Arvesen, whose leftist paper was the main outlet for Grundtvigian ideas in Norway. In 1875, Arvesen wrote a long article critical of missions. The heathen should be christened, but not Europeanized, and their new churches should be independent. Skrefsrud, Arvesen felt, represented a necessary revolution in missionary activity. Soon after, Skrefsrud's first letter appeared in the paper, which became the mouthpiece of the Santal Mission in Norway (Nyhagen, 1990, I: 235-44). Because of its position among Grundtvigians, it was read well beyond the district. Yet theologically, Skrefsrud had as much in common with the Pietists as with the Grundtvigians. Thus some Grundtvigians felt Skrefsrud had become one of them,[21] while others never accepted or even liked him.[22]

The second meeting, in 1873, was dominated by the Vonheim

teachers; at the third meeting, Skrefsrud spoke. One of the themes that year was language: Skrefsrud strongly supported the Neo-Norwegian movement. In the 1880s these meetings became more political in tone (Ramberg 1994: 132-3).

No account of the Norwegian scene at this period can ignore Björnstjerne Björnson. Far more than Ibsen, whose appeal was more intellectual, Björnson was the national poet of the period. His early work was romantic, and his decision to settle as a farmer was influenced by a romantic idea of the countryside. When Skrefsrud came in 1873-4, Björnson was close to the Grundtvigians in religious matters. Then, inspired by Darwinism, he broke with Christianity.

Björnson's personality was overwhelming. Typically, he wrote articles to leading European newspapers explaining Norwegian national claims and arguing for an international judiciary to prevent war, yet the same week wrote to local newspapers about bad service at the local telephone station, while pursuing his campaign for washing daily. He put his finger into everything. When Filseth, the editor of *Gudbrandsdölen*, visited Björnson in Rome in 1899, he had met a Danish girl he liked, but was too timid to follow up the affair. Björnson packed him off to Copenhagen and he returned duly engaged to be married.

None can be compared to Björnson on the Norwegian scene in the late nineteenth century. Yet he was not a leader in the conventional sense. His initiatives changed radically from one period to another. Politically, he turned from the extreme Left in the 1890s to become a moderate. At each turn of his fancy, he lost friends and gained others; but from 1870 to 1905, he remained at the centre of the cultural and political scene. He and Skrefsrud had in common their capacity to take their own stand at all times as against all comers.

## SITUATING SKREFSRUD'S NETWORKS

Skrefsrud's kinship with the Lundes was a link too good to ignore by a missionary in search of support. The Grundtvigians welcomed him when the orthodox did not, and once he had spoken at the 1874 meeting, he was placed with them whether he liked it or not. But there were other, political, factors. The Norwegian Missionary Society was ruled by the orthodox of the State Church. To many liberals, they seemed to care more about the doctrines of a few converts than about the moral and material condition of the people.

If people wanted to become Christian why stick to a stingy theology, which would be abracadabra to them? Skrefsrud came in handy at a point when the Grundtvigians needed to prove their legitimacy as church members. Now they had a real alternative to the orthodox Mission Society.

Skrefsrud had worked to gain support in Britain, and further his linguistic studies in Germany: he saw his trip to Norway as a visit to friends and family, and had no illusions about the Norwegian Church. He must have been pleasantly surprised at the enthusiasm of his relatives and friends at Lillehammer, as well as by the Pietists in Christiania. Starting in Lillehammer, Skrefsrud laid the foundations of a network that became his most reliable support in the years to come. It included the Lundes and his father-in-law, D.Onsum; it was Lunde's wife Karen who had first taken in Grundtvigian ideas and inspired her husband and relatives. Then there was Fagstad, the merchant whose shop he had robbed as a youth, and his daughter Klara. While at Lillehammer, Skrefsrud visited the Fagstads daily, and for a short while Klara became his fiancée, but it seems her family was against the marriage.[23] The Onsums had already lost a daughter in India. Still, Klara became central to the mission's network, as secretary to Lunde, when the latter founded the support committee in Lillehammer in 1877. All these people, like most Grundtvigians, belonged to the political Left—the large and inclusive Liberal Party. The Norwegian Missionary Society was seen as an instrument of the Right. Now the political Left had a Mission of its own.

When Skrefsrud came out of jail in 1861, a group of Pietists attached to Enerhaugens Samfund—the foremost of the Working Men's Clubs founded by Halling to combat socialist influence in 1851—formed a prayer circle to support him. Later, they continued to follow his work. They assembled in the home of the carpenter Pedersen every second Monday. When Skrefsrud visited them in 1874, they changed the prayer circle into a Women's Club, one of the first support committees for the Mission in Norway. Skrefsrud says he enjoyed 'some of his happiest hours' among the Pietists.[24] But some of them, he felt, did not understand Grace, instead dwelling on Sin—Skrefsrud wanted Christianity to be a religion of Light (Nyhagen, I: 245).

The first Norwegian support committee was started in Drammen[25] in 1874. Its leader was the lay preacher Nils Paulsen

Bergskau, who had founded his own Free Church. This church with a dozen members, was never a success, but Paulsen was central to the support of the Santal Mission for many years. Born in 1815, he was a carpenter, but in 1840 he fell sick, was converted, and joined the revival which a Danish lay preacher, C.L. Clausen,[26] had started in the Drammen area. Paulsen soon began to preach himself, with considerable success (Heggtveit, II: 566-7). He was an avid reader, but suffered from lack of schooling. Friends helped him to attend the Teacher's Seminary from 1845 to 1847, where he met people who were to become important in Norwegian evangelical circles, such as O. Skullerud, the future editor of Halling's journal, who founded the Circle of Brothers, an important faction in Norwegian low-church circles. Paulsen taught in several places, ending up at the school of an industrial concern close to Drammen. His wife was the adopted daughter of the family at the nearby paper mill that had been founded by Hauge. The secretary of the support committee had married into the same family. Clearly this, too, began as something of a family concern! But due to illness Paulsen quit teaching in 1858 to buy a farm near Drammen, when he started his church that year. He was theologically unorthodox and undogmatic, decidedly low-church, and became one of the leaders of the Free Church movement.

In Edinburgh in the 1870s, Dr. Graham received several visits from Norwegians eager to create a Norwegian Free Church. They seem to have represented the remains of the Haugean movement, as revived by Lars Oftedal. Skrefsrud found many of his Pietist friends deeply engaged in the Free Church movement.

The editor of the Christiania journal *Aftenposten*[27] asked Skrefsrud to publish his autobiography: Skrefsrud promised to comply, but the book never came. A long biographical article did, however, appear in the popular *Skilling-Magazin*,[28] and was reprinted by several other journals, in Norway and in Chicago.[29] Even more important, an influential weekly, *Almuevennen*,[30] which had some 22,000 subscribers, wrote about Skrefsrud and reprinted his letters. Between them the two papers made the Santal Mission generally known to the Norwegian public. By the end of the year he was known wherever Norwegian was read.

Skrefsrud also contacted the University in Christiania, and gave his Santali Grammar to Professor M.J. Monrad, with a long dedication in Latin. He wanted to publish some linguistic work under the auspices of the University, but this was refused in view of his past. Here as in Berlin, he claims that the University asked him to collect ethnographic material (Nyhagen 1990, I: 255-6). Before leaving, he again spoke to the prisoners of his old jail.

Little had been done, while he was in Norway, to create a support structure for the Mission. But friends and relationships were made, and activated when Börresen came in 1876-7. Contributions started coming in, some through the local priest, but the clergy were sceptical. Arvesen took care of contributions at first, then turned to Lunde, and in 1877 he, Fliflet, and Fagstad started the support committee at Lillehammer, followed by Christiania. Skrefsrud's visit to Norway had been more useful than he expected and probably realized at the time. The theological differences between the two wings of Skrefsrud's supporters might have broken the alliance. But these years, in Norway, religion and politics move together, as is indeed true of much social and political history of the nineteenth century, in Britain or in India.

Skrefsrud visited Denmark only briefly, but met Kalkar, who had refused to finance Börresen's and Skrefsrud's work. Since then he had corresponded with them, written of them in the DMS journal, and forwarded money collected for the Mission. Kalkar was now quite interested, but sceptical of a Mission in which none of the missionaries were ordained, and one that had no links with any recognized Church. Skrefsrud later turned to Kalkar for help in solving this problem, by ordaining Börresen in the Danish Church.

Skrefsrud participated in a Grundtvigian meeting at the Sagatun Folk High School. Grundtvig had been against missions, and one of his followers, V.J. Hoff, had just published a brochure to that effect. Now Skrefsrud met him and persuaded him to change his mind (ibid.: 256-8). In making the Mission known and respected, Skrefsrud had prepared the ground for later work.

## CONSOLIDATING THE MISSION: 1874-1877

Skrefsrud had failed in several recruitment efforts, but now a new missionary came back to India with him. Thord Bunkholdt was born in Telemark in 1852, of a family of yeoman farmers. They lost their farm, and when Thord was twelve, he lost his father. At seventeen, he was employed by a school for difficult youth. Its director, Mikkelsen, was an active Evangelical, and Bunkholdt went through something of a conversion there. By Mikkelsen's help he studied to become a teacher, and taught at the institution; later, he wanted to become a missionary. Mikkelsen advised him against the NMS seminary in Stavanger, and suggested he go to see Skrefsrud when the latter came to Norway in 1874. Bunkholdt announced his intentions, and was accepted by Skrefsrud. By November that year Bunkholdt joined Skrefsrud and Mrs. Börresen in Berlin for the passage to India.

Bunkholdt learnt Santali quickly and was put to work in the girl's school. He also looked after the boys after school hours. He had tuberculosis, however, which restricted his work at first. A doctor had seen him before he left, but thought India might be good for him. Indeed, his health improved. He was a good horseman, so in his spare time he rode to nearby villages to look after the congregations. He also read languages and theology. He was timid and taciturn, but reliable (Nyhagen 1990, I: 268-71), and ready with a balanced opinion when others got excited. He was very different from Skrefsrud, but they seem to have got on well.

The Mission was nevertheless desperate for new collaborators. On his begging tours to Bombay Börresen met Köbke, a Dane from Christianshavn like Börresen, but of German origins. He had been a seaman, but had settled in Bombay as a missionary and married an Indian. He was fluent in Marathi, English, German, and Danish. In the Bombay City Mission he did social work among destitute Europeans, Anglo-Indians, and seamen. Skrefsrud wanted him for his Mission, but was refused (ibid.: 271-2).

When Skrefsrud and Caroline Börresen came back from Europe on 23 December 1874, things had changed. While they were away, Börresen had increased the strength of the congregations. They had left a congregation of 300; now there were 2,000 Christian Santals, spread over 144 villages. Skrefsrud and Caroline were greeted with flags, singing, and great festivity. Börresen had built his 'cathedral' an enclosure of twigs and branches, for a congregation of 600; now it was too small, and in 1874 he doubled it. 'The cost of this', he writes, 'is not much but the ventilation is considerably more than we need especially during the rainy season'.[31]

The main problem was to find 'pastors' for the new converts. They were to conduct the Sunday service, hold two daily assemblies, and teach the children on weekdays. No wonder such men, unpaid, were hard to find. Each congregation also had its elders, charged with maintaining moral standards and deal with conflicts (ibid.: 260). They, too, were unpaid. Each village had a 'church', a hut made of branches. Democratic as it may have been, this system was extremely vulnerable. Everything depended on the enthusiasm of the early converts, and it shows their eagerness that it worked at all.

At Christmas Andrew Campbell came to Benagaria before taking up his duties with the Scottish mission at Pachamba. He was impressed by the Christmas crowds. Later, six chiefs from the Pachamba area visited Ebenezer, and according to Mission history, they all converted (ibid.: 259-60). The missionaries now recruited eight cathechists, charged with evangelizing and visiting congregations. They were elderly, proven men. They, and some of the leaders, received some pay, whenever their religious duties prevented them from working their fields (ibid.: 260-1). Skrefsrud's idea had been that everyone should be self-supporting, but this soon proved impractical. The congregational democracy was supplemented by a monthly meeting—called the *kulhi durup* to keep close to Santal tradition—where elders, leaders, and others who wanted to be heard, participated. These assemblies, starting with Lord's supper on Sundays, continued in the evening and into Monday mornings, ending with the payment of monthly wages, baptism, and marriages. In many ways this appealed to Santal tradition. But as it gained in importance, less room was left for local self-government. In the last instance, the missionaries dominated the central meeting and the influence of the Santals diminished.

Discipline, however, was still largely left to the congregations. Beatings with a stick occurred; punishment was also by fines, in the Indian tradition. These practices hardly conformed to European ideas of congregational discipline. The baptism of children was, of course, not yet prevalent. Instead, the Santal name-giving ceremony was replaced by blessing the child in church, this practice continuing until Skrefsrud's death. The Santal Mission did not take to the custom, common in other missions, of using European names (ibid.: 261-4). This certainly showed respect for Santal tradition, but the missionaries may have been unaware of the close links between naming and worship of the bongas.

Skrefsrud says they celebrated the Lord's supper once a month, but others contest this.[32] They modelled their practices on the Scottish Presbyterians: seated, men and women separately on each side of the aisle, they received the Lord's supper through the hands of four selected elders, who were served first. Thus the missionaries did not act like the orthodox Lutheran pastors who administer the bread and wine. Skrefsrud says they accepted the 'body and the blood' of Christ according to the scriptures, but adds that they did not bother about the how or the why: 'we know that we get whatever the Lord has destined for us.'[33] Services were in Santali and Bengali; the latter disappeared in due course while the Bengali Bible, however, remained in use.

The Christian Santals contributed to a fund to aid the destitute. Each village had a committee of four in charge of such contributions, which they sent to Ebenezer. The *nawai*, the harvest festival, was transformed; instead of sacrifice to the bongas contributions were made to the common funds. But such efforts to create an economy of self-help faded as leadership was centralized in the *kulhi durup*. Other missions were far more effective in this respect (ibid.: 266-7).

The problem of dealing with a large congregation became overwhelming. Börresen tried to solve the problem by recruiting more catechists, 30 men and 10 women in 1875 alone. Their salary had to be reduced from 6 to 2 rupees a month to accomodate the increase: later, the wages were increased to 4 rupees. But catechists could not baptize converts or administer the sacraments. On 9 April 1876 the first Santal 'pastors' were ordinated by Börresen. They were Siram Soren and Surju Murmu.

## BÖRRESEN AND EUROPEAN SUPPORT

In the spring of 1876 it was decided that Börresen should go to Europe: the Mission needed money. Börresen's fund collection tours were successful, but the Mission was expanding. The tours occupied Börresen three months of the year, and the best months for travel were also the best for evangelization. It was he who did the main work in the field. A new economic base was needed (ibid.: 289-90). The effort to find new funds was also due to strain in the relation between the IHM and the Baptists. Questions concerning a deed 'conveying the mission property' to the BMS on Börresen's and Skrefsrud's death had been raised, and matters were getting complicated (Hodne 1966: 111). Yet the Scandinavians wanted to retain the BMS link until they were sure of making it on their own.

Börresen built a series of links to non-Baptist congregations and individuals in Europe, and one feels he consciously avoided the Baptists. He planned to go to Britain and America; Scandinavia was secondary to his plans. What they wanted was to raise a fund large enough for the Mission to work from the interest that accrued. Thus some ten to twelve thousand pounds were needed. This was extremely ambitious, yet Börresen was optimistic: his magnificent beard, he told Skrefsrud, would surely impress people even more than Skrefsrud's youthful figure.[34]

When Börresen arrived in London in the summer of 1876, he put these ideas to the BMS. They found the plan incompatible with the missionary spirit. It would estrange the missionaries from dependence on God's grace, and put too much power in the hands of those who controlled the funds. Börresen did not stay long in England, feeling that most of the people he needed to see would be away.[35] Yet he did participate in the Mildmay meetings in London.[36] Börresen was not deemed important enough to speak, but met influential people. The oriental linguist Robert Cust had a special interest in Indian tribes and in missions, and urged the CMS to turn to the aboriginals. They called a special conference to discuss it, where Börresen took part, meeting the missionaries Puxley, Storrs, and Shackell (who had all worked among the Santals), Yule, the administrator who played an important role in Santal history, and Sir William Muir, who had visited Ebenezer in India and had given political support to the IHM. Börresen made a good impression and the assembly felt that 'now was the time to enter through the open door' (Nyhagen 1990, I: 293-4).

Börresen then went to Germany to see his children, continuing to Denmark and Norway before returning to Britain in October. He went straight to Edinburgh, to Dr. Graham, with whom he had corresponded since 1874. It may have been Graham who convinced him of the impossibility of raising a large, permanent fund. Instead, Börresen and Graham established support committees in Edinburgh, Glasgow, Aberdeen, and Dundee. Graham was secretary and treasurer in Edinburgh, looking after the relations between the various committees (ibid.: 289-92). In Dundee, A.R. Grimond, a rich jute merchant, was a major supporter. The support structure proved efficient and lasted well.

The Scots were to dominate his links to England, too, when Börresen returned to Britain in January 1877. In London he gave a number of talks in churches and assembly halls as well as at 'drawing room meetings'. Sir William Muir, though an active CMS man, agreed to head the London committee. Robert Cust and General Colin Mackenzie were other prominent members. For the role of secretary they chose another Scotsman, W.L. Watson, a partner of James Findlay & Co., an important firm with large interests in India. Watson himself had tea-gardens there. Watson had met Börresen in Calcutta in 1870, and had contributed to the mission since. He became their main contact in London, and arranged for the shipping of men and goods to India. In 1877 he went to Denmark, and joined Börresen for a trip to Norway. Like Graham, he remained one of their best supporters, and visited Benagaria on his last trip to India, in 1896. He died in 1903 (ibid.: 292-3).

The men who headed the support activity came from several backgrounds. Some, like Graham, were indefatigable Christian activists, but shared an Indian career with men like Muir, Cust, and Mackenzie. Another group were retired missionaries, who also had worked in India. There is a link here, between the colonizing enterprise and the culture of charity among the Evangelical middle classes in Britain. India was in a way the ultimate object of charity, an experimental terrain for the unity of Christianity and progress. In the British context, certainly, the mission became the conscience of the colonial system (Comaroff and Comaroff 1992: 184). For those who were not missionaries, it was as if the mission represented a way to pay a debt that their work had left unpaid. This is less true of Scandinavia, where none of the leaders of the support structure had particular links to India.

Börresen's visit to Britain was a success, and for years Britain was the most important source of funds for the Santal mission. Though Börresen was at Mildmay, he does not seem to have been influenced by the fashion for 'holiness' and a more inward-looking religious mood in English Evangelical circles. He would probably have shuddered at the idea that true religion could change at all.

From Norway, Börresen expected little, but he established important contacts. Paulsen became his special friend, and was the first Norwegian to contact Hertel in Denmark about possible collaboration. Hertel was sceptical, since Paulsen was a freechurchman and no Grundtvigian. He contacted Lunde, who saw Paulsen as an 'agitating sectarian' and a doubtful ally.[37] But Klara Fagstad, writing separately, felt that Paulsen was a liberal offshot of the old

Haugean tradition[38]—an acute observation indeed (Nyhagen 1990, I: 245-51).

Paulsen worked for the Mission until his death in 1894. Active in debate, in 1881 he clashed with Björnson, who supported modern bible criticism. 'To ride the goat in Peer Gynt or stand by the bridge of Augedal telling tales, such are the things you are fit to do: but if you want to deal with the Bible, yours will be the fate of the man who wanted to climb the Skagastölstind,[39] said Paulsen. His attacks on Björnson almost led to a court case, even if our citation seems to show that he confounded Ibsen and Björnson. After his own Church was dissolved, Paulsen helped found the first Free Church congregations in Horten and in Moss. He disagreed with Luther's view that 'the child is in the throat of the Devil till Baptism tears it away': for Paulsen, 'Jesus comes and triumphs over he who controls death'. In other words, the Devil is not Lord of all that does not belong to God—a liberal deviation from orthodoxy. Yet, Paulsen was politically conservative, and in this he differed from most of Skrefsrud's pietist friends.

## A SWEDISH MYSTIC

Börresen did not want to go to Sweden. 'But the Lord sent Miss Rapp and a rich merchant and they asked me to go to Malmö and my travel to Uppsala was very hard for me, and by the Grace of God I went there and found such wonderful friends'.

Sweden was at that time rather different from Norway and Denmark. The Norwegians got their Constitution in 1814: in Denmark, peaceful demonstrations led to the end of absolute monarchy in 1849 (Giverholt 1969b: 530). Developments in Sweden were slow and gradual: parliamentary reform in 1866 left a two-chamber system, with nobility and bishops in the higher chamber—a system which lasted until 1970. During our period, these lords still had considerable power (Giverholt 1969a: 407), and the Church was dominated by High Church tendencies.[40] The distance between them and the low-church and various free churches was much greater than in the other Scandinavian countries (Molland 1969e: 369).

Börresen's special friend in Sweden was Waldemar Rudin, Professor of Theology at the University of Uppsala. Profoundly marked by Pietist revival in his youth, Rudin grew away from it, inspired by contemplation and mystic experience, and he criticized both Pietist moralism and the orthodoxy of the High Church. In theology and church politics, Rudin was something of a rebel, but he was respected, and his University position explains why Börresen dedicated much of his correspondence to the question of recruitment.

Rudin gives an image of himself: 'I saw a wanderer, a holy pilgrim. He bore an oriental cape, was barefoot, but his face, like that of a king or a priest was highly awe-inspiring, and turned upwards and onwards. Such a one should I be, dress myself thus every morning. A pilgrim, a stranger, with heaven mirrored in heart and face, wanting nothing of the earth but shelter for the night. But since the whole world is wandering, one often associates with other humans along the way and should be able to serve them' (Söderblom 1923: 9).[41]

Born in 1833, Rudin was the son of a lieutenant who married the daughter of a minor noble and higher officer, and rented a farm on his father-in-law's land. But he was sacked from the army and left his family when the boy was three years old. Rudin was raised by his mother and her family. His mother worked as a teacher or lady companion, and was often absent: he was eleven before he got to know his father, settled to 'a humble, but honest life'. There was no strong religious influence; yet at the age of nineteen, Rudin underwent a conversion, influenced by Captain Berger, officer, painter, and friend of his father. At Uppsala University, Berger introduced him to Pietist circles. He met H.J. Lundborg, who later founded Fosterlandsstiftelsen, corresponding to the Home Mission in other countries (ibid.: 9-20). Rudin's conversion was gradual, not the 'miraculous' event that Skrefsrud's and Börresen's had been. He was now seen as a *läsare*[42] or Pietist. Still, he was a mystic and an ascetic, turning away from the world, rather than from sin (ibid.: 20-1). Among the major influences was Kierkegaard, of whom Rudin wrote an excellent biography. He translated Baxter, read a number of mystics,[43] felt close to Beck and the Swabians, and was influenced by C.H. Bergman, preacher to the Swedish court and another mystic. Like Lundberg and the Pietists, he criticized the official Church, but his love of ritual made him feel close to High Church views.

This contradiction marked Rudin's career. When ordained in 1859, he did not become a priest, but worked as an organizer in Lundberg's Home Mission. From 1862, he led their new Mission School, training missionaries mainly for East Africa. But in 1867, he published a translation of one of Beck's sermons in the Fosterlandsstiftelsen journal.[44] 'The good which is in the Lord and the good that moves in you will meet', wrote Beck, seeming to deny the sinful nature of man: worse, to Rudin's Lutheran critics it seemed he supported the doctrine of good works.[45] Rudin added fuel to the fire by a sermon addressed to the Pietists against those who thought themselves saved. There was intense debate in the Fosterlandsstiftelsen. On New Year's Day, 1869, Rudin wrote to the board: did they want him to stay? They voted, 9 for and 9 against. The chairman's casting vote decided in Rudin's favour, but he felt it was time to leave (Söderblom 1923: 43-68).

Sympathizers offered him a calling, where he served three years—his happiest, he says. In 1872, he was invited to a professorship in exegetics at Uppsala. His engagement in missions was rekindled when he met Börresen in 1877, and he started a support committee in Uppsala (Nyhagen 1990, I: 328). Their correspondence is saturated with biblical imagery. Thus Börresen writes 'How can we sing in a foreign land . . . But we are freed by Christ from the duties of Babylon'.[46] Babylon is, of course, the profane world : the allegorical phrase alludes to Evangelical solidarity.

Börresen, like Rudin, was no rationalist: it was God, not the missionaries who would save the Santals. The leader of the CMS mission had been visiting, and he 'took part in the meeting of the Elders, and . . . said, if the Santals are not converted by such men I heard today, they will never be converted. . . . Christ has to raise the witnesses from the people themselves. Then there will be Truth and Strength'. Indigenization was still central for Börresen.

Soon after, Skrefsrud wrote[47] telling how he was inspired to become a missionary by professor Fjellstedt's book, *Skovstjernen*.[48] He mentioned the role of the University in training missionaries. Those who go to the Mission Field 'have been reared in greenhouses and therefore are not suited to follow the leaders of the congregation', he said. If only 'the University could be like a plant nursery for knowledge and faith, as well as a manly desire for action (its candidates) should be the best suited for the task of converting the heathen'. Learning alone would not do it, nor subjective faith, 'The Mission seems to me a far heavier task than the work of a pastor at home. He has to demolish heathendom, to build a congregation on the national way of thinking of the people, and that without seeming to decry but building since the heathen will not let himself be vanquished if you tell him that all that he has is bad. I think the wisdom of a serpent coupled with the simplicity of a dove is nowhere more needed than in the missionary field, where a thorough knowledge of man is a *sine qua non* for progress.'

In 1880, Börresen wrote again,[49] as the Fosterlandsstiftelsen wanted to establish a Mission among the Santals, just south-west of the IHM. 'They cannot stay in a civilized place and work among the Santals. This is a mistake we have seen among people working among the Gonds. . . . If the brothers from Sweden will work among the Santals, they have first to live in a hut before they can build a house.' It is clear that he did not want competing missions close to their own field. And they had invested a lot: 'Our new station Dumka is ready and will be opened on 21 November. . . . It is the main station in the Santal country. We had to build Dumka because both the Jesuits and the British wanted to build there . . . (and) because the judge and the collector will be there. Now we start another station in Jagdi or Daiman. This will be more among the people where everything is still in darkness. And we will have to start from the bottom again.'

But there was a scarcity of suitable missionaries, as is clear from a letter Börresen sent next year.[50] 'The tigers are becoming lambs and they sing. Our son is now 13. We hope he will be given to us by the Lord himself. He hopes to work here in the vineyard of the missionaries'. Then, Rudin's son and his own could become friends – there is only three years' difference between them'– and perhaps Rudin's son could join the Mission. 'Skrefsrud . . . did not find anybody suitable when he was back home himself. Somebody was to come, a trainee from the Danish (mission) school. There was a Norwegian doctor from America. This couple was miserable – he had a hopeless woman. They shocked everybody by their behaviour and had to leave after a couple of months . . . there was Jensen, who came back with me. He was ordained by bishop Martinussen, and we were glad to have him. . . . He has been here three years, but his health has been very bad, as he started his studies too late and overworked himself. He has headache and the whole nervous system is in disorder. Last year he could do nothing. . . . When we sent away the Danish student, the leader of the Mission School asked us why. I criticized him for sending from the school candidates who are not capable'. He turns to another candidate, who has told Graham he wants to'try'. Börresen wants nothing to do with such men. 'If you are called by the Lord you don't have to ask about the climate'. To qualify was not easy: only in the field did it become clear whether the candidate was fit for the job. Motivation was crucial, also health and mental fitness together with moral armour.

## LUDVIG HERTEL: CONVINCING A GRUNDTVIGIAN

Börresen had not really expected support in Denmark, going there mainly to visit his sister in Copenhagen. But he went to a meeting of the Home Mission, where he met its leader V. Beck and spoke about his work among the Santals. Beck, who had seen foreign missions as a monopoly of high-church priests opposed to his own work, fell completely for Börresen. 'It is the Lord', he wrote later in the Home Mission's journal, 'who wants to give this Mission to the newly awakened Danish congregation, as a gift of Grace'.[51] The Mission's ideology suited Beck's ideas. The Heathen should be baptized as soon as he would accept; many converts would be Christians in name only, but among them one should work on Home Mission principles. This, he felt, was how Europe had become Christian, and this was what Börresen was doing among the Santals.

The next day Börresen spoke in St. Stephen's Church. Kalkar opened the meeting, with many Danish Church leaders present, and many listeners recalled Grundtvig's words about the seventh star[52] of Christianity, the great congregation to come. Could it be that it was to appear among the Santals? Contributions were called for and started to come in. Soon other Church leaders spoke out for the Mission, and when Börresen came back to Denmark in September, he spoke at several important meetings. Then, at a meeting at Paaby parsonage in Jutland, he met Ludvig Hertel, a young clergyman central to our story (Nyhagen 1990, I: 295-8).

Hertel's father had been a pastor in South Jutland, and moved north after the Prussian conquest of 1864. He, like many Danes, felt the loss of the Danish province strongly, and was active in the nationalist movement. His son continued this activity, intimately related to the Grundtvigian movement, and became a Grundtvigian.

He felt the meeting with Börresen as a new calling. Soon after he wrote an article in *Höjskolebladet*, the main organ of the Grundtvigians,[53] where Börresen was described as one of Europe's leading missionaries, a new *Ansgar*—the saint who christianized Denmark. Hertel remained enthusiastic and uncritical of Börresen all his life, and became the kingpin of the Mission's support, not just in Denmark but in all Scandinavia. His collection of letters[54] is the most important source for the Mission's history during his time. Nyhagen describes Hertel as a touchy, rather suspicious person, of a lively temperament. The relation with Börresen was steady, but with Skrefsrud—as temperamental as Hertel—there were several clashes, which Börresen did his best to smooth out.

Hertel began by writing to Skrefsrud, sending him a copy of his book on the Santal Mission. Skrefsrud thanks him,[55] as the book is correct in all except minor detail, but 'You should not touch my earlier life, as it will do no good to our work'. He warns Hertel against rumours about the Mission's theological position. They try, he says, to follow the precepts of 'the original church', but 'clothed in a Santal form, so it may become a '*Santal church*'. Skrefsrud was clearly concerned with the allegation that the mission was not Lutheran, and he stressed how Santals believe in the Trinity, the personal nature of God's Grace, and the Devil. Luther held that a child could only be saved through baptism; Skrefsrud, however, stresses the individual consciousness of grace as a *sine qua non* for baptism. The latter, however, is the Baptist position. For orthodox Lutherans, baptism cannot depend on worthiness since we are all unworthy of God. But, Skrefsrud says, the Mission kept to the Apostolic Credo:[56] there should be no problem for a Lutheran in supporting the Mission.

Later, Skrefsrud gradually modified his position. Börresen baptized many,[57] and 'I have advised Börresen to follow Lutheran practice in everything except . . . infant baptism, which should remain optional'.[58] He argued, now, that this was to avoid intimidating the Santal Christians, some of whom wanted infant baptism, while others liked to wait. 'I have nothing against infant baptism, but it is the only point where I had doubts—there is no longer any opposition from my side'. 'In what you say about the dangers of logic', he continues, as Hertel seems to have held the Baptist view logical but wrong, 'you are completely right, as many have been stranded on this reef. But I don't think it is a danger for me, as I never allow reason limited by its own rules of thought to enter the realm of the infinite, which would only lead to conclusions based on analogy with what is finite. I cannot deny that besides philology, philosophy is my dearest interest, and I think even more than I read about the problem concerning spirit and matter, idealismus and realismus, the subjective and the objective.'

By October[59] Skrefsrud had sent an explanation of his views, and his 'reconversion' to Lutheranism, to Kalkar. To Hertel, he was more personal: 'Do the reasons for the alteration of conviction, or rather the temporary rejection of conviction, seem to you weak or strong?' But then he affirmed: 'I am again standing purely on Lutheran ground, and there is no danger that I ever again should change it, as I now *know*, why I am a Lutheran'. He went on to say that Börresen had baptized twenty-five children in Thakurpura.

'We believe in the Resurrection, the Absolution of sins by baptism, and the Christians know that in baptism, they enter into a pact with God and swear to be true to him.' Skrefsrud wanted Hertel to realize that the conception of baptism as a sworn-in treaty was an adaptation to Santal ways of thinking. 'They always say', he explained, 'if somebody has done anything wrong, that he has acted against the treaty': the idea of baptism as a treaty came from land grants by rulers to their subjects. Any difference between the way Lutherans saw their pact with God, and the Santal conception of treaty, was explained as a matter of cultural translation rather than theology. For Santals, oaths were the main way to affirm an obligation (Carrin-Bouez 1991c). He did not say that it was the bongas who wreaked vengeance for perjury. His stress on adjustment to Santal culture was in tune with a series of other remarks in defence of the mission, which, curiously, related to a number of Grundtvigian positions.

'You have heard so many rumors . . . for example, that (the converts) refuse the Bible as the Word of God, that (the Missionaries) teach conversion after death, and say that our Christians need nothing but the word of Tradition', wrote Skrefsrud. Refusing the Bible as the Word of God refers to the Protestant trope, whether the Bible is the speech of God written, so to speak automatically, by human hand, or whether the texts reflect divine inspiration but are composed by human agency. Bible criticism, ascendant at the time, made fundamentalists wary of those who, by implicating human agency, were 'refusing the Bible as the Word of God'. They included romantics like Schleiermacher—or Skrefsrud—who stressed the spirit rather than the words of the Bible. It is to this criticism Skrefsrud refers later, saying they are accused of treating the Bible as 'just another book'.

Conversion after death refers to specific or universal access to salvation. Orthodox Lutherans hold that only baptized members of the true Church may be saved. Skrefsrud never accepted that all heathens go to hell, but to the orthodox this implies an unacceptable 'conversion after death'. Skrefsrud defended himself of the charge, which, however, was justified given his Baptist views. The word of tradition refers to Grundtvig, who accorded the 'living word' a crucial role in the Church. Grundtvigians did not hold tradition as the only source of faith, but this was a common accusation against them by the Home Mission, Pietists, and orthodox Lutherans. He also refers to accusations that the missionaries think 'one may live a merry life and still be a good Christian'. In view of their opposition to dance and drink, this is hardly just. The point here, however, is that the same criticism was made against the Grundtvigians. Skrefsrud, then, was tailoring his arguments for a Grundtvigian audience, proposing an alliance against common enemies, which implicitly relativized the problem of baptism.

It was probably Hertel who made Skrefsrud return to the Lutheran fold. It may have been a matter of strategy, for Hertel made it clear that Danish Lutherans would never support a Baptist missionary. Yet Skrefsrud resisted the pressure for a while. 'Those who believe that heathen children dying without baptism will not be saved—that I will not support' he writes.[60] 'Whether heathen who have not been baptized will go to hell after death, that is beyond our judgment. . . . God will not condemn those who have not heard the word. . . . Why I let myself be baptized again? Because it was a matter of conscience with me, as I was not sure of my own baptism. Why I don't baptize children? Because they should be able to answer the question regarding the Credo. I have baptized children of five years and I believe they have lived truly. . . .' Skrefsrud's Haugean background made him doubt his own baptism. He was baptized by a rationalist priest, whom he felt had not the Grace to perform the act, and he was not sure to have got the absolution baptism should confer. It was later, in jail, that he received absolution from Christ himself. He stressed that his position was a personal one, 'Börresen can do as he likes.'[61] Hodne felt that Skrefsrud's Baptist views go well beyond the question of baptism itself. He certainly valued the inner voice central to Baptist tradition. When visiting Britain in 1874, he did so as a Baptist missionary (Hodne 1966: 146-7), and it was not a question of doctrine, but of autonomy and power which led to the break with the Baptists.

When Skrefsrud talks about his own personality[62] it is for a definite purpose: 'My way of expressing myself has been sharpened not only because I am an autodidact but also since I have never lived in society since I was sixteen years old.' These letters show Skrefsrud as an archetype of the 'modern individual', whose subjective identity and views result from his reflections about his particular trajectory. Yet they also show his dependence on an audience, a mirror to reflect and attest to the reality of this particularity. Skrefsrud's independence leans on the recognition of at least a few others whose opinion he respects.

## A VIEW OF MISSIONS

The same alliance is proposed against the Danish Missionary Society. The Mission should be a matter for the congregation, not a Missionary society. The best men of the congregation, 'in whom it trusts and who feel themselves called', should go out to convert the Heathen. Skrefsrud and Börresen certainly did not wish to be paid servants of a society, but the argument also fits Grundtvigian ideas. One should judge such work according to its ideals, says Skrefsrud, not in terms of an annual report 'where one can see how much each Christian has cost'. 'I can assure you', he continues,

> that missionary work with all its suffering, of which there is ample if one is a true missionary, is the most interesting life in the world. One throws oneself therein, one hardens oneself to perseverance, one follows up one's work with an eagerness which will never allow itself to be beaten. His interest anoints his tongue, and intensify . . . his efforts to the point where the Heathen feels reality and truth in what he says . . . But in this, he must after all use all the instruments and use their own expressions, similes of their own daily life, and put forth the food in their own vessels—one has to distinguish betweeen Christianity and European customs. . . . One should not abuse their gods and their religion, but only show how the ancestors, in the course of time, forgot the true religion, and that it has been kept in the Bible, which is not a book for any tribe or nation but the common property of Man. To become a Christian is not to become another caste but only the propitiation of Him as the common father of Man.

'I have been preaching' he says in another letter,[63] 'that the Heathens should not forget the demands of their gods even if they are disappointed by them. How much more should we, then, keep to the true god.' Here, indeed, Skrefsrud seems to accept that Santal beliefs really are a religion, and not mere superstition. We are close, here, to Grundtvigian ideas of Nation, Congregation, and Tradition.

The Santals, like the Nordic peoples, should become Christian without—in modern terms—losing their identity.

For this endeavour, it was crucial to have native priests. 'As soon as one can get native priests one should use them, for among the Heathen something of the idea will always stick that one becomes an outcast when Europeans baptize them, while when natives do it, they do not feel the same. . . .'

## INDEPENDENCE AND LUTHERAN LINKS

The final break with the Baptists came in 1877. The disagreements had developed over several years, and there is a period of transition till 1881. The turning point is the Trust Deed of 1880 which makes Skrefsrud and the Börresens responsible for the property and rights of the 'Santal National Church'. Skrefsrud writes to Hertel[64] about the deed. He stresses that the wards have no real power, and that 'they have not done what certain English and Scottish wanted them to do', which may well relate to a clause that the IHM and its property should revert to the Baptists on the trustee's death or demission. Yes, he admits, 'the wards could ask us to leave our Mission if so they wish'. But, he underlines, the land is held on the condition that it is used for Mission work. And 'we must have free hands to choose our successors. If we cannot get aid on these conditions, we will be short of money . . . and the Mission must be given to a society: the trust deed is so made that this is possible'.

Clearly, Skrefsrud was exasperated by the conflicting demands of the Baptists, who wanted to retain control, and the Scandinavians who wanted all links with the Baptist past to be severed. 'I am getting tired of all these conflicts and losing my appetite for work. The wards have affirmed that the Mission should be run according to Protestant Evangelical principles so that it may be transmitted . . . to another society, whether Anglican, Presbyterian or Lutheran. I have found no better expression.' We see, here, his answer to the pressures resulting from the break, with the need to utilize to the full the new Danish support.[65]

'We need at least four more stations to cover the field. I hope that Denmark will be able to raise the money.' But Skrefsrud assures Hertel that their conflict with the Baptists would not hurt British support. 'Regarding our independence, we should not fear anything as long as I am in charge of the trustees'. By stressing his distrust of the Norwegians, he clearly wants to incite Hertel to maximal efforts: 'I will come only to Denmark if I come, the Norwegians are not worthy of doing the work of the Lord among the Santals. I am not talking about the Grundtvigians or about some honest exceptions, but about the priestly class and of the people who let themselves be led by the noose. Such small hearts can only be found in Norway. The best thing that can be said about us Norwegians, is that there is a good deal of good material in us, that foreigners, not least the Danes, can make something sensible from. Otherwise we remain provincial, born-at-home all our life, bitter members of parties without common sense'. As if to sum up, he says: 'Strength as such does not fear any danger, and is not keeping watch'. Then, to exemplify: 'Regarding myself, the Lord has left me on such a bumpy road that I have had to seek refuge in "the belief of children"[66] since knowledge is an objective regard and not a subjective relation'. Qualities other than university studies are needed to be a missionary.

Then Skrefsrud criticizes their own report, which 'will not give a learned impression. . . . Please tell me what you think of it. . . . It will be a good thing if I come to Denmark soon'. It seems that he is conscious of Börresen's weaker points, and wonders what effect they will have on a Danish audience. Should he come himself to correct any misunderstanding? Finally, Skrefsrud notes that Siram's children, among others, have now been baptized. The reader, of course, may wonder why the pastor has not seen to this earlier. Intended to reassure Hertel, the remark also shows that the transition to Lutheranism is still imperfect.

While Börresen was in Denmark, Skrefsrud wrote to Hertel[67] about his plans to have Börresen ordained by the Danish Church, clearly a move to legitimize the Mission in Danish eyes. 'You should not be afraid that I think you will make a Grundtvigian of Börresen', says Skrefsrud. 'All you Christians must stand together, especially during these discussions which concern five or half a dozen . . .'. He saw that Grundtvigians might find Börresen too Pietist for their liking. Of Börresen, he said: 'The water is not deep where the waterfall is the whitest'—beautiful speech is no proof of deep thought.

Skrefsrud asserted that 'our purpose here is to build one Santal Christian Church, on the model of the first church, not the translation of a translation. So you can see (that) we will not include anything that is not original. If we are failing in our task, then working through the instinct of the Santals, we will succeed'. Of course, he was himself the translator of this instinct for his Scandinavian audience, who had no other way of knowing the Santals.

'If the Danes have confidence in Börresen and our Mission, they will ordain him', he affirmed. Danish churchmen were sceptical of Börresen's credentials. Many doubted—with reason—his theological knowledge. To be an Evangelical preacher among the Heathen was one thing, to be ordained a priest in the Danish Church, something else. Skrefsrud interpreted the implicit message as: what is good enough for the Heathen is not adequate for the Danes. He was bitter that the Danes wanted to reap where they had not sown. He asked Hertel to arrange the ordination, even if the Grundtvigian bishop was too 'snobbish' to do it. He would never ask anything else from the Danish Church, but did not want to leave the Santals 'without a recognized support when we die'.[68]

In January 1878, Börresen was a priest, and Skrefsrud calls Hertel 'Friend and Brother'.[69] Now, Skrefsrud wants the church to make Börresen a bishop.[70] The question remained of the relation of the Danish to the Santal Church. 'Were we right', asked Skrefsrud, 'to start an isolated congregation?' Hertel called Börresen an 'infant soul'. Yes, admitted Skrefsrud, 'If he thinks he is among friends, he can be fooled: if he knows he is among enemies, he can be superb'. Hertel felt the need for someone to look after the accounts: in 1878 Muston, having given up his indigo business, took on this responsibility.

Finally, in 1879,[71] Skrefsrud returned to the project of making Börresen a bishop, then declared his love of Denmark. 'The Mission should be tied more closely to Denmark than to any other country. Norway, as a country and a Nation, has no part in it. I feel more attracted by Danish love than by the cold indifference, nay, the warm opposition of Norwegians. I shall not start a conflict regarding apostolic succession.' At the same time, he wrote to Rudin in Uppsala, asking about the arguments for apostolic succession, which the Swedes practice. He wanted a bishop as head of his Santal church, while remaining independent of outside ecclesiastic powers. The implied bargain was: the Danish Church may have Santalistan, but only if it accepted his chosen bishop. If not, he implied, there may well be other interested parties. . . .

On the question of missionary recruits, Börresen was charged with questioning candidates.[72] Skrefsrud admits, to Hertel, that the University of Copenhagen 'is well to the fore scientifically'. But, 'it is a negative wonder that the candidates coming from there should not bring greater (intellectual) treasure, unless they feel it safer to retain it in their own head. I won't agree with you that such men are among the best in Denmark, for (they) . . . should be the equals of the best anywhere, especially in the field of philology. Such men as Westergaard are among the best in oriental linguistics, and his works on Sanskrit are the best that exist in the field. They stand next to the superb Sanskrit encyclopaedia of Röthe and Böttling'. There is a double edge here. Copenhagen graduates were not the best choice as they would not put their knowledge to use in the mission field. Here, the practical missionary is speaking. But it must not be thought that practical orientation is at odds with erudition, so Skrefsrud tried to show off his learning.

Finally[73] he asked Hertel not to publish his journal of the Mission more than quarterly, or they will be too busy to furnish the necessary material. A year later he proposed the name *Dahkwala* (postman) for the journal. Hertel wanted the older pupils at Ebenezer to write in it, an idea put into practice later.[74] By March 1880, Skrefsrud received the first issue of the journal, and liked it. He told Hertel they now had their own printing press in Benagaria.[75]

## QUESTIONS OF MARRIAGE AND THE CALLING

Jensen, a Danish candidate for the Mission, asks whether he should get married before coming out. No, says Skrefsrud,[76] it will be hard for him to learn the language if he does. In October,[77] Skrefsrud congratulates Hertel rather drily on the latter's engagement. He has, he says, given up his resistance to Jensen's marriage, and Börresen has taken him on. . . . A month later,[78] Skrefsrud wonders if Mrs. Jensen will be lazy, which would be 'a great calamity'. He refers, here, to what happened when Sundberg, the Mission's first medical doctor, came to Ebenezer in 1877. He liked the place but his wife did not, and they left after a few months.

Like Skrefsrud, John Sundberg was born to a poor family in the East Norwegian countryside. His father died early, and he was adopted by the janitor of the Realskole[79] at Lillehammer. He was offered free teaching there, but had to earn money as a child, working as a boatswain and a fiddler. He excelled in languages and became Skrefsrud's Latin teacher when the latter was in jail. Later, Sundberg went to sea for many years, living in Peru a while. Then he settled in

Chicago, where he studied medicine, and became a friend and follower of Thrane, the socialist leader. By 1874, on graduation, he taught at Texas Medical College. From there he wrote to Skrefsrud asking about work in India. Skrefsrud was delighted to have his old friend, and Börresen felt God had finally answered their needs for a doctor (Nyhagen 1990, I: 354-5). But it did not work, and Skrefsrud blamed Mrs. Sundberg.

Hertel has difficulty finding work as a priest, partly because he was so busy with the Mission. His fiancée wanted him to drop it and get a proper job. Skrefsrud warns Hertel[80] that his fiancée is not worthy of him, saying he is suffering from 'marriage illness'. 'If your fiancée is not changing her mind, you should not have her. Don't believe I am speaking from theory, I have been through the fire myself'.[81] Hertel wants to come to India as a missionary, but Skrefsrud retorts: 'if, because of your fiancée, you should come to the heathens, it would make no sense. I think that you have a special call for the mission. . . . That you have not given up the mission for your fiancée, shows that you have a greater role to play'. Hertel's fiancée feels the mission makes him proud. To Skrefsrud, this is just 'Frauenlogik' (in German)—the logic of women. He tells Hertel that Jensen has got a little boy and has no time for work. Then we learn that Hertel's ex-fiancée has written to Mrs. Börresen, and by February,[82] she has broken the engagement. 'I have told you . . .', says Skrefsrud, 'as nicely as possible that I don't think your fiancée is a suitable match for you. I hope you don't ever think about it again . . . she does not suit you and so the grief should part from your heart . . . it is when the soul is searching what it doesn't really want . . . that it is feeling grief. I hope you will find a place where you can work for God'. But in the mission there were five Europeans and no money for more. Maybe Skrefsrud's advice had an effect, for he wrote:[83] 'To see that you are able to control yourself in regard to sex, has been a pleasure for me. A man should feel deeply but when necessary he should bear the pain (of separation)—few women can do the same . . . The Lord will choose for you. There are better things in the world than to be married, and we must be led to the Great Goal that God has set for us.'

The next letter[84] refers to Hertel's remarks on the Zenana mission. As if following this line of thought, Skrefsrud says: 'Mrs. Börresen has wished that you should go to Norway and Lillehammer.

What do you think of the plan to go there at the Mission's cost ?' It is the first of several remarks targeting Klara Fagstad, whom Skrefsrud had wanted to marry in 1874, as the spouse for Hertel.[85] Several letters deal with Hertel's personal affairs: in the break with his fiancée, he should see 'the leading hand of God, with people who seem to fit each other like a punch in a blue eye.[86] 'What have you done about my suggestion that you go to Norway?' asks Skrefsrud five weeks later.[87] 'You say you will not easily be in love again. It is not my intention that you should not find a wife: but you should look well. It is not for nothing that Mrs. Börresen wants to send you to Norway'.[88] Three weeks later,[89] Hertel finally found a calling, and Skrefsrud wishes him well, tells him he now needs an active and loving wife, and urges Hertel to go to Norway. As if the allusion to Klara was not enough, he praises the Norwegian landscape, and a little unexpectedly, even his countrymen. They are stable, their reasoning is sound, but they are stubborn and need to learn about the world. A couple of weeks later,[90] Skrefsrud is thanking Hertel for the invitation to visit him. 'But whatever you do, don't fall in love again before you know that the object of your love will suit you'. He is pleased that Hertel is going to Norway. But Hertel's answer must have been a surprise. 'The news of your marriage . . . with your ex-fiancée' writes Skrefsrud,[91] 'will not prevent you from receiving our warm congratulations'. The plans for marital alliance between the Danish and Norwegian support structures of the Mission have failed, in spite of Skrefsrud's efforts, writing from another end of the world.

Marriages, in the missionary milieu, clearly are not simply the 'love marriage' identified, among many Indians, with Western culture. Jensen's marriage is seen as an encumbrance, but finally it is his health that cuts short his missionary career. Sundberg's wife is a 'calamity'. We remember Mrs. Body, whose qualities, or lack of such, kept her husband from being taken on by the IHM. True, she married Cornelius on her husband's death, but for this he was sacked from the Mission. Among our missionaries there were the Börresens, whose marriage certainly worked well enough in missionary terms. Yet perhaps the following excerpt from one of Börresen's letters[92] is rather telling: 'My wife has been very sick for two months. She has been close to death. Now she is better. I hope she will be there a long time and able to work a long time.' The marriage of the Starks, whom we shall meet later, was clearly a love marriage, and stands out as an exception. James Long, too, seems to have lived in a relationship of love and trust with his wife.

What exactly, then, was required of the missionary wife? Above all, she should be willing to share his life and work to the greatest possible extent. She might do so by providing homely comforts in the field, or participate actively in the work, as Caroline did. Above all, the missionary wife had to symbolize a conception of Christian womanhood. A particular moral stature, implying fidelity and chastity, was certainly needed and did not, we assume, fit Mrs. Body. But almost as grave as a bent towards the body was 'laziness'. This is what Skrefsrud feared in Jensen's marriage, citing Mrs. Sundberg as an example. The view of womanhood was framed by the Protestant Ethic, and Klara Fagstad's seriousness, intelligence, and capacity for work made her a perfect candidate for the role of a missionary's or a pastor's wife.

## CONVERTING THE CHIEFS

In his first letter to Hertel,[93] Skrefsrud presents an overview of events in the field:

> Last year, Christianity was despised and hated by the Great, and loved by those of little importance. The opposite has been true this year. The powerful have accepted it, while the poorer have kept back. Last year the Christian element in our district was the weaker one, because some of the greatest chiefs were heathens, while this year, the Christian element has won the majority of superior positions. The people are baptized, and heathendom is now seen here more as the paganism of old days. Last year there were persecutions; this year, the Christians have the upper hand. . . . Last year, the chiefs could not decide for Christianity, whereas this year, I met a lot of them in a large meeting affirming they will become Christians. Though they are not yet baptized, and some of them perhaps not too soon, our district is a mark burnt on the whole country. . . . as soon as (it is known that) they are from Nankar, they are called Christian and nobody from the far-off districts will eat with them . . . we feel that in our district Christianity has triumphed, and all will sooner or later become Christians. Yes, some Santals have even left their village because they could stand the Word of God no longer. Thus there was a chief who some years ago ran away from his own village because his relatives had become Christians. We followed him, however, and he again picked up his gear and disappeared in the mountains some thirty miles from here. But sometime ago we visited him, and he then said he would no longer resist, he is now a very lovable Christian, and the first crop of the new station Dumka, where the judge is.

Skrefsrud adds that the chiefs now act truly and efficiently in the interest of the Mission. The congregation close to Benagaria is strong and able to defend itself, while the strength of more distant groups is variable. He praises the work of the two native priests. In another letter,[94] Skrefsrud says: 'I have talked to the Heathen chiefs about the future of Santalistan. They all agreed that Christianity will be their future religion, and ... admitted that serving the gods was good as long as they were in darkness.'

What are we to make of these changes? Certainly, the mass conversions of 1873-4 concerned mainly poor people, and this letter seems to indicate that support from chiefs and leaders came only by 1875-6. Could it be that the chiefs were waiting to see whether the Christian influence would last? By the time Skrefsrud was registering a change in attitudes, the community of converts had increased steadily for two or three years. Nevertheless, while the missionaries perceived a changing attitude among powerful Santals, many who would not be baptized 'too soon', never were. Probably, what Skrefsrud sees is acceptance of the missionaries and their converts as a real presence in the region, rather than a changing attitude towards Christianity as such. Good relations with the missionaries might be politically useful: we do not see this attitude as evidence of a deeper ideological change.

But some chiefs did convert. 'Ramdas, the superior chief from Baromania, has brought an old uncle, the Chief of Kendpahari, to the Lord. . . . Another chief, who lost his village but got it back by our help, came one day to say it was the Lord who helped him, so he will no longer serve the gods but serve God. He has been taught for sometime and will be baptized'.[95] It is clear that Skrefsrud and Börresen did not start by converting the chiefs. In the beginning, and especially during the famine year 1873-4, they worked from the bottom, rather than the top, of local society. Was this accident or strategy? Certainly, from their home backgrounds they were used to thinking of the poor as material for conversion, and to oppose, as Pietists often did, the religious simple folk to profane authority. It was Börresen, however, with his Home Mission style, who effected most of the early conversions: Skrefsrud, with his intellectual ambitions, seemed to have taken great pleasure in the company of chiefs and dignitaries. He seems to think and act as a chief among chiefs.

Asambani[96] is a large valley between Kargata and Paspari in the East and close to Gando in the West. It is between Ebenezer and Dumka surrounded by large villages where live some of the main chiefs. We do not have many Christians there and among them few are influential. The Heathens here are famous for their conservatism and their hate and persecution of the Christians. They have brought their persecutions so far, they will not allow them to get water from the wells. They have provoked divisions between baptized and unbaptized women as well as to convince weak Christians to become reaccepted among the followers of the gods which took place when the Christians gave a dinner to the Heathens. When the enemies of the Lord heard that we had bought Asambani,[97] they held a council, in order to prevent anybody here from becoming baptized.

One said that if we were coming to the other side of the mountains he will cleave our heads apart. Another assured that he will dishonour us in such a way that we will run away from where we came. Even if we did not fear such talk, we found it wiser to do what we could to counteract this badness. A good means presented itself: in fact two superior chiefs had married their daughters to Christians who had led themselves to be reaccepted among the Heathens, and the large crowd of superior chiefs had, on that occasion, eaten with the apostate Christians while the same chiefs again had eaten with other heathens, (so) the whole country has become polluted. We waited till the end, the National Assembly of the Santals, and put this matter to the Assembly, asserting that if the superior chiefs have acted according to law, anybody should be allowed to eat and to marry with Christians and the hate and strife should cease. If they were acting contrary to law, then we demanded that these superior chiefs and every body who had eaten with them . . . should be (considered) polluted as Christians. We argued thus in three meetings of the council and it created a lot of commotion . . . one shouted that those who have eaten with the Christians should be outcast. But this was not done since the guilty were among the richest and they did not know how many would be implicated.

Many Chiefs, then, and no doubt commoners, too, wanted to cast out the converts, no longer accepting them as proper Santals. Should we see this as a parallel to the *bitlaha*, marking the ethnic boundary? Or is Skrefsrud right when he often uses the term 'casting out' for this process, which would seem to imply Hindu influence and a tendency for Santals to accept certain hierarchical implications of caste? We cannot answer this question easily, for with all their ethnic distinctiveness the Santals had known about Hindu castes for centuries. What is clear is that Skrefsrud reacted, not only in defence of his converts and his idea of a Santal nation, but also against the idea that Christians should be treated as inferior by the Heathen. One wonders if his reaction would have been similar, if it had been the Christians who had taken the initiative to exclude the other Santals. Thus he never seems to condone the suffering that discrimination from non-Christians implies, as a parallel to the suffering of the early Christians, as some of the missionaries among south Indian untouchables seem to have done (Cederlöf 2003). He continues:

> Therefore, they had smaller meetings in the district but could arrive at no result, since they found our conclusions correct, and did not know how to throw out their richest chiefs. At last, they called a general meeting and sent for their foremost superior chief, Kharup Pargana to help them to arrive to a conclusion. . . . One chief there asked to be baptized. Karoo Pargana[98] told him—'remember that you are a superior chief. You are nothing less than that. I shall soon send you off with your silly wisdom'. Next day, more superior chiefs came, and the matter was brought up again. The day after, it was suggested that Karoo Pargana should write a document with me for the future.

Skrefsrud presents the contents of the latter:

> Whereas the superior chiefs, deputy superior chiefs, and chiefs, whose names are written below, have introduced eating, drinking and marriage with Christian Santals, so we hereby decide that there should be no ban on eating, drinking and marriage with Christian Santals, but this should not imply any need for baptism. Let those who want be baptized, and those who do not, will not be baptized. There follows the names of those who have introduced this law, then the names of all the judges, and finally the names of those who as representatives signed the document, namely, two heathens and two Christians.[99]

The heathens were Karoo Pargana and Mongot Manjhi; the Christians were Nitai Pargana and Skrefsrud, the latter acting as the chief of the Christian community. Skrefsrud tells Hertel that the two chiefs who threatened to crush Skrefsrud's and Börresen's heads, have been severely punished.

The document seems to confirm that what was happening was political change: the Christian community, with Skrefsrud as its spokesman, was recognized as a presence in local affairs. Acceptance was mainly a matter of avoiding conflict and—a theme which remains important to this day—division within the Santal community. As we shall see, this does not mean that conflict and division were avoided, but there was a countervailing tendency to try to bridge the gaps and solve the conflicts. Skrefsrud's faith in the document soon proved too optimistic: another persistent trend in Santal politics was resistance to central authority.

Skrefsrud writes, presenting what he sees as the gist of the chiefs' comments,

> we have made the road, and we must walk it. We have eaten with them and married them. We cannot possibly reverse this nor even readmit them if they are outside. As our forefathers have not left any law regarding this, since our laws of excommunication and reintegration regard only moral faults, while the difference between Christians and us regard religion, in fact we serve the gods and they the real God that we accept as our creator, so it must be free to eat with or marry the Christians. The conflict is over.

Conflict was however, to return, time and again.

Skrefsrud's enthusiasm, then, was misplaced. Yet there is something here which differs from most missionary accounts. Among the Satnamis, for example, the missionary Oscar Lohr was received cordially by the guru and allowed to speak for four hours—yet after this promising start, he was reduced to picking up a few converts from the school he had already run for sometime (Dube 1998: 70-7). What Skrefsrud described was something else: a lasting political engagement with the chiefs, where political moves and countermoves followed each other, in a context where Santal chiefs and the missionaries were confronted as opposed, but basically equal, kinds of powers. He was describing the debates in a political idiom —in spite of occasional outbursts of Evangelical rhetoric. Moreover, in the scenario he presents, the colonial power is surprisingly absent. While this may not have been the truth, but partly at least a product of Skrefsrud's own insistence on seeing the Santals as a 'nation', his description makes us feel that he, at least, was convinced by his own construction of the political situation. We may see the missionary as framed by the colonial enterprise, and to us it may seem clear that the Santal chiefs were not as independent or powerful as they or Skrefsrud apparently thought. And yet the process of accommodation between Santals and missionaries seem to have proceeded, at least in part, as if the parties were independent players in a power game detached from the larger colonial scene. For the missionaries, this definition of the situation conformed to their need to be independent players, and to position themselves as intermediaries between the Santals and the colonial regime. This may also have suited the Santal chiefs, who may have found in these new sahebs an excellent measure to circumvent or put into parenthesis the colonial administrators they already knew.

Such reciprocal manoeuvres between chiefs and missionaries bring to mind the situation the Comaroffs (1991) describe among the Tswana. But there is a difference: the Tswana chiefs ruled real chiefdoms, which Santal chiefs never did. The role the chiefs assume in Skrefsrud's account goes well beyond their usual powers. They, like the missionaries, may have jumped at this occasion to be taken seriously as representatives of something bigger than themselves. If they made Skrefsrud a chief, to an extent he did the same for them.

## NOTES

1. The *Times*, 16.03.1874.
2. *Daily Review*, 25.03.1874.
3. Lately as Assistant General Inspector of Health in the Bombay Government.
4. *Fosterlandsstiftelsen*.
5. His daughters continued the work for the Santal Mission for some years, but then it quietly faded out.
6. Dr. Lazarus printed the early mission reports, free of charge, at his Medical Hall Press. He had a hospital in Benares.
7. The BMS' *Juvenile Herald* wrote: 'Next month we shall have a portrait of Mr. Skrefsrud, and we feel sure it needs only be known that we are doing this, to secure a very large sale'.
8. £ 300 from Newcastle, £ 400 from Edinburgh, and £ 500 from Birmingham. These were large sums then.
9. Moody was invited by Pennefather and Bainbridge for a tour of Britain, but both died and the tour got off to a poor start. The breakthrough in Newcastle turned the tables, and success was even greater in Edinburgh and Glasgow, February to April 1874 (Bebbington 1989: 162-3).
10. Bebbington 1989: 163, citing Kent 1978.
11. Letter to J.G. Blom, 14.12.1873; letter to R. Petersen, 17.02.1875.
12. Like the British Inland China Mission.
13. *Morgenbladet*, 13.12.1910.
14. Starting with Verdens Gang (1868) and Dagbladet (1869) in Christiania.
15. Bö provided the timber for the building, free and freely delivered.
16. She was the sister of Skrefsrud's wife Anne.
17. In 1878, he wrote: 'The Man at home, who is closest to my ideal of the refining effect of age is Christopher Bruun . . . since humanity in him is transcended by the Godly . . . and especially, since he lives a Godly life, as if it were just a passage to perfection beyond' (Skrefsrud to Lunde 4.10.78, cited by Nyhagen, I: 236).
18. This statement dates from 1888 (ibid. 236), but their discussions predate the formulation of the 'Santal National Church' which Skrefsrud and Börresen used later.
19. Neo-Norwegian is a new form of Norwegian introduced by Ivar Aasen from 1848, based on the 'archaic' dialects of Western Norway closest to old Norse.
20. Per Bö, the rich farmer who had donated the building materials for Bruun's school, was the organizer.
21. Nyhagen notes A.M. St. Arctander as an example (1990, I: 235-6, 240).
22. Among Grundtvigians opposed to Skrefsrud, Nyhagen mentions Viggo Ullmann (1990, I: 240-1).

23. Some thirty years later, Hanna Fagstad writes: 'As regards Klara, we know, we that know her best, that she was much too weak to support all the sacrifices . . . implied in being the wife of a missionary' H. Fagstad to Hertel 5.12.1903, cited by Nyhagen, I, 242n.
24. Skrefsrud to Pedersen, 4.10.1879, cited by Nyhagen, I, 244n.
25. A timber and wood-processing town some twenty miles west of Oslo.
26. Clausen later became a leading figure in Norwegian-American church life. See chapter 8.
27. Founded 1860, later to become Norway's most important newspaper, which it still is.
28. 10.10.1874.
29. *Norden*, 19.11.1874.
30. *The Commoner's Friend*. Its editor was J. Chr. Johnsen, who supported the missions (Nyhagen 1990, I: 315).
31. H.P. Börresen to A. Graham, 14.10.1874.
32. Muston, in the *Daily Review*, 27.04.1874.
33. Letter from Skrefsrud, *Faedrelandet* 19.08.1876.
34. L. Skrefsrud to C.B. Lewis, 03.05.1876.
35. Skrefsrud to Graham, 18.05.1876.
36. Among the speakers were Hudson Taylor, Grattan Guinness, George Müller, Horatius Bonar and Lord Radstock (Nyhagen 1990, I: 291).
37. Th. Lunde to L. Hertel, 10.08.1880.
38. K. Fagstad to L. Hertel, 12.08.1880.
39. Drammens Blad, 17.09.1881.
40. This is quite visible in ceremonies, where the Swedish church, like the Anglican, is far removed from the austerity associated with Lutheranism. Another difference, which interested Skrefsrud particularly, was the apostolic succession of the bishops.
41. Rudin's biographer N. Söderblom, known for his peace overtures during WWI and for his ecumenical work, uses a number of Rudin's letters and manuscripts but does not give exact references.
42. 'Reader'. The term was (and to some extent still is) current in Sweden—from a time when common people who 'read' were mainly religious.
43. Madam Guyon, Fénelon, Tersteegen, Jakob Böhme, the Marquess of S.T. Martin and Franz von Baader.
44. Budbäraren, August 1867.
45. Orthodox lutherans felt that Beck and the other Swabians were influenced by calvinist and catholic thinking.
46. Börresen to Rudin 1878, no date.
47. Skrefsrud to Rudin, 21.02.1878.
48. The book is named after a small white flower, 'star of the wood' common in the Scandinavian forests. The metaphorical sense is clearly light shining in the darkness.

49. Börresen to Rudin, 29.01.1880.
50. Ibid., 10.01.1881.
51. *Dansk Indre-misjons Tidende*, 1884: 67.
52. Grundtvig had written of the 'stars' of Christianity as a series of cultures leading towards Christian perfection: Greece, Israel, the old Norse world: the sixth star was modern Europe, with the seventh yet to come.
53. 1876: 493 ff.
54. In the Aarhus City Library.
55. Skrefsrud to Hertel, 26.03.1877.
56. It is not clear which Credo Skrefsrud refers to here, as commentators have stressed. The formula may have been chosen to please Hertel. At first the candidates were asked to repeat the full Credo at baptism. Later, they were asked: 'do you believe in the Trinity according to the Apostolic Credo as you have learnt ?'.
57. Skrefsrud to Hertel, January 1879.
58. Ibid., 08.02.1879.
59. Ibid., 09.10.1879.
60. Ibid., 05.06.1877.
61. A letter written much later by V. Jacobsen, another Danish supporter, to J. Vahl, indicates that Skrefsrud doubted infant Baptism since his youth. Thus he accepted 'the faith of the Baptists, which in fact he fundamentally opposed, but which was the only faith that would rebaptize him'. Jacobsen says Skrefsrud told him so in 1881. In Skrefsrud's open letter to Kalkar in 1879, he alludes to early scruples and 'unusual circumstances and course of life' as well as his reading of the biblical texts (Hodne 1966: 144-5).
62. Skrefsrud to Hertel, 23.09.1879.
63. Ibid., 30.08.1879.
64. Ibid., 08.02.1879.
65. These concerns are stated very clearly in Skrefsrud to Hertel, 05.05.1879.
66. no. Barnetro. In Evangelical circles, 'belief is more important than knowledge.
67. Skrefsrud to Hertel, 09.07.1877.
68. Ibid., 20.08.1877.
69. Ibid., 06.11.1877.
70. Ibid., 04.01.1878.
71. Ibid., 08.02.1879.
72. Ibid., 09.07.1877.
73. Ibid.
74. Skrefsrud refers to Hertel's idea in a letter to Hertel 23.01.1880.
75. Skrefsrud to Hertel, 10.03.1880. By June, Skrefsrud took the press to Dumka (Skrefsrud to Hertel, 21.06.1880).

76. Skrefsrud to Hertel 20.08.1877.
77. Ibid., 05.10.1877.
78. Ibid., 06.11.1877.
79. The Realskole, a German term, an alternative to the classical Gymnasium, stressed contemporary learning.
80. Skrefsrud to Hertel, 11.08.1878.
81. Ibid., 11.09.1878.
82. Ibid., 08.02.1879.
83. Skrefsrud to Hertel, 05.05.1879.
84. Ibid., 17.06.1879.
85. Klara is not the sole reason for the trip, as Mrs. Börresen wants Hertel to form women's committees.
86. Skrefsrud to Hertel, 02.08.1879.
87. Ibid., 22.07.1879.
88. Ibid., 30.08.1879.
89. Ibid., 23.09.1879.
90. Ibid., 09.10.1879.
91. Ibid., 23.01.1880.
92. Börresen to Rudin, 29.01.1880.
93. Skrefsrud to Hertel, 26.03.1877.
94. Ibid., 11.08.1878.
95. Ibid., 09.07.1877.
96. Ibid., May 1878.
97. This refers to Skrefsrud's buying the zamindari rights to the area, briefly discussed by Hodne (1966: 332-5) who feels Skrefsrud did it to keep others out. Santals resisted zamindars and tax-farmers whenever possible.
98. Kharup would seem to be the same as Karoo Pargana who was a heathen and against baptism.
99. Skrefsrud to Hertel, 04.01.1878.

# 6

# Contested Minds: Christian Austerity and Santal Pleasure

The colonial encounter changed the Santal life-world, not just its religion or economy but also its ideas of space and time. For the Santals, time is shared by all, and to claim more time, like claiming wealth, goes against egalitarian values.[1] The missionaries wanted converts to plan their time, to allocate it as a scarce value, in the Western way (Lakoff and Johnson 1980: 7-9). Time must not be wasted. Moreover, daily prayer and Sunday service, as well as the Church assembly, introduced a new rhythm in the converts' life. The Christian calendar was explained in sermons and, later, in the Christian newspapers. Such events were intended to discipline behaviour: absence from Church was a serious matter. At the same time, missionaries worked on the past, wanting to construct a new social memory. Their teaching projected the Santals into a foreign, biblical history as seen by protestant Evangelicalism, and a new geography where Jerusalem, Egypt, and Norway were salient points in a strange continuum.

The converts still lived in villages pervaded by traditional perceptions of time, a life-world dominated by agriculture and heathen beliefs, except when sending their children to school and attending the service. The *Sohrae*[2] festival for the healthy reproduction of cattle, was frowned upon by the missionaries as it involved dancing, heavy drinking, and sexual licence, and was also important for finding a bride. The end of the year was marked by another festival, drinking rice-beer and eating rice cakes with kin and friends, while offering to the ancestors. Converts could not participate, and sometimes feared for their crops since no bonga would ensure their growth. And when the rainy season came, Christians were banned from watching ojhas go from village to village with their disciples to sing, dance, and beg. This ritual wandering, which lasted a week, was experienced as a mystic and initiatary voyage in the sky.[3] Converts were allowed the leisure of going to the market, but could not gamble on cock-fights or drink with relatives. Moreover, it was probably hard for Christians to get help to sow and transplant during the hot season, since they could not invite helpers to beer parties.

Santals refer to alternating work and pleasure, but evoke an inner time devoted to intimacy with the bongas. To long for a bonga lover is to short-circuit time since all become bonga one day. Traditional Santals say Christians are no longer in the bongas' eyes, they are Santals no more, which means belonging to a clan and respecting its deity. Christians should feel God watching their actions; but were supposed to have escaped from the bongas' eyes.

## SEDUCTIVE BONGAS AND THE BONGAS' TRUTH

Even though the bongas watch over humans, they do not administer justice: they only punish human transgressions. They attempt to seduce humans, whom they later kill. Often, a bonga appears from still water and offers a mirror to a girl. If she looks at herself she is dragged into the water and trapped in a cave before the bonga rapes her—punishing her for her narcissism, even as the rapist bonga is also an interested party. Other bongas seduce married women by looking like their husbands. In a tale about a blacksmith's wife, the husband has gone to a distant market. When the bonga knocks at the door, the wife believes her husband has returned, though the bonga's chest is more hairy, a detail the wife fails to note. When he makes love to her, she feels he is stronger than her man, but is seduced. The bonga when satisfied kicks her womb several times, and she dies the next day. Here, the seducer is punishing a woman who should have been chaste. Again, rather than administering justice the bonga is taking advantage of human weakness. The bonga lover's behaviour evokes marriage by elopement, when the boy takes the girl away against her will. We are in a world of power and conflict, without the construction of impartial justice attributed to an ideal king—or to God.

Male bongas overpower women by violence and sex, then kill them, while men in love with female bongas may acquire supernatural powers. But the latter will try to keep the man in the other world when he asks for leave to return. In one story, the bonga accepts on the condition that she may bear his son. The man begets the child, and returns to the world with the powers of a great yogi, able to wake the dead. In such tales, the man engenders a spiritual lineage in the other world. Another young man falls madly in love with a bonga who teaches him the art of healing. When he wants to return, the bonga asks a son from him. The son is born and the man returns to become an ojha. But he is often possessed by his lover, running to the mango tree where they first met. Fearing madness, he runs to the Mission, where a Christian teacher ties his arms and legs to exorcise him. Actually exorcism turns out to be literacy. Finally, says the story, the man becomes a Christian and escapes his bonga. The Mission compound appears as a refuge against bongas, but is the young man still a Santal? Can Santal identity be maintained when one is no longer in the bongas' eyes? (Carrin 1993, Bodding 1925),

Skrefsrud caricatures the Santal relation to the bongas as superstition and false belief: bongas do not help in sickness or difficulty. He feels Santals have a pragmatic relationship to their deities, sacrificing to them to avoid disaster. Skrefsrud is wrong: the relations with the bongas are psychologically salient and evoke those with kin.

Sometimes, female bongas protest the machismo of human husbands: one night a young man, driving his buffaloes, saw a girl standing by a *pipal*. She was stuck in the branches of the tree. The young man freed her, and asked her to come with him to his house. His parents gave her a mat, and the girl slept apart. Next morning she rose early, collected the dung from the cowshed, swept the courtyard and fetched the water. The boy's mother was delighted and they decided to keep her as the boy's wife. That night the two slept on the same cot and 'made their minds one'. Later the girl said to the boy: 'We are now husband and wife. We are here, not for a day, but forever. If we ever quarrel you should not kick me: if you do, I shall leave you'. Later, the boy married her, they had a child, and the house grew rich. They had another child. But one day the husband kicked his wife and she wept bitterly. She took her two children, and when they reached the middle of the field, they all burst into flames and vanished. When the others saw it, they were scared as they felt she could have eaten them, but she had disappeared. Later, the house grew poor (Archer 1974: 281).

Sometimes, the psychological salience of the relation between bonga and man takes a different turn. A female bonga appears in the guise of a relative, often the hero's *hili* (elder brother's wife). When he tells his real *hili* of these nightly apparitions, she says, 'Did I have to become a bonga that you be aware of my existence?' ironically alluding to the potential erotic relation between them. In fact, such stories are often narrated to convey a message and to strengthen mutual affection or desire (Carrin 1995).

The malevolent bongas are like humans: they desire wealth, magic powers, or sex. Far from being moral, they trap men in situations such as incest or illicit relations, or tempt them to enrich themselves by supernatural means. They induce humans to transgress taboos, but their amoral strategies are perceived as uncomfortably close to humans. Unlike the Christian God, a Freudian would see them as close, not to the superego but to the id.

## THE TRAINING OF AN OJHA

The ojhas are specialists in dealing with bongas. A novice realizes his calling when he dreams of female deities, who will inspire him and reveal the identity of agents of illness. To become an ojha, boys learn invocations and some knowledge of medicinal plants from a guru. Later, the disciples are trained in drawing ritual diagrams. Initiation starts with possession, and there are several techniques. One of them is to sit on a cylindrical stone used to grind spice, until the boy falls down possessed. The disciples learn to name and identify different bongas. In the month of *dasâe*, the guru takes his students for a week of ritual wandering. He presents them in the villages, where they sing of how they must climb the mythical strings that link the sun to the earth, to attain the flower of knowledge. They describe how the master dismembers their body, then reconstitutes it. This transformation implies sexual conversion as the boys return half male, half female. Ojhas are invested with feminine sensitivity which makes for possession by a bonga or tutelary goddess. The initiation is a secret ritual where the ojha transfers his bongas to the disciple. He also invests his disciple with the third eye of Shiva, to protect him against malevolent powers. All ojhas venerate Kamru guru, the first teacher who learnt magic from a blacksmith in Hazaribagh.[4]

The ojha shows some shaivite features, such as the trident and the *joto*,[5] whose powers are mentioned in the Santal texts. He uses them to control bongas and Hindu goddesses. He can sacrifice and knows the invocations[6] and exorcism formulae.[7] His knowledge of plants enables him to collect them in the forest and awake their curative powers through invocations. When healing, the ojha prepares for possession, sprinkles some drops of oil on sal leaves and scrutinizes them, naming a malevolent bonga or witch for each spot. He then declares which agent he suspects. This may be the patient's family bonga or that of his father-in-law. Other candidates may be the *sima* bongas who live at the boundary of the village, or worse, the forest bongas who attack women or hunters. If the ojha suspects a witch, his diagnosis must be confirmed by the *jan guru* or witch finder.

The *ojha* may also offer his own blood to satisfy a malevolent spirit. He pricks himself with a thorn on his thigh and his stomach. This *sitka mayam*, menstrual blood, evoking his femininity, is sprinkled on rice while he recites invocations[8] to appease the bongas. He enumerates possible names. If the patient's pain does not cease, he catches the bonga in the pot with his *trishul* or exorcism stick,[9] or even in a diagram[10] and returns the malevolent agent to the forest. Exorcism implies knowing the names of more than 160 bongas and their invocations. Exorcism is generally associated with impurity: in some rites, the *ojha* should be impure in order to trap a malevolent deity in his matted hair, the only part of his body that remains pure. The *joto* may also spit fire in the night to neutralize witches and malevolent spirits. The fire is linked to Shiva's eroticism and the matted hair may disrobe witches (Carrin 1986).

## WITCHCRAFT

The origin of witchcraft parallels the origin of the ojha's knowledge. Once, Maran Buru taught men to cure sickness, but women hid themselves behind the trees, observing him secretly. Another myth says women wanted to get the ojha's knowledge and spied on him to access his powers *(siddhi)*. They did not succeed, but wrought witchcraft, which is seen as stolen knowledge transformed by its improper use.

Women are seen as malevolent powers, whose ability to seduce men makes them dangerous. Several myths describe how women get tired of men 'who are always barking at them like dogs'. In one, women fearing to be killed, say, 'let us see who kills whom'. Such killing is seen as vengeance rooted in kin conflicts and gender relations. The power to be a witch appears at puberty, and many a girl is supposed to learn witchcraft as soon as she is menstruating. An elderly woman, often her aunt or mother-in-law, will teach her witches' songs. Archer (1974: 294) quotes two songs which relate initiation to nakedness. In one of them, the girl takes her clothes off and learns from her mother-in-law how to eat her husband. To 'eat' men, *jom*, is the favorite activity of witches. The wife's complicity with her mother-in-law comes from their shared distance from the husband's clan, affines not fully accepted in the lineage (Carrin 1996b). Woman's magic power is linked to menstrual blood, a poisonous and polluting substance, which makes her subject to the ambiguous power of the *roa*, the soul which lives in the womb. It may leave the body to convey negative substances to the dreamer,[11] and witches learn to use it for this purpose. Santal men consider all women as potential witches, since all have menstrual fluid.

A Santal proverb describes the witch as one who has not found room in other people's eyes (Carrin 1996b). Witches in their turn cast their evil glance on their victims' houses, crops, or children. They are ostracised because of their envy. The ojhas know many malevolent bongas, which the witches worship; but they can be controlled by benevolent ones. The ojhas stress their ability to control witches, and in their witch stories reveal a world where the natural laws are inversed. Their bodies are distorted and ugly; their feet are turned backwards; they give birth from the anus; and they excrete by the mouth. They enjoy transgressing religious norms and hold their nocturnal assemblies in the sacred grove, an offense against the bongas. They pollute the grove by copulating with minor deities, drinking alcohol, and eating human flesh. There is no land of witches: they stand at the five corners of the world. Their ubiquity is frightening.

The society of witches emerges as a parody of the social world. Witches are supposed to leave their human form in bed at night and go in their magical carts to attend the witch assembly. There, they listen to a chief witch[12] who commands malevolent bongas. She names the next victims, and other witches must obey her orders. Since witches form a hierarchical society, their initiation proceeds by degrees. After hearing witches' songs, the novice should qualify for full membership by eating a member of her husband's family. Sometimes she kills him taking the form of a wild animal during the hunt. In other cases, witches kill by disease, sowing its germs at the door. The training of a witch ressembles that of an ojha: but while the ojha's possession identifies malevolent agents, the witch submits to her cannibalistic tendencies.

Witch stories are stereotypical, evading the social complexities of the actual situation. The victim grows ill gradually, getting emaciated and vomiting blood, while witches cut and cook his liver and heart, which they share in their nocturnal assembly. Such acts are mentioned with horror by the Santals and were so considered in Skrefsrud's time. But while men say witches have no excuse for witchcraft, women defend it as the only way to take revenge against men. Witch stories are told by men often pretending to have surprised their activities or heard their conversations. For a woman to tell such stories is highly improper and may be seen as a provocation. If anybody falls ill, it may be proof that the 'witch's talk has become true'. Ojhas say that witches, like female bongas, get satisfaction from eating their victims.

Witchcraft crystallizes rivalries that oppose rich and poor, sexes and generations, implying that hate and jealousy may trap women in desperate symbolic acts. They may express their hate by putting menstrual rags in the husband's grain bin. Even if this does not kill him, such magic stands for murder resulting from hate. Witches are often old women, especially widows, who have inherited land and are envied by their kin.

Although Skrefsrud treats witchcraft as superstition and pays little attention to it, it appears that conversion was an escape for women accused of witchcraft. Curiously, Skrefsrud was seen as well versed in withcraft by the Santals, who threatened suspected witches with 'Kerap' who knew a 'better witchcraft'. Skrefsrud himself claims to have ended the activity of the *jan guru* in Nankar, not just demonstrating their treachery but banning them: the chiefs in council had accepted a 'law' against them.[13] He does not see witches as a 'satanic' deviance, for he is aware that witchcraft may mask quarrels about inheritance or land tenure, or jealousy among kin. Like many Santal women, he thought witchcraft might represent women's vengeance in a world dominated by men.

But why did Santal men tell Christian women that Kerap could send them to the land of the *ekagudias,* the terrible creatures who had only one leg? Perhaps they thought he must know witchcraft as he was a good orator, and able to make them accept his plans. And he was close to a foreign God whose powers seemed limitless since he could treat serious disease and save lives, cures he himself attributed to God rather than to the efficacy of medicine.

1879 has been a very bad year for the crops, says Skrefsrud in a letter to Hertel.[14] As always in such situations, the witches are responsible. The Santals know that some years are bad, but why should the scourge return?

> . . . it must be the witches who have brought the trouble. They were seeking advice from wise men from afar . . . (but) since Kerap did not believe in them, they could not find out anything. It follows that Kerap was in league with the witches . . . (and) even protected them against the wise! What was to be done now? . . . some of the sharper chiefs found out that one should threaten the witches with Kerap, that he would bring his black art to find the witches and send them to the man-eaters living on an isle in the Ocean, if they did not stop eating cattle and men. They assembled their people and let the women (those thought to be witches) stand in the middle and said to them . . . (that) he (Kerap) would carry out his punishment if they did not of their own will stop practising witchcraft—and it helped! Next day, all the cattle were well again and (the sickness) did not come back. And the chiefs themselves believed that these threats were the reason why the cattle sickness in the villages came to an end.

It is interesting that Skrefsrud does not refer to this episode as a miracle wrought by God, as Börresen almost certainly would have done. Skrefsrud does not seem to put great store in miracles, rather he takes for granted that God has it in his power to influence worldly matters. Was not his own conversion a miracle?

Looking at the event in terms of Santal history, it is remarkable that the suspects were not killed—as often happened in witchcraft affairs, before and after—but that Kerap's 'powers' were used publicly by the chiefs. Perhaps this was a compromise worked out by Christian chiefs who wanted to avoid a massacre. If so, we may be as impressed with the political nerve of the chiefs as with that of Skrefsrud.

## TAMING THE BODY

If witchcraft shows us the implicit conflict marking gender relations in Santal society, this does not imply sexual repression. The idea of sexual pleasure in Santal stories and songs is remarkable. As long as prohibited relations are avoided, there is no ban on pre-marital sex. The longing for a village lover[15] is sung in a number of love songs *(don seren)* at weddings. Usually, a girl does not marry her village lover and meeting becomes harder when her marriage arrangements are made. Yet, she may still meet him, though the families may prevent the meetings as the marriage approaches.

A number of metaphors describe feminine beauty: girls are the marigolds, rabbits, peacocks, deer, and silver fish that boys try to capture. Boys may say a girl sparkles like a white cloud. Archer (1974: 109) says a girl 'must be solid and supple, with small hips and hardly any waist'. Her body is important but her face should be beautiful, too. Her nose should be small and straight and her eyes neither too small nor too big. In describing how women got a clitoris, Santal stories implicitly assume female pleasure in sex. One day five women went to bathe in the river. Four of them put aside their vagina when bathing. When they came back one girl was missing. Maran Buru came with her vagina and shared it between the four. Since then women have a clitoris.

In contrast to feminine charm, masculine seduction rests on more diffuse criteria. A boy should have a smart way of walking, regular features, and a sound voice. A charming boy is often a good singer, a flute player, or a drum player. When ready for love he is as ravenous as a tiger, the girl an oriole bird. Songs tell us that boys and girls do not mature at the same time: often a boy wants a girl not yet ready for him. The girl often protests she is too young when trying to drive the boy away. Courtship may result from long friendship or a single encounter. Yet seduction becomes obsessive and mixed with the fear of separation. Santal romance is highly emotional and both sexes take the initiative to make love in the forest or during fairs or markets. If a boy cannot win a girl by sweet words or by playing the flute he may try to take her by force, which is an offence, so he must pay a fine. Besides the forest, the back of the house is used as a metaphor for sexual intercourse.

While the missionaries accepted a certain pre-marital freedom they opposed adultery. In Santal narratives even old couples enjoy sex and allow each other some freedom. Such stories were obscene to the missionaries and Christian education implied strict censure of sexual jokes. Skrefsrud, and later Bodding were aware of the Santal passion for romance expressed in love songs or licentious forest songs.[16] They avoided translating them, though Bodding lists 'obscene' terms in his dictionary. By setting them apart the missionaries missed their central place in expressing Santal emotions. For them, sexual allusions were obscene, and they did not imagine how they could express feelings beyond the realm of sex, such as the anxiety of separation, the coming of age, as also attachment, or procreative powers.

The missionaries seem to have disliked Santal dance, reacting against its erotic overtones. By banning rice-beer and dance they controlled seductive display amongst youth. But they could not prevent marriage by elopement or the escape of the converts' wives, especially if they came from non-Christian families. But the missionaries liked Santal music, and especially the twelve tunes, each corresponding to a particular theme. Skrefsrud used them and with Sibu Besra he composed hymns with great success.

It seems that in Skrefsrud's time, Santal boys felt that village girls were theirs by right, with hardly any right to refuse. This had to clash with Christian morals. Skrefsrud alludes to heathen promiscuity but does not condemn Santal youth. Perhaps he remembered his own past and felt that Christian education would bring youngsters to the serenity of Christian marriage. The school, and especially the girl's school, played a major role in taming the body. Caroline insisted on hygiene and on discipline, which was often administered corporally. The strongest reactions were reserved for sexual offence, as when schoolboys were accused of having accosted (or raped—such episodes are not described precisely) schoolgirls. The school was surrounded by high walls to sequester the girls, at a time when Skrefsrud's sister-in-law Karen Lunde campaigned for mixed schools in Norway. The sympathy Skrefsrud felt for youth seems completely absent from Caroline's mind. Her eagerness to marry off her graduates—sometimes even before they finished school—must be seen as a way of containing sexual desire.

Skrefsrud does not condemn Santal sexuality, except for adultery at festivals. He defends Santal customary law, and says that only physical defects or impotence suffices to annul a marriage–'madness or defects on the part of the wife constitute no case for divorce'. Skrefsrud criticised some forms of Santal marriage, such as elopement, but felt the way to fight them was with Christian union. He disliked polygyny, but was impressed by the freedom Santal women enjoyed. Yet many a Heathen woman married to a Christian seems to have missed her freedom as she could no longer dance, chew tobacco or drink. She felt estranged from her heathen family who sometimes tried to take her back.

At Skrefsrud's initiative, the 1875 conference of the various Santal missions[17] took up the problem. Frequently, it was said, converts found their wives being taken away and given in marriage to non-Christians. In other cases, a converted wife would find her husband taking a co-wife without her consent. Some missions allowed divorce if one partner converted, but Skrefsrud felt marriages with non-

Christians spread the Christian message. According to him, divorce was possible among Santals only if both parties agreed. Thus Christians could bring to court cases of 'illegal' divorce or the 'forced' abduction of a spouse. Other missionaries supported his view, and several such cases came before the courts. Only in cases of blatant infidelity should divorce be allowed (Nyhagen 1990, I: 276-7).

Christian marriage in the Mission was often arranged by the congregation, decided by the families, or, in the case of the schoolgirls, by Mrs. Börresen. Yet the missionaries stressed that the best Christian couples result both from mutual attraction and family decision—like many Western marriages at the time. Skrefsrud acknowledges[18] that Santal marriage is stable and involves co-operation between husband and wife. But he remains silent on Santal happiness, which depends on being jolly and enjoying life day by day. He fails to see how Santals take life with a certain humour. Christian love (*dularia*) was a sublimated version of Santal pleasure (*raskau*). The respect for Santal culture that Skrefsrud proclaimed was compromised by his refusal to acknowledge the sources of pleasure that played a central role in being a Santal.

In spite of certain liberal attitudes – there is no record, for example, of determined attempts to cover the women's breasts – the colonization of the body (Arnold 1993) is present in more subtle ways. The body emerges implicitly in the missionary discourse in the same way it is explicitly characterized in Norwegian Evangelical circles today. It is the seat of 'old Adam'—pre-Christian man, home to most temptations Christians should control. Promiscuity, drunkenness or pride all result from the strong body, and when the body is weak—in poverty, hunger, and illness—man may learn in humility to replace carnal pleasure with the joys of the soul. Skrefsrud was convinced that healing was God's work and when the first doctor joined them he had to leave soon after. Any death or healing was God's will. This fatalist attitude had its counterpart in Santal thought, where Thakur was measuring everyone's life span. Many conversions are, in fact, explained by famine or illness.

## THE JOY OF DRINKING

Among Santals, beer is a pleasure, *raskau,* and a central value in life. As with the Subanun (Frake 1962) drinking defines socialization, regulates ritual cycles, and punctuates social events such as transactions or contracts. Libations of rice-beer and *mahua* liquor are offered to ancestors and bongas. Santals know high caste Hindus hold them impure for indulging in alcohol and sex, but answer that Hindus frequent liquor shops or brothels secretly. Educated Santals may abstain from alcohol, but traditional villagers enjoy their rice-beer and associate it with good speech and tobacco. Still, drunkards are not accepted, and there are cases of divorce where the wife complains of abuse by a drunk husband and the culprit is then turned out of the village.

It is the women who brew beer. Today, yeast is bought in the market but used to be prepared by the ojha, who collected the plants and ground them, an operation associated with possession. The first extract is offered to the ancestors, then to guests, and finally, to the family. The symbolism of fermentation evokes fertility and sexuality, alluding to the first incest, induced by drinking the beer that Maran Buru taught the first siblings to brew. Similar associations surround tobacco, which sprouts from the buried flesh of a girl that her brother refused to eat—eating symbolizes sexuality. Her fermented flesh becomes the essence of tobacco. Fermentation alludes to a slow and mythical cooking, a portent of fertility.

The Santals use different names for rice-beer, from the occasions where it is served. Central are the betrothal and marriage ceremonies: both parties drink to conclude the first marriage negotiations. When the bridegroom and his party come to take the bride, they are offered the 'the bridegroom people's beer'. The families drink when they erect the marriage pole and when they remove it. More beer is drunk when the bridegroom is dressed, and yet more when the bride's father receives the bride price. At funerals, the affines must bring the beer with which the chief mourner nourishes the deceased's 'flower-bones'. Rice-beer evokes the reproduction of the lineage. Traditionally, large quantities of meat and beer were offered to guests who might number a couple of hundreds. Affinal kin from other villages brought beer, rice, and goats, and expected to receive even more, equal to the value of several cows. Partners often had to borrow. This logic of reciprocity escaped the missionaries who saw such lavish spending as a sign of Santal improvidence.

Rice-beer for bongas and ancestors ritualizes exchange, standing as an emblem of tribal values. Today, it is drunk whenever *jharkhandis*[19] are present. Whenever an offence has been committed, the fines imposed often include beer. Beer is paid to the midwife after delivery, to the marriage negotiator, and to the ojha coming to his patient's house to cure him. Santal women are free to sell their beer at markets. They also make and sell the *sal* leaf cups from which the beer is drunk. For them, an entire economic activity disappears when beer is banned. Selling beer gives them an opportunity to meet and talk.

Towards the end of April women go to the forest to collect *mahua* flowers, which symbolize fertility, and are given to women by the *naeke* during the ancestor festival. The flowers are distilled to a strong alcohol which aid the journey into trance and is drunk by ojhas when they invoke the deities. In Santal poetry the *mahua* flower is compared to the ring of Maran Buru: as the ring is close to the finger, so the flower strengthens the trance.

The liquor shop was usually kept by low-caste Sundis, often close to the men's work. In the context of colonial labour, liquor offered Santal workers respite from their ill-paid toil. Tales describe the moneylender taking his debtor to the liquor shop the better to abuse him. Alcoholism aggravated exploitation, which helps to explain the missionaries' condemnation. In 1880, Skrefsrud writes to Hertel about the problem.[20]

> There has been much noise as the police took several villagers who had brewed alcohol and brought them to the magistrate at Rampur Hat, where they were given a considerable fine, and also threatened if they did the same again . . . For the Santals had their Christmas—like our heathen ancestors[21] — and as it chiefly consists in everybody, large and small, men and women, intoxicating themselves for five days, and the Santals in the regulation district are not allowed to make alcohol, they are in great need. Drunkenness is the favourite sin of the Santals . . . only because we watch our chiefs . . . so closely is it possible nearly to eradicate drinking. And if we don't even try to abolish the same sin among the heathens, then our Christian superior chiefs, who have to judge between man and man, stand in great danger—wherefore we did abolish, a few years ago, the sale of alcohol in our district. But since nine liquor shops were left in the regulation area nearby, I have now asked the magistrate in Rampur Hat to close them, as I hope he will do, since he is both a believer in Christ and a friend of ours. . . . Since I knew that several villages were making alcohol, they all got punished as I told the police. . . . In one village, they wanted to beat up the police. Two policemen had come, and they had to send for me . . . (they) told me 'the Santals have more respect for you than for us'. When the moral influence has an ally in the heart of the people itself, then . . . (it) will be stronger than the constraint.

## THE ETHNOLOGICAL QUESTIONNAIRE

In 1877, Skrefsrud responded to the ethnological questionnaire of H.H. Risley.[22] Skrefsrud aims here, as ethnologist rather than missionary, at presenting the Santals as laborious and reasonable despite their superstitions. He wants to show how tribal laws are coherent, and can be trusted by the British administrators. His answers reveal an acute sense of observation, but he also consulted elders, especially Kolean Guru, with whom he had written the *Mare Hapram ko* (1887), later translated as *Traditions and Institutions of the Santals* (1942).

Skrefsrud starts by stressing how Santal religion differs from Hinduism. 'They believe', he says, 'that there is an invisible god, creator of heaven and earth, whom the old traditions call Thakur. Thakur is acknowledged both by the greatest European and brahmin scholars (and) admitted to be an aboriginal word in later times borrowed by the Hindus. The Santals do not worship Thakur, as he does them no harm.' We see here the missionaries search for an aboriginal monotheism. Skrefsrud interprets the Santal origin myth to state that the worship of Thakur was replaced by that of Maran Buru about AD 13, during their sojourn in Champa. 'They discussed the matter, they do not recollect whether it was twelve days or twelve years, and finally decided to change their religion.' Thus the democratic Santals, we understand, may again discuss and return to monotheism.

'Their principal bonga is Maran Buru, the Scandinavian Loke who, according the Santal traditions, induce Pilcu Haram and Pilcu Budhi to Ṣin by making them drunk.' The identification with Loki is suggestive: it would be hard to state more clearly the parallel between the conversion of Santals and that of his own forefathers. In both cases, original monotheism had degenerated to polytheism. Then, 'as immigration to the Santal Parganas took place about one hundred years ago, they changed their religion', which, we suppose, became what he now saw before him. Skrefsrud interprets the worship of the bongas as a kind of pantheism. 'They sacrifice anywhere, in the holy grove, in the house, in the field, in the forest, as the case may be, according the object of sacrifice.'

'The Santals have not as a rule taken to Hindu deities, only here and there one sees a Santal who offers to Kali or Sib or Durga, they employ a Hindu priest to do this sacrifice.' Skrefsrud states that Santals have no idols and emphasizes that, unlike Hindus, they have no priestly class. 'Sacrifices for the welfare of the community are done by the priests but the family worship is offered by the father of the house.' The Santals, he says, 'eat the sacrifices', but, besides animal victims, some priests connected with forest, hunt or rice-fields, offer drops of their own blood to appease the malevolent bongas.

Skrefsrud says the Santal have recently practised human sacrifice to a mountain god. 'No one can tell the name of the god. But, it is certain that the god is not the goddess Kali. The Santals call this god Buru bonga, mountain god. The reason for human sacrifice is alleged to be the desire to become rich or to be able to conquer an adversary or enemy.' He feels the custom is recent: 'we have traditions . . . (that) they commenced as soon as they crossed the Damodar river. They believe they have learnt it from the Hindu rajas and the Paharias. The victims were kidnapped when found alone.' Skrefsrud names the *parganas* who practised it a generation earlier: 'Bogma pargana in Lachimpur, Godda district did it very often. But he was martyrized (*sic*) to death by the Santals during the insurrection of 1855. Each man whose relations he had sacrificed was giving him a cut with his battle-axe, thus killing him slowly'.[23]

Skrefsrud then turns to agricultural rituals, important for the fertility of women, and seems to respect their role in the agricultural cycle.[24] He enumerates them: the sacrifice of a fowl at sowing, when the paddy becomes green, and when the millet[25] is ripe. Skrefsrud notes the two levels of sacrifice; public ones by the priest in the sacred grove, for the whole community, and private ones where the family head offers the first crop to ancestors and clan deities. Skrefsrud tells Risley how the cattle festival, *sohrae*, allows married men and women to have illicit sexual relations: 'so long it is not near relatives, such cases are not sanctioned with heavy punishment'.

Among private sacrifice, he notes the *abge bonga* which is secret. As a private god, '*abge* . . . helps the members of the family in all their troubles'. As many Santals have converted, he says, they have disclosed the name of the *abge*, and the deities have taken revenge on them. 'Some are not known, because so many have become Christians', he adds. Here he implies that converts have forgotten their *abge*. But did they not, rather, prefer to keep it secret from the missionaries? Skrefsrud notes that women are not allowed to eat the meat of animals sacrificed to the *abge*.

Skrefsrud remained surprised by 'superstition'. 'The Santals believe in gods, in trees, in water, in stones but they (the deities) are supposed to live there . . . and the Santals worship these gods in order they may not harm them': 'The souls of ancestors are worshipped with prayers and sacrifice, but the Santals are in great dread of the ghosts of the dead'. He criticizes their 'fancy that the dead speak to them in their dreams'. They 'do not practise austerities, and nobody thinks chastity to be a particular virtue'. The hook-swinging festival—which celebrates the austerities of Shiva—is, he says, 'a festival for sexual intercourse; when they dance . . . (and) suitable matches are determined'. Skrefsrud had clearly not grasped the peculiar combination of austerity and sexual prowess that Shiva incarnates.[26] In Bengal today, men often practice hook-swinging to obtain male offspring.

Skrefsrud does not seem to be shocked by premarital love among the Santals. Here he is more liberal than most contemporaries. But he dislikes the lack of self-control produced by drink, and the semi-public promiscuity that results.

> Legally a man can only have one wife . . . he is, however, with the consent of his wife, allowed to take his deceased brother's wife or to get a second wife if his real wife is barren. Those who take a second wife for any other cause are looked upon as 'goats'. And, if the real wife defends her right, such women are not allowed to come into the house. . . . I know only four cases in over one hundred villages in which a Santal had, for licentious causes, taken a second wife during the lifetime of his real wife. The first wife is always the real wife.

But polygamy was not unusual then, nor later, and Skrefsrud may be overstating his case to make the Santals more respectable, and to stress the traditional base for the Christian marriage he had introduced. 'There is no prostitution among Santals' he claims, except where they are in contact with soldiers and similar groups. The few who had lent themselves to it were excommunicated.

Interestingly, Skrefsrud minimizes the importance of prohibitions on cousin marriage and other kinship rules. 'Some people have said', he states, 'that he (the Santal) may not marry any of his maternal aunts or their daughters nor the daughters of their maternal uncles to the third generation as long there are people who know the relation. Here exists no such prohibition'. This conforms with the findings of later ethnographers, and Sona was married to a member of her own clan, though Skrefsrud admits that such alliances are banned. But his point introduces another theme: as Santals are prepared to forsake their gods, and some have no gods at all, there is no barrier to intermarriage between Christians and Heathens. He cites the meeting where 'parganas of twelve taluks came together and decided that Santal Christians and Santal Heathens could eat, drink and intermarry. . . . They wrote a document and signed it and that document is in our possession.' If the religious divide was no barrier to marriage, why bother about kinship rules? Skrefsrud came to define Santal endogamy as defining identity, stressing how Santals avoid brahmins and other high caste Hindus. He describes the *janam* ceremony performed some days after birth to admit the child into the tribe or nation. From that day, the child has a clan and a sub-clan and may be present during the rituals associated with the deities worshipped by these groups.

Skrefsrud pays particular attention to various kinds of oaths. 'The Santals will not even, now that they have learnt as much bad from the Hindus, speak falsely if they take any oath.' He apparently wants to stress the soundness of Santal customary law. The Santals have many oaths. 'On my uncle or nephew, I affirm this to be true or false.' 'If what I say is false, my mother is my wife.' Or the juror says 'I put my hand on my chest and swear. If I speak falsely, let the tiger eat me.' Sometimes, says Skrefsrud, he will take live coals in his hand, declaring that if he speaks truth, he will not be burnt. 'Terrible causes and consequences are attached to all these oaths. The whole family will die.' But he criticizes the role of the ojha, who drinks heavily to get inspired, and denounces witches and the witch-finders.

In Santal religion, Skrefsrud looked for a figure to express the monotheist principle, which he felt sure had once been present. Maran Buru is the higher bonga who created humanity. But he bestows pleasure, drink, and lovemaking on humans, that missionaries could not reconcile with their own stern God. To translate the name of God he chose Thakur, who seemed properly divine since he did not receive sacrifice. He was invoked when Santals were taking oaths. He becomes a benevolent figure for the missionaries, while the Santals hold him responsible for the fire rain that destroyed the world. In some narratives he parallels Jom Raja, a version of the Hindu god of death, Yama.

While Skrefsrud's version of the Creation myth has Maran Buru as the creation god, A. Campbell[27] collected another version (1916a) where Thakur came first and appears as Thakur–Jiv or 'God the spirit'. He is also known as Chando bonga—the sun and moon.[28] Thakur-Jiv charged Malin Budhi with creating humans from clay. She made two and laid them out to dry. Sin Sadom, the day-horse —an emanation of the sun—trampled them to destroy her work. This was reported to Thakur who asked Malin Budhi to throw them into the sea, then blessed her to again create the first human pair. They became geese, who went to Thakur and said: 'You gave us being but we cannot find a place to stay.' He ordered the water animals, crab and lobster, to bring up the earth from the bottom of the sea, but they failed. Finally, the worm ate the soil of the seabed and excreted it on top of the ocean. Thakur Jiv caused a *karam* tree to grow, then *Sirom* grass, *dubi* grass and all kinds of trees and herbs. The geese made their nests in the *sirom* but Raghop' Boar, a sea monster, ate them. On hearing this, Thakur sent Jaher Era, a female deity, to guard their eggs. From them two humans were born, Pilcu Haram and Pilcu Budhi.[29]

Here Thakur is the creator while in Skrefsrud' version he destroys humanity by fire-rain. Thakur later introduces bongas as guardians of men, and teaches men to work, unlike Maran Buru who, in Skrefsrud's version, shows them how to dance and make beer. Both versions still co-exist as they did in the nineteenth century. While most Santals refer to Maran Buru when they worship the bongas, some Christians prefer Thakur as creation god, probably since he seems closer to a monotheist figure.

## RESISTANCE AND THE KHERWAR MOVEMENT

By 1875 the missionaries had succeeded in founding a viable Christian community, but there was still resistance. A Santal chief, Ram, took Skrefsrud to court, accusing him of plundering his house, taking him by force to Ebenezer, holding him captive, and menacing him if he would not accept baptism. Ram was sentenced for defamation to one year's prison and a fine of Rs. 700.[30] But he was not alone. In 1875, when the missionaries made the government close the drink shops, resistance increased.[31] They were invited to hunt meetings, to impress and frighten them (Jörgensen 1920: 102-3), and 'the heathen believed they would have the government's permission to chase the Christians from Santalistan, since the Santal Parganas were the land of the bongas from old'.[32] Such ideas, of course, were not completely at variance with those of some British administrators, who preferred to deal directly with the tribal groups. Yet many of the officials who took this view, were themselves Evangelicals or others who saw the missionaries as working for the tribal cause. Börresen's behaviour at one hunt meeting has become missionary myth: he accepted the invitation, only to state: 'Your missionary is here: kill him if you like' (Nyhagen 1990, I: 277). Skrefsrud, at another meeting, found the Santals far more determined to fight (Jörgensen 1920: 104). In some areas, Christians were threatened: they must either return to their old religion, or be chased from the village. Some Christians fled, while others brought such cases to court.

The most important resistance in this period was the Kherwar[33] movement, which appeared in the winter of 1871-2. In 1874, the Kherwar leader, Bhagrit, was enthroned as a Raja and declared himself chief of all Santals, to liberate them from colonial rule and missionary influence, and regain the lost kingdom.

Bhagrit came from the village Tardiha in Godda district. He had taken an active part in the 1855 rebellion, and in 1868 was jailed for two years for rebellious activity.[34] There he met Matudin, whose influence was crucial in Hinduizing the movement[35] (Nyhagen 1990, I: 283-4). It spread quickly and people were slaughtering impure animals everywhere. They assembled in numbers, armed with bows, arrows, and other weapons.

Close to Tardiha, where Bhagrit built a temple for his followers, was a CMS station from which the missionary Stark reported on the events. He was born in Calcutta in 1834. His father died early so he went to La Martinière,[36] whose principal A.W. Christopher was on the CMS committee. The boy was fascinated by CMS work among the Yoruba and Abekuta in West Africa. When he graduated, he worked in a government office and lived with his brother, headmaster of the CMS school at Amherst Street, Calcutta. He tried to get into Bishop's College, and to the CMS seminary at Islington, but Cuthbert of the CMS told him there was no need to go there. Thus he continued to hope for admission to the mission, living with his brother, who later moved to Bhagalpur. Here Droese, the German CMS missionary, took him on as a teacher in 1853, when he was nineteen years old. Later, Droese opened a school for Paharia boys and Stark was put in charge, since he had picked up some of their language. His first acquaintance with Santals came when they were brought as prisoners to Bhagalpur after the rebellion (Moorat 1925: 1-11).

When the Santal Parganas[37] were formed after the rebellion, several new posts of assistant commissioner were created. Stark was offered one but refused, as he wanted to be a missionary. He was soon disappointed. He and his brother had often officiated in Church when Droese was away, but now the missionary put a stop to the practice. He told Stark that the object of the CMS was 'to raise Indian helpers, or to get out English Missionaries direct from England' (Moorat 1925: 13). Moorat here shows her resentment at the treatment of the Anglo-Indians,[38] belonging fully neither to the colonizers nor the colonized. Stark resigned, but one Angus McKenna got him a job at Doveton College, Calcutta, which he held till 1867.

Just before the mutiny, Eliza Sutherland arrived in Calcutta with her mother and sister. The girls had grown up in Transvaal, but their father was an officer during the Sikh wars, and then the family stayed in Serampur. They knew Stark's mother, so now they lodged with her. They arrived on 12 March: by the 28 Alfred had proposed to Eliza. They were married on 10 September, and lived in college lodgings. But after eleven years, Alfred was sacked.[39] He then met E.C. Stuart, CMS secretary in Calcutta, and was taken on as secretary at the mission's Calcutta office (Moorat 1925: 21-37). Storrs, CMS missionary to the Santals, realized his experience of the area, and Stark was put in charge of a boarding school for Santal boys at Taljhari. After six months, he was preaching in Santali (ibid.: 41). He effectively led the mission station from 1870. In 1872, he was transferred to Pathra; he did not get on with Storrs' successor. Stark was charmed by the 'truthfulness and simplicity' of the Santals, in spite of their 'proneness to bribery and weakness for drink' (1925: 50). Santals and Paharias, notes his daughter, 'could not live peaceably together' (ibid.: 57).

Here too, 1873-4 was a famine year. Like Börresen, Stark was in charge of relief work; 'Stark's road' was among the results. But, notes Moorat, the Bengali officials served their own interests, and neglected the Santals, 'whilst Hindu traders got the monopoly, these bought at Government rates, and sold at their own'. This, she implies, provoked the Kherwar movement. Stark managed to prevent an attack on the magistrate's *kacheri*[40] until the magistrate, back from on tour, saw to it that rice was fairly distributed. But corruption had created a climate of distrust (ibid.: 76-7).

A leader rose up among them, whose name was Bhagrait; he feigned to be a religious reformer, but all the time he was really sowing sedition. He told the people not to pay rent for the land. "Who made the land and all the grain it produces?" he asked them. "The one above", was the reply. "Then why should we pay the Government? It is ours, given to us by the one above. Let those of you, who will, follow me by this

> sign. . . ." Bhagrait got an astonishingly large number of followers, who called themselves 'Bhagraitias' or 'Safa Hor', which means 'pure people'. In many villages not a fowl or pig was to be seen; and it was an open secret, that, when the rising took place, those who were found with these 'impure creatures' would be put to death. (Moorat 1925: 77-8)

The Starks heard of this from the local converts, and noticed 'a change in the behaviour of the people. Daily large numbers would pass our house armed, as we had never seen them in past years, carrying bows and arrows, spears and dreadful-looking tomahawks'. They never molested the missionary or his family, but friendly converts advised them to leave. 'Wait a little; you have sown your corn', a Santal is reported to have said, 'see who will reap it. By such and such a time we will send you by beat of drums to that happy land of which you are always speaking and singing' (Moorat 1925: 78-9).

> Bhagrait had got up a shrine on Tardiha Pahar, a hill that stands out high and prominent, and can be seen miles away. On the summit of the cone-shaped hill he had set up three large stones; there his followers were invited to bring their offerings and tributes. Crowds of Sonthals went up with their offerings of milk and ghee . . . and money. The former were poured on the stones, and the money was placed on the ground in front of Bhagrait. He was dressed in 'tussar' (a kind of country silk) and had a secretary and a *vizir* (Prime Minister). After the offerings . . . had been presented, they would come to him and make their *johars* (Santali obeisance) . . . Bhagrait even went to the length of bathing in milk, thinking that would make him fair like us. (Moorat 1925: 79)

The *vizir* asked each man the number of ploughs he had. 'On receiving the reply, he would tell them: 'Put down four annas for each plough'. The Secretary would be instructed to give them receipts and numbers, and to inform them that they had paid their dues, and so would have nothing more to pay to the government.

This, in fact, is the best description we have of Bhagrit's proceedings. We see clearly, here, the royal model, as well as its link to the sanctuary. We remember, too, that the taxation system he uses here is the one that Sidhu and Kanhu had demanded, prior to the rebellion. A plough is a measure of land worked (Campbell 1988: 538), and thus does not include the fallow on which Santal agriculture depended. They found it unjust to pay tax for land that bore no crop that year. Bhagrit, like many a modern revolutionary, was organizing his raj even before the fight had begun, and was also laying its financial foundations.

Moorat, however, sees it differently.

In this cunning way, Bhagrait was fast becoming a rich man: he received piles of money daily and was to have been anointed and styled 'Nawab Badshah' or emperor. The Sonthals were told the day on which they were to assemble on the hill for his anointing: the date was fixed for the general rising and massacre of ourselves, the magistrate, Indian Christians and Babus . . . . Some of the Christians went to Tardiha Pahar in disguise, and on coming back told father what they had heard. The Magistrate's house at Godda was to be Bhagrait's, and our home at Pathra would be given to the Vizir. They advised father to leave . . . (He) wished to send mother with their children to Calcutta, but she would not agree. (Moorat 1925: 79)

Stark wrote to the C.M.S. secretary in Calcutta: 'If you don't hear from me again, you will know by my silence that I have been killed; the Sonthals are rising'. Sir Richard Temple, Lieutenant-Governor and on the CMS committee, saw the letter, 'and was greatly concerned, as it was the first information he had received of any trouble in that district' (Moorat 1925: 79-82). The Commissioner of Bhagalpur was told to investigate. 'He invited father to breakfast, and, after the meal was over, he took a letter from his pocket and asked father if that was his writing . . . Mr. Boxwell, the commissioner,[41] then asked him if he could substantiate the statements made. Father replied: 'Yes, if the magistrate will give me a policeman or two.' (Moorat 1925: 82) The policemen followed Stark in civilian clothes and 'witnessed the tribute given' to Bhagrit. Next day, the commissioner, the magistrate and the missionary all went there on elephants.

When they got there, they found the Police had not carried out orders, but were awaiting their arrival at the foot of the hill dressed in uniform. This, of course, alarmed the Safa Hor . . . and thus they could not be taken unawares. On getting to the top of the hill, Mr. Boxwell and Mr. Grant[42] had Bhagrait arrested and ordered the policemen to break down the false shrines: but not a man could be persuaded to break them for fear. So these gentlemen and father had to put their hands to the work themselves: they lifted off the stones; then others joined in their removal . . . . There was great excitement among the Sontals, when their leader was arrested. (Moorat 1925: 84)

In fact, the Commissioner put off the trial until he could get troops from Bhagalpur. The Santals were besieging the Court every day. Yet Bhagrit was sentenced to two years' imprisonment.

'When his term was over and he was free again, he gave out that he had been with Chando Baba receiving orders about the welfare of his people, which he had now come to carry out. Many of his followers rallied round him again . . . Bhagrait, unknown to us, planned another massacre at Pakaur, as we found out providentially in time'. There were rumours that Bhagrit wanted to kill Mrs. Stark and her children, while Stark was in Calcutta on a missionary conference. They spent the night in prayer, and later stated that they had been saved by a miracle (Moorat 1925, 84-5; Nyhagen 1970, I: 286).

Soon after, Moorat tells us, 'Bhagrit committed an act of violence against an old man'. This time he was jailed for five years, and died of cholera in jail in 1879. Many of his followers refused to believe in his death, 'but said that he had been translated to heaven and would return from God to be their King and give them back their country. This they preferred to believe, till the lapse of years compelled them to admit their mistake. This idea kept the Santal country disturbed from 1873 to 1878' (Moorat 1925: 89).

## INTERPRETING THE MOVEMENT

Moorat, like her father, saw the Kherwar as a political movement. Others, like the missionary Andrew Campbell and Boxwell, the Commissioner of Bhagalpur, saw it as a religious revival. It may well have been provoked by Santal disenchantment with the traditional religion, as Bodding thought. But he knew the movement mainly at a later time, when it had effectively become non-violent (Nyhagen 1990, I: 283). Skrefsrud and Stark, who knew the movement in Bhagrit's own time, were afraid of another Santal rebellion. Skrefsrud writes[43] that Bhagrit held no god responsible for the creation, so the Santal Parganas belonged to the Santals who had cleared the jungle and made it habitable. To free them from their oppressors, they must win the favours of Singbahni, the moneylenders' god, by giving up the bonga cult, purifying themselves and their houses, and getting rid of impure animals such as pigs and poultry. They must also stop drinking and dancing. According to the only text on Kherwars found in the Santal Archives,[44] Bhagrit's followers did not plunder like Sidhu and Kanhu, but behaved like true ascetics. But they did threaten with violence those who did not follow their teachings.

Moorat's account, however, makes clear that Bhagrit wanted to introduce the same taxation system as Sidhu and Kanhu, i.e. taxation by the plough, the land unit Santals used and which excludes fallow.

This points to agrarian claims as an important base for the movement, and ties it to the strain of peasant insurgence that unites most of the unrest on the tribal fringe of Bengal. What is striking in the missionary comments on the Kherwar, is how they prefer to stress the religious or the ethnic factor while minimizing economic hardship. This was certainly not, in Skrefsrud's case, because he ignored the economic difficulties of the Santals, as both his work for land reform and his comments on the scarcity of land show. Rather, we feel, he was convinced of his own role as the Santal's benefactor in these respects, and refused to see that another religious movement could have similar goals.

One centre of the movement was the Sultanabad area, where Dhunu, chief of village Sidpur, was one of the leaders. He is supposed —apparently the information came from Börresen—to have said that as soon as the head of the Raja of Maheshpur fell, there would be no more taxes for the Santals.[45] Like Bhagrit, he was jailed in the autumn of 1874. But the Kherwar movement continued to exist clandestinely.

When Skrefsrud returned from Europe, the Santal Parganas remained unruly. The military was again sent to Maheshpur soon after. 'There has been a half insurrection', wrote Skrefsrud to Lunde, stressing that Christians were still persecuted. The movement calmed down for a while, but in 1876 there was a resurgence. Skrefsrud wrote to Boxwell[46] about the *parwana* circulating through the Santal Parganas which—he felt—was a signal for a new revolt. Again, Sultanabad was central to the movement, with many new adherents slaughtering pigs and poultry. The chief of village Haripur had declared—says Skrefsrud[47]—that the insurrection would start as soon as Dhunu got out from jail. Thus Dhunu was kept in detention, though he was very ill. Typically, Skrefsrud asked the authorities to hand Dhunu over to him. This they finally did, stressing that Skrefsrud would be held responsible for any trouble. Dhunu was brought to Benagaria where he was looked after and gradually got better. In the end, everything went as Skrefsrud hoped: Dhunu asked for baptism.[48] But Dhunu's conversion did not check the Kherwar movement, as Skrefsrud had hoped. He asked to have Bhagrit too, but he, instead, was freed in 1876, and soon planned new action. He was soon jailed again, for real or supposed crimes, and died in jail, of cholera, in 1879.

This did not put an end to the Kherwar movement, however. In

1880 there were widespread protests against the survey. Jadu, Bhagrit's brother, went to the authorities and refused collaboration unless all Santals, traditional, Kherwar, and Christian, were united. According to the official, W.B. Oldham,[49] they said the true religion should win, and all Santals should adopt it. The official sent them to the missionaries, and in January, 1881, a great meeting was held at Ebenezer to discuss the matter (Nyhagen 1990, I: 286-7).

## THE KHERWARS AS MATERIAL FOR CONVERSION

Skrefsrud seems to have been optimistic about converting the Kherwars. This is surprising, since Bhagrit's movement and imprisonment were known to him. Yet he writes to Graham as if these events never happened.

Another very remarkable thing has taken place quite lately. There is a Santhal sect, called the Kherwars, or Saph Hor (purists), which has sprung up during the last ten years. These people, with their acknowledged leader, an over-chief,[50] went to a magistrate and told him that they would not allow the census to be taken in their villages till he made the three sections among them—the heathen, the reformed heathen and the Christians—one: and they told the magistrate, if the heathen are in the right, let us all be heathen; if the reformed heathen, then let all embrace their doctrine; but if the Christians are right, then let us all become Christians, as we are in search of truth. The magistrate told them they should go to the missionary, as that was not *his* (the magistrate's) work. The purists answered, that it seemed strange that he could not judge in those matters; to which the magistrate rejoined, that if he were to judge such matters, the missionaries to whom God had given that work, would have to take to the plough, or become magistrates. He advised them to discuss with one of our intelligent Christians, who was present, which advice they followed, and they discussed the claims of Kherwarism and Christianity for two days, which resulted in their leader appointing a day in January when they would come to us and put themselves under instruction, saying that if they became Christians, all of them (many thousands) would embrace our religion, as the Kherwars, they said, would go one and the same way. We do not know what will come out of it, but it is very remarkable, and we would request you all there to help us, and pray that all these people may join our ranks and enlist under Christ's banner. The Christian who had this conversation with them is confident that they will carry out their promise, and leave Kherwarism for Christianity.[51]

Börresen, too, was optimistic.[52] One of the leaders of the Kherwar insurrection had converted.

He could find no peace with his *bonga* despite his sacrifices, and went to a Brahmin. He followed the Brahmin's advice, and tried daily sacrifice, but in vain. He thought of his rebellion, when they wanted to kill all Hindus, Christians, and Muslims, and would all become kings. He was put in prison, got the message, 'your saviour is born', and started to pray to the real God. . . . He went to his god, and asked him to kill him if he had any power. There was no answer. He pulled down the god he had made, threw him in the river and came here to look for Jesus. He was crying from pleasure when he heard that Jesus was a friend of the sinners. He found peace in Christ. And then his wife and son, who had been walking twenty miles that day, came. Everything went well, and they were baptized. . . . I asked him if he wanted to wait a little, but he said no. So he was baptized with his whole family.

The Christians hoped, then, that the January 1881 meeting would prove the occasion to convert the Kherwars. This did not happen. Rather, from their own point of view, the Kherwars carried the day, and perhaps the whole move was a brilliant piece of propaganda on their part. The meeting was a great disappointment to Skrefsrud, who changed tack completely. A few days later, he wrote to Smith, Assistant Deputy Commissioner, who had sought his advice on how to deal with the Kherwars:

1. When you have found them (the leaders) substitute for what I did, a sound public flogging, the more Santhal spectators the better and have soldiers near if necessary, and let it be clearly known that the men are flogged for libelling the Govt. by setting afloat such absurd and indecent rumours.[53] 2. Tell the people that everyone who will propagate this falsehood hereafter will be similarly beaten. 3. Send away the worst of the ringleaders as state prisoners after the flogging. 4. . . . deal with the Kherwars according to their deserts, and do not treat them any longer as a harmless, if not praiseworthy, social religious movement, because the religion is only a means towards an end . . . [which] is nothing short of . . . their former Champa autonomy.[54] (Hodne 1966: 286)

Elsewhere, resistance continued, but apparently the opposition against the survey abated, at least in Nankar taluka. Elsewhere, the military had to be stationed at strategic points. In Hazaribagh, the Kherwar resurgence was led by a Hindu, Dubia Gosain. He knew the Santals well, and his orders were followed. Some of the disturbances related to the survey operations. In Jamtara, the unrest started early: in December 1880, the official bungalow was burnt.[55] The missionaries, Cornelius and Paterson, had to be protected by the military. In Dumka, too, extra forces had to be deployed, while at Katikund the local official was attacked by about one thousand Santals, and had to declare there would be no survey in the area, in order to escape with his life.[56] This was the first real survey of the area, and the fact that it was to be done by night did nothing to allay Santal suspicions. The practical reason was that one expected people to be at home at night: but there were rumours that the population would be marked by burning special tatoos on them; others that they were to be sent away, the men to Kabul[57] and the women to tea gardens in Assam. Skrefsrud felt the rumours were started by the Kherwars for their own purposes (Nyhagen 1990, I: 287-8).

In the following years we hear less of the Kherwars, and Skrefsrud felt their influence declined in the 1890s.[58] But in 1883, Börresen accused them of the sacrifice, by decapitation, of a twelve year old boy in a village in Jubdi taluka.[59] The accusation figures, however, only in *Santalen*, *Dahkwala* and in a letter to Dr. Graham. Börresen apparently never thought the story worthy of official attention. Or did he not believe the rumour himself?

There were 40,000 Kherwars in the Santal Parganas according to the 1881 census. The category did not figure in 1891, but by 1901 74,000 Santals claimed to be Hindus. Nyhagen thinks these were mostly Kherwars (1990, I: 288). In 1921, Bodding felt the sect was losing ground. 'We had', he said, '. . . something approaching a famine two years ago, but very little was heard at the time of any fresh activity on the part of the Kherwars' (1921: 222). Some, he thought, had returned to their original religion while others had converted to Christianity.

Bodding describes how the sect has divided into three separate groups, mostly found in Pakaur subdivision, in the north of Dumka subdivision, and near Godda. The first group is called Sapai, referring to the original stress on avoiding pollution, who perform name-giving ceremonies and marriages between themselves. The second is called Samra as their guru, Bariar, came from Samra village. He prayed to Chando, and his disciples sang devotional songs and taught new adepts to give up bongas and offer sweets, songs, and money to Chando. They have exorcisers, adds Bodding, who behaved like ojhas, invoked the bongas, and sacrificed animals. No one else was allowed to share their sacrificial meal. Sometimes the guru asked for a pig which was buried alive. The third group is called Babajiu and represents the original sect.

Such splits are still typical of tribal movements, and are often related to the emergence of charismatic leaders. All three groups worship Ram Chando. Ram is a Hindu deity, and Chando is Santali for sun (and moon), used to refer to a single god, who, says Bodding, is identified with the Sun (ibid.: 224). All are vegetarian, and do not keep fowl or pigs, do not drink beer, nor eat the flesh of dead buffalos. Their exorcism, purification, and vegetarianism show Hindu influence. To show Christian influence, Bodding quotes a song mentioning 'Chando the father, Chando the Son, Chando the Soul or Spirit'. The archive text stresses that the Kherwar gurus used the words 'It is your faith (patiau) that will cure you' when they were healing disease. This, too, would seem to show Christian influence.

In 1922 Bodding again wrote of the Kherwar movement, discussing its origin and practices. The movement aimed at a return to original Santal culture and religion. It was announced through visions that their present oppression was a punishment for abandoning Chando and venerating minor spirits. Bonga cults were apostasy, and the leaders called for return to monotheism (Bodding 1922), which would bring back the golden age. This monotheism was perhaps inspired by Vaishnav and Shaiva gurus, as noted by Gossner missionaries describing the visit of Kabir Panthis to Oraon villages. We find similar claims among the Tana Bhagat after 1914 in Chotanagpur (Roy 1915, Dasgupta 1999).

Both Fuchs (1965: 56) and Bodding (1922) say the Kherwar leaders had contact with missionaries. Bhagrit told his followers he would petition Chando and pray for them (Fuchs 1965: 55). Bodding says his precepts were close to the ten commandments, which are indeed mentioned in the Santal text. During the 1874 famine, when the British imported rice from Burma, Bhagrit claimed the rice had been given by the Santals to the bongas; now it was returned by the foreign rulers. They might eat it but pigs or fowl must not pollute it. As for the rebellion of 1855, Bhagrit held that Sidhu and Kanhu were right in wanting to reconquer the country for the Santals, but explained their failure by the sin of taking women from other castes, so that God had withdrawn his aid. Bhagrit's followers were strictly monogamous and married only among themselves.

## HINDU INFLUENCE

The Kherwars seemed ready to abandon bonga worship: but were they Hindus? They certainly did not develop a version of the goddess cult, as some Hinduized tribes have done (Hardiman 1995, Carrin 1997). They promoted an egalitarian ideal and criticized differences of prestige or wealth between clans. The movement was probably influenced by the Chuar revolts. The Chuars were active both during the Bhumij rebellion (Jha 1964) and Birsa's movement in 1895. In the Chuar revolts, like the tribal movements, agrarian claims encoded the desire for a lost kingdom, present in Santal poetry and clan myths. Royal claims are expressed when the *pargana* is enthroned 'like a king'. Though the ritual may be recent—Carrin observed it around 1970—it shows how Santal ideas of kingship are wrought in a Hindu idiom. This royal model, which pervaded the 1855 and 1861 rebellions, Bhagrit's and Birsa's movements, is also found in the *karam* ritual, which the Santals celebrated on occasions such as marriage, the initiation of an ojha, or the installation of a chief. Here, they questioned the relation between prosperity and kingship, asceticism and poverty. Central to the *karam* myth are the alternative roles of king and renouncer. We remember Mandho Singh, born of a Santal mother, who wanted to Hinduize the Santals. They refused to follow him: though Santals have borrowed many Hindu elements they oppose central Hindu values such as purity, hierarchy, and caste.

This denial is expressed in satire describing Hindus as stupid. One folk-tale[60] (Bodding 1925: 88), shows how a brahmin makes a fool of himself by judging people according to status and caste. A vulture symbolizing the power of divination comes to him, giving him one of his feathers, to be used 'like spectacles' to see the real value of things. When the brahmin uses it he sees the truth: his wife is mean, while low-caste and poor people are goods.[61] In *Why We Should Know Our Neighbours' Deities* the narrator acknowledges a link between kingship and Hindu gods, attributes the origin of epidemics to Hindu goddesses, and mentions the *bhuts,* harmful spirits ressembling malevolent bonga.[62] Thus, he notes, a woman who dies in child-birth becomes a *curin,* a kind of *bhut,* if she is a Hindu and a bonga if she is a Santal.

The relationship of bongas to popular Hinduism, notably to goddesses such as Manasa, is ambiguous. The latter causes snakebite but reveals invocations against it to the ojhas, becoming their main tutelary deity. But while the opposition of vegetarian and blood-drinking deities is central to the Hindu pantheon, Santal ritual stresses the exorcism of malevolent bongas. In Santal invocations, written at the time of our missionaries, epidemics are attributed to Hindu goddesses: Durga, Sita and Kali all appear as malevolent in Santal eyes. Shiva is ambiguous: he is the companion of witches, but also the ancestor of the first ojha. As Ishvar Bonga, he protects the cattle, while as Mahadeo, he controls malevolent deities and shelters witches. As a couple, Shiva and Parvati are malevolent, the latter being a bad influence on Shiva.

Though Santals generally oppose the hierarchical implications of Hindu thought, hierarchy appears in Santal ritual through the different roles occupied by bongas or Hindu deities. Thus the messenger, the disciples, or the devotee are all inferior to a chief bonga, while the witness is a superior bonga like Maran Buru. The thief may be Santal or Hindu, but is always inferior. The Hindu goddesses popular among Santals are blood-drinking, linked to Kali or the Tantric world. They include the *jugini*, who are avid of sexual relationships in the graveyard, or the *curin*, spirits of women who died in child-birth.

Generally, bongas are subordinate to Hindu gods. The Santals of the Rajmahal hills performed hook-swinging as Mahadev devotees around 1870 (Oddie 1995), as Skrefsrud acknowledged.[63] A Santal text, probably written during the early 1890s, mentions the rite[64] and tells of Santals who join to obtain magic powers.[65] Man (1867) also observed this festival held during the rains and, says Archer, associated by Santals with annual romance.

Santal villagers invoked Hindu deities at Skrefsrud's time: he mentions Kali and Mahadev.[66] In the Santal archives, we find numerous lists of Hindu gods supposed to manipulate the bongas.[67] The ojha often have Hindu tutelary deities, and Bodding feels the Santal ojha has borrowed many elements from his Hindu counterparts in the region. Still, 'Much of the practices of the Santal ojha seems to be essentially outside the Hindu fold . . . (but) the ojha's special bongas seem to be of a nature somewhat different from that of the ordinary Santal bongas' (Bodding 1986: 10). Although the name is borrowed from the Hindus, the Santal ojha is clearly a Santal institution bridging the gap between popular Hinduism and their own religion, centered around cults of the bongas.

The ojha is certainly an ascetic, supposed to practice healing as *dhorom*, without much pay, though the missionaries criticize those 'humbug' ojhas who take money so that their patients must borrow (Bodding 1986: 12). 'Whenever these ojhas are unable to effect a cure, the bad result is not, of course, due to their own lack of ability, or the insufficiency of their remedies. The responsibility is elsewhere, with the powers behind the scenes. The 'eaters' (that is to say the destructive power of bongas and witches) have gained the upper hand, the ojha will say, and he considers himself free from all responsability.'

Yet the field of ritual action of the ojha extends beyond the art of healing. Through his knowledge, the bonga world is not a haphazard collection of deities, but a world in which the social conflict between the Santals and their Hindu neighbours can be symbolized.

## RETHINKING SANTAL MYTHOLOGY

The various reform movements show the innovative capacity of the Santals, but these movements also reinvented Santal traditional religion. Some Santal myths of the colonial period deal with Hindus and Hindu gods, and are still told in villages, while others are found in the Santal archives. These narratives focus on four main themes: origin and redefinition of work; currency and commodities; labour and human sacrifice, and the transformation of human sexuality and reproduction.

The Santals say their ancestors, during the golden age, did not have to work, and death, as such, did not yet exist. One myth tells us how death was introduced to the world by Thakur, who scrapes his body to make a ball of dirt, symbolizing death.[68] Then appears a Hindu raja and a leopard acting as tax-collector. Thus the coming of death is accompanied by taxation and labour. Another version tells us the first ancestors worked in the forest. Clearing the forest marks the fragmentation of territory, the split into sub-clans, and the fragmentation of time. In yet another version, the ancestors submit to division of labour: men hunt, while women dig for tubers. The migrations disturbed the peace of the golden age, and some Santals settled permanently. They are compared to silkworms preferring to sleep in their cocoons, while the true ancestors still migrate. Finally, Maran Buru appears, teaching them to sow and plough. The original twelve clans split into some 160 sub-clans, and the totemic reference is altered. As migrations end, the ancestors must work.

In Skrefsrud's time the archive texts describe death as a labour camp.[69] There, men and women are employed by Yama Raja, the king of death, to make new human beings from the bones of old. They seem to view the reproduction of society as a kind of artisanal work. Hammers and nails are used by the recently dead workers: they are constantly driven by a chowkidar (evoking colonial labour).

Human sacrifice too is presented as a metaphor of labour. A story written at the turn of the century describes a large number of Santal workmen engaged in the building of a bridge. To ensure a solid foundation, the 'Captain Saheb' secretly calls a Santal chowkidar in charge of one of the gangs. He is given a bribe and calls three of his men; they get hold of a fourth, push him violently under the foundations of the bridge, and before he can complain, bury him under sand and gravel. The obvious parallel to the Western reader is of workers laying down their lives for their enterprise. The victim is anonymous, his selection haphazard. The Santals are no strangers to human sacrifice, with the king or *pargana* as sacrificer; but here, the saheb takes their place. The story accuses the British of cruelty and corruption. The simile of death as a labour camp, emphasized in the story of the bridge, shows us labour sacrificed in the interest of capital, as a metaphor for colonial society. Such images came uncomfortably close to truth (Carrin-Bouez 1993).

The institution of the adopted son-in-law shows how the notion of labour is tied to a network of social obligations. In the encompassing society, contractual labour does not imply this social field. There labour is split from the social contexts that give it meaning. For Santals, it becomes unnatural, or even supernatural, as in the following story. A bonga makes an old man recruit him as a servant. The bonga has a secret ambition: he wants the *joto*, matted hair, that the man has stolen from him. As he works for the old man, the *joto* produces wealth, becoming a symbol of surplus. The servant bonga works by magic, but one day he leaves the old man's house and the wealth disappears. The bonga stops the game he has staged, but when the surplus is gone, the old man dies.[70] In another version, a Santal steals the *joto* as he believes it will make him rich. The bonga becomes the thief's servant to get it back. Later, the bonga finds the *joto* in the granary of the thief. He places the *joto* on his head and goes, leaving his hair floating in the wind.

Surplus here equals survival. Bongas grant both to humans. The servant bonga may be a metaphor for the working son-in-law, bongas like affines being outsiders. Both play an inferior role but manipulate the rules. Thus, the son-in-law gains his bride. She has powers of reproduction, the only real surplus in Santal society. Sometimes humans secretly worship a bonga to become rich. He steals the crop of rich peasants to distribute to the poor. Santal criticize such worship but also regard the rich as anti-social beings. Sometimes, the bonga of the surplus demands human sacrifice. One story[71] states that a man enriched by a bonga must offer a human sacrifice two years later. The man sacrifices his son but as the bonga wants more victims, he orders his men to kidnap other people's children. Finally, the parents' victims take revenge and kill him.

Work is generally seen as negative. Death is an employer and work entered the world with him. Opposed to it is pleasure and the wholeness of time and space associated with the golden age. Despite missionary efforts, the Santals never adopted a protestant work ethic. Work, in that sense, was a new concept in Europe, too. The strict delimitation between work and leisure is not a feature of pre-industrial Europe: it is the factory with its sonorous calls to work, which introduces the opposition between labour and leisure to most Europeans.

Facing the alternative of becoming Christian or Hindu, the Santals try to recompose elements from the two religions. They tend to privilege Hinduism, with which they have lived as neighbours for centuries. But they refused Hinduization since they do not accept the low status accorded them in the caste system. Christianity is associated with schools, hospitals and labour, Hinduism with cults where the Santals join in only 'to look'.

Some texts written by Santals explain why they could not really become Christians. As to Jesus, who becomes Isor Baba, the Santal solicit his apparition in vain. In some stories, he has thaumaturgic powers and controls a 'Hana Puri', land of the dead, which ressembles to a fault the Kamarupa, land of the *yogis*, which the Santals already know. In one story, Jesus meets a Muslim and tells him he has preached the promise of Paradise for the Santals but they answer: 'You promise like a moneylender without even counting the years!'.[72] In this ironic remark we see the refusal of reckoning time, whether relating to finance or commerce in souls. The Santal parody the moneylender and refuse linear time, associated with work. In myths of death, Santal are more fascinated by the Hindu idea of reincarnation than by Christian anxiety about the last judgement.

The Santals know about *yogis* and appreciate stories of how to obtain supernatural powers. Such power was the only means available to fight Christians and their art of persuasion. The *yogis*, mostly Shaiva, were astute, with supernatural knowledge, control of magic, and bestowed fertility on women. But in Santal folktales, they never forget their services and return for payment. In one tale, Jhades Yogi gives a fruit to a barren queen who becomes pregnant on eating it. She is happy to give birth to twins. But later the *yogi* returns, taking the younger boy as his disciple. He learns many tricks but wants the knowledge of the *yogi*, which lies in the soul of the ascetic. He learns from birds that the *yogi* has hidden his soul inside a small bird living on a certain island. Overcoming all sorts of obstacles, the boy finds the bird and, twisting its neck, releases the soul. He then kills the *yogi*, but as he runs away, the *yogi's* head runs after him, spitting fire like an ojha.[73] The boy's voyage symbolizes the quest for supernatural powers, a theme so recurrent that Assam and Kamrup, the land of the *yogis*, becomes a magical and dangerous land of death. In Santal myth, Shiva is the father of the first ojha, Kamru Guru. The goddesses Durga and Manasa are his younger sisters. Manasa revealed the *mantars* to the first ojha. Through Kamru, there is continuity for the Santal between the powers and knowledge of ojha and yogi.

The drift towards Hinduization was balanced by a revival of the tribal ethos. The coming of new exploiters wrought for the Santals a nostalgia for their golden age, which probably gave its symbolical thrust to the Kherwar movement. As tribals partly deprived of their lands they needed to legitimate their right to territory, so they anointed Bhagrit as their king.

## NOTES

1. Anti-social elements are suspected of secretly worshipping 'thief bongas' who steal grain from other villagers' threshing-floors to give to their devotees.
2. In October/November: coincides roughly with the Hindu Dussehra.
3. After climbing the 'gossamer's threads' woven by the first gurus between earth and sky they reach the sun's door and are dismembered and reassembled by their guru, as an initiatory step.
4. Bodding (1986:124) derives Kamru from Kamarup in Assam, as Carrin was also told in Orissa in 1978. This does not imply that the ancestors were there but rather that Santals have heard tales about the land of Kamarup.
5. Sometimes, an ojha's hair becomes matted like that of a Shaiva ascetic when inspired by his tutelary deities.
6. *Mantar.*
7. *Jharni*, from *jhar*, to blow. For an analysis of *mantar* and *jharni* see Carrin-Bouez 1992 and forthcoming.
8. The invocation may describe the evil deeds of the spirit and his abode, The ojha first alludes to the covetousness and desire of the spirit for blood and, in a second invocation, tries to negotiate with the spirit threatening further action if he does not cease to torment the patient.

9. To catch the spirit the ojha sometimes puts a red cloth with sweets in a pot and when the bonga manifests his presence the ojha gets possessed and closes the pot.
10. *Yantra*.
11. Though men, too, have a *roa* they are less vulnerable since they are closer to the *ji*, the other vital force which dwells in the bones and is highly positive.
12. *Dain bonga.*
13. Jörgensen rightly stresses that no Santal council had this kind of authority, but accepts that the influence of the *jan gurus* had diminished seriously in the district (1920: 123).
14. Skrefsrud to Hertel, 09.10.1879.
15. The village lover is often a lasting romantic alternative to the spouse.
16. Forest songs are not allowed to be sung in the village. It is said that they are composed by divorced women, still longing for sex—a somewhat macho construction.
17. This conference was held at Ebenezer, 13 October 1875. Representatives came from the CMS, the Scottish Free Church Mission, and the Baptists from Midnapur (Nyhagen 1990, I: 274).
18. In his answer to Risley's ethnological questionnaire.
19. Members of the Jharkhand party, representing tribal and subaltern interests.
20. Skrefsrud to Hertel, 23.01.1880.
21. He refers here to the Norwegian Jul (Yule in English), a great occasion for drinking and dancing well into the nineteenth century.
22. The document we have refers to 240 questions but shows only Skrefsrud's answers.
23. For further discussion of human sacrifice among the Santals, see Carrin 2005.
24. In nineteenth century England, the best frequented Church festivals were those that coincided with older, agricultural rituals.
25. *Panicum rubateum,* L.
26. For British and Missionary views of this festival, see Oddie 1995.
27. A Scottish Free Church missionary active from 1874 and author of the first *Santal-English Dictionary*.
28. For the Mundas, the god appears as Sin Bonga, sin being a word for daylight.
29. Some narratives added to the myth explain how different plants are used by humans. Thus *dubi* grass is used by Santals to settle cattle deals. The seller gives some sprigs of the grass to the buyer.
30. Letter from Skrefsrud to J. Boxwell, 30.03.1876; letter from Skrefsrud to Oplandenes Avis, same date; *Annual Report of 1875-6*: 7-9. All cited by Nyhagen, 1990, I: 277.

31. Jörgensen (1920: 102-3) seems to imply a link between the closing of the drink shops and increasing resistance, but he does not say so explicitly.
32. Skrefsrud to W. Smith, 05.06.1875.
33. The name designates the Santals and is linked to their golden age.
34. G.N. Barlow to the Secretary, Govt. of Bengal, 07.10.1874 (BJP 1874, vol. 255).
35. J.N. Boxwell to the Commissioner, Santal Parganas, 01.10.1874 (BJP 1874, vol. 255).
36. A school for poor English and Anglo-Indian boys.
37. The CMS missionaries called it Santalia, as opposed to the Santalistan of the Scandinavians.
38. It is not clear whether Stark was entirely European. His 'father' died in 1830 and so cannot have been his genitor (Moorat 1925: 1-2). The reticence with which Stark was treated would be easy to explain if he was Anglo-Indian, as Nyhagen in fact states. So would the tone of his daughter's writing. Mary Moorat's second husband, the Lieutenant G. Sircar, was certainly Indian or Anglo-Indian.
39. His daughter explains that the new headmaster, Sims, brought a number of new teachers out from England.
40. The magistrate's office—from which the famine aid was also administered.
41. Moorat is wrong here: the Bhagalpur Commissioner in 1874 was G.N. Barlow. The story, too, may be family myth, for on 02.09.74, Stark wrote to Barlow about Bhagrit's enthronement (BJP 1874, vol. 255, cited by Nyhagen 1970, I: 284).
42. The magistrate at Godda.
43. In the *Friend of India*, 08.11.1880.
44. *Babajiu ko Reak' Katha*, Santal Manuscripts 1448 Y. A long text written by Sagram Murmu [See Andersen, Carrin and Soren (forthcoming)].
45. H.P. Börresen to G.N. Barlow, 02.09.1874.
46. Skrefsrud to J.N. Boxwell, 29.02.1876.
47. Skrefsrud 1881: 35.
48. Ibid.
49. Oldham to the Commissioner, Bhagalpur, 01.02.1881 (BJP 1881, vol. 1647).
50. This probably refers to Jadu, Bhagrit's brother.
51. Skrefsrud to Graham, 29.12.80, published in Graham 1881: 14.
52. Börresen to Rudin, 24.11. 81. He may be referring to Dhunu.
53. The indecent rumour, according to Skrefsrud, was that the purpose of the census was to put marks on the breasts and private parts of every Santal woman.
54. Skrefsrud to Smith, Ebenezer 08.02.81. Copybook, Dumka. 'Only one

meeting 'he says '. . . has been sufficient to expel the above rumours and thus preserve perfect peace'.

55. W. Rattray to the Deputy Commissioner, Santal Parganas, 14.12.1880. (BJP 1881, vol. 1647).
56. W.B. Oldham to the Commissioner, Bhagalpur, 29.01.1881 (BJP 1881, vol. 1647).
57. The British had invaded Afghanistan and occupied Kabul in 1878 and again in 1879.
58. Skrefsrud to the Deputy Commissioner, Santal Parganas, 14.03.1892.
59. *Dahkwala*, 1883: 244-5. Also *Santalen* 1883: 147; Börresen to Graham, 04.09.1883.
60. *The Brahman and the Vulture.*
61. Bodding 1925-9, vol. III: 88-95.
62. Santal Archives, 1448 D. 0152.
63. In his answers to the Ethnological Questionnaire, 1877.
64. *Corok'puja.*
65. Man (1867) saw a Hansdak engaged in hook-swinging. Carrin observed the ritual in Mayurbhanj, 1978, where Santal devotees tried to get rain: it worked. Archer, too, notes that Santals participate in the hook-swinging (1974: 133).
66. In his answers to the Ethnological Questionnaire, 1877.
67. See Carrin, forthcoming b.
68. This theme is also found in the myths recorded by Elwin among the Baiga of central India (1939).
69. *Hana Puri Reak' Katha*, Santal Manuscripts, 1686, file II, 1964.
70. *Bonga do hor thene gutilen rean*, Santal Manuscripts, 1451, 1577.
71. Stories of this kind are common. One such story is in Santal Manuscripts, 1448, 0116.
72. This story was told by one of Carrin's informants in Orissa.
73. Bodding 1927-29, vol. III, 47-83.

# 7

# A Christian Santal Community

## PROTEST AND PUNISHMENT

Since 1874, when Börresen dispensed with the Managing Committee, some two thousand baptisms took place until 1878, and then two and a half to three thousand annually from 1878 to 1882.[1] The numbers seemed incredible in those days.

The Danish recruit, Berg, baptized his first converts on 6 November, 1885.[2] Yet in Haripur, where he was stationed, resistance was strong. The place 'hides all kinds of heathen hearts, both soft and hard.' Thus one day, he meets 'an old heathen of the stone-hard kind, who held that he had never sinned, never had deserved punishment, and would certainly be saved just like the rest of us. He reasoned rather like a European free-thinker, and argued that none of us can know anything about the hereafter. To appeal to his conscience seemed in vain . . . to appeal to God's word is just to get for an answer that 'it is all pure invention'. Berg feels better about his Hindu gardener, who really feels for his religion, and built an altar for Hindu gods in the servants' hut. It certainly embarassed the missionary to find these 'bongas' on his own domain. He made him remove the images, but felt that the young man, hindered only by social pressures, was closer than many others to the truth. He also found two intelligent young men in the village, with whom he talked of matters regarding Europe that would interest them. They even visited the readings of the Elders, but one day they did not come to church. Berg, asking why, learnt that they had prayed in their own homes, 'just as he has taught them'. The missionary asked them to do so, but on a weekday, so they may come to church on Sundays.

But in June 1879,[3] there was opposition, Christians refusing to go to Church or send their children to school. Skrefsrud heard

rumours that the elders gave us six rupees and that we kept some of the money. The Christians felt they were feeding us by sending their children to school—I found that the Christians who love Mammon have invented this. They are now in a terrible condition as I have asked them to prove this in Council, and that (if they are right) I and Börresen will go to prison for it, and back to Europe with shame. Or, if they cannot prove it, they should themselves go to jail, like people who have fallen upon the flock like gaping wolves and strewn the poison—among all the Christians. Already the Christians have hurried back to the churches and the parents are again eager to send their children to school. This has been an insurrection, and needed a strong hand.

The Christians, he said, felt the accusations had done harm, and some friendly heathen chiefs 'said that not even the heathen will say such things about their benefactors. How much less should the Christians do it!' He was not sure how far to take the case: 'it must be done in such a way that everybody realizes it has been a terrible lie'. The missionaries were awakened from their illusions, but 'the heathen have again had a chance to defend us and show the respect and confidence they have in us, which cannot fail to bear fruit in the long run.'

The opposition abated,[4] and the Church was again full. The same 'sickness' of not going to church had been present in Asambani, 'but when they heard about our strict counter-measures . . . I hear from Jensen that it has got better there too. . . . The Christians are reporting against each other. Nothing serious. I may therefore suppose there is nothing. Too little eagerness to come to the house of the Lord is the most important'. Yet in his 'complete report' on the insurrection,[5] Skrefsrud made a series of judgements of Santal character, which perhaps reflect his disappointment with his chosen people:

1. First, I have to say that the Santals are highly impulsive people. They are sticking together like sheep and lack individuality. 2. The Santals are afraid of loving people as they are not yet driven by principle but by impulses. Their sense of freedom is always based on licence. 3. The Santals are gullible so they tend to believe rumours without proper reason, especially if these seem to fit their natural and acquired tendencies. 4. The Santals do not think of tomorrow and cannot see the use of whatever gives no fruit today. 5. The Santals in their ignorance and lack of sense are extremely stubborn so that the clarity of conviction itself becomes dark for them. 6. The Santals let themselves be ruled by their women, who could be better than they are.

Skrefsrud gives some reasons for the new pessimism:

some elders . . . heard that Hindus who are travelling, presenting the word of god, get twelve to fifteen rupees a month, and by their false nature they could not see why they should not get the same. . . . Their fantasy soon helped them to the conclusion that monthly wages must be equal for preachers of all religions, even if they are of different quality. This was soon seen as reality. 'Such and such an amount of money (has been given) for us, the elders and the Christians. Börresen and Skrefsrud are taking it.' The missionaries were greedy; 'would they keep our children in school without getting some advantage from it? Why should we feed such people? Why should we let our children remain in school? Let us take them out.'

'Among a people like the Santals, who make an insurrection every fifty years, this was of the greatest danger to the Mission, and once Börresen came back deeply concerned from a council of elders. As he had to go to Dumka, it fell upon me to deal with the case . . . I first called the three elders separately. I demanded, according to Santal custom, that they should either tell me from where they had (the information), or prove their allegations. Their statements conflicted with each other as one did not know what the other had said. . . . None of them could prove the truth of what he had sown in the community. Then, I called a general meeting where I let the elders inspect the accounts. Then, the Council corrected them and they had to take back what they had said and . . . write their confession in the protocol. Then, I suggested they let their children go back to school and pay the fees . . . And I stressed our efforts among them, and gathered the Church meeting, and it was decided that every Christian should send his children to school, which was written down and signed. Then, the elders were suspended and have not yet been readmitted by the community. (They) . . . had in the Santal way to ask forgiveness of the villagers and give them a meal. Those responsible for the insurrection will be prevented from partaking of the Lord's supper.

This report tells us more about punitive measures than the elders' views, but there is a sense of equity offended by the missionaries who seem to enrich themselves at the cost of the Santals. The demand for equal pay points to a political consciousness rather like that of nascent union movements, with a desire for equality with Hindus and, to an extent, even with the Sahebs.

Yet Skrefsrud feels he can control the situation.

'I am in many things, for I am not only preaching the Word of God, but also I am the first in social and other affairs among the Santals. Since I am working to improve the condition of the Santal people, I have ample enemies but deep marks are left, that not even time will efface. I put my fingers into everything that may bring down the bongas and raise Thakur in every consciousness, and in all that can raise the Santals to a cultured people, since they have a big heart and warm feelings. But I can assure you I have enough to do here. The Santals are a stubborn race, in the fullest sense of the word, and one must both pull and push to get them where one wants. And even then, it is slow work.[6]

The urge to control seems, with Skrefsrud, to take precedence over other goals. The dynamics of the missionary encounter seem to produce results beyond what the missionaries are capable of turning to their own benefit.

In 1880, Skrefsrud returns to the land question.[7]

> Today an old man . . . asked me to help him to get back the lands that he has given to a money-lender as he had signed a document by which the money-lender got the land. The money-lender told me that the magistrate had nothing to do with it. I told him that his land was lost for ever and . . . that it could be even worse if he did not come in time and take counsel from the great advocate John. He has suffered from the money-lender. If he had spoken to the magistrate beforehand the money-lender would not have fooled him.

Skrefsrud's point is moral. His reforms, seen by some as an effort to protect Santals against encroachment (Hodne 1966), had left the peasant with new and frightening responsibilities. Private property rendered the Santal peasant master of his own fate, though not yet imbued with the spirit of capitalism. Skrefsrud pursued his reform, yet wanted to 'protect' the Santals. His memoir on customary law had been essential to the land reform George Campbell introduced in 1872 (Hodne 1966, Carrin 1996a). But it was not as beneficial as they thought. When R. Carstairs became Commissioner of the Santal Parganas in 1886, he found that it had led to large-scale transfer of land to non-tribal people. More than 40,000 such transactions had been made, mostly to merchants and moneylenders, and dispossession was a pressing problem. Carstairs introduced a ban on transfer of land to other 'races', which became law under Sir Andrew Frazer in 1907 (Nyhagen 1990, II: 232).[8] But only the Bengal Tenancy Act of 1910 gave the Santals some protection against encroachment.

## THE ROLE OF SANTALS IN THEIR CHURCH

From the start the missionaries were thinking about the indigenization of the Church. Still, from the 1880s, we see a gradual loss of control, not only by Skrefsrud and Börresen, but also by the Santals. The first Church organization was rudimentary. Till 1876, when Siram and Birju were ordained, the term pastor was used for leaders of congregations, without any ordination. Pastors and elders played an important role, preaching from village to village, dealing with daily problems, and guiding the converts' religious lives. They were given considerable freedom to act on their own initiative, and were much less subject to discipline than what Liebau (2003) describes for the Tranquebar mission a century earlier.

New stations were founded. Asambani, 13 miles from Ebenezer, was in the charge of Jensen, the Danish missionary, from 1878 to 1881. When Jensen, sick, returned to Europe, he was replaced by the Santal Suna. The Annual Report of 1881-2 mentions seven stations, of which only Ebenezer, their main base, was led by a European, Börresen; all the others had a Santal as the head. Even if Skrefsrud and Caroline were absent that year, the numbers are telling. The confidence of the missionaries in their Santal collaborators is shown by the case of pastor Surju, who decided on his own to move his station from its humid location to a hill nearby. Börresen and Skrefsrud performed the early baptisms, but from 1880 more and more conversions were obtained by Santal pastors and baptism was performed by them. Börresen stresses[9] their importance: 'If we now had more Europeans, I would not know what to do with them . . . I am absolutely certain that we should count on only a very restricted number of Europeans, and that we should raise the Santals to their task, as we have already done and are still doing. We should be their teachers, advisers and tutors, but the Santals should be converted by the Santals, so that as a Nation they can hear the Word of God from the mouth of their own people.'

Several letters show the responsibilities of the Santal co-workers. 'Since I was myself completely snowed under by work', says Börresen,[10] 'Surjo . . . baptized the eleven Heathens and so has got a new branch to look after. They live some fourteen miles to the south of here, so every Saturday one of the Elders goes to stay with them on Sunday and preach for them, and he comes back on Monday. The Elders here in Nankar take turns in this task, which they see as their duty.'

But there was already nostalgia for the earlier years. Hatia died in 1882. 'When we gather the Elders for council', comments Börresen, 'we see numbers of dear faces among them, who, like Hatia, have dedicated themselves wholly to the Lord'. Yet, these men were now old, and 'we doubt very much that we may again have such powerful witnesses of the Lord'.[11]

A community of Christian Santals was indeed being created, but was not invested with socialist, egalitarian values, as we find among the Catholic Mundas.[12] Mutual help—digging a canal or building a house—must be secured from Christians. Traditionally, village co-operation implied drinking and joking together, activities the Mission frowned upon. Archer notes in the 1930s[13] that while Catholics allowed drinking and dancing at Christmas, the CMS banned public drinking, but accepted the 'more decorous types of tribal dances' (1984: 701).

Börresen describes[14] how, as chairman of the local charity committee, he wishes he had more money, as poor widows are numerous. Contributions are made during the service, and people give as much or little as they want. The pupils have no money, so they 'save a little of their rice each week and bring it to church on Sunday—and this helps quite a bit. But only such are helped as are unable to work, and have nobody to look after them, children, that is, who can take care of their elders.' Aid is given to none able to help themselves: and the Mission as such spends no money on the poor. In this the Scandinavians are no different from their Evangelical counterparts in Britain and elsewhere (Bebbington 1989: 120).

The service at Benagaria had been announced by drums, in Santal fashion—often cited as an example of the Mission's openness to Santal custom. The initiative to replace the drums with a bell came not from the missionaries, but from their Danish supporters.[15] A committee was formed on Caroline's birthday[16] to provide the Benagaria church with a font. But the contributions—Hertel stresses those from 'occupied' South Jutland—by far exceeded expectations, and so it was decided to offer a bell, which was duly sent, and should have arrived by Christmas 1883—except that it was lost in a Calcutta warehouse and only found in the spring. The bell, no doubt, was given with the best intentions. But it may also stand symbolically for the gradual increase of European customs that was just beginning to be felt in the Church.

## THE VILLAGE SCHOOLS

From about 1880 the Deputy Commissioner at Dumka, W.B. Oldham, tried to take up the old idea of schools run and partly financed by the Santals themselves, using the *jog-manjhis* as teachers. But the government wanted Hindi or Bengali as the language of instruction,[17] and opened the first schools for Santals in 1881 (McAlpin 1909) .

It seems that the educational work of the Mission was declining at this time. In 1880 there were 32 village schools, by 1881 only 28 (Jörgensen 1920: 128). Börresen claims they have about one hundred schools, with some 3,000 students, by the time Skrefsrud returned from Europe (Hodne 1966: 310). The government, urged by Oldham, now supported missionary schools with grants-in-aid, and Börresen was quick to take advantage of them. So did the Scottish

Free Church missionaries, who increased their village schools from 4 to 23. But if close to a hundred schools got started, it is doubtful whether they really worked. Börresen himself could not inspect them, and sent the elders, who tried their best, taking care of religious instruction and implementing a certain measure of control. It cannot have been very effective. Börresen did not realize 'the impossibility of procuring competent teachers' (Hodne 1966: 310). This may be why it was decided to close some schools in March 1886. Secular schools were left to the government, as they were uneconomic (Nyhagen 1990, II: 136-7), and ambulatory schools were started to visit the Christians and teach their children.[18] Still, the Annual General Report for Bhagalpore Division, 1886-7, claims that more than one hundred village schools were opened in the Damin through Oldham's scheme, and many may have been schools Börresen had started, and now ceded to the government.

When Carstairs became Deputy Commissioner in 1886, he found some 700 schools in the district, most teaching in Hindi or Bengali. The Santals, if present at all, were often relegated to a corner where they tried to pick up whatever they could without any help (Nyhagen 1990, II: 234; Carstairs 1912: 291-2). The IHM and the CMS were teaching in Santali, but their schools were few. Carstairs wanted Santali as the language of education, with the Roman alphabet, as Skrefsrud had used it, and Oldham had proposed for the Jubdi area in 1882.[19] Carstairs wanted to use it in all schools meant for Santals, and this was accepted in 1888.[20] The preparation of school books and other materials was left to the missionaries. These reforms brought some improvement, but progress was slow, well into the twentieth century (Nyhagen 1990, II: 234-5).

## CHRISTIAN MARRIAGE

In 1873 Skrefsrud got a licence to perform marriages between converts. He allowed marriages with non-Christians, but could not avoid conflicts between the communities and within such mixed marriages. Skrefsrud bothers little about Santal marriage rules, and Christians seem to be married by the missionaries without taking them into account. We do not know whether Christians followed the preference for marrying the cross-cousin,[21] but agnatic ties were little affected.[22] Adoption was problematic as it involved placing the child under the protection of his adoptive father's bonga. A Christian adopting a child from another clan must declare it at the *kulhi durup*. A heathen child must be baptized, and at baptism the clan could be changed. If a Christian girl could not show the father of her child, a husband was found for her as for a heathen girl (Archer 1984: 703).

A Christian could not take a second wife, except when the first one left him. The Scandinavians then allowed remarriage by the 'innocent' party. Converted women returning to their heathen family were readmitted by a communal meal.[23] Church weddings were not marriages from a traditional point of view, since they excluded the rituals held in the bridegroom's and bride's houses. In spite of Skrefsrud's tolerance of marriage between Christians and Heathens, Archer (1984) is categorical some generations later: the non-Christian must convert before marriage. The change seems to have been gradual but may be dated to the first decades of the twentieth century.

Marriage between Christian Santals and Hindus are not banned but are abhorrent to Santals. If a boy applies *sindur* to a Christian girl's forehead, he must pay a heavy fine to the girl's father. The most important difference between tribal and Christian law is divorce, since by the Christian Marriage Act (1872) Christians can divorce only by petitioning the Court in Bhagalpur, a heavy procedure for most Santals who must thus stay united for life (Archer 1984: 705). In Skrefsrud's time, too, it was hard for Christians to divorce.

'Some time ago, a young man who has gone to our boy's school was baptized. He was married and lived with his wife many years, when the word of God converted his soul. . . . But his wife . . . did not leave him. After some time, they both went to her family, where the man let his wife stay for some days. Later, when he sent for her, her mother would not let her go, since (her husband) had become a Christian. The man had several meetings with the chiefs of the district. They supported the mother. . . . The man complained to the magistrate . . . and asked to get his wife'. The magistrate sent for the wife and asked her, 'if the man had done anything against her, and she answered he had always been good to her. The magistrate asked if she wanted to join him, and she answered that if he would kill her, she would not go, since he had become a Christian. The magistrate put her in jail. In the evening she was released and asked if she would go to her man, or live in jail'. She went to her husband. Skrefsrud concludes: 'the heathen have again suffered a loss'.

Hertel held that the woman should not be forced to go back, as he supported the freedom of women. Skrefsrud argues[24] for 'equality in social matters between Heathens and Christians, (and) as hundreds of chiefs and councils here have decided to stand on that equality I would not allow that woman to be taught by her mother.' 'Another man asked me', he says later,[25] 'to help him to get back his wife who has gone with another man. I answered him that I had just gone for a similar task for a man whose bride had run away with another man. He said that infidelity was becoming too common in the country and that something should be done. . . . I told him that the rightful bride of Christ has been promised us from the Cross. . . . The Bride is the Church'. Divorce was not a question of freedom for women or men, but involved breaking a bond as solid as that between the Lord and his Church. The Grundtvigian rhetoric cedes to an orthodox, or pietist one.

'A short time ago', Skrefsrud continues, 'we had a great victory over the Heathen. . . . The Borkiari chief's sister was married to a superior chief, while sixty villages under him are becoming baptized. But later, because of his father's anger, he sent her back to her brother.' The Borkiari chief took the superior chief to court, and the latter had to take his wife back, or pay her a pension. The father of the superior chief came to the magistrate when he heard of the judgement. 'Let us live peacefully with these Christians. We will not be able to do anything about them' he said. The father ate and drank with the Borkiari chief, then brought the wife back. 'Thus one of the most important chiefs had to keep his Christian wife'. Others will follow, says Skrefsrud.

All this points to the problem of reaching the women. 'More missionaries are needed to further Christianity.[26] This is very true for the women as they have influence over the men. . . . Mrs. Börresen, he says, is making good workers of her schoolgirls, and teaching Santali[27] to village women 'in order to help them better themselves'. They need a woman from Europe. . .' but she must have character and grace, and this is not found among many'.

## SKREFSRUD AS A LINGUIST

Skrefsrud was an exceptional linguist[28] who contributed greatly to the preservation of the richness of Santali. He started to learn languages in jail. In India, he hired a Cochin rabbi to teach him Hebrew and a pandit from Benares for Sanskrit, studying Persian and Arabic as well to prepare his translation of the scriptures. He soon mastered Santali and developed a special liking for it. From the beginning, Skrefsrud used metaphor when preaching. He hunted with the Santals, and transposed the parables of the Gospels in images from daily life: thus, the wounded bear withdrawing to his lair is likened to those who resist the call of Christ, who, like the hunting priest, has 'brandished the branch', rallying the faithful.

The first Santali grammar had been written by the American Baptist, J. Phillips (1852),[29] but it does not show the complexity of the verbal system. He also wrote a Manual of Santal Mythology, with an appendix on the Mosaic account of the creation and fall.[30] Phillips started by using the Roman alphabet, but pressure from the publishers made him choose Bengali characters for his later publications. Then, Puxley of the CMS published (1868) a Santali vocabulary using the Roman system introduced by Forber and others for Hindustani (Bodding 1932-6, I: 15-19).

Phillips introduced Skrefsrud to the Calcutta School Book Society, and encouraged him to write his own grammar (1873). This remains the best attempt at describing Santali before the coming of structural linguistics. Bodding criticizes the use of the model of an inflectional language to describe an agglutinative one,[31] but employs Skrefsrud's grammatical categories for his translation of folk tales thirty years later. Morgenstierne and Myklebust (1958) note that Skrefsrud was one of the first to use a laryngoscope to classify phonemes. His system of transliteration is still valid, with minor modifications introduced by Bodding (1929-30).

During a Managing Comittee meeting in 1868, it was decided that Skrefsrud should devote much of his time to literary work—Bible translation in particular. On his return from Europe in 1874 he threw himself into this work. In 1874, a printing press was installed at Ebenezer, publishing in Santali.[32] The first hymn book had appeared in 1872. There were only 18 songs, several written by Skrefsrud to popular Santal melodies.[33] In 1876, Skrefsrud had a new book ready, with 43 psalms.[34] It is typical of his efforts that he was not content to translate European hymns, but tried to create Santali Christian poetry. He had also written three small school books. This, and his grammar, was the sum of his literary work to that date (Nyhagen 1990, I: 282). His Bible translation progressed slowly, but he did publish the Gospels and some ritual texts in the *Girja Puthi* in 1885. Next year came Luther's cathechism and a translation of a Bible history by the Norwegian Vogt. Pontoppidan's exegesis and his text of daily readings were projects which came to nought, but Skrefsrud edited a new hymn book in 1886, with 171 songs. School books were another project where results did not come up to expectations. A translation of Aesop's fables was the only concrete result of those years.

Skrefsrud accepted a commission from the government to write a comparative grammar, to include seventeen languages of the Kolarian family.[35] The initiative came, almost certainly, from George Campbell, who wrote about tribal languages himself (1865, 1874). In July 1879, Skrefsrud was conversing with native speakers of Birhor and Munda,[36] and writing on Larka (Ho). We have from his hand a sketch showing his acquintance with Ho, Munda, Kharia, and Bodo. In 1889, he published a short introduction to Bodo, a Tibeto-Burman language. In 1879 he writes,[37] that the Danish linguist, Jacobsen, has asked about his work. He has sent some samples, and comments: 'It is certain that my future should be dedicated to literary work . . . so that others will not have to struggle with the same difficulties. You will receive copies of whatever I publish: 1. My dictionary is going to be published. 2. The comparative grammar of eight Munda languages. 3. The New Testament in Santali, and the Bible History'. He hoped[38] that his comparative grammar would solve the problems of transition between the languages (the way one language changes into another). Implicitly criticizing Risley's work, he says we cannot know from language the race[39] to which the Santals belong.

While Börresen was in Denmark,[40] Skrefsrud wrote six grammars but still had eleven left. 'Nothing has been written on these languages . . . I compare them in one grammar, not only showing their similarities and differences but also accounting for original form and meaning as well as the processes they have gone through, (their) separation and establishing their independence.' His efforts to account at once for the evolution of each language and the coherence of the language family, were close to the limit of what was possible in comparative lingustics then, thirty years before Saussure conceived of structural linguistics. Needless to say, the work was never completed.[41]

In 1903 A. Campbell published the first Santali-English dictionary, 'a handy companion to the traveller'.[42] From his arrival, Skrefsrud had started to collect Santali words. In 1869, he had collected twelve thousand[43] with the gloss in Santali. By 1875 he hoped to have the dictionary printed[44] but that did not come about. The optimism is typical of Skrefsrud, and after 1883 he found little time for this work. But in 1884 he wrote[45] that he had not yet decided whether to put quotations or just the meaning of words. By 1885, when his health forced him to a long stay in Calcutta, he visited the zoological and botanical gardens to check on Santali terms for animals and plants.[46] When he handed over the project to Bodding it had grown to 30,000 words, and became the basis for the latter's dictionary.[47] Bodding used Skrefsrud's notes to develop the applications of each term. He also turned the vocabulary around, making it English—Santali, a task just begun by Skrefsrud. As published, in five volumes, the dictionary has more than 60,000 words. It came out from 1929 to 1935.

## TRADITIONS AND INSTITUTIONS OF THE SANTALS

In 1871, Skrefsrud and his Santal guru, Kolean, worked together on a compendium of tribal tradition, the *Horkoren Mare Hapram ko reak' Katha,* which was published in Santali in 1887. It was to preserve, for the Santals, what would soon, with conversion, be forgotten. Skrefsrud wanted to introduce the book in the mission schools, but Börresen would have nothing of it. There was enough heathendom among the Santals as it was, without teaching it at school! (Nyhagen 1990, II: 128-9).

The *Mare Hapram ko* opens with the 'ancestor's story', Kolean's version of the creation myth. It is not a trivial matter which version is used, and they differ between regions (Bouez and Carrin-Bouez 1974). The story would rarely have been told as a coherent oral text. It is one among several sacred stories of the Santals—such as the *binti*—but Skrefsrud presents it as a parallel to Genesis, a tendency still found among Christian Santals. The creation myth is told at different points in an individual's life cycle, mainly when the child is shaved and when the deceased's flower-bones are taken to the river Damodar. The ancestors' story, as told by Kolean, takes place in primordial time when the earth was under water. Thakur, glossed as the Lord, creates the aquatic beings—crab, crocodile, tortoise and others. Then he forms two birds from his sweat.[48] They lay eggs on the water from which are born a human couple, who are carried by Thakur to a place called Hihiri Pipiri. There, 'they had no clothes, they were both naked; still they felt no shame, and they lived in great peace' (1942: 5). Maran Buru appears, teaching them to brew beer and inducing them to drink. While incest is still central to the story, the siblings declare to Maran Buru the following morning: 'We are awfully ashamed; we are both of us naked; last night, when we were drunk from beer, we did something bad'. Such guilt is absent from the version Carrin collected among non-Christians in north Orissa. In the *Mare Hapram ko*, incest is a step to the discovery of nudity: 'the siblings made a skirt and a loin-cloth from ficus leaves'. The first pair gives birth to seven boys and seven girls who marry and form clans. Then several countries are mentioned, where the ancestors stayed for 'who knows how many years'. But when they reach Khoj Kaman, they become 'very bad' and Thakur is angry: 'Mankind does not listen to my word, therefore I shall make an end of them'. He sends a fire rain but rescues one pair of ancestors who shelter in a cave.

After destroying the world, Thakur stages a new one where the ancestors meet other Munda groups as well as Hindu castes. The narrative moves towards an externalization of the mythic elements, describing in detail the battle of Champa in which the Munda groups confront the Hindus. Then comes the story of Mandho Singh, who wants a Santal wife but nobody will give their daughter to the son of a Hindu. The ancestors fight Mandho but borrow certain Hindu customs such as the use of *sindur* at marriage and cremation.

Kolean describes the rites of passage from postnatal purification to marriage and death, and specifies the various gifts and exchanges. He describes the marriage ceremony at length, but omits the sexual jokes exchanged by affines. He deals with the different forms of marriage, but notes that widowers and divorcées are not appreciated. Polygyny is tolerated, but Kolean stresses the problems between co-wives. As for forcible marriage, the boy should be found, beaten, and made to pay a fine—his behaviour is likened to the uncastrated forest animals, or worse, to malevolent bongas. If a girl cannot name the father of her child, a husband must be 'bought' for her: he will then adopt the child. Kolean stresses the need of adoption to normalize the child's status, but omits that it will have the father's bongas. We get a harmonious picture of husband and wife living together, sharing farm work and daily tasks, pleasure and sorrow, but 'very little is done in the way of punishing children' (1942: 94). The wife's side is thought better, but if the husband dies, the wife and children go to his family. The narrative describes the Santals as a moral community, where marriage is crucial and spouses share responsibilities, and relatives support each other in times of difficulty. Yet the morality emerges as an implicit dialogue between Santal and Christian sensibilities.

Despite solidarity, 'it does not go equally well for all there' (1942: 106). Some have cattle and servants, others must pay their fathers' debts. Kolean seems less egalitarian than modern Santals, and, like the missionaries, justifies poverty as caused by the lack of wisdom and foresight. 'They have no sense, they are foolish and they are also lazy, they have no children either. And their womenfolk waste away all, or they themselves squander all by drinking beer or they cause themselves to be fined on account of transgressions' (1942: 107).

Influenced, no doubt, by Skrefsrud, Kolean praises temperance, hard work and the moral virtue of saving. His vision of work as a daily labourer seems idyllic compared to other testimony from the Santal archives. 'One kind of poor people do not become absolute paupers, because they have no necessary work of their own, they work for wealthy people. Thereby they get their subsistence and people also feel compassion with them' (1942: 108). Compassion, here, seems a Christian template, for Santals are more sociable than moralist.

'They jest together about a thousand matters', says Kolean, but the age has been spoilt, probably 'because we have got much confusion in connection with the bongas', and implicitly he blames polytheism: 'You Europeans have only one bonga. You are very fortunate, because you worship the Thakur who has made us' (1942: 158). Thus, they forget their songs and dances, though he mentions several. In the present age, women do not honour men, sons do not respect fathers, drink causes conflict, and the rage of a woman 'is as when your shoulder blade is shot through with an iron arrowhead' (1942: 173). Formerly, there was no moneylender—today Santals must defend themselves against oppressors.

Kolean discusses the hierarchy of chiefs, but says the 'village headmen have become utterly greedy' (1942: 129). Formerly, Santals were keen to tell the truth; now they lie and even swear falsely. To kidnap children for sacrifice, or to rape women, has become common. He also comments on the recrudescence of witchcraft: 'As to witches, formerly we drove them away after having treated them disgracefully; only now and then have we killed them. . . . The ancestors of old did not call this murder; therefore they did not punish those who beat them to death'. Clearly, Kolean defends Santal ethics, implicitly deploring those who go to the 'smooth verandas', i.e. the courts.

'Sin Bonga is a good bonga, but Thakur is superior. He sees everything' (1942: 132). Christian influence is evident here. While Thakur is the Lord who establishes order in the world, the bongas are unpredictable, reflecting the feats and failures of the ancestors. When Kolean describes the flower festival, he quotes the speech of the possessed boys—each bonga gives his name, and Jaher Era, the lady of the sacred grove, introduces herself with poetic speech, recalling a mythic country of abundance where Santals are conscious of their ties with the bongas (1942: 102). But Thakur is different: 'Here then, Lord Father my Thakur . . . tell us, show us, we are blind, ignorant human beings; when we speak, it stops in our throat, we are choked with the words'. This declaration of human helplessness sounds strange in the Santal context, as does the appeal to an omniscient Thakur. Are we dealing with a reinvention of tradition by Kolean, perhaps under Skrefsrud's influence? Were Christian ideas already finding a place in Santal religion, filling the space left by a lack of theodicy? Such expressions are not found today in regions outside Christian influence, nor have we come across them in the Santal Parganas.

This way of addressing Thakur construes a relationship between God and his devotee which is alien to the bonga world. In the *Mare Hapram ko*, ritual becomes more than sacrifice, producing a new ontology where the devotee seeks more than his reflection in the bonga world. Clearly, *Mare Hapram ko* purports to structure the life-world of growing boys and girls: they should remember the time of the ancestors but also learn to be critical of village dignitaries: thus we learn that formerly the *jog manjhi* kept the youth in strict order but nowadays, they are corrupted, accepting rice-beer to keep silent on transgressions. *Mare Hapram ko* proposes an ontology of the Santal world, but a disenchanted world, where improvement is difficult because of poverty and envy. Kolean presents the Santal as a moral community proud of its traditions and oral literature, but threatened by moral corruption and witchcraft which is 'the great trouble with us Santals'. Today, says Kolean, witchfinders must prove by all means, including secret agents, that they are right. They 'act very deceivingly . . . they hypocritically blacken people and take their money' (1942: 168). Similar criticism is made of possession. Now it is faked: 'The ancestors have said that when those to be possessed are inspired, they become unconscious, they do not remember anything. But nowadays the possessed remember everything'. More explicitly, Kolean explains how one man—Biram—told him he had received excellent beer by pretending to have been possessed. Still, Kolean admits some bongas to be true: they reveal themselves, and cannot be caught. They are the bongas of the sacred grove and they warn the villagers: 'You have done this or that wrong; now observe religious abstinence and do so and so; otherwise it will go bad with you'. Revelation, here, acquires a positive value not present with possession. Kolean seems to imply that Santals expect more from the bongas than they can offer, preparing the way for Christianity to provide the real answer to their religious quest. There is a shift in Kolean's account, from the vanishing past of the ancestors, towards a new conception of a universe centred on Thakur. While Skrefsrud uses the material to 'prove' the original monotheism of the Santals, we can see how the *Mare Hapram ko* introduces a monotheist principle in a polytheist world.

Kolean's voice emerges clearly through the text, more so than Skefsrud's. The relative effacement of the Western subject might seem to make the dialogue into a monologue – if we forget that Skrefsrud's questions and writing frames Kolean's discourse. 'Skrefsrud . . . told me', says Bodding later, 'that the book contains absolutely nothing of his own, the whole being a faithful record of Kolean's words and language' and he adds: 'I cannot, however, help thinking that Skrefsrud had something to do with the arrangement' (Bodding *in* Skrefsrud 1942: 1). Thus the book answers questions posed in western terms, it is part of a 'global interview' (Comaroff & Comaroff 1992: 10). But we may at least situate the protagonists. Skrefsrud's interest was to establish a fixed body of custom for future use, thus reifying Santal culture and masking its diversity. Kolean participated to a large extent in this reification. The process of reinventing Santal tradition is thus clearly visible.

This does not mean that Skrefsrud's questions are innocent of intent. His interest in Santal custom, especially the *rites de passage*, is motivated by his desire to adapt the latter to his plan of conversion, leaving alone, as far as possible, all elements of the indigenous culture that do not contradict Christian values and principles. This ideology, which set Skrefsrud and the mission he created apart from many other missionary enterprises, stems from historically specific ideas rooted in German and Scandinavian romantic thought. The ideology of the Santal mission was built on the idea that the Santals were a 'nation' having the same rights to its own cultural expression as, for example, the Scandinavian peoples. This respect for the indigenous culture avoided some of the cultural collisions that missions created elsewhere, but wrought contradictions in the creation of a Christian community among the Santals.

We now understand better why Skrefsrud wanted the book introduced in school. Far from constituting a repository of heathen tradition, the *Mare Hapram ko* in fact secularizes it and opens it up to critical discourse. It does, in part, for the Santals what the debates of the Bengal Renaissance did to Hindu culture, and like the missionaries taking part in the latter, Skrefsrud must have expected the discourse to turn towards Christianity. The book did, in fact, become part of a critical appraisal of Santal culture, but the missionaries were not alone in benefiting from it. The Kherwars did, as did those who reinvented tradition later. Even today, Santals often refer to the *Mare Hapram ko* to legitimize their interpretation of old customs, implicitly accepting its criticisms. As a modern informant puts it: 'Bongaism is not a moral religion'.

We do not know how consciously Skrefsrud had planned this, but he certainly forged the inner criticism that emerges in its description of traditional religion.

## TRANSLATING THE NEW TESTAMENT

Skrefsrud's linguistic efforts were meant to prepare him for the translation of the scriptures. He notes the difficulty of determining the true meaning of Santal words, alluding to Christian notions such as baptism or grace.[49] Central, of course, was the name for 'God' in Santali. The AFBM used 'Ishwara', but for Hindus it meant 'Shiva'. The CMS and the Scottish Free Church Mission used 'Chando', also of Sanskrit origin, which in Santali means both sun and moon. Gradually, they came to prefer 'Isor', the term for Jesus. In 1872,[50] Skrefsrud urged all missionaries to translate God by Thakur. This, too, is a Hindi loan word: no Santal word begins with a cerebral *th*. Yet Skrefsrud maintains that the word is of Kolarian origin.

Skrefsrud claimed to have started translating the New Testament in 1871, but this translation was never published. Börresen was sceptical of the progress of Skrefsrud's work. The CMS missionary, Cole, however, translated the four Gospels and printed them in 1877, followed by the Acts in 1879. In 1880, the Auxiliary Bible Society proposed a conference of Santal missionaries to discuss a version of the New Testament acceptable to all. Skrefsrud refused to attend: he doubted the proficiency of the others in Santali. Thus he wrote to Stark of the CMS, that 'neither the Bethel mission nor the missionaries of the SFCM[51] were competent to discuss theological terms of importance for the translation' (Hodne 1966: 225). 'Such production', he says of Cole's translation, 'ought not to go under the name of God's word';[52] it could not pass 'even the lowest standard of criticism'.[53] This made collaboration impossible. The idea of a conference was dropped, and a committee was formed by the CMS missionaries with Cole as chief translator.

Skrefsrud proposed that he and Stark should come to Calcutta together to discuss the matter with Wilkins, the secretary of the Auxiliary Bible Society. Stark was not seen as erudite, though he knew Santali, and the proposal must have surprised many, including Stark himself. Nyhagen feels he was chosen for other reasons: Skrefsrud felt he could dominate Stark, who was Anglo-Indian[54] (1990, II: 381), and whose status was low. The reference to a low-status CMS man was perhaps meant to infuriate Cole, whose incompetence was thus more than hinted at. But Skrefsrud may have liked and respected Stark, a true fieldworker, respected by the Santals, and of humble origin like himself. Anyway, Stark turned down Skrefsrud's offer, like his CMS superiors and probably out of a sense of loyalty to them.

Other missionaries seemed better qualified. Cole had already published translations,[55] and though Skrefsrud spoke scathingly of them, Börresen used them.[56] Another missionary in whom the CMS had great hopes was John Blaich from Württemberg, who had been educated by the Basel Mission. He and N. Roth had started an independent mission in Assam, helped by Graham and financed from Britain, when the CMS refused their services. But in 1876 he was recruited and put to work among the Santals. He learnt the language thoroughly: 'I venture to say that in another year or two no one (including the much boasted Skrefsrud) will be so thoroughly acquainted with Santali' wrote Storrs in 1878.[57] Then there was Andrew Campbell, the Scottish Free Church Missionary, who had come to the CMS to head their grain bank for the Santals in 1872.[58]

He not only knew Santali but had an intimate knowledge of Santal customs. Skrefsrud knew Campbell, but they did not always agree, and Campbell sometimes seems to have been put off by Skrefsrud's arrogance (Nyhagen 1990, II: 382).

During his visit to London in 1881, Skrefsrud met the Editorial Sub-Committee of the British and Foreign Bible Society, and criticized strongly existing translations. He offered his own translation of the New Testament, which, he said, was practically complete. The BFBS quickly ordered Calcutta to stop all translation work and to wait for Skrefsrud's manuscript. But no manuscript came. At first, Skrefsrud excused himself, saying the work must await his return to India, but in January, 1884, the BFBS requested Calcutta 'to ask Skrefsrud to fulfil his promise and submit his translation to a joint revision committee'[59] (Hodne 1966: 226). It was formed, with J.L. Phillips—son of the author of the first Santali grammar—as convenor, and with Skrefsrud, Campbell and a couple of CMS missionaries, as well as Haegert and Cornelius.

In June 1884 it was noted[60] that Skrefsrud 'had not replied to several communications made to him by Dr. Phillips, James Brown, and the Secretary of the Bible Society'. The possibility of his serving on a committee or of submitting his translation was ruled out. Perhaps the committee was not acceptable to Skrefsrud'—Hodne hints that Haegert and Cornelius, both sacked from the IHM, were at issue here. The committee was reorganized, with Cole as chief translator. He found the work too slow, however, so in 1887 he proposed to retain his own translations, and add the parts translated by the committee. Most of this version had been published by 1899 (Hodne 1966: 227-8).

Meanwhile, Skrefsrud handed over his work to Bodding. The Benagaria New Testament came out in 1906, and from then on the two versions existed side by side, the CMS using Cole's version and the IHM and the Scots using the one by Bodding and Skrefsrud. In 1966, as Hodne wrote, a common version was finally in press (ibid.: 228).

## THE GIRL'S SCHOOL: MOULDING CHRISTIAN WIVES

While Skrefsrud and Börresen's letters reflect the polemics of missionary debate, Caroline's letters are more matter-of-fact, as when she describes the letters she has received from her girls while in

Europe.[61] One tells of a trip they made with Börresen 'to a place where he was baptizing a number of Santals. It was so lovely there in the mountains . . . but there were still so many Heathens, that we were quite sad, and with one heart and soul we cry, praying to God, that he will soon convert them all.'

Malti, the daughter of Naran, the village chief, had just been married to a boy at the school. This seems to be another marriage arranged by Caroline to produce a couple dedicated to mission work. Malti wrote: 'Everything is well with your Sunday Schools. The women are so nice in coming regularly and precisely and, O, how we look forward to your coming back, and to what you will be saying, when you see how much they have learnt by heart, but we long so much for the day when we shall see your faces again. That I went back to the School, since Anpi is so ill . . . you (already) know. Everything is going well at the school, even the new pupils listen to my voice, and so, do not be anxious . . . all is well'. 'My husband' continues Mrs. Börresen, says what a pleasure it was to him, when Malti said she would return to the School . . . 'That is the right spirit', says Börresen. 'She doesn't ask will I get anything for it? . . . But she sees that there is a need, and so she comes. . . . It is as if the responsibility for the school and everything has become so established with the older girls, that they all stand guard to see that nothing happens.' 'It may now be seen', says Caroline, 'what my grown-up girls are made of. The responsibility. . . brings forth the strength that is in them, and promises well for the future'. This sense of responsibility cannot be simply the result of the iron discipline that ruled Mrs. Börresen's school. Somehow, Malti, like Anpi or Sona, seem to have internalized the Mission's project as her own.

Caroline praises her husband, who has opened several Sunday schools for girls in the villages. 'How he finds the time to think of everything, I cannot understand. When I once told Skrefsrud of my astonishment, he answered: 'God is doing that to teach us that he needs neither you or me as long as he has Papa!'. Though Skrefsrud may criticize Börresen's intellectual capacities, he seems ever ready to acknowledge his spiritual superiority.

## MARRIAGE CEREMONIES AMONG THE CHRISTIANS

In August 1879,[62] Skrefsrud told Hertel that Mrs. Börresen's oldest pupil was marrying. This must be Anpi, who was born in Manbhum in the early 1860s. Her grandfather lived in Nankar, so she came there with her parents. She ran away from home, to be taken in by Mrs. Börresen's school. She was bright, and became one of the school's best-loved pupils. When she married a catechist of Dumka in 1879, he was moved to Benagaria, so that Anpi could continue to help run the school. She was active in the congregation until she died in 1943, and was one of the converts best known to the Scandinavian audience. She corresponded with Paulsen in Norway and with the Danish dowager queen, Caroline Amalie. In 1879 Anpi sent the Queen a pair of slippers and a quilt, made by herself and the other schoolgirls, as a Christmas present. The Queen gave Anpi a cross of gold inlaid with precious stones, which Caroline, Bodding says, bought from Anpi for the royal sum of Rs. 20. (Nyhagen 1990, II: 135-6). Clearly, Caroline wanted to keep to the established order, with herself in control of links to Western dignitaries.

Sona, Anpi's close friend, remained at school until she married in 1881, the day before Skrefsrud and Caroline left for Europe. Gulu Murmu, her husband, was the son of Suna, also called Bokta,[63] since he had taken part in the hook-swinging festival. He lived in Birbhum. With his parents Gulu was baptized in 1874. Gulu was the eldest of three brothers, who all went to the school, and 'learnt as much as one could learn at that time in Benagaria'—says Bodding, critical of the pioneers' work (Bodding 1919: 20).

Sona's marriage was 'held in the usual Santal way', says Bodding. Since Gulu's parents were dead, Nimai 'doctor'[64] represented his family. 'But he made the mistake of uniting two from the same tribe'.[65] Both Gulu and Sona were from the Murmu clan. 'Neither Gulu nor Sona knew they were from the same tribe, before they were married. It has not been easy for them' (1919: 21). This is intriguing to the anthropologist. Was it really possible for Gulu and Sona not to know their respective clans? Was this lack of basic Santal knowledge due to their schooling? Or should it be explained by the fact that they were, practically speaking, orphans? Was Sona seen as adopted by Anpi Marandi, and no longer a Murmu (Anpi speaks of her like a daughter)? Anyhow, what was obvious to Bodding forty years later was apparently not so to an ojha at the time, since the marriage was allowed.

Gulu was about twenty-four when he married. He worked occasionally in the printing press, but also taught in one of the village schools. They stayed in Benagaria but then Gulu went to Assam with Moltke, head of the colony, to serve chiefly on hunting expeditions. While Gulu was in Assam, Sona worked at the girl's school. But when he returned, Börresen sent them to Chondorpura, Gulu as catechist and Sona as teacher. They were effectively in charge of the station, except for a short while when 'another European was staying there'.[66] When Bunkholdt took over in 1886, Gulu and Sona moved to Mohulpahari, where Sona continued her school work.

On Saturday, 17 October 1885, a young man from 'a blessed family'[67] married a girl from Mrs. Börresen's school. The schoolboys were free on Friday to gather leaves and vegetables in the forest, while the girls made plates and cups from the leaves. On Sunday, teachers and boys decorated the church. Friday night they slaughtered, for about four hundred were to be fed—two hundred scholars, and all the women from the Sunday schools, since the bride had been teaching there. It was a send-off party too, as the couple was going to Assam. The meal was held after the ceremony, but all did not eat together. The women ate in the girl's school yard—surrounded by high walls—except the bride who joined her husband at the head of the dignitaries. The boys ate with the male visitors at the boys' school. This must have taken care of any tendency to flirting and jokes between the sexes, making the wedding most unlike a traditional Santal marriage, where the couple's parents joke and allude to their children's future sexual acts. The dual structure of the traditional marriage, husband's and wife's clans, was replaced by a hierarchical representation of the Christian community centered on the schools. It is striking how many marriages Mrs. Börresen arranged between orphans or other youth cut off from their families, creating couples who owed everything to the Mission rather than to their Santal identity and clan.

## LETTERS FROM SANTALS

In the 1880s a number of Santal Christians, urged by the missionaries, wrote letters to friends of the Mission in Europe. Some were published in *Dahkwala*, *Santalen* and *Johar*. They give an impression of the conditions in Santal country as seen by the Christians, though they were clearly influenced by what the missionaries wanted them to write. The missionaries want their supporters to know at least some converts as individuals, a concern also manifest in the use of photography. As Börresen took Siram to Assam in 1885 to relieve

Surju, the resident pastor there, they made a detour to Calcutta to take Siram's picture with his family. It took three days to do so, but 'some of the friends want them (the photographs), and Dr. Graham in particular'.[68]

One of the first of these letters was sent from Benagaria in 1881 and published in the first number of *Dahkwala*. It is signed Sinjo[69] and was sent to Helvig. Sinjo says she is learning crotchet, and talks of her garden, full of beans, jhinga fruit and pumpkins, as well as flowers. Some days before, wild elephants went through three villages, destroying a house. She describes the wildlife, insisting on the presence of tigers, who 'take away animals and even kill the shepherd, while the jackals howl in the night'.

Moki sent a letter in 1882 to Kate, Börresen's daughter, then at school in Germany, reminding her that they had met when Kate was a child. She talks of Börresen's birthday, when he had a headache. Another letter from Moki, sixteen that year, was to Mama, whom she hoped to see at Christmas. 'Papa is alone with his Santal children'. They prayed for Mama to join them. Moki also wrote to Rose, one of Moltke's sisters, in 1883. The letter is typical: 'I was very glad to get a greeting from you. You ask me how are the girls. They are all well, and we are very glad and praising God, that he will protect us. Your big brother came here from Assam. He was not well, but now he is better. We are going to Dumka, and your brother is going with us to hunt. Dear Rose, we have travelled in the country for one month. We were very happy. We brought the Word of God to many Heathen. Thank God there was no sickness. We pray for all of you not to forget to pray for us'. Anpi also wrote three short letters to Rose, and one to Jana (1883), another of the Moltke girls.

Anpi also describes these tours:[70] 'We were telling God's Word to the Heathen, they were listening gladly and we hope many will convert. I was with Mama in Dumka in 1880 to tell God's Word . . . There are 71 girls in the school. Three of them have become teachers. The big girls go to teach the (village) women on Sunday afternoon. The women give them tea and home-made cakes. We have a very nice time together. Papa invited three elders and their wives and gave them tea. They were drinking and singing'. Rose also got a letter from a young boy, Dilmo. 'We have been travelling and eating a lot of meat. It is very hot here in the country and it is not comfortable. Next week we go to Dumka. During Christmas came a man who gave us much pleasure with his five children . . . Bunkholdt and the girls were playing and had fun. Your brother was not playing. He was sick.'

These letters offer a few glimpses of life in the Christian community. Nature and the seasons are recurrent themes, but so is food, which crops up again and again. Moltke's role as a hunter seems to be appreciated by the girls, more, perhaps, than by the missionaries. Companionship is clearly important, on the tours of the country, and we often hear of singing and 'having fun', even of 'play' as in the case of Bunkholdt. Such tours and amusements must have been welcome breaks, for life at school was by all accounts strenuous, highly disciplined, and rather dreary.

The letters show the youth active in teaching and proselytization. The Mission was still run on the snowball principle: the converted should convert others. While the letters were inspired by the missionaries, and written by those most trusted by them, one still gets an impression of enthusiasm among the Santal Christians. Was it religion alone that brought such enthusiasm ? Or was it pride in a new skill, in writing and reading, and the importance allowed them in the Mission's scheme? Was it the pleasure of having an important message to spread, or was its content significant in itself ? One point is clear: the schoolgirls had a role to play, probably far more important than their place in traditional Santal society.

This may also have been true of the elders, who sent Graham a letter, dated Benagaria 16 August 1883: 'We elders would like to tell you about our work. We are walking about the country and telling about God to the Heathen. And we hope that in good time we will be able to let people come to the Lord. We are working hard. People are coming to the Church. This year the crops are good, the rains have been good . . . it seems to be a good year.'

Letters like this were certainly strategic in convincing Graham of the missionaries' engagement. But some were more personal in tone, like one Sinjo wrote him, on 30 December: 'Take my greetings to those who are left free by the Grace of God . . . how relatives and friends are able to free you I don't know. One thing I must tell you is that my little son Anandu with whom I played . . . has left me. He is now playing with God . . . Papa told us that you are our friend, we are very glad. We have been told that you are very old. We are happy that by the Grace of God we are spreading the seed of God in the country. I have baptized some people. Be well . . . Perhaps my years will diminish because I am very sad . . . Pray that the Lord will deliver us and comfort us in our sorrow.' These Christian expressions convey feelings it would have been hard to express traditionally, where sorrow tends to be repressed. In March 1884,[71] Sinjo wrote to Dr. Graham, 'I am very surprised that you can love us so much . . . We came from the darkness of sin. Our earlier friends have not loved us as much'. We detect a certain stigma here, as if the Santals feel unworthy of such attention. Was this feeling general among the Christians? Sinjo also writes to the Countess Rantzau in 1886, describing the service, the good meal afterwards, the forest, and the wildlife. Important here is the trust the missionaries have in the converts, giving them the opportunity to express their new conviction in their own way. The adoption of the new faith thus engendered a sense of individual purpose.

While in Norway, Bunkholdt received a letter from his schoolboys.[72]

> When we got your letter, we were very glad. When we read of the ship you were sailing on, how long, broad and deep it was, we were surprised. If we could have gone with you, how would we have been overjoyed! We would perhaps not have been able to sleep, but looked around us day and night, not stayed inside the ship, but on top of it, so we could look around to all sides. What you told of the isle of Ceylon, the city Colombo, the cinnamon gardens, the palm woods, the houses of the natives, the temples of the heathen and their twenty-seven feet long idol, both gladdened and surprised us . . . . Dear Saheb, in our country it is now very hot. It has not rained a single day. This month they usually transplant the rice, but this year they have sown nothing . . . . We remember you very much and long for you . . . . We greet you very, very much.

It is not only the mission's supporters who are hungry for information about a larger and different world, the Santals have the same craving. And, if Norwegians and others felt a sense of adventure reading about missionary exploits, the Santals, too, devoured the various stories that their missionary connection offered.

## ADOPTION AND CHARITY

Links to individuals were also established by a support committee 'adopting' a convert, usually an orphaned child, sending money to support it. A letter from Caroline to Rudin[73] shows how this was done. Mission friends in Uppsala want to adopt a child of ten, in addition to the five they are already supporting. 'You can choose between three small girls', writes Caroline, 'whose mother died in greatest poverty'. The father could not take care of them and he was asked to send them to the school. 'They have some ailment of the skin, but they are very sweet.' A fourth, Sanya, the daughter of a widow in Assam, was brought back three years ago by Caroline. A fifth is Tripsy, who has become Christian through her uncle, a travelling elder. The mother ran away with another heathen, so the elder's sister brought her up, and Tripsy has difficulty at school. She was very sick last year, but her uncle prayed with her, and she was sure she would get well. She did. Caroline asks Rudin to choose.

Two years later,[74] 'Mariam is dead, and little Puke also died in the arms of Käthe. The smallest of the three sisters finally died. Tripsy was very ill but is well now.' Then she proposes other girls, Randan, and 'Sauri, a daughter of pastor Surju and Gangha, daughter of the son-in-law of pastor Gorjo. The mother has just died from cholera.' We see how the care of such children becomes an act of charity, not a collective responsibility, even in the case of a pastor's child. We also understand how close death could be.

When Börresen took Siram and some settlers to Assam in October, 1885[75] they saw the devastating floods in the lowlands of Bengal. The water had washed away everything and hardly anyone could remember such a calamity. The government was collecting money, but he feels private charity would have been better. Still, 'whether the Missionaries over there have done anything . . . I have not heard. It is the English Church mission (the CMS) and sometimes the Baptists who work there, but the papers say nothing (of such aid) . . . . The Bengalis have probably never been hit so hard as this year, and yet they continue to close their hearts. They cry to their Gods and are lost. Whether the Missionaries take the opportunity to invite them to salvation . . . I do not know: but one might hope so.' There are obvious echoes here, of the criticism Börresen suffered when baptizing 'rice Christians' in 1874: clearly, he hoped his colleagues would now realize he was right.

## THE BEGINNINGS OF THE TEA INDUSTRY

When the Santal Mission decided to acquire land in Assam, they just managed to get in before tea boomed. Tea was grown in India from 1835, but commercial production began only in 1850 in

Darjeeling, while the first garden in Jaipalguri was opened in 1874 (Bose 1993: 54). Production was small in the 1860s,[76] and a depression in 1866-9 burst many of the early companies (Tomlinson 1993: 122). But production rose sharply from the late 1870s. The number of tea gardens in Bengal peaked at 235 around the turn of the century,[77] then declined, though acreage and production continued to increase (Bose 1993: 54).

Tribal people dominated the labour force on plantations, where the worker's place was as a servant rather than an employee (Bhowmik 1981). The first Darjeeling plantations used Nepali labour, but the annexation of Jaipalguri from Bhutan in 1865 opened up new lands, which the government offered cheap to planters—as they did in Assam later. Tribal labour was induced to migrate from Chhotanagpur, hit by famines and land encroachment. Most were 'initially cajoled and coerced' to make the move (Bose 1993: 96). These 'wild men of no caste' were constructed as Dhangar, coolies fit only for labour and ready to do any kind of work. Fetishizing the tribesman,[78] this created a 'market for aboriginality', which set the context for the missionary view of migration as an opportunity for the Santal. Dhangars were first recruited to the sugar colonies in the second quarter of the nineteenth century. Then, it was hard to recruit labour for tea in the tribal areas of central India. But by the 1850s overseas migration was restricted by government—mainly due to the frightening death rate of tribal workers during the passage—and Dhangars became available for work in Assam. In 1878-9, about 25,000 coolies came from Chotanagpur. By 1891, some 20 per cent of the tribal people of Ranchi district had gone to the tea gardens, and between a third and a half of the immigrant workers on the Assam plantations were from Chotanagpur (Ghosh 1999: 16-31). Those from the Santal Parganas are not included here.

Hunter writes of plantations in which the whole family gets employment, and 'every additional child, instead of being the means of increasing his poverty, becomes a source of wealth. The labour is the lightest known to agriculture, and as soon as a boy can walk he can earn his living . . . in a few years the emigrants return rich men' (1975: 134-5). Yet in the 1870s and 1880s, plantation wages were about half the going rate for agricultural work in Jaipalguri, so locals were not interested. Plantation workers were free, not indentured as in Assam, but economic conditions tended to exclude return to the area of origin. The labour force was regularly replenished from the tribal areas until the 1930 slump (Bose 1993: 96-7), and Santals remained an important part.

## SANTAL EMIGRATION AND THE FOUNDING OF THE ASSAM COLONY

In October 1880,[79] Skrefsrud had returned from Assam where he wanted to establish a Santal colony. The contract with the government had been signed, and Börresen had gone there with forty Santals. Something had to be done, says Skrefsrud: the land is poor in Santalistan and the population growing. Some Christians have gone to Murshidabad and others to tea gardens in Darjeeling and Assam. Some heathens go to Mauritius; there is a danger that the Santal tribe will dissolve.[80] Thus the missionaries had long been looking for new lands. In 1874, the South Australian government had offered good conditions for the Santals in the Northern Territories, but the distance was too great.[81]

Graham took an interest in the project, and asked his Indian friends if there was room for the Santals in the Central Provinces. There was not, but then he wrote to a relative, T.H. Stevenson, magistrate in Lakhimpur, who replied positively. The missionaries found it an excellent place for the Santals. But it was far — 700 miles—and so migration would be very costly. One Scottish benefactor offered to pay for the first migration. It was refused. 'We therefore bought a land-map of Assam and asked Mr. Hunter[82] if there was not another place closer . . . we found out that Dahi, close to the Bhutan or Goalpara were uninhabited and very fertile.' They wrote to the Deputy Commissioner, T.H. Campbell and asked for his conditions.[83] The Assam government welcomed the idea. Campbell wrote to Graham: 'The movement is sure to extend in future years, until the large unproductive wastes . . . are converted into smiling fields and orchards, interspersed with villages inhabited by a happy and contented people, whose presence owing to their religious training, will prove a source of great strength to our administration'. Campbell said the place was uninhabited, writes Skrefsrud, 'and that he would be glad to receive the Santals. His conditions were good but not as good as those we could get in Lakhimpur'. The missionaries then played one local administrator against another, until 'the Assam government could give better conditions than Mr. Campbell. Now our problems were over and our most hopeful prayers had been heard'. The missionaries engaged in quite a political enterprise to negotiate land on behalf of their converts.

Skrefsrud makes us understand that Christian Santals would be isolated from heathen and Hindu influence, and cites the economic advantages of the scheme. With some Santal chiefs, he visited the area in 1880, then wrote to the Deputy Commissioner in Dhubri demanding some concessions. The Santals should get land in the Duar Guma, north of the cultivated land and extending towards Bhutan. They should get leases in perpetuity and pay a fixed rent through their *manjhi*, chosen by the people and confirmed by the Government. He would be given 10 to 15 *bigha* of land rent free. Conflicts should be regulated through the headmen and the *pargana*, having the same powers as in the Santal Parganas. Like a political agent, the colony superintendent would be independent of the district administration. The demands were granted.

In 1880, Börresen went to Assam to found the first settlement, with forty Santal volunteers (Graham 1881). To Graham, who believed the converts went there as teagarden coolies, he stresses that they are settling their own lands.[84] 'We left Ebenezer on 18 October for Calcutta, and from thence proceeded by the Eastern Bengal Railway to Sara-Ghat, crossing the Ganges by steamer; we then took the Northern Bengal Railway steamer 5 miles, tonga 13 miles, steamer 5 miles, bullock cart 1 mile, and at last steamer 30 miles to Dhubri. From this place the Santhals walked 30 miles northward to the district called Goma Duar, of which we have taken possession, and the Government lent me an elephant to travel and use as long as I remained there. The whole journey can be done in three days and two nights from Rampur Hat'.[85] It was strenuous, however. 'Of the 11 days travel I was in bed 5 nights, the others were spent in travelling', writes Börresen of another journey later.[86]

One night was spent in a government bungalow which was but a bamboo hut on poles. Börresen, sleeping on the floor, was troubled by rats, who wanted 'to destroy my sun hat, and nearly made a hole through it'. He kept banging on the floor, the rats 'took no notice' of these 'proceedings', and in the end, he got used to them and slept. As they arrived, hungry and thirsty, on their new land, they found their effects had not arrived, but some babus living there 'went and prepared a very nice supper for me . . . and you may be sure I thanked God more for these little attentions on their part than otherwise for

1000 roupies'. The Santals, too, had trouble finding rice and other necessities for the first few days. Still, Börresen stresses, the next day was a Sunday, and they did not miss their two regular services.

'On Monday, 25 October, we all walked into our new country, I alone being on an elephant . . . About a mile from the last village, we came upon a site where there is a kind of garden or grove of trees, and we called the place Thakurpura (the city of God); but there is no road thither at all, and we had to make our way through the dense jungle grass, which is some 16 feet high, and each stalk 3/4 inch thick'. The grass was too fresh to burn, so they had to cut it, a tremenduous task. They could not clear space for the whole village, so they just cut a clearing for the church. Yet Börresen was enthusiastic: 'the country is most beautiful, being one of the finest I have ever seen . . . covered with beautiful parks . . . to the north and north-east the background is made up of the Himalaya mountains, so that the scenery is altogether charming.' Börresen did not believe the planter's reports on rainfall, but soon learnt that the latter was right. When the settlers came the climate proved disastrous and the death rate during the first years rose to 14 per cent (Bodding 1910a).

'The land . . . is about forty-five miles long by six to eight miles wide. All this tract is free of heavy forest, by which it is skirted on the north and north-east sides . . . The northern boundary abuts on the Himalayas in Bhutan, and if we require more we can get the whole of Dheerang. . . . It is all waste land, and so much of it, that if the entire nation of Santals were to emigrate there, there is land for them all'. The soil was the richest Börresen ever saw, and would bear three rice crops a year, or else jute, oil-seed, tobacco, or wheat. The Santals got it very cheaply, and he expected that two acres well worked would earn more than six in the Santal Parganas, or in Murshidabad, where so many Santals had gone. The country was unhealthy but Börresen felt the problem would cease once the jungle was cleared.[85] The land was tilled when it belonged to the Bhutanese. 'I was told', says Börresen, 'that at that time the Bhootan Raja and his people lived in great comfort and glory, but subsequently the English dispossessed them, as they were always quarrelling and at war.' Yet it was hard to clear the forest. They borrowed another government elephant to haul timber, but it refused this kind of work and ran away with four big trunks—they found it after twelve days, but the timber was lost. They gave up on building a church—meant to house the people in the initial phase—and built barracks instead.

There was just a single tea garden close to the colony, and three in the whole district. The one close to them was in a poor state, from want of labour.[88] Their colonists, Börresen says, will not work in tea gardens, but he hopes the coolies will come under the Mission's influence. 'Something like a new mission field is open to us, as there are no missionaries whatever'. And Börresen, ever practical, goes on to stress the expense involved. Their friends in Europe should be told that 'we shall be very glad to toil on here, and bear the heat and burden of the day . . . while they need only send us a little of their surplus'.[89]

This seems to have worked, for soon Skrefsrud was thanking Graham[90] for a hundred pounds. He, too, was optimistic: 'the gospel will . . . be extended to the hill tribes of Assam, the Mech, and also the half-hinduised Raj Bongsos.[91] These people have entreated the Santhal brethren, when they were in Assam, to allow them to come and live among them, and that they even will live under the protection of God *without* their gods, and learn about our religion. It is remarkable what an influence the brethren gained over those people'. This may have been optimistic, as standard practice in Assam became to use bands of local forest people to catch labourers absconding from their indenture contracts.[92]

In December 1880, Skrefsrud[93] went to Assam with the first permanent settlers, taking the cattle with them. They did not use the route Börresen had taken, but trekked by way of the Rajmahal hills. 'It will be difficult to . . . *procure* cattle, owing to the price being so high in Assam itself, so that we shall have to buy cattle here . . .'. 'The brethren' felt it would not be too difficult to take the cattle to Assam. Clearly, the missionaries listened to the converts in practical matters.

In his letter to Graham, Börresen mentioned the Danish doctor, Arendrup, who was the first to take responsiblity for the colony. He had just graduated from the University of Copenhagen. Skrefsrud stressed that he 'belongs to a very old and highly connected family'. He came to India on his brother's ship, to see the world. Börresen showed him the churches,

> walking over hill and dale . . . to see both heathen and Christians, and, in Santal fashion, to partake of the latter's hospitality, sitting on the ground and eating with his fingers curry and rice, served on leaf plates; and he told me . . . that the difference between heathen and Christians, between those who have enjoyed an education in

our schools and those who have not, is so marked, that an outsider like himself could hardly believe that they belong to the same race. There was something so innocent, and at the same time so intelligent, in the faces of the Christians . . . that he was greatly struck by it. And having seen the work of the girls . . . he assured me that they were far in advance of the generality of pupils in his own country. This was very encouraging to hear from a man like him.[94]

There is deference, here, to the high-born doctor. It is striking, even in recent Mission literature, how Christians are made to look different from the Heathen, better groomed and dressed, and smiling towards the camera. In comparison, the unconverted look stern and wild, with dishevelled hair.

Arendrup died in 1882. Börresen rushed to Assam, and wrote[95] of the unexpected death. Arendrup had asked if he might come back to Benagaria, but it was to no avail. He got sick as soon as he got back to Assam, though in Benagaria he had 'looked as well as he ever did . . . but to our Doctor he had said that he would not live long'. Arendrup had told Börresen, when he took the job in preference to better-paid work in the tea gardens: 'I will rather stay here and let myself be converted by the Santals, than become a ruin in the tea gardens'. Börresen piously hoped it had worked. Arendrup may exemplify a spirit typical of the times. There is a quest for adventure, but this is not yet the innocent pastime it is now, and the danger of sudden death is very real. Sometimes, as with Arendrup who 'suffered from depression', the death wish does not seem distant.

In 1882 Skrefsrud left for Europe, and Borresen was left to start the colonization. But all is well:[96] 'all are happy, everything looks flourishing, they have had a good deal of rain, they should be able to sell a good deal of their harvest this year, which will enable them to pay the land revenue and start remitting their loans to the Government.' The settlers had built their church, a circular enclosure capable of holding a thousand, and school was held daily for some fifty girls and sixty boys. To Hertel, who relayed a proposal from Danish supporters to buy draught animals for the settlers, Börresen stressed that such aid should pass through the Mission: only they could distribute it to the most needy, and do so free of interest. Eight families had oxen, yet there are nine who had none. And the tigers took their oxen. While he was there, in full daylight, 'the Tiger came loitering out of the bush and threw himself on a big buffalo ox, killed it and dragged it away. The owner . . . was standing near by . . . the man will be unable to plough'. Still, the tiger did not benefit from his kill, for the Christians fetched the carcass and shared the meat—whatever the tiger said, 'when he came to find his ox, only the mice will know', concludes Börresen.

The management of the colony was not simple. Three of the four superintendents died of fever between 1880 and 1897. Carl Moltke, a young Count who came out without any formal engagement, took care of the colony for a while, but returned to Denmark in 1884.[97] In a letter written[98] as Moltke was taking charge, we discern a certain scepticism on Börresen's part. 'While it will be hard for him in the beginning, it should work. He has learnt a good deal of Santhali, and loves the people dearly, and he also has a good deal of energy, so by the help of God, in whom he trusts, it should work.' He had some mental trouble, and was never clear in his religious views. He stayed three years, but may have spent as much time hunting as running the colony. He wanted to return to Assam, but Börresen was not keen. Then, the Count died, at the age of 30, in 1886 (Nyhagen 1990, II: 108-9).

Börresen's scepticism does not apply to his Santal collaborators, nor the project as a whole:[99] 'All is going well in Assam. All honour must be given to Siram as a pastor; Lakaj is the writer, a superbly capable young man full of life. He deals with all the accounts . . . he writes excellently, and talks some English. His letter-writing is in European style, and he will be of great use to Count Moltke. His wife is a teacher in a girls' school. Dr. Arendrup's assistant, Nimaj, is a capable young man, and Arendrup had full confidence in him. He was here with us for many years. All these young men were raised here with us'. The pride is almost audible in Börresen's voice. His Santals—for the pride is tinged with paternalism—make it possible even for a mediocre white administrator to manage.

## LIFE IN THE COLONY

Three years later[100] Börresen gave more details about life in the colony. They had a good harvest that year, though the rain had brought some illness. He came there with Siram, who was going to work as a pastor, and his family. They arrived on a Sunday morning for the service, where Surju preached. Börresen confined himself to greetings from the old country. Afterwards, says Börresen, he shook everyone's hand: at first he tried to skip the children, but they cried . . . 'It took a lot of time', he remarks drily. Though he missed

Moltke's hospitality, his cook was given so much food that he had to invite others to eat with him. The first day Surju, the resident pastor, was invited: next Siram and his family, then the teachers, and so on. One notes the implicit hierarchy. Next Sunday Siram preached at the Lord's supper.

The congregation lived a simple life, says Börresen, without conflict. Two families, however, were ostracized. The first since they don't come to the Lord's house, and also because the man socializes with the Heathen and sometimes drinks. They have had to build their house at some distance from the village . . . the children receive no schooling, since the parents won't send them. And so they live there alone and isolated, though Siram and the Elders visit them and entreat them to seek the Lord. . . . There is no sign of that till now.' The other family comprised a widower and a widow, who wanted a happy life together in this world.

> The man has four children and the wife three, and then the man is suffering from such uncommon idleness . . . he prefers to sleep all day . . . though he has an extraordinary appetite and demands food whether there is any or not. The wife, on the other hand, has a great appetite for work . . . . Now she has no liking left for the idle man and she scolds him to make him plough. He has good oxen and she too, so if only he would work, they could be well off; but the one thing he can be moved to do, when she scolds, is to take his stick to beat her. So much for the expected happiness of their marriage. The result is, that she gives him no food, and so his daughter has to look after her lazy father. Therefore the brethren have excluded them, until they will be reconciled and live in peace. Three of his children and one of her daughters have been sent with Surju to my wife[101] and since the man is sick now, and his wife won't nurse him, the main chief has taken him into his house till he heals. So there are new efforts made to make peace . . . but till then they remain excluded. Those two families apart, everything is well . . . All work hard but have blessed fruits of their work, some have tried planting sugar cane, which does very well.[102]

In 1888, Col. Maxwell found a colony consisting of 111 houses, with 590 inhabitants and a cultivated area of 1,886 *bighas*. By 1902 there were 5,075 *bighas*, and by 1910, 4,486 inhabitants, of which 1994 were Christians, 3,678 were Santals, the rest Rabhas and Bodos.[103] Strict rules banned drink and worship of bongas. School was compulsory. By 1906, 600 Santals had settled outside the boundaries in order to escape these rules (Bodding 1910a).

In 1889, Halfdan Bahr took over the management of the colony. In January 1887 he had married Börresens daughter Ingeborg. Bahr was born in Stavanger in 1858. Though from an academic family, he studied gardening, and from apprenticeship in the Botanical Garden at Christiania, he went on to Copenhagen, to Kew, and in 1883 to Calcutta's Botanical Garden, where he became manager a few years later. We know little of his life before he met the missionaries, but Nyhagen says Calcutta had not been 'fortunate' for his spiritual life. Due to his health and the lowland climate he then applied for a similar job in Darjeeling, which he got.

Halfdan and Ingeborg apparently left the mission for more secular surroundings, but in Darjeeling they were influenced by a Baptist priest, H. Rylands Brown, to become active Evangelicals. Somewhat earlier Bahr suggested to his father-in-law that he might take care of the Assam colony, but Börresen declined. Now he accepted. Bahr had no religious function, however. Siram ministered to the colonists' spiritual needs (Nyhagen 1990, II: 142-3).

When Bahr took over the colony in 1889, it was in a bad state. He rebuilt decayed villages, founded new ones, instituted loans to help immigration, and went on tour in the Santal Parganas to persuade Santals to migrate.[104] He also had a new bungalow built in Thakurpura, renamed Grahampur, to honour their Scottish friend. The map of the colony (ibid.: 428) shows most villages named after missionaries: Kerappur, Börresenpur, Carolinepur, and also Sirampur —certainly a later development. Like American townships, the colony was seen as a new country, created by missionary activity.

By the early 1890s, the Colony's problems were solved, and the Mission's future seemed a family affair, with the next generation lined up to take over. This was not to be. In 1893 Bahr had to take a long leave, and Skrefsrud took over. Next year Bahr had to go to Europe, and Börresen would not at first let him return to Assam. In 1895 he did so, but died the next year (ibid.: 194). Dr. Raya, a Bengali working for the mission, who had some medical training, was in charge of the colony for nine years. He was the secular administrator, while Siram was responsible for the religious side. In 1906, Muston took over the colony.

As early as 1897 an arrangement was made with the Forest Officer of the district: for eight days' unremunerated labour in the Government reserve, the colonists might remove dead *sal* posts and branches for firewood and building (Bodding 1910a: 37). The missionaries called it 'permit' work. We should remember that the right to firewood and other minor forest products has usually been refused by the Forest Department, even to this day.

## PROBLEMS WITH THE GOVERNMENT

The missionaries had not foreseen the negative attitude the Assam government was to develop towards the colony. A year after its establishment, the government wanted to reduce the area drastically, to liberate land for teagardens. The advances made to migrants for draught animals were withdrawn, and the payment to the *manjhis* reduced, while local police were sent to control the colony. A tea garden was established at Mornai, within a quarter mile of the Santal villages. Börresen, fighting these measures in Skrefsrud's absence, saw the Assistant Commissioner at Dhubri,[105] who promised to keep out any further tea gardens. Börresen felt that the government 'will never succeed in making people migrate into this country. . . . They have no gifts for that. I told them that straight: they will surely give in, and we will get all our legal rights'. Börresen is optimistic; in fact he had difficulty coping with the situation. On his return, Skrefsrud demanded in a letter to the Viceroy that the territory should remain intact, since the scheme was built on a number of self-contained communities. His protest had some effect, but no measure was taken to relieve the colony from its neighbour, the Mornai tea garden.

Skrefsrud forbade the colonists to work in tea gardens and tried to make life difficult for the planters. He had no illusions about conditions there and wanted the colony to be different. How far the missionaries succeeded in this, is another question, especially when the Mission itself took to tea. The Chief Commissioner proposed they should buy a small tea garden; in 1890, the Mornai and Tamarhats plantations, then in financial trouble, were taken over. Yet at one time, it was the tea garden manager who kept an eye on the colonists and assisted them in case of need (Bodding 1910a: 15). Could the Mission colony, then, remain different from the plantations, and to what degree?

In 1905 the government again wanted to reduce the area of the colony, referring to a clause enabling the government, if colonization was slow, to resume unoccupied land and grant it to outsiders. Skrefsrud and Bodding protested, and finally, the Lieutenant-Governor supported the missionaries: the area of the colony remained intact.[106]

Bodding acknowledges the heavy price the colonists paid in money, labour, health, and human life, but stresses the benefits. 'The Santals up there had no fear of the cheating moneylenders, they became honest, straightforward, and independent characters who stand for right and justice'.[107] Bodding went there several times and took photos, using a magic lantern to show them to Santal audiences in the old country. The technique was new, and the Santals seem to have been fascinated by the concreteness of the images, making the unknown known and countering the negative stereotype of Assam. It certainly helped recruit new migrants.

For the tea gardens, the prospect of cheap labour was tempting (Bodding 1910a: 29). Bodding's mode of recruitment contrasts with that of the tea gardens, where reforms to ensure voluntary enlistment led to a proliferation of unlicensed recruiters. Their practices are graphically described by Ghosh (1999), citing a report from Singhbhum in 1890, that the recruiters 'delude persons by sexual considerations, and a good looking male or female generally is able to secure many recruits of the opposite sex'. One recruiter induced a girl 'by promises of keeping her himself to accompany him to his house'. There, his lawful wife was to pick a quarrel with the newcomer . . . 'and a grand row ensued, in the course of which the *arkatti*[108] left the house in anger, taking no. 2 with him, and proposing to her that they should go . . . to Assam. . . . With the girl's ready consent they went . . . to Calcutta, where the man took her to a depot and deserted her, returning home to his lawful spouse richer by some Rs. 20 or Rs. 30'.[109] (Such tactics, incidentally, are still in use.) The planters did not care about Santal morals: 'whenever the Colony women came to fetch water . . . coolies were on the other side, ill mannered or downright obscene'. According to Bodding, this was why the missionaries bought the neighbouring tea gardens. 'It was not a financial affair', he says, and they 'gave the exploitation of the tea garden to a foreign company: they had already agreed to work the garden on the same principles as we ourselves would do' (Bodding 1910a: 30).

Bodding remarks that the Santals tend to influence their surroundings, rather than be influenced by them. Still, he felt they were losing their identity due to contact with Hindus and Muslims. He urged evangelization: 'those who become Christians might ensure the survival of the tribe and become the true founders of a regenerate race of Santals'. He stressed the importance of family migration: 'whenever their wives are servants in Hindu families they never come back'.[110] The simple life of the Santals did not exclude the temptations of alcohol and sexual freedom.

Bodding justifies the colony: the colonists are better off than other Santals, though he is conscious of taking away their 'amusements' so they require 'substitutes or something better' (Bodding 1910a: 39). But the situation was more complex than he thought. The autobiography of a headman, Chotrae Desmanjhi, provides a Santal point of view.

## A SANTAL AUTOBIOGRAPHY

Chotrae had taken part in the 1855 rebellion. His father was a priest of the boundary deities. Later Chotrae converted, and wrote his autobiography (Murmu 1938) around 1907. Published in 1917, when he was 88, it presents his view of life in the Colony. He notes the decay of custom and the despair of poverty after the rebellion, as also the wave of unrest, accompanied by a revival of Santal traditions. Chotrae kept away from revivalism, as he felt that the chiefs were only too keen to use the tribal deities to affirm their own power.[111]

The missionaries open schools and dispensaries, but deprive converts of traditional drinking and dancing, imposing puritanical ethics. Chotrae tells us how difficult it is to leave the old gods, so strongly linked to Santal clan identities. Even the Christians, he says, do not want to abandon their gods when they are dying. He notes how missionaries introduce strife to Santal society by their intolerance of elopement and divorce. Though he shows much regard for Börresen, Chotrae stresses resistance and shows how Skrefsrud's successors manipulated Santal belief to their advantage.

An anecdote shows one of the causes for resistance: 'An elder named Singai had been listening to the story of Christ, but his mind stayed like a stone. He also thought that Bahini Bonga, his clan deity, would not allow him to convert. Then he felt he was dying and was very afraid, but still he did not want to get baptized. He went to the mission and there found Raya,[112] who told him about Christ. Raya explained that Christ was the true bonga. Singai answered that as he had never ceased to sacrifice to the bongas, they could not abandon him. His death was rather pathetic. When he saw Jom Raja, the god of death, and his soldiers armed with knives, he thought the terrible figure was an accomplice of Satan, master of the Christian Hell. Fearing death, he asked himself loudly why his mind did not awake to the Christian faith. Then he understood that he was, above all, a

Santal, and that all would be well.' In the end, conversion amounted to no longer being one's true self.

Chotrae notes the conflicts created by the missionaries, opposing converts to heathens. It was partly to distract converts from heathen influence that they wanted to found an Evangelical community in Assam. Chotrae, who followed Skrefsrud there, explains why the project was doomed. Though the missionaries moved thousands of Santals to Assam, hundreds died on the way, and many ended up in the tea gardens. Chotrae tells us that neighbouring planters put pressure on the missionaries, since they were eager for cheap labour. He criticizes Skrefsrud for underestimating the danger from the planters, for whom the poorest Santals often worked, under conditions even worse than in the 'old country'. When they faced such harassment, the settlers deeply regretted their neglect of the bad omens they had met on their way to Assam. Though he stresses exploitation, Chotrae explains the problems of the colony in terms of the missionary ignorance of Santal psychology.

As Christians they were not supposed to believe in omens, which they still saw as a necessary precaution against the evil eye. Skrefsrud wanted to sacralize the Colony by allowing the Santals to take some earth from Santal Parganas and mix it with the soil of Assam. But to be effective this ritual should have been dedicated to the bongas. A tribal territory needs first to be occupied by deities and the idea of 'virgin land' stands for no man's land. The missionaries underestimated the symbolic value of dedicating a territory to deities over which a *desmanjhi* had powers. Without the *bongas*, the chief's status seemed hollow, even if his juridical status was the same as in the Santal Parganas. And then the Santals—a migratory race, as Bodding and Skrefsrud put it—had a number of customs linked to migration. The Santal chief must hold a *sarjom* branch representing the ancestors and submit to the local *abge* by sacrificing an animal. Christianity could condemn such practices but not eradicate the felt need for them.

In trying to create an evangelical setting in Assam, the missionaries ignored the symbolic load carried by the country. They ignored the association of Assam with death in popular Hinduism. Chotrae does not mention this, but Assam is a land of exclusion. Here fled the incestuous, thieves, and murderers who, if not killed, were driven away and—in modern times—had to work in the tea gardens. This image pervaded Santal thinking, so that when the missionaries spoke of 'virgin' land north of the Brahmaputra, the place was charged with ambiguity. Assam is the land of the dead, an image of death which negates the Christian one.

The main impression one gets from Chotrae's autobiography is that the Santals had not fully succeeded in integrating Christian elements in a religious syncretism. He feels the missionaries are benefiting from people's anxiety about death: 'One should not talk about it', he says; 'if we have sacrificed to our deities all our life, they are not going to abandon us'. In separating the Santals from the bongas, the missionaries deprived them of becoming ancestors after death. And they have no other certainty about the afterlife.

We may identify two opposed views of death from Chotrae's book and from Santal tales: a temporary death, an erratic journey to the magical land of Assam from where yogis and ojhas return as magicians able to cure others, and the death of ordinary people transporting them to a labour camp where their despair is expressed in the loss of individuality and sexual identity. Labour, the main value of the Christians, lends its imagery to the myth. We are in a world where pleasure, condemned as immorality, is eradicated. The missionaries indulge in describing the death of children and the saved who go to Isor Baba's land, but fail to convince Santals of the beauty of Paradise. Only educated converts could assimilate the rhetoric of paradise as fusion with the Christian God. In the same way, Satan could find no place in the Santal worldview.

The missionaries compelled Santal people to abandon their traditional values for a economic improvement. If the Assam project was not a failure on economic or social grounds, it stands for the Santals as a western utopia, the paradise in the tea gardens. Yet a new Santal community was created, one which was founded in the common hardship of Santals and missionaries, and in which the latter, no longer strangers, stood as inventors of another world.

## NOTES

1. Children were not baptized until 1878. Thereafter, children were included, so the rate of conversion diminished. Yet the numbers were impressive, compared to other missions in India.
2. Berg to 'Santalen', 10.11.85, published in *Dahkwala*, no. 1, January 1886: 20-4.
3. Skrefsrud to Hertel, 17.06.1879.
4. Ibid., 30.06.1879.

5. Ibid., 15.09.1879.
6. Ibid., 09.10.1879.
7. Ibid., 21.06.1880.
8. Carstairs remained as Commissioner till 1900, and wrote *Harma's Village*, a historical novel describing the Santal Rebellion, published posthumously in 1935.
9. Börresen to Graham, 10.03.1883, *Dahkwala*, July 1883: 102. We use Hertel's Danish translation.
10. Börresen to Hertel, 23.11.82, *Dahkwala*, no. 2, February 1883: 22.
11. *Dahkwala*, no. 8, 1883: 8-9.
12. Hoffmann, the leader for many years of the Jesuit mission at Ranchi, was influenced by German ideas of Christian socialism. He formed cooperatives, and organized social assistance to the needy.
13. Some of Archer's cases relate to the beginning of the century as he heard narratives from old people and consulted judicial information in the Bhagalpur record room.
14. Börresen to Hertel, 23.11.82, *Dahkwala*, 2 February 1883: 21-2.
15. *Dahkwala*, 01.01.1883: 11.
16. 27.03.1882.
17. Letter from J. Beames, Commissioner of the Santal Parganas, to the Secretary, Govt. of Bengal, 09.11.1887.
18. Santalen 1886: 86; *Annual Report* 1885-6: 28-9.
19. A.W. Croft, Director of Public Instruction, to the Secretary, Govt. of Bengal, 19.02.1882. Bengal Educational Papers 1882, vol. 1630.
20. The Secretary, Govt. of Bengal to the Commissioner, Bhagalpur, 02.03.1888. Bengal Government Papers 1888, vol. 3167.
21. Archer says Christian Santals follow traditional rules of exogamy, which contradicts Skrefsrud's assertions in the ethnological questionnaire. On Santal non-Christian kinship today, see Gautam (1977) and Bouez (1985).
22. Archer's (1984) data here refer to a period from the 1930s to the 1950s.
23. The *jom jati*, 'eating the community', implies that the convert has left the tribe and must be readmitted by ritual commensality.
24. Skrefsrud to Hertel, 09.10.1879.
25. Ibid., 21.06.1880.
26. Ibid., 15.09.1879.
27. This refers probably to teaching them to read and write, as we know Sona and others did later.
28. Bodding (1919) says Skrefsrud was proficient in 40 languages though he was too busy to study them deeply.
29. From the Baptist Free Will Missionary Society, who worked from Balasore in Orissa.
30. Hodne 1966: 219.

31. Wenger, author of a Bengali grammar, influenced Skrefsrud and is thanked in his introduction. The influence of Latin is clear in the use of modal categories such as 'benedictive'.
32. The 1875 conference discussed how to write Santali. Graham wrote about a 'Universal Syllabic System', invented by Hunt from experience with North American Indians, enabling illiterates to read and write in three days. Hunt sent Harbinson to the CMS missionaries in 1876. Cornelius went to see him, but Skrefsrud did not. Storrs says Harbinson had 'little education and even less judgment'. After living on the CMS two years, Harbinson wanted to start his own mission, but Størrs was against it (Nyhagen 1990, I: 272). Harbinson seems to have been as arrogant as Skrefsrud—perhaps it was as well that they never met.
33. They also used the hymn book of the Orissa baptists, and ordered 500 as late as 1875 (Nyhagen 1990, I: 265).
34. Like the older edition, it had an appendix including the ten commandments, the credo, the Lord's prayer, and the texts read at baptism and the Lord's supper.
35. Like many linguists, Skrefsrud used this term for those Indian languages now classified as Austro-Asiatic (Zide 1966).
36. Skrefsrud to Hertel, 20.08.1877.
37. Ibid., 08.02.1879.
38. Skrefsrud to Hertel, 05.05.1879.
39. In fact, he felt the Santals are Dravidian by race. Modern physical anthropologoists rather point to their Mongoloid cheekbones.
40. Skrefsrud to Hertel, 02.08.1879.
41. Sten Konow comments on the project in his introduction to Skrefsrud 1942.
42. Skrefsrud to Campbell, 11.04.1903.
43. Third Annual Report.
44. Skrefsrud to R. Petersen, 17.02.1875.
45. Skrefsrud to Graham 07.08.1884, cited by Hodne 1966: 222.
46. Annual Report 1885-6: 4. This may have been the occasion of meeting Bahr, Börresen's future son-in-law.
47. Bodding's preface to the dictionary. The manuscript of the dictionary is in the University Library, Oslo. Santal-English, 1445p, English-Santali 1-775.
48. Here Kolean Guru is clearly influenced by Puranic myths, where gods, goddesses, men and animals are made from the sweat of Shiva. Elwin notes similar influence among other tribes (1949).
49. *Third Annual Report*; *Fifth Annual Report*.
50. *The Christian Spectator*.
51. Scottish Free Church Mission.
52. Skrefsrud to Stark, 01.05.1880.

53. Ibid., 05.05.1880.
54. For the colonial tendency to assimilate the country-born to the 'mixed race', see Stoler in Stoler and Cooper 1997: 101-16.
55. He had also published a couple of papers on Santal culture. See Bibliography.
56. He ordered 50 examples of Cole's translation in 1880, saying he hopes to order several hundred when the translation of the New Testament is completed (Nyhagen 1990, II: 380).
57. Storrs to H. Wright, 07.05.1878, cited by Nyhagen, 1990, II: 382.
58. In 1878 he became a missionary.
59. Proceedings of the Calcutta Auxiliary Bible Society, 16.01.1884.
60. Proceedings of the CABS, 18.06.1884.
61. Caroline Börresen to Hertel 23.11.82, published in *Dahkwala*, 1 January 1883: 1-2.
62. Skrefsrud to Hertel, 02.08.1879.
63. i.e. *bhakta*, devotee.
64. The term Bodding uses here refers to a 'medicine man', i.e. an ojha.
65. Actually, the same clan.
66. This nameless person was of course Pahle (see chapter 8).
67. Börresen to Hertel, 04.11.85, published in *Dahkwala*, 1 January 1886: 6.
68. *Dahkwala*, 1 January 1886: 6-7.
69. One of the early 'pastors'.
70. 04.07.1883, we do not know to whom it was addressed.
71. Sinjo to Dr. Graham, 05.03.1884.
72. *Dahkwala*, 1 January 1886: 26-7.
73. Caroline Börresen to Rudin, 21.11.1886.
74. Caroline Börresen to Rudin, 19.07.1888.
75. Börresen to Hertel, 04.11.85, published in *Dahkwala*, 1 January 1886: 7.
76. Only 4 per cent of British imports came from India in 1866.
77. In the early 1900s, Indian tea supplied 59 per cent of the British market (Tomlinson 1993: 122).
78. Later, tribals were classified as 'class I' coolies, as more resistant to malaria. Only they were to be employed in malaria-ridden districts, while Bengalis (Class II) or coolies from Bihar and the North-West Provinces (Class III) were used in more healthy places. For the recruiters, aboriginals brought higher prices. (Ghosh 1999: 31-4).
79. Skrefsrud to Hertel, 04.10.1880.
80. There had in fact been considerable Santal migration, to present-day Bangladesh and to Nepal, for example. Their large spread has not led to a dissolution of the feeling of community among Santals, however.
81. Skrefsrud to Hertel, 04.10.1880.

82. Government statistical officer who wrote *The Annals of Rural Bengal* and other works.
83. Skrefsrud to Hertel 04.10.1880.
84. Börresen to W.L.Watson, London: 22.11.1880.
84. Graham 1881: 3-4.
85. Skrefsrud to Graham, 29.12.80, published in Graham 1881: 2-3.
86. Börresen to Hertel, 23.11.82, *Dahkwala*, 2 February 1883: 22.
87. Graham 1881: 7. He was wrong here, as later experience was to show.
88. 'The most frequent complaint of the planters was . . . the scarcity of labour' (Ghosh 1999: 44).
89. Graham 1881: 9-10.
90. Skrefsrud to Graham, 29.12.80, published in Graham 1881.
91. i.e. Rajbansis, a Hindu caste usually seen to be recruited from Hinduized tribals. For the Mech, see Gait 1926.
92. Ghosh 1999: 43-4. The practice may not yet have been common when Skrefsrud wrote.
93. Skrefsrud to Graham, published in Graham 1881: 13.
94. Graham 1881: 12-13.
95. Letter from Börresen to Hertel, 13.09.82, resumed in *Dahkwala*, 1 January 1883: 4-8.
96. Börresen to Hertel, 13.09.82, *Dahkwala*, 1 January 1883: 2.
97. Moltke's parents were important donors. This may have influenced Börresen to accept him. His parents may have felt, like many parents of youth sent to the colonies, that this was his chance to prove his calibre.
98. Börresen to Jacobsen, 02.11.82, *Dahkwala*, 1 January 1883: 3.
99. Ibid.
100. Börresen to Hertel, 04.11.85, *Dahkwala*, 1 January 1886: 5-10.
101. That is, to Mrs. Börresen's school.
102. Dahkwala, 1 January 1886: 8-9.
103. For Rabhas and Bodos, see Karlsson 2000. The Santal Mission later worked among the Bodo (Nyhagen 1990, II: 11-22; Hodne 1992: 351-71).
104. The Bahrs were assisted by the Mission's first single female missionary, Signe Tillisch, from a well-known Danish family. She had joined one of the new Protestant monasteries, Vemmetofte Kloster. Born in 1842, she was no youth, and in 1895 she returned to Denmark (Nyhagen 1990, II: 193-4).
105. Börresen to Hertel, 13.09.82, *Dahkwala*, 1, 1883.
106. Nyhagen 1990, II: 306-9.
107. Letter from Bodding to Skrefsrud, Mohulpahari 22.10.1906 (Grahampur Mission Library).
108. *Arkatti* is the term used for the recruiting agent.

109. Deputy Commissioner, Singhbhum to Offg. Secretary, Chief Commissioner, Assam: Bengal General Proceedings, 1890: 103. Cited by Ghosh, 1999: 47-8.
110. Women migrating singly were often described as prostitutes by the authorities (Bates and Carter 1993: 164).
111. In what follows, we are relying on Carrin's discussions with her informants in Orissa and Bengal, as well as Chotrae Desmanjhi's text.
112. This is 'Dr. Raya', a Bengali with some medical training, at one time in charge of the Assam colony.

# 8
# The End of an Era

## SKREFSRUD'S SECOND TRIP TO EUROPE: 1882-1884

Since 1877, the IHM relied on modest funds from friends in India, and even more modestly from the Santal themselves. Börresen's visit in 1876-7 brought support from Denmark, but most of the money came from Britain. Clearly, without more financial muscle, the enterprise was doomed. It was natural, then, to turn to Scandinavia, and now it was Skrefsrud's turn to go. He counted on Denmark, stressing his bitterness towards Norway, whose state church and its priests were pompous, bureaucratic, self-righteous, and narrow-minded. As Lunde puts it: 'Because of Skrefsrud's entire circumstances the Santal Mission has become, in this country, a kind of protest against the State Church, against the rigid orthodox as well as the partly high-church, partly low-church pietists and against the Norwegian Missionary Society which is wholly governed according to the views of the State Church priests'.[1]

The main problem for orthodox Lutherans was the fuzziness of the missionaries' confessional views. Lunde got several letters complaining that the priests accused the mission of 'false teaching'. He knew 'no better advice than to answer . . . that we intend to convert the Santals in spite of the Norwegian priests'.[2] Skrefsrud was irritated by the Norwegians: 'In Scandinavia they cry: don't help the Santal Mission, for *one* of their three missionaries is a Baptist. The Baptists cry, do not help the Santal Mission, for *none* of the missionaries are Baptists. . . . At least the Baptists show themselves better trained in logic than the Scandinavians, for they build their warning on 'none' while the Scandinavians reason from 'one' only, and that 'one' contested by the Baptists'.[3] This letter, it is true, was an answer to Hertel's advice that Skrefsrud declare himself Lutheran. But in 1879 Skrefsrud wrote:[4] 'It is still something of a riddle for me, why my compatriots should be working against my missionary efforts right from the start, since after all I don't stand in the way of the success of (their) mission work in Africa; neither have I asked for their help in Santalistan'. But then he hints that his work merits support from Norwegians as well as Danes. The letter created a stir: Schiörn, a priest defending the NMS, attacked Skrefsrud, who wrote to Hertel:[5] 'I shall quite peacefully let both sides write till they have finished: then I will answer calmly, but make some revelations which will not be palatable.' Such remarks are revealing. Skrefsrud affects to be above the squabbles of the Norwegians, but is also eager to vindicate himself. There is little of this in his relations to the Danes or Scots. Deprived of respectability in Norway by his criminal past, he can succeed only by becoming a hero. The emigré can be excused for his flight only by flagrant success.

Skrefsrud had not foreseen the opposition from the NMS. As one of their workers reported, the Santal Mission was at first supported mainly by 'the Grundvigians and their hangers-on', but now seemed to be gaining influence 'even among serious Christians'.[6] Inside the NMS, some began to feel the Santal Mission was closer to apostolic practice. Did the NMS not ask too much of its converts before it would baptize them?[7] Others, however, doubted the Lutheran credentials of the Santal Mission, recalling its Baptist past. Lunde protested, citing the declaration that Skrefsrud had made to Kalkar.[8]

Skrefsrud did not want to go to Norway. To Hertel he wrote that the Norwegians were not 'worthy of taking part in the wonderful work of God among the Santals . . . Such narrow-mindedness as exists in Norway can exist there, and only there'.[9] But when Skrefsrud was coming to Europe in 1881, the Christiania committee urged him to visit Norway. He did so for four weeks. It was a success, and he returned the two following years, staying some seven months in all (Nyhagen, II: 26-7).

## NORWEGIAN RADICALISM OF THE EARLY 1880s

The milieu in which the Christiania committee worked was the world of prayer-houses and the Enerhaugens Samfund, the Working Men's Club that Halling had founded to counter Thrane's socialist influence. It was an important venue in the nascent Norwegian labour movement, in spite of its Christian ideology. Here the sociologist Eilert Sundt gave many of his talks. Skrefsrud first spoke at the prayerhouse in Hausmannsgaten. It was a packed house and many tried to follow the talk through the windows. The journal *Östlandsk Tidende* asked: 'Why doesn't the bishop . . . offer the largest church in town to this, the first man of our Church ?'[10] This wave of sympathy inspired Skrefsrud, who ended his talk saying 'If I had a thousand lives, I should be a missionary in all of them'.[11] Then he spoke at the Enerhaugens Samfund.

The Christiania committee was still a humble affair, run by honest men of good will but with little organizational flair. They were, however, looking for someone of stature to lead them, and found Oscar Nissen. It was he who organized Skrefsrud's visit—having just taken up his chairmanship. He was a friend of Björnson, an arch-radical, enthusiastically adopting one cause after another. In 1864, we find him volunteering to fight against Prussia, an ardent Scandinavist. In 1870-1, as a young doctor of medicine, he is in Paris, in a sanitary corps of the Communards. Later, he becomes a founder of the Teetotaller movement in Norway. He works among Christiania prostitutes, then leads the first strike of female workers, the girls of the match factories on the outskirts of the town. Later, he is a founder of the Labour Party, the editor of its main journal and, finally, its chairman. His work for the Santal Mission is but an episode in his life, and one may wonder why missionary work would interest such a man.

This was an epoch of intensive cultural debate in Norway, as exemplified by Ibsen, Björnson, Alexander Kielland, and Jonas Lie.[12] Björnson, we have seen, was close to the nascent Grundtvigian movement; Kielland criticized the Pietists and Puritans vehemently in his novels.[13] All four contributed to a radicalism reaching well beyond intellectual circles. The Grundtvigians started to have some influence through Bruun's school, but were not yet a faction of importance in the Norwegian Church. Björnson turned free-thinker; yet in 1879 he published a poem in praise of Skrefsrud:

To Skrefsrud

I honour you, because you were discarded,
yet heard the voice and gained your victory.
I honour you, since you, still charged with wonders,
respond from faith, and from your inner force.

I honour you, since you were fit for thirsting,
for feats of spirit through both need and fight;
I honour you, because you are the greatest,

son of the Gudbrand Valley in your time.

I do not share your faith you forceful dreamer;
that divides not, when the spirit message bears.
For all that flows about me, great and noble,
adore I, since I God adore.

In 1882 Björnson invited the missionary to his farm near Lillehammer. They met again in Paris, 1883, where Skrefsrud apparently tried to convert Björnson,[14] without success. Yet friends they remained. This did not go down well with Skrefsrud's friends: when Björnson gave a lecture in 1886, the proceeds of which went to the Santal Mission, they protested against contributions from an 'enemy of Christianity'. Skrefsrud cited the German Lutheran, Harms: 'If Satan himself offered me a contribution for the Mission, I would accept it, since he would thereby contribute to the destruction of his own Kingdom'. 'Björnson', added Skrefsrud, 'could surely not be worse than Satan?' His acceptance was in the spirit of the support, for Björnson had spoken of the magnetic power inherent in certain personalities—such as Skrefsrud. The gesture was made consciously, for Skrefsrud's fame in Norway was being threatened by the attacks of the young missionary Pahle.

The support comittee at Lillehammer also belonged to the Left—the liberal party—but to a different cultural milieu. Lunde, who led the committee, supported the general vote in his early years, but by the 1890s he had doubts.[15] He began as a radical, but died as a moderate. In spite of their different careers, his development ran parallel to that of his brother-in-law. In 1886, Lunde is among the main contributors to *Framgang*,[16] a new journal at Lillehammer, founded by the Vonheim circle as a left-wing alternative to the conservative *Lillehammer Tilskuer*. Lunde specialized in political articles. When, in 1890, the paper's radical editor, Johan Filseth, broke with the conservative Bruun, Björnson and Lunde helped him found yet another left-wing journal.[17]

Another matter of debate at Lillehammer at the time, was common high schools for boys and girls. Lunde was interested, but it was his wife Karen, Anne Onsum's sister, who published the notes she had written for her husband. 'This Lord of creation had decided', she writes, 'in spite of the beautiful words he entertains at all kinds of occasions concerning the rights of woman—to say he had no use for my 'mumblings'. So here is what I had intended Mr. Lunde to say'. She concludes that co-education would come sooner or later, in view of the female demand for education (Ramberg 1994: 143-4).

In 1888, Johan Castberg, on the Left of the Liberal Party, was organizing the labour associations—as an alternative to socialist agitation—in larger units. Lunde was on the committee in the county around Lillehammer (Ramberg 1994: 168). He was an activist for a railway through the Gudbrandsdal valley, which later became the main line to Trondheim (ibid.: 176).

Reading the correspondence one wonders whether Klara Fagstad is not the most central personality of the Lillehammer group. It may well be she, corresponding with Hertel, who incited Lunde to form a committee; they were the first Norwegians to whom Hertel wrote for mission support (Nyhagen 1990, II: 251). Then, when Hertel's fiancée threatened to leave him, Skrefsrud promptly advised him to go to Lillehammer. Later, Klara visited Hertel, but he was already married. One may discern a note of regret in their correspondence, however, and Klara remained the contact Hertel preferred in Norway. She was a favoured correspondent of Skrefsrud too. Nyhagen calls her the *primus motor* of the work at Lillehammer (ibid.: 330).

Skrefsrud visited Sweden in 1883 and preached in the Gothenburg Cathedral. The visit was arranged by the Inspector of Customs, Kullgren. The latter has described, in his unpublished autobiography, how he tried for years to awaken the Swedes to missionary work. The High Churchmen, says Kullgren, thought this activity to be beneath them, and the Pietists were only interested in the Home Mission, working among the poor in Sweden itself. Kullgren was the mainstay of the Mission's support until the Heuman affair in the late 1890s. Yet Swedish support was never as solid as in the other Scandinavian countries.

## PARLIAMENTARIANISM AND THE SCHISM IN THE NORWEGIAN LEFT

1884 is known in Norwegian history for the triumph of parliamentarianism. This had been the main issue keeping Liberals together under the leadership of Johan Sverdrup, a left-wing intellectual, close to radical writers such as Björnson or Kielland.[18] The intellectual wing of the Liberal Party was the public for whom they wrote. They alone could never have won the majority, but

Sverdrup forged an alliance between them and the Agrarians, descending from the peasants of the 1814 parliament, who had won a majority in 1833. They stemmed from the Haugean movement, and most Pietists voted for them. We may call them populists: they opposed the bureaucracy, as spenders of public money and as a social class. They opposed the priests: some were Freechurchmen while others wanted more influence for laymen in the Church. They introduced local self-government in Norway, substantially reducing the officials' power. The core of the movement were affluent farmers and provincial merchants.[19]

The introduction of parliamentarianism in 1884, defying the veto of the Swedish King, started the process leading to independence from Sweden in 1905. The Conservative government, from the class of officials and old merchant families, was replaced by Sverdup's Liberal ministry. But no sooner was victory gained than the proposal to name Kielland a national poet, with a honorary stipend, drove a wedge through the governing alliance. Björnson and Ibsen had received such honours: the radicals saw it as scandalous if Kielland did not get them.[20] The low-church wing, however, was shocked that a Christian state should grant such an honour to a declared atheist who had made his reputation mercilessly criticising their own circles. The revival movement led by J. Oftedal was particularly hostile to Kielland. Kielland never became a national poet (Storstein 1949: 119). Björnson was furious: he was a friend of Nissen. Björnson's atheism broke some of the respect the Grundtvigians had for him, including Lunde and his friends. The days when Björnson could write a poem in honour of Skrefsrud were gone.

## A CRITICAL AFFAIR

As Skrefsrud found growing support in Norway, a scandal, known as the Pahle affair, threatened to compromise everything. Johan A. Pahle was a young theologian recruited through Nissen, an idealist, and a teetotaller: while still at school, he decided to become a missionary (Nyhagen, II: 112). For all we know, Pahle did not differ radically from the Johnsonian views of the state Church. But his idealism implied a sceptical view of others. 'One says one thing, but thinks another: one teaches something but lives something else' he wrote to a friend.[21] Even Nissen admits to Rudin,[22] that Pahle withdrew from contact with fellow students, living more in the ideal than the real world. Pahle received his degree in Theology in 1882, then wrote to Skrefsrud. He was accepted as a missionary, and accompanied Skrefsrud to India in 1883. He travelled by Gothenburg, becoming a friend of Kullgren. On his arrival, Pahle was taught Santali by Skrefsrud, and got on well with the boys at the school, which Skrefsrud wanted him to take over.[23] But soon there are notes of dissonance. In February, 1884, Kullgren states[24] that he has received a letter from Pahle, which 'being of a most particular nature' is not fit for publication[25] (ibid.: 112-13). In a letter to Eckhoff,[26] Pahle described the contrast between his expectations and what he found at Benagaria. He had thought the missionaries would be living simply, but they lead a life of luxury. Coming from a poor background, and working his way to a University exam, Pahle was shocked by the comforts of colonial life (ibid.: 113 and n.).

Pahle was given to extend the Chondorpura station and build a bungalow there. Here he clashed head-on with Börresen who wanted to advise him. The quarrel led to Pahle's dismissal. But the pioneers gave a more general reason: Pahle was not suited to be a missionary.[27] He was dismissed in 1885.

Pahle was in no mind to take his dismissal lightly. In a series of letters to mission supporters in Scandinavia, he stated his criticism in no uncertain terms. Some of the rumours he mentions seem to come from Fritz Pettersen, the railway employee who had married Börresen's sister but had come to look askance at his brother-in-law's work. Börresen had, in fact, tried to prevent the marriage, since Pettersen did not live like a true Christian. But Pahle seems to have accepted Pettersen's criticism—including the rumours, from the time when Skrefsrud and Börresen worked for the Gossner Mission, that there was an illicit relationship between Skrefsrud and Caroline Börresen. This was shocking enough to supporters in Scandinavia,[28] but Pahle also said the missionaries were rich landowners, with considerable private incomes in addition to what the Mission paid. The latter sum—this was true enough—was fixed by themselves, and Pahle felt that financial control was far from satisfactory. Finally, and this must have vexed Nissen, there was wine at the table in Benagaria.

It is true that Skrefsrud had visited Europe twice in the company of 'another man's wife', and had spent a long convalescence in Cannes with Caroline. It may well be, as Skrefsrud said,[29] that the he felt like a son to the Börresens and treated Caroline 'like a mother'. He always referred to her as 'Mama'. But she was only eight years older than him and one may wonder, with Paulsen,[30] why they were not more careful to avoid such rumours.

Nissen was a man of action. He must have got the news by telegram, for by 8 January 1885, he called the Christiania committee, inviting the Drammen committee as well as Pauss and Eckhoff. They talked till two at night, and concluded by suspending all transfer of funds until the matter was cleared. They contacted their counterparts in Denmark and Sweden (ibid.: 115).

The decision was soon contested. Paulsen was absent, and took a firm stand for Skrefsrud and Börresen, going to see Nissen a week later. The Lillehammer committee protested: by holding back the money, Nissen had taken sides. From Kristiansand, too, came criticism: it would not do to ask Pahle, the accuser, to provide the proof. Lunde wanted to call Skrefsrud to Norway to defend himself: then he read Pahle's accusations and felt like hushing the whole thing. He trusted his brother-in-law—of whose faults he was not unaware—far more than Pahle: the latter had over-reacted, was vindictive, and his tone more than anything else proved that the pioneers were right. Reading Pahle's letters today, one gets the impression of a young man unjustly treated, responding in a rage. But what strikes us, since similar accusations about the opulence of missionary life were made by Söfeldt seven years earlier, is the shock these recruits from a modest, puritan background experienced at the luxury of colonial life.

Perhaps the Onsums, and Fagstads, belonging to Lillehammer's upper class, were less shocked. Should they have given or offered their daughters (Anne and Klara) in marriage to a man of no substance? It was enough that he was an ex-convict. Paulsen, the teacher turned farmer, was no poor man either. Nissen, on the other hand, though a doctor and a bourgeois was no less condemning as he was dedicated to the service of the poor. All this gains importance when we relate the crisis in Santal Mission circles to the broader political conflicts raging in Norway those years.

Nissen did not write to Hertel, but to Vill. Jacobsen, who expressed his confidence in Börresen and Skrefsrud, and criticized the decision of the Christiania committee. The Danish committee met on 26 February and came to the same conclusion. Their declaration was penned by Birkedal, the chief of the Grundtvigians. Rudin, of the Uppsala Committee, received a letter from Pahle, but

Rudin believed in Börresen, and warned against accepting Pahle's accusations without proof. But the Gothenburg committee, led by Pahle's friend Kullgren, took them seriously. Like Nissen, Kullgren froze funds for India. He wanted a meeting of representatives from the three Scandinavian countries, and proposed to send two trusted men to investigate on the spot. Meanwhile Hertel, who stood by Skrefsrud and Börresen, published Skrefsrud's 'answer' in *Dahkwala*.[31] Nissen answered, explaining Pahle's criticism in *Santalen*,[32] but concluded by hoping Pahle would again work for the mission (ibid.: 116-17).

Pahle had mentioned this, but contacted other missionary societies, even before the break with Börresen. He tried to join the CMS mission to the Paharias before leaving India: but they contacted Ebenezer, where Skrefsrud and Börresen advised against him. He asked Eckhoff to inquire about work for the NMS or the Schreuder Mission, and thought of going to America as a priest.[33] Borchgrevink, the NMS leader, answered positively and it seemed that Pahle might go directly from India to Madagascar: but the NMS board wanted to clarify the reasons for Pahle's dismissal from the IHM (ibid.: 117-18).

Nissen meanwhile wrote to Pettersen for his views on Pahle's accusations, but apparently he never answered. Perhaps he preferred not to get involved. Börresen was his brother-in-law: he may not have liked the missionaries nor they him, but the seriousness of Pahle's accusations was something else. Muston wrote to Nissen in support of his friends, and Berg, the missionary who came out with Pahle, supported the pioneers.

Skrefsrud sent Nissen an old letter from Krüger, with whom he had worked in the Gossner Mission. Krüger had supported Batzsch then, and one might think he would side with the critics. But 'openly before God and every man' Krüger 'never saw you doing any bad thing in Purulia about (which) you asked me, neither did it come to my mind of thinking so'.[34] Finally, the brothers Allen, wards of the Trust Deed, were convinced of the integrity of the missionaries and found Pahle's accusations groundless (ibid.: 118).

To Skrefsrud, these letters should suffice: if the Christiania committee still wanted proof, they must send somebody to investigate. Börresen suggested to Birkedal that they do so.[35] Finally, Bunkholdt was now going to Scandinavia on holiday, and would be available for further information. But then Vahl, in his journal,[36] published a letter from Börresen, referring to Pahle as working 'against God's kingdom on Earth'. This was strong stuff in the Evangelical milieu, and the Norwegians were angry. Nissen criticized the Danes for publishing such letters, and promised an explanation, though he still wanted time to investigate (ibid.: 118-19).

Then Bunkholdt came, and at a meeting in Gothenburg representatives from the three countries discussed the affair. Nissen was absent, as well as Hertel and the Lillehammer group, but the gathering included Beck, Jacobsen, Rördam, and Vahl among the Danes, Rudin and Kullgren from Sweden, and Bodding from Norway. They acquitted Börresen and Skrefsrud on all points, but the decision was to be published only if necessary. Then, one of the Norwegians—we don't know who—told the journal *Fädrelandet* about it. Soon, 'everybody' was talking.[37]

By now Pahle was back. He went to Nissen, upholding his accusations. Then the Swiss *Evangelisches Missions-Magazin* published another criticism of the Santal Mission, penned by A. Stern, a former missionary to India whose source was Hägert (who had broken with Skrefsrud and Börresen years ago). Nissen wrote to Stern for information about Skrefsrud's alleged landholdings. A meeting was called at Christiania, where Lunde and Pauss participated. They wanted to confront Pahle and Bunkholdt, but Pahle did not come. Instead he sent a list of questions for Bunkholdt, but the latter found several of them of 'a private character' and no interest to the Mission. Bunkholdt's situation was difficult: 'it was only too easy for him to choose his words in such a way that those at Ebenezer would be shocked' (ibid.: 120). Skrefsrud, in fact, reacted negatively to some of Bunkholdt's words.[38] Still, the meeting concluded in favour of the missionaries (ibid.: 120). They and their supporters had won the day, and Lunde[39] and Klara Fagstad[40] now turned against Nissen, who withdrew. The conflict had raged in mission circles not only in Scandinavia, but also in Scotland, where Graham made his own investigations, and in America, where the journal of Hauge's synod criticized Börresen sharply.[41]

The affair tells us much about the way Skrefsrud used his correspondence to influence matters. The network he had built—with Hertel and the Lillehammer circle as nodes—allowed him to build his defences strategically. He was successful, but the affair took a lot of his energy and made him bitter. He was too far away to understand the links between this affair and other events in Norway, so crucial to our understanding of the changing position of his and other missions in Norwegian cultural and political life.

## A PARALLEL CASE

As the Pahle affair shook the Santal Mission, the Scottish Presbyterians struggled with a similar conflict. Mary Pigot had taken charge of their orphanage and zenana mission in Calcutta in 1870. She was 'a quarter Indian', her mother being Eurasian. She was respected till William Hastie became principal of the Presbyterian college. He soon quarrelled with a teacher at Pigot's orphanage, Kali Charan Banerjee, about Hastie's book *Hindu Idolatry and English Enlightenment*.[42] Hastie wrote that 'Any reply deserved by these insolent Babus would have to be delivered from the tip of my boot.' He told Banerjee and Miss Pigot to stay away from each other. He wanted to control the orphanage and zenana mission, but she opposed these attempts.

Then, at a picnic Hastie saw Banerjee and Miss Pigot sharing a park bench, with Banerjee's arms 'resting over Miss Pigot's feet'. Rumours said Banerjee had been seen at an orphanage window 'with his arm round Miss Pigot's waist'. Then came the allegation in an anonymous pamphlet[43] that supporters of the zenana mission were 'the auxiliaries of the Jesuits in Calcutta' (Ballhatchett 1980: 112-13).

Hastie stated his accusations to the Foreign Mission Committee of the Church of Scotland. They reacted differently from Nissen, however: when Miss Pigot came to Edinburgh to defend herself, she was told 'to go back to Calcutta and defend herself there' (ibid.: 113). She sued, but was awarded only one anna in damages.[44] Miss Pigot was friendly with Indians in general,[45] and the *Bombay Guardian*, radical and nonconformist, felt she 'might have been tried before a native with more satisfactory results'.[46] She appealed, and in 1884 she won her case: Hastie had to pay damages of three thousand pounds. He went home and spoke to the Edinburgh Committee for eight hours, in vain. They sent a commission of enquiry to Calcutta.[47] Miss Pigot, cleared, was awarded a pension by the Church of Scotland. Hastie later became Professor of Theology at Glasgow (ibid.: 115-16).

The Scottish mission left its conflict to the courts: no such attempt was made by Pahle or his opponents. Conversely, the Scots were content to let the matter be decided in India: the Christiania committee clearly wanted to control the case. Should we assume that the Scandinavians did not trust their courts? Perhaps they wanted to avoid public scandal. The Scots Church acted as if its reputation could not be tainted by a conflict between two of its missionaries. But the Scandinavian mission had no church as its base: its reputation, and capacity to raise funds, rested on the personal honour of its founders. If Börresen and Skrefsrud were not what they were supposed to be, the whole structure would collapse.

## THE MISSION IN NORWAY, 1884-1889

In Norway, the break between the liberals and the low-church Left had profound effects on the Santal Mission. From now on, the mission was a low-church affair, but this also implied a demand for democratic control. Were the supporters, who provided the money, to have an influence in the field? Should the Christiania Committee coordinate the work? Or was it just one among several groups of supporters? Thus far, Skrefsrud and Börresen, who wanted no meddling from the committees, had had their way. But neither they nor their supporters, painfully aware of the weakness of the present arrangement, were content. Klara, who stood by the founders, saw this clearly. In an anonymous article in *Santalen*,[48] she compared their mode of work to the NMS. 'The Santal Mission', she wrote to Hertel, 'has no voice speaking for it, what couldn't it be if it had a position like that of the Missionary Society'.[49] She was concerned by the distrust of the priests, and felt they must hire travelling emissaries to raise public interest (Nyhagen 1990, II: 153).

It is easy to see why priests looked askance at the Santal Mission. Many supporters of the Mission were active freechurchmen. The conflict was sharpened by the events of 1884, for few priests were Liberals. A couple of years earlier, Gisle Johnson had published a manifest against radicalism (Nyhagen 1990, II: 147-8). The NMS was conservative, too, so even if Nissen wanted to quit after the Pahle affair, he was urged to continue. Politics was everything, and the supporters wanted to have Nissen around, to keep the Left for the Mission.

Nissen tried to work towards a national level integration of the support committees, but a national meeting at Moss in 1884 only sharpened the opposition between State Church members and dissenters. He planned a new meeting in 1885, but the Pahle affair came up. In the autumn he asked Pauss to take over, but Pauss wanted a priest on the committee, to gain confidence from the Church. Nissen opposed this, but next year he wrote from Germany to lay down his chairmanship. He felt his left-wing views hurt the Mission, since many saw liberals as fallen Christians. He had no word from Börresen for two years. But finally, Nissen had become a free-thinker,[50] and was now active in the Social Democratic movement. When he defended the prostitutes in 1887, he had to leave the Temperance movement, which he had led from 1879 to 1887 (ibid.: 153-4).

Pauss took over from 1887, and wanted to reconcile the parties. No great organizer, he wrote to Hertel: 'The Organization here is still the same excellent one, that is, none'.[51] He soon got a priest to join. Gustav Jensen was influenced by Haugeanism through his father, and by Grundtvig through his mother. He soon became the real leader. Börresen and Skrefsrud were pleased with the new committee, which kept the supporters together, but did not expand the activity forcefully, even if, as Klara had suggested, a few travelling emissaries were taken on. Yet popular support remained strong. There was fascination with the mission as a window to an exotic world to which Scandinavians had limited access, compared with the people of the main colonial powers.

## A CHANGING RELIGIOUS CLIMATE

Norwegian State Church circles play no part in the Pahle affair. Skrefsrud is supported by Grundtvigians and the Pietist Free Church milieu. With Nissen leave the radicals, whose Christianity is related to humanitarian views rather than any confession. The liberal Danish churchmen—Grundtvigians, Pietists, and Liberal mainstreamers—support Börresen and Skrefsrud, while in Norway their Mission is the object of a strange reserve in Evangelical circles. Is it truly Lutheran—or is there still something of Skrefsrud's rebellious spirit about it, making it 'not quite. . . ?'

But the spirit of the times is changing. The Norwegian alliance between Christians and Radicals belongs to a larger trend, nourished by a belief in progress, where technology, development, and conversion to Christianity all contribute to the creation of a new world. Common to atheists and Christians is a feeling of moving, in Manichaean terms, out of darkness into the light. In Norway, Björnson is the typical representative, and in praising Skrefsrud he is paying tribute to this common perspective. From the 1870s, led by Oftedal, Norwegian Pietism dissociates itself from the Utilitarianism that characterized the Haugeans. Even Kielland admitted the Haugeans' dynamic force, stressing the difference from Oftedal's 'rabbits'. The former incarnated the capitalist spirit: the rabbits did not. The contrast between Haugeans and rabbits may be compared with that between traditional Methodists and the holiness movement rising in Britain with the Keswick conventions of 1875. Led by the Pearsall-Smiths, an American couple, it had its beginnings at Mildmay and elsewhere (Bebbington 1989: 155ff). The rabbits and the holiness movement opposed the earlier, rationalist spirit, in Britain often called 'meliorism', very similar to the ideas of progress that had united Björnson and Skrefsrud in Norway.

This world-view changes in the second half of the century, at different times in different countries. Rolt (1970) puts it, for England, at the close of the Great Exhibition. In India, the mutiny is crucial. In Norway, the obvious year of change is 1884.

A new ethical relativism was associated with Keswick. Social theorists began to feel that cultural values vary with historical experience, and Evangelical teachers that duty depends on knowledge. Both were marked by the historical relativism of German Romanticism, which was 'spreading slowly into the Anglo-Saxon world. The holiness movement was part of the most far-reaching cultural shift of the century'. But it was far more intellectual in tone than Oftedal's movement. Keswick partisans referred to Wordsworth's cult of the transcendental beauty of nature, and Hardy's idealization of the countryside, making theirs a neo-romantic revival (Bebbington 1989: 168-9). Such artistic developments did not appear in Norway until the 1890s, with writers like Krag and Hamsun. One outcome of the holiness movement was to reduce evangelical investment in Christian activism, such as in foreign missions. Another, central point, was the demand for a 'second conversion', distinguishing between true and not-so-true Christians.

At the 1879 Missionary Conference at Bangalore, the trend towards education continued. But there were also new kinds of doubt. Rajahgopaul, an active Indian, said that the majority of mission school pupils did not convert but 'live false hypocritical lives'. We see here the new concern with quality, rather than quantity, of conversions (Copley 1997: 23-4), related to the holiness movement. By the Calcutta conference of 1882, the primacy of education over itinerating was clear. But at the same time, educationists found that educated Hindus showed little interest in converting (ibid.: 24-6). This growing scepticism, coupled with a demand for 'true' conversions, set the tone for the last decade of the nineteenth century. This did not affect the Santal Mission at first. But by the 1890s it wrought a new climate among missionaries, stressing the quality of Christian life among converts rather than the quantity of conversions.

*The Annual Report of 1889-90* puts it rather succinctly:[52]

> The Santhals have been willing to admit that there is only one true God, and it is also told in their traditions, that their ancestors adored Him, but that later generations abandoned Him to propitiate the bongas. Now we have generally got the following answer, as we entreated them to turn back to their ancestral God and believe in His Son Jesus Christ: Though we do not believe any more in our Gods, and though we are convinced that Christianity is the only true religion, we do not feel any urge to become Christians, since we cannot imagine any other form of happiness than eating, drinking, getting drunk and dancing, briefly, live the life we like to do.
>
> When we have answered that life is not made of pleasure only, but rather chiefly of sorrow and need, and that it is of great advantage to those who have given their heart to God that they can turn to Him with all their grief and worries, they have answers ready like the following: 'As regards always praying to God, it must surely be worst of all, for in our experience some of the most terrifying moments in our life have been when we had to approach the Bongas and propitiate them, and we always try to get away as fast as possible from that hoary business—how terrible then it must be to be always close to the great God and propitiate Him.

For the Santals, the main thing was to appease the bongas who can never be close to men. To get closer to one god was a foreign idea to Santals, as bongas are not to be trusted by ordinary men.

In the beginning, says the report, the Santals were negative: they feared the missionaries had 'political and worse' motives for conversion, and dreaded the wrath of the bongas if they were to convert. But as the missionaries became better known, and helped the Santals against zamindars and moneylenders, enmity changed to trust. Part of the willingness to hear the Gospel was, therefore, due to sympathy for the missionaries. But 'the fortress of Satan' was not yet taken. 'No sooner were they past their troubles with their oppressors, than their enmity, . . . turned to indifference.' Still they rejoiced, for the 'new stand was a defensive rather than an offensive one, and so the door was open for the more earnest among them to listen to the call of Christianity'. Yet the missionaries were anxious, for while these influences might bring the people to Christ, they might also harden the people 'like Pharaoh in the old days'.[53]

This anxiety was new. Their success had for years obscured the question their missionary colleagues had been asking: what was the quality of the conversions? Were the Santals becoming Christians in name alone? These doubts increased during the 1890s. Yet in the report, they are grateful that with 'drought, cattle sickness and other suffering of different kinds, with which God has visited them, they have had no time to get completely hardened, but have been obliged to seek aid from somebody or other, and since they continued to be in need in spite of the numerous fowl, pigs, and goats they sacrificed to their Gods . . . they have gradually been brought to understand . . . that it is not to the powerless gods they should turn for help, but the living almighty God'.[54]

The report is not signed, but the style is Börresen's. Indifference is the enemy and the supporters at home should know the missionaries are sensitive to this danger. But it is naive to think heathens will convert from conviction: the effort to side with the Santals against their oppressors have born fruit, as have the manifestations of God's wrath, since fear of God is fundamental to faith. Thus 'rice Christians' are not easy conversions but gifts from God. Critics have felt that such Christians must be hypocrites, 'who would stay with the flock only for as long as they were fed', but the report affirms that many of those 'baptized during the famine of 1873-4 have shown themselves to be among the most earnest, reliable, and active Disciples of Christ, while some of those who were baptized in better times have caused us a lot of anxiety and trouble. We must be grateful if the percentage of serious Christians among those baptized last year, when there was no famine, shows itself equal to that of 1873-4'. This is a familiar point with Evangelicals: 'In a sinful world like ours we must thank God that such things as poverty, sorrow and suffering exist, otherwise we fear that few, if any, would seek God. We think that it is mainly by such means that we are brought to inquire about spiritual matters.'

Börresen reassured his audience. The endeavour was to make sure that those who asked for baptism 'do so from pure motives, and we always impress on (them) . . . that they should withdraw rather than come with ulterior motives, since they will then be subject to a Higher Judgement. Yet when they insist, 'we have no right to refuse them, whether they are in need or not'. Still, there is a new stress on how hard it is to be a Christian: 'since Christianity demands . . . either a 'for' or an 'against', and it has been easy to see how those who still cling to their old faith have felt this, as also how they have tried to the last to resist this requirement.'

We feel these reflections stem less from experience among the Santals, than influence from wider Christian circles, where the urge for conversion was giving way to an emphasis on earnestness and 'holiness'. Christianity was no longer the spiritual aspect of general progress: there was a need to assert 'true' Christianity. But the report also discerns 'a more general movement towards Christianity, which made us hope that the awakening we were longing for, and for which we had prayed, was now at hand'. Then follows an account, village by village, of this movement.

The first example is a failure. In Chittragaria, 'a very corrupted village', the chief's assistant was seriously ill. Two of the Europeans went there to preach for him, with high hopes, since he had wished to convert. 'But alas, the heathens got hold of him, took him to another village, sacrificed to the Bongas for him, and told him the witches were "eating" him, and so they made him forget the living God and trust in men'. He died a heathen. Still, one missionary continued to work in Chittragaria, while the other 'was led by fate to another village, Tarachua'.

Tarachua was a very conservative village: 'not a soul had been baptized there all these years'. But Ihade, a man from there had been learning carpentry at Benagaria for years, and was influenced by the Christian carpenters to have himself and his family baptized. But in Tarachua, 'one old woman gave vent to the general feeling, when she told Ihades' wife she could no longer take water from the common well, since she was polluted and had become outcaste'. Ihade complained to the manjhi, and a meeting was called, where Ruhui, known to the missionaries as a firm and reliable person, proposed to fine the old woman, 'since it might well be that before long Ihade would be followed by others, who would not like to have their women treated as outcasts'. This was accepted, and a few days later Ruhui and his friend Tunui came to ask for instruction. They and their families were baptized. Both were 'of a peaceful but strong character . . . who did not hide their lights' and soon seven more families converted. The Christians in Tarachua are among the most active in the congregation, says the report. While most villagers adopted a 'wait and see' attitude, Ruhui and Tuhui turned to their kinsmen in other villages, converting several families.

In Kuamul too, 'fate' intervened. Only a few villagers were Christians and 'two of them a shame for our congregation'—we suspect drink was involved. 'A Christian . . . met an eager and pronounced enemy of Christianity, whose name is Sido. . . . Sido said he was going to the Market, but the Christian answered 'No, you are going to Hell if you do not turn your heart towards God'. 'This rather rough and abrupt way of addressing a man turned however by God's grace into the means for Sido's conversion', and he then converted eight more families, including the brother of the previous Manjhi, who left in anger years before to escape the "endless praying and singing."

Then there was 'the most remarkable victory' Christianity had won that year. In Aturia lived Jolha, an epileptic. Indigenous diagnosis was ambiguous: either his illness was due to witchcraft, or the bongas had inflicted it upon him. Jolha paid for both kinds of treatment, but to no avail: then turned to the missionaries. It worked, and Jolha was converted. When he and his wife returned to the village, they spoke to their kinsmen, including most of the village. Pores, one of its most influential men, was converted. 'And now the fight began in earnest. We, and those who were baptized here, prayed and preached: the heathens danced and drank like crazy. But by God's grace the Devil lost the battle'; of 27 families in the village, 25 converted, including the chief.[55]

Christianity spread towards the south and south-east, where the Kherwars had been strong. 'There are signs', says Börresen, 'that makes us hope that dawn is near'.

## A NEW TYPE OF MISSIONARY: HEUMAN AND BODDING

In 1885, Börresen returned to the problem of recruitment. He wanted Europeans at only a couple of stations. 'We want to work with Santals. . . . In the missionary field, a man will be seen just as he is . . . fifty natives cannot propagate as much as one bad European can destroy. Nobody should work in the vineyard, unless he is called.'[56] He talks of the endurance needed, of a missionary who returned to Ebenezer more dead than alive from a tour. 'I am sure you will agree when I want to reduce the number of Europeans. Our dear Bunkholdt is a good man, but . . . not strong enough to propagate the Word to the masses of the Heathen'. They need 'a man who knows farming: not too young, with some experience and a heart for the people'. They are indeed getting excellent recruits, but rather different from what Börresen had asked for. They were young, and they were trained theologians.

Ernst Heuman, the Swedish recruit in whom they had high hopes, joined them in 1886. He learnt Santali quickly and his grammar, based on Skrefsrud's, was ready by 1888, and published by the Royal Danish Academy in 1892 (Nyhagen 1990, II: 131-4). He took charge of the boys' school at Ebenezer, and by 1890 was seen as the likely successor to the bishopric Skrefsrud hoped to procure for Börresen. He married Börresen's second daughter, Käthe, in 1889. Yet he soon realized, as Pahle had done, that what the missionaries told their supporters was far from the truth. Unlike Pahle, however, he preferred, he wrote to Rudin, to pray to God for improvement (ibid.: 134).

Then there was Paul Olaf Bodding, born in 1865. His parents had known Skrefsrud since he came out of jail in 1861. They were Haugeans and ran a bookshop in Gjövik, a small town south of Lillehammer. The father was a friend of the Onsums, and a frequent visitor to their farm. The Boddings had long been childless, but kept praying for a child, promising that any offspring they had would be dedicated to the Lord's service. As Paul Olaf grew up, he felt the urge to become a missionary. Bookish and intelligent, he had a gift for languages (ibid.: 181-2). When Skrefsrud came to Gjövik in 1882, he heard about Bodding's son, and said: 'I have been praying to God that he should find me a successor. Who would have thought he should hear me thus, that he should be the son of my best friends?' (Santalen 1915: 246-7). Paul Olaf met Skrefsrud, and started his theological studies in the wake of the missionary zeal that followed Skrefsrud's visit. In 1884 he asked to be taken on at once. The answer was positive; but Börresen and Skrefsrud wrote to the Christiania committee that Bodding would become a better missionary by training in the field than at the University (Nyhagen op. cit., 183).

Bodding wanted to go to India in February 1885 but his parents felt he should finish his studies first. He wrote to Nissen that there was no question of giving up his calling,[57] but Skrefsrud feared

Bodding was swayed by Pahle's accusations.[58] Bodding was active in the students' missionary society, keeping in touch with members of the Christiania committee. He graduated in 1889 and was accepted by the Mission that summer. After practical training, he was ordained in November. But this went straight against Börresen's wish. Sharp letters were exchanged between Pauss and the Danish missionary, who was in Sweden at the time. 'The main thing', wrote Börresen, 'is that we are fitted by Jesus our powerful bishop to become his true servants'. His opposition was not due to dogmatic differences: what was at stake was prestige and power. The pioneers had no need for assistants with formal qualifications superior to their own. Bodding arrived in January 1890. Skrefsrud knew of his linguistic and literary abilities, and was not disappointed. A couple of months later, Bodding was put in charge of the Santali journal, which first appeared in May. He could not yet write or read the language, but was responsible for the content, translated by Heuman and Skrefsrud, as well as for production and distribution (ibid.: 185-6). Later that year Bodding was put to work on the dictionary.

The journal, *Hor hoponren Pera*,[59] was perhaps the most original of Skrefsrud's literary work. It is still published under a different name. It contained articles on history and religion to acquaint the Santal with the outside world—from Greek antiquity to the Norwegian religious revival, with rather less in between, save for the Mughal conquest of India. It was written in the Evangelical idiom, for those educated at the Mission schools, in an elaborate language. It brought letters from readers, writing for religious guidance, or reporting on the progress of Christianity in their locality. Non-Christian Santals are largely absent. The journal presents a Christian community rather more harmonious—we must assume—than reality.

It is interesting to compare the *Hor Pera* to another missionary journal in the vernacular, the *Orunodoi* of the American baptists in Assam. That journal followed the strategy we know from Long's work in Bengal, to produce a forum for general cultural debate in which the religious content was discreetly present. It succeeded perfectly in attracting an elite leadership, but conversions were not forthcoming (Sharma 2003). The *Hor Pera* was altogether more evangelical and its readership more popular: it spoke directly to the converts.

Bodding's fiancée, Clara Braathen, came in December 1891, and they were married a few days later. She, too, came from a Haugean family, living and working at the Eiker Paper Mills, founded by Hauge himself. Clara brought the bell that had called the labourers to work there, donated for the church at Mohulpahari. She died from pneumonia in April 1892, and was buried to the sound of the Eiker bell (Nyhagen op.cit.: 186).

## TOWARDS THE JUBILEE

Börresen returned from Europe in February 1890. He had long wanted to build a real church at Ebenezer, but they were short of money. Now, their Scandinavian supporters agreed to help. Börresen was the architect, and planned for congregations of two to three thousand. Sending the plans for approval, he stressed there was to be no pulpit, nor altar: 'Our friends at home should know for sure, that we out here follow no outward forms'.[60] He wanted no tower, but Skrefsrud insisted: 'I cannot imagine a beautiful church, one to inspire devotion, without a tower pointing towards Heaven',[61] he had written to Hertel. Finished in March 1891, this was said to be the largest Protestant church in northern India. Börresen had built fast and well, but the cost turned out to be Rs. 30,000, and in spite of contributions they had to borrow extensively. The church was consecrated on Easter Day with some 1,800 present. There would have been more, but for an influenza epidemic which cost many lives, followed by grasshoppers, provoking famine. There was no longer any hope of government intervention,[62] but contributions from Scandinavia helped (Nyhagen 1990, II: 187-8).

Bunkholdt had managed the girls' school when Mrs. Börresen was in Europe, helped by Anpi, who also managed the bungalow in Caroline's absence. But Bunkholdt was suffering from boils, and in 1894 he had to go to Japan for treatment (ibid.: 193). Berg, the Norwegian who came out with Pahle, had married in 1886, but his son died, and his wife suffered from the climate. They returned in 1892.

At Christmas 1891, they had a visit from J.C.H. Storjohann (1832-1914), founder of the Norwegian Mission to Seamen, and a central figure in the 1890s revival in Norway. Like many burghers of Bergen, he was of German origin. He was meant to succeed to the business, but wanted to study, passing his theological exams in 1860. He became pastor of the seamen's church in London, then secretary of the Christiania Home Mission. Storjohann copied the American tent meetings, held factory services, was active in school work, and built prayer houses that were to become central to the Norwegian religious landscape. He had started a seminary in Christiania, and wanted to train Santal missionaries there. Skrefsrud, who knew him from his visits to Norway, was not convinced, and though he was eager for Storjohann's visit, others, Klara Fagstad among them, were sceptical.[63] Storjohann was on his way to America, on a world tour. He had a grant from the Christiania Committee for America, which Klara criticised.[64] Börresen, too, was sceptical of the visit.[65] The Grundtvigians looked askance at the Home Mission, whose ideology impregnated the seamen's churches. But Skrefsrud liked Storjohann.[66] He wanted to visit America himself, but had no time yet, and seems to have been glad to find an eager and effective stand-in. Storjohann was accompanied by four Norwegian seamen and a couple of Scots (ibid.: 191-3).

In 1892 the IHM celebrated its twenty-fifth anniversary. There were now six to eight thousand Christians, and the influence of the Mission reached well beyond. 'Oh, if You could have been here', wrote Skrefsrud to the Baroness Reedtz-Thott, 'as Papa stood on the pulpit before 3,000 Christians and several hundred heathens, who had to sit on the Verandah—and some fifty chiefs among them . . . at the end he could not speak a word for heartfelt emotion and tears! It was worth a whole life's work to be there . . . What a change in these 25 years!'[67] But Börresen was old, his wife past middle age, and even Skrefsrud, at 52, was feeling tired.

## NORWEGIAN LUTHERANS IN AMERICA

Lutheran America, as Storjohann and Skrefsrud came to know it, was profoundly marked by the Civil War and the issue of slavery. Among Lutherans, the ethnically German and conservative Missouri Synod sided with the South. It was followed, in part, by the orthodox Norwegian Synod, whose leaders asked Gisle Johnson of the theological faculty at Christiania for advice. Slavery was not contrary to the Bible, the latter concluded, but insurrection was: the Confederation was wrong in seceding but right as regards slavery. This answer arranged nothing, and the pro-slavery party was at odds with most Norwegian immigrants, who espoused the Northern cause. They formed a Northern regiment,[68] and with victory the orthodox Lutherans were further discredited. This tendency was strengthened by the move towards the West, the main dynamic force in post-war American life. The migrants were not receptive to the old New England churches—Congregationalists, Presbyterians, and Unitarians: the West was soon ablaze with Evangelical revival, dominated by Methodists and Baptists. Both creeds were later brought to Norway by Norwegian-American preachers (Andersen 1975: 114). The lay preacher's mass meetings became a regular feature of American life. Foremost among them were Moody and Sankey, who had made a lasting impression on Britain and Europe in 1873.

The Norwegian migration to America occurred at the same time as that of the Santals to their various destinations. In both cases, migrants fled from overpopulation, land hunger, and poverty. Both migrations involved, at least in the early years, long, difficult, and dangerous voyages. But the different futures awaiting the migrants are striking: while the Santals were largely indentured into hierarchical structures where they were little better than slaves (Tinker 1974; Ghosh 1999), the Norwegians settled as independent farmers, escaping the stratification they came from. Their different destinies reflect the place of the two groups in the colonial order.

The first Norwegian immigrants were Quakers, in 1825, but Lutherans soon dominated the new settlements. In the next forty years, 77,874 Norwegians emigrated, mostly to America (Andersen 1975: 4). Before 1865, most came from the countryside, but after the Civil War migration diversified. 18,000 came in 1869, a peak year. By 1887-8 they were 20,000 a year (ibid.: 10-12). In 1910 there were 16,50,000 people of Norwegian descent in America (ibid.: 88)—about as many as in Norway itself—concentrated in Minnesota and Wisconsin, while Illinois, Iowa and the Dakotas held significant Norwegian minorities. Typically, the Norwegian migrant was a farmer, but there were important urban colonies in Chicago and Minneapolis.

Three leaders stand out as founders of Norwegian Lutheranism in America: Elling Eielsen, Claus Clausen, and J.W.C. Dietrichson. Eielsen was a Haugean lay preacher, who found himself imprisoned in Denmark under the law once used against Hauge himself. Encouraged by a Haugean merchant in Drammen, Eielsen sailed for America in 1839, and in 1846 founded the Evangelical Lutheran Church in America, known as Eielsen's Synod. By 1914 it had 40,000 communicants in 350 congregations. It changed its name to Hauge's Synod in 1875, after a break with the domineering founder, and established a seminary in 1879. By 1891 it had its own foreign mission, concentrating on China (Andersen 1975: 104).

Dietrichson had been ordained in the Norwegian Church before coming to America in 1844. There was soon conflict between him and Eielsen, who 'may have wondered whether Dietrichson aspired to be a bishop in America. Dietrichson, on the other hand, looked askance at lay activities and expressed misgivings over the propriety of Eielsen's ordination' (Ibid., 105). The schism between high-church and low-church was clear: priests ordained in Norway 'resented and feared the self-assertiveness of the former peasantry, or *bondestand,* in America'. Dietrichson had a hard time in his parish, he had a lawsuit brought against him, and several fights with members of his congregation (ibid.: 105-6). He left for Norway in 1850, but others followed, and founded the Norwegian Synod in 1853.

Clausen, a Dane, had been a Haugean lay preacher, but was influenced by Grundtvigianism through W.A.Wexels, a pioneer of such views in Norway. He came to America in 1843, and settled in Muskego, Wisconsin, where a Haugean leader donated land for the first Norwegian church in America. Clausen soon had difficulty with Eielsen's criticism of the Church (ibid.: 105). He joined the Norwegian Synod, moved to Iowa, and was elected to the state legislature. By the end of the 1850s, he was excluded from the Synod for his Grundtvigian views, but was readmitted in 1861, confessing his 'error'. He insisted that slavery was sinful, and was again excluded in 1868. Two years later he became president of the newly formed Conference of the Norwegian-Danish Evangelical Lutheran Church of America (ibid.: 107-8). He retired, ill, in 1872.

Then there were the Augustanas, the Swedish Lutherans in America. Their Norwegian members left to form the Norwegian Augustana synod in 1870. The Conference joined in 1890 with the Augustanas and the Anti-Missouri Brotherhood, which split from the Norwegian Synod on the slavery question, to form the United Church, uniting the majority of Norwegian Lutherans in America. But rifts soon appeared, and the Conference's seminary, Augsburg, was a central issue. The Anti-Missourians wanted their school, Saint Olav's, as the main college of the new Church—leaving Augsburg as a theological seminary. But Augsburg was more than that, built as it was on a consciously 'anti-humanist' platform. Then, the United Church seemed to move towards a Presbyterian stand, with an authority over its congregations unacceptable to parts of the

Conference. Thus, in 1897, the Lutheran Free Church seceded (Hamre 1986).

This fervent activity on the religious front was a dominant feature of Norwegian-American debate in this period. But there was also an ultra-liberal or even freethinker opposition, ax exemplified by the Unitarian Kristofer Janson (Draxten 1976)[69] or the old socialist leader, Marcus Thrane (Leiren 1987).

## THE BEGINNINGS OF AMERICAN SUPPORT

The Santal Mission was known in America before it was heard of in Scandinavia. From 1869 *The Morning Star*, the journal of the Freewill Baptists who worked among the Santals in Orissa, brought news from Ebenezer. The *Missionary Herald* of Boston wrote about the mission in 1873. Skrefsrud's visit to Europe in 1873-4 was reported in Scandinavian papers in America,[70] and when Börresen came home in 1876-7, major newspapers such as *The Evening Post*, *New York Observer*, and *Independent* wrote about him. Probably the first contribution from the New World came from a Danish Sunday school in Illinois on the last day of 1877 (Nyhagen 1990, II: 210-11). They heard of the Mission from the Grundtvigian journal *Kirkelig Samler,* whose editor Jakob Holm, an enthusiastic supporter, came to America in 1876. By 1879 the Danish Church in America sent money from their annual meeting. Among Norwegians Marcus Thrane, the old socialist leader, in 1882 criticized Storjohann— then in America—and Skrefsrud.

Then, in 1882, Skrefsrud met Oftedal, an Augsburg professor and brother of the leader of Kielland's 'rabbits', at the NMS general assembly in Bergen. Oftedal was not the only American there; H.G. Stub of the Norwegian Synod was critical of Skrefsrud, partly because of the latter's link to the Freemasons, unacceptable to American Lutherans. Skrefsrud and Oftedal became close friends. But it was the lay preacher H. Bottelsen, a baker in Hamar and Christiania, who invited Skrefsrud to America. In Christiania he had been chairman of the 'little' home mission.[71] An active freechurchman, he had gone into the building trade in the 1880s, and the economic crisis hit as he stood surety for several friends who went bankrupt, trailing Bottelsen with them. Then Skrefsrud came, helping him regain faith. Bottelsen went to America, joined Eielsen's flock and published, anonymously, a book about Skrefsrud and his Mission.[72]

Towards 1885 he moved to Minneapolis where he became steward at the Trinity Church, influencing its pastor, M. Falk Gjertsen, to support the Santal Mission. In 1893, Giertsen joined the United Church.[73]

In 1891, two Minnesota Norwegians wrote to *Santalen* that America would support the Mission, if Skrefsrud would come. He answered he would go as soon as the Bible translation was finished. Meanwhile, Bottelsen formed a committee with Oftedal and Falk Gjertsen among the members. All were Norwegians, mostly from the United Church. They soon invited Skrefsrud. He could not come, but Storjohann did, and his visit was a great success for the Santal Mission.

Bottelsen returned to Norway, and was replaced by a colleague of Oftedal at Augsburg. They again invited Skrefsrud. He left Ebenezer in April, 1894, reached Copenhagen by the end of the month—we are now in the steam age—and arrived in New York on the 19 May. On the 17 May he made the main speech on the national day—the passengers went in procession around the ship. At Brooklyn, then a Norwegian centre, his picture was on the front page of the Norwegian newspaper, and he spoke to large crowds. He preached at the Trinity Church, built by laymen in protest against the orthodox Norwegian church and in the Danish Church before leaving for Minneapolis.

Skrefsrud preached incessantly, three times a day, then cut down to preserve health, but held 364 meetings in America—about one a day, deducting four months of illness. One of the first was organized by Oftedal, who impressed Skrefsrud greatly. He participated in annual meetings of the United Church, the Augustana Synod, and Hauge's Synod. The Norwegian Synod stood aloof (Nyhagen 1990, II: 217-21).

Skrefsrud used Norwegian almost everywhere. Even in distant places, several thousand came to hear him. By November, however, he was down with pleurithis, and stayed four months with the Falk Gjertsens, speaking only occasionally. Incidentally, the priest's daughter became his fiancée, but again there was no marriage.[74] By March he was active again, speaking at various Norwegian seminaries. The tone was that of revival meetings, and he was instrumental in starting the revival that shook Norwegian America in the 1890s. Skrefsrud met old friends,[75] and several of his brothers and sisters now settled in America. When Skrefsrud came, a majority of the

United Church, mainly the Augustanas and the Anti-Missouri Brotherhood, opposed a minority that was centered on the Conference. Skrefsrud was unable to hide his sympathy for the minority, led by Oftedal and Georg Sverdrup, a close relative of Norway's first parliamentary prime minister. The majority reacted, fearing he would be a spokesman for Augsburg. The visit was not arranged by the mission committee of the United Church, they said: it was a private affair. Several congregations refused his visit and would send no contributions through the Minneapolis committee. He tried to play neutral, but in vain (ibid.: 222-6). The criticism of one orthodox leader, H.A. Preus, may serve to explain central issues (1990).[76]

Preus accused his opponents of being 'reformed'. Calvinism was heresy to him, and only details distinguish papist from calvinist heresies. The Augustanas had joined the General Synod, which was open to contact with Anglican, Reformed, and Methodist Churches (Preus 1990: 137-8). Preus calls it 'Unionist', referring to the Prussian State Church, formed in 1818 by merging the Reformed and Lutheran churches. For strict Lutherans this was a catastrophe never to be repeated.[77] The pastors of the Norwegian Synod are chosen by the Synod, though theological orthodoxy is combined with determination to build a free church. Among the Augustanas, the pastor is elected by the congregation—a two-thirds majority is sufficient to dismiss him—and represents his congregation in the synod (Nichol, in ibid.: 13-17). The idea of a congregation dismissing a minister by vote scandalizes Preus. Two strains emerge here: theological questions, seen as expertise demanding proper training; and practical interest, defending the priest's position, and, implicitly, the stratification between the bureaucrat class and the peasants, as it existed in Norway. Sverdrup, liberal rather than conservative, held that the Church must be 'of the people'. For Preus and Sverdrup, as for Skrefsrud and Börresen, such differences relate to deeply felt ideals, and we see how the missionaries' lack of interest in theology becomes a theological stand.

Apart from the crucial point of priesthood and lay activity, Preus stresses other doctrinal errors, concerning absolution, the Sabbath, slavery, regeneration through the Word, and millenarianism (Preus 1990:155). To the orthodox the Gospel constitutes absolution. Here, God forgives; humans can only spread the word. The Reformed view is that the Word is only declarative, which Lutherans see as a

Catholic error (ibid.: 157-8). 'American Sabbathism' identifies Sunday with the Sabbath of the Third Commandment. To Preus, Sunday is chosen by man, not God, and secular authoritities should not legislate on the holiness of Sunday (ibid.: 131). Slavery is not banned by the Bible; it comes under the Fourth Commandment (ibid.: 161-73). Then, the Word itself regenerates man. Baptism is not, as the Augustanas held, needed for Regeneration. One may be saved without baptism but not without the Gospel (1990: 156). Chiliasm, a form of millenarianism is the belief in the return of the Jews to the holy land, introducing the millennium. Preus, accusing some Augustanas of holding this doctrine, finds no base for it in the scriptures (ibid.: 160-1).

The tenets of Lutheran orthodoxy emerge clearly here. The Bible is the only religious authority, since its every word is God's own. Luther's writings are canonical and must be referred to whenever the Bible is not clear. A clear line is drawn between secular and religious spheres. Due respect is owed secular authority, but its interference in religious matters must not be tolerated.[78] The importance of the Word relegates all sacraments to a secondary role. And though it is accessible to all, Christ wrought the priesthood to guide the Congregation.

Skrefsrud never defined his theological position, but in America, where the synods fought to represent true Lutheranism, he sided with the Conference, and Sverdrup's unorthodox views may serve as a guide to Skrefsrud's. He denies the individual agency that is often seen as central to any Protestant doctrine of human responsability (Asad 1996: 271). The Holy Ghost expresses itself through the congregation, and salvation comes from the faith God creates in man. The agency is God's, the individual just an intermediary. Sverdrup stresses the contradiction between the congregation and church hierarchy, but criticises the individualism of the pietists, such as Eielsen's flock. To Preus, laymen cannot judge theological matters. But for Sverdrup, right and wrong are questions of faith, not theological expertise.[79] 'The Church', he says, '. . . craves for Freedom, so its members may freely confess their Faith'. This implies doctrinal freedom, since God may bestow different visions of reality, all equally true (Hamre 1986: 32). The Church in the larger sense cannot be equated with a single church or sect. Training at Augsburg differed from that in the orthodox seminaries, for Sverdrup was highly critical of the 'humanist' tradition.[80] Skrefsrud is said to have thanked God that his friends kept Augsburg when they formed the Lutheran Free Church in 1897.

Skrefsrud's visit had created a base of support in Norwegian America. From 1895 the American committee had its own newspaper,[81] and sent several missionaries (Nyhagen 1990, II: 226-9). Skrefsrud was impressed by America. The independent spirit of the American congregations inspired him, contrasting as they did with the State Church Christians he knew. Sverdrup's ideas of the Church, and his theological stand, were probably closer to his own views than anything else he had seen. Here, perhaps, was realized the dream he once had of the Santal National Church—albeit, it is true, without the Santals.

## DECEPTION AND CONTROVERSY

Suddenly, Börresen telegraphed Skrefsrud to return immediately. In October 1896 he was back, and found Börresen exhausted: he had a stroke a few months later. Several letters from Scandinavia had reached Börresen, complaining about Skrefsrud's long stay in America. There was also serious conflict between Caroline Börresen and Heuman.

The girls' school was characterized, in 1892, by the Inspector of Education as the best in Bengal.[82] Heuman managed the boys' school, which had been in a sad state when he took over. Now it grew steadily. In 1891, he opened new lodgings for the boys, financed by the Swedish YMCA and other Swedish sources. An excellent teacher, popular with the boys, he took an interest in the schools run by other missionaries. In Darjeeling he met Blaich, in charge of the CMS school at Taljhari, and was impressed. They taught up to an officially recognized examination opening the way for further studies. But this meant using Bengali, while Skrefsrud held that Santals should be taught in Santali, so as not to educate Santal boys 'away from their own people'. Skrefsrud and Börresen disliked boys who tried to put on 'Bengali manners', shoes or socks, or the flowingly draped vestments of the Babu.

Heuman had to admit that the CMS schools were of a higher standard than his own. Still, he felt Skrefsrud's policy was basically correct, and said so. But he felt they should adopt the basic plan of the government schools. In 1892 he held a public examination at the elementary level, with Skrefsrud's approval, and by 1893 his boys did better than at any other school in Bengal. Next year the first of his boys passed the Middle School Exams. Heuman did not want to go further yet; they still avoided English, which Skrefsrud had abandoned in the 1870s, fearing that the boys would become 'preposterous clowns'. Bengali, however, was needed if the exams were to be recognized by the government.

Heuman was in the spirit of the times: missionaries now saw education as more important than itinerating. But this implied that schools must have more than an academic function. As Heuman put it: 'The more I get to know the people, the more I am convinced that education is currently both the most important and the hardest part of our work out here—I think not merely of the education of the young, but that of the whole congregation. If among the young that we educate, there should . . . be established numbers of Christian couples, who would be planted all over the country to become examples of Order in their inner and external lives, then they would be a mighty levering force for the whole life of the congregation'.[83]

But Heuman's valuable work would soon be ended by conflict with the founders. During the rains of 1895, one of the schoolboys was accused of accosting one of the girls—a minor—at Caroline's school. She submitted the boy to three hours of interrogation and 'made him confess', as Nyhagen puts it. She demanded a compensation for the girl's family. But the boy's father would not pay, as both he and most of the congregation were sure of the boy's innocence. Caroline took the case to court, and asked Heuman, who believed the boy, to abstain from appearing as a witness. But he came, and in spite of a verdict in the girl's favour, Caroline got Heuman removed from the school. He was given a post at the out-station Tilabani, where he read a letter Skrefsrud had written to *Santalen*,[84] regretting the shortcomings of the school under Heuman's leadership (Nyhagen 1990, II: 239-43). Heuman went home in 1898, left the mission for good, was ordained in the Swedish church (ibid.: 257-61), and later became Bishop of Tranquebar (Brundin 1926).

In 1892, there was a breakthrough in conversions in the Sultanabad area, which, we recall, had been a centre of Kherwar activity. Entire villages were suddenly asking to be baptized. There were near-famine conditions in the district that year, which, says Nyhagen, 'had woken them up spiritually'. Sibu Besra (1850-1908), ordained by the Mission in 1884, was in charge here. Son of a chief who chose to remain heathen, Sibu had gone to the boys' school at Ebenezer. He soon became the Mission's best orator, and wrote a large number of hymns and songs, which are still sung. Sibu had a busy time catering to what was a real mass movement, with about 2,000 baptized in a very short time. He had won the confidence of Santals in his area, and Börresen insisted, against Skrefsrud's and Bodding's advice, that he should remain in sole charge at Sultanpur. The situation looked promising, and Sibu's way of dealing with it impressed the old missionaries. But, 'Sibu could not stand the pressure of such a movement. His success destroyed him' (Nyhagen 1990, II: 195-6). Exactly what happened is not clear, but Jörgensen says he let the elders do most of the work, while he himself spent his time—and earned good money—deciding quarrels among the heathen (1920: 170). Apparently, Sibu also 'put on airs' and thought himself the equal of the older missionaries. He was removed to another station, but those who replaced him could not stop the converts from returning to their original religion. Much later, the area was like a 'swidden' to the missionaries, where no attempts at evangelization would work.

The optimism of the missionaries had lasted a long time. But around 1895, there was growing concern about the spiritual condition of the converts. 'What we miss now', writes Börresen in 1897, 'is that first, burning Love among the first Christians, which made them all seem like lighted candles.'[85] Bodding had not been slow to register the problem. 'The conditions are not magnificent, but rather dark, and we must work with hope towards (another) hope' he wrote in 1894.[86]

There were other deceptions. Bunkholdt died in 1897, in Assam. Frithjof, Börresen's only son, joined them in 1898 but died in 1900. After Bahr's death, Ingeborg became Bodding's second wife in 1897 but ran away on the wedding night with the Mission's coachman, a Muslim: she was still living with him and their five children in Nepal in 1919. Perhaps surprisingly, Caroline continued to correspond with her, and sent her money—facts which only became known as Käthe, now Heuman, protested against Bodding's third marriage. This made Bodding a bigamist, which eventually led to his dismissal from missionary activity, and, incidentally, provided the opportunity for his vast ethnological work.

Skrefsrud's letters of the last five years of the century show this pessimism, mixed with hope, as he heard about revival in Norway and hoped for something similar among the Santals[87] (ibid.: 231-2). As he gradually took over Börresen's duties, his running of the mission reflected doubt in the moral and spiritual qualities of the converts. He began to move Santal religious workers around, sacking some others.

Börresen had been far more ready to trust his Santal collaborators than Skrefsrud. In 1899 Skrefsrud thought that he had caught several of the Santal leaders on out-stations 'misusing their position, turned money meant for the station to their own private use, and other such charges'. In some cases, says Bodding, the accusations were probably true, 'but not in all the cases, and certainly it was not true of Gulu', Sona's husband. With a dozen other leaders, Gulu was called to Benagaria, where he stayed several months. 'In Benagaria they went about as Elders, and there were meetings held with or by them'. Bodding is critical, for 'there were certain less desirable elements, who were able to make their influence felt' (Bodding 1919: 22). He felt, twenty years later, that Skrefsrud was far too suspicious—one feels he was getting rather paranoiac.

The question of moral authority versus domination in the mission field reads like a microcosm of the colonial situation in India. Why, asks Guha (1998: 63), did the establishment of British paramountcy in South Asia fail to overcome the resistance of its indigenous culture to the point of being forced into a symbiosis? Colonialism, he feels, could continue as a relation of power in the subcontinent only on the condition that the colonizing bourgeoisie failed to live up to its own universalisic project, as formulated in the Bengal Renaissance. The colonial state, he says, was an intrusion into indigenous society, despotically structured with 'no mediating depths, no space provided for transactions between the will of the rulers and that of the ruled' . . . this '*immediacy* proved to be an essential factor both in the constitution of dominance and in the construction of the political domain' (ibid.: 65). This meant dominance without hegemony: order became a more decisive idiom than improvement. The failure is not obvious at first, neither in the mission field, nor in India as a whole, until the end of the nineteenth century. The laws themselves were characterized by double standards—one for the whites and the other for the natives. The rule of law in colonial India had its origin in the pervasive power of the ideology of law in British political thought (ibid.: 67), as is noted by Thompson (1968) discussing the class manipulation of the rule of law. Rabindranath Tagore cites instances of racist discrimination in juridical affairs, referring to Kipling's imagery of India as a zoo where the natives had to be kept under control by the whip combined with 'a promise of bones for food and even a little affection that was owing to pets' (quoted by Guha 1998: 71).

The situation worsened by the end of the nineteenth century: there was no longer a real advance but 'merely a gesture in the direction of the past'. Guha looks at the literature of the eighteenth century as 'mercantilist historiography', an effort to educate Indians in liberal values. The colonizer had the dual role of conquistador and scholar, which again recalls Skrefsrud's role among the Santals in the mission's early phase. In the age of industrialism colonial historiography acquired a new look. James Mill (1818) was considered the first historian of India. Guha stresses how central to the logic of Mill's history was the denunciatory chapters on Hinduism (1998: 76). Mill demonstrates the absolute inferiority of Hindus to Muslims in every respect and of course the superiority of British to Muslims. While Skrefsrud stresses the equality or even, in some ways, superiority of Santals to Hindus, there is never any doubt that they can and will be 'improved' by (his and Börresen's) European influence.

The 'bad faith' of the Victorian historiography of India derived from the political philosophy of improvement; but the idea of colonialism as a civilizing mission was losing its credibility as colonialism had its records judged by an increasingly subject population. In neo-colonialist historiography, says Guha, the colonized have no desire of their own, a strategy aimed at characterizing colonialism as hegemonic dominance. The same paternalist effect is evident if we look at the position of the Santal missionaries in first half of the twentieth century, as when Rosendal, the senior missionary, argued against Gausdal's proposals for autonomy in the 1920s (Hodne 1992: 417-21).

## THE SPIRIT OF THE NINETIES

In the last quarter of the nineteenth century, European Christianity was changing. In Britain, the Holiness movement had led to new standards of spirituality: much more than a right and moral life was asked of the 'real' Christian. The spirit of 'self-help', as typified by Samuel Smiles' books, had been strong: men like Skrefsrud and

Börresen were, in a sense, religious counterparts of Smiles' secular heroes. They were certainly fighters in the 'battle of life', where to win without a struggle was perhaps to win 'without honour.'[88] Here, we are clearly dealing with the 'protestant ethic' as Weber saw it.

Moody and Sankey took the spirit of the camp meeting to Europe, producing a revival which influenced Evangelicals in Britain and Germany, and strengthened the Home Missions in Denmark and Norway. The background to this new wave of revival in Europe was industrial expansion. The Church had difficulty in reaching the growing population of the new industrial suburbs. But efforts were made, through Home Missions, social work, Christian Working Men's Clubs, and, from 1878, through Booth's Salvation Army. Several Evangelical activists saw a parallel between the teaching of the Gospel and Socialist ideas, forming Christian Socialist organizations. There were attempts, notably in Germany, to form a Christian Labour Party opposing the Socialists.[89] All this tended to favour a low-church approach, opposing the theological research that was forging new links with the history and sociology of religion. As a result, popular Christianity and academic theology grew further apart. This in its turn led to a new brand of conservative theology—in Germany at first—which differed from older orthodoxy in having to elaborate its theoretical and academic base (Holmquist and Nörregaard 1939, II: 1-32).

In India, too, the new spirit of 'social purity' is felt. Slum work and the suppression of vice were part of the new mood. The 1868 Act, providing for the control of prostitution, yielded to liberal and Evangelical pressure in 1888. That year Alfred Dyer, a Quaker activist in the purity movement, settled in Bombay as editor of the *Bombay Guardian*. His views were seconded by the *Sentinel* and the *Banner of Asia*. The latter, too, had a European editor, though when moving to Bombay as a Salvation Army officer he changed his name from Ward to Man Sukh Lal, adopted Indian dress, and married an Indian wife.

There was no shortage of scandal. Fanny Epstein was a Jewess from Whitechapel, born in Warsaw, believed to have been 'abducted' by one Alexander Kahn, formerly of the brothel trade in Buenos Aires. He brought Fanny to Bombay, but when her father and the National Vigilance Association tracked her down, the police found her in charge of a 'saloon bar' which had been given to her by Kahn; she was doing well and had no wish to be rescued. Her evidence saved Kahn from a conviction, in 1891, but her brothel was sold at a loss (Ballhatchett 1980: 126-8). In 1893, the Calcutta Missionary Conference held a large meeting to campaign for social purity. 'The most shameless characters', said Bishop Thoburn of the Methodist Episcopal Church, 'in the city are not Indian but persons imported from Europe . . . devoted to the propagation of vice in all its forms' (ibid.: 131).

Though one Indian journal accused the 'puritywallahs' of hypocrisy, the authorities took the criticism seriously. Could brothel-keeping be made a punishable offence? The Calcutta police protested: there were 20,000 prostitutes and brothel-keepers in the city, far more than they could deal with. But brothels could be closed if the public complained: a series of such complaints followed in 1893-4, and many European-run brothels were closed. The Bombay Midnight Mission patrolled the street of European prostitutes at night, 'knocking on doors and windows'. The residents complained, and the police played neutral. Dyer, Man Sukh Lal, and others spent time in jail for public disturbance—but others replaced them. The suicide of a barmaid led to rules banning European women from selling alcohol. Curzon, then Viceroy, noted: 'the spectacle of the service is open to the eyes of natives . . . and occasionally . . . incidents occur which are profoundly degrading to the prestige of the ruling race' (ibid.: 131-9). Sin was no longer an unavoidable part of human nature; in the colonial setting white respectability must not be stained.

Hindu sensibilities had evolved. Rajput and Muslim court traditions had accepted concubines and dancing girls as symbols of luxury and power. The emerging Hindu middle class, however, rejected such practices, substituting an ideal of family respectability partly shaped by European influence. The new Hinduism and Evangelical Christianity were competing to present the most convincing image of moral respectability.

The distance between British and Indian elites continued to grow, in spite of efforts to reduce it, notably under the Liberal Viceroy Lord Ripon. 1882 brought one of the bitterest controversies of the period. The Law Member, C.P. Ilbert, proposed a Bill to remove all 'invidious distinctions' between Indians and British in terms of law. As it stood, the British could only be tried by a British judge. To Ilbert, this made no sense. 'Imagine', he wrote, 'its being suggested to a Parisian magistrate on behalf of an English pick-pocket!'[90]

Liberals like Mill supported the Bill. The first Indian was due for promotion to Sessions Judge. The question was pressing (Metcalf 1995: 204-6). But as the British in India realized they might be tried by an Indian judge with none of their own race in charge, all hell broke loose. A ferocious campaign was staged against the Bill, there was even a threat to kidnap the Viceroy. Most of the Civil Service sided with the opposition.[91] Ripon compromised. The Bill was a continuation of the liberal policies of pre-Mutiny years, but India had changed. The belligerence of its opponents, says Metcalf, expressed 'an increasing fearfulness, linked to a newly perceived vulnerability' (1995: 211). It was a shock to the British, says Mason, to be confronted with educated Indians who 'thought and talked like an Englishman and claimed to be judged by English standards, and the shock roused a great deal of irritational anger' (Mason 1985: 285-6). The racial conflict was strengthened by the ban on child marriage, introduced in 1891, which launched Tilak's political career, protesting against it. We find no reference to these conflicts in the writings of our missionaries. Only in the 1890s do we see any real change in their relationship to their converts.

In the field, Skrefsrud and Börresen were faced with new men, like Bodding or Heuman, who built their conservative position on rationally argued theological knowledge. Only superficially did their views ressemble those of an earlier generation of Bible readers. Skrefsrud had read widely, but knew little of the new theology. In the Home Mission and the new revival, they found much to agree with, but Skrefsrud tried to keep aloof from the conflicts of the new generation, except in America. Börresen's devotion seems immune to such new-fangled oppositions, though one suspects that his apparent naïveté hides a conscious choice. Yet the ideology on which they had built their mission seemed to fit the spirit of the times. Like the revivalists, they opposed bureaucracy, the priesthood, and academic theology. Their distant base in India helped them to transcend the conflicts of Western Christianity. To Western friends, they were survivals of an earlier age, when simple faith could still move mountains.

Skrefsrud and Börresen were both trained mechanics. The older man had, in Berlin, certainly entered the 'labour aristocracy' as defined by Hobsbawm (1964). Skrefsrud, by all accounts an excellent craftsman, was well on the way when he chose to become a missionary instead. His early interest in Thrane's socialist movement, probably inspired by his patron the coppersmith and mechanic Erik Bu (Nyhagen 1990, I: 91), underlines this point. Such skilled men, forming the upper crust of the working class, furnished a strong base for the Evangelical version of a Protestant ethic, coupled with a conservative and economically liberalist economic stance. Their peculiar mixture of religion and belief in progress was anchored in such views. But by the 1890s the labour aristocracy was threatened, as their place was taken by better-trained men from middle-class backgrounds. Gradually, the idea of letting a skilled mechanic take over a branch of the firm—a position Börresen had been offered—became exceptional: trained engineers would take that place. Similar trends were visible in other trades, as firms grew bigger and managers and technicians formed a new stratum between the skilled worker and the boss (Hobsbawm 1964: 272-315). The Holiness movement was not based among the fading labour aristocracy, but among the growing middle classes. The romanticism of the movement fits this picture, and explains the break with the Samuel Smiles syndrome: the movement urged its followers 'to turn aside from struggle as a futile assertion of the self in order to discover the rest of faith' (Bebbington 1989: 166). In all this, it was not an isolated phenomenon but represented the spirit of the times.

Trevelyan stresses the unreflecting confidence that characterized the Victorian English: they dominated world commerce, and the Royal Navy was supreme in terms of military power (1964: 224-6). France had been Britain's only rival, and a poor second. But by the end of the century and of Victoria's reign, Russia, Germany, and the United States were expanding their naval and military strength: British hegemony was seriously challenged. 'As anxiety mounted, the British turned for reassurance to a ringing show of self-confidence' (Metcalf 1995: 167). To James Morris, the apogee of the Empire was Victoria's Diamond Jubilee, 1897, celebrated as a festival of Empire. He stresses the 'almost feverish enthusiasm' (1978: 24) of the proponents of 'New Imperialism' (1978: 29). But 'these were brittle times . . . the grand Victorian synthesis of art, morals and invention was already fading, and with it would fade the certainty and optimism . . . there were many Britons in 1897 who . . . saw omens of disillusionment to come. The times were too gaudy to be safe' (Morris 1978: 30). This account rings true. The Indian Empire 'is not a moribund organism', Curzon protested in 1904. 'The impassioned character' of the denial, says Metcalf, 'surely reveals a good deal more than the words themselves' (1995: 168). To Morris, the mood cracked during the South African War, which broke out in 1899. But well before that, older groups were pushed aside by the rising middle class. The aristocrats were still in power, but new men brought a new mood, such as Salisbury's colonial secretary Joseph Chamberlain, a manufacturer from Birmingham, and a Unitarian to boot. His efforts to rationalize the Empire failed, but were typical of a trend (Morris 1978: 54, 58-9).

This underlying tension forms the background to much of Kipling's work. His India was part of his youth: he left in 1889. Looking back, it is clear that most of his Indian heroes belong to the earlier period: Campbell would certainly have been a man to Kipling's liking, and we feel Skrefsrud would have been, too.[92] In many ways, Skrefsrud and Börresen succeed in the kind of venture Kipling describes in 'The Man who Would be King'—for a while they create their own domain, at the limits of colonial control, where their power rests on local support, as much as on the presence of colonial force. Campbell had seen the Sikh wars and the Mutiny, more than enough to understand the fragility of colonial rule and its dependence on the respect of the ruled. By 1897, British domination was taken for granted, and it was to this easy confidence Kipling spoke. His views on race belong here: the white man bears the burden, but there is 'neither east nor west . . . when two strong men stand face to face, though they come from the ends of the earth'.[93] Race is less important than manhood. In 'A Saheb's War', the Sikh soldier devastatingly critiques the British military record in South Africa. Kipling, here, is contesting the racial snobbery that tarnishes the Imperial image as the century closes; but his literary weapons are drawn from the past. The changes were real. It had been an India 'where personal relations still counted for much', and 'the provincial Governments consisted of perhaps a Lieutenant-Governor and three secretaries' (Mason 1985: 297); now it was a bureaucratic machine, with the British entrenched at safe distance from the natives. The individual heroism of our missionaries has no place in the rationalized Empire that Chamberlain and others are trying to create.

While the neo-romantic spiritual drive gained the upper hand in Britain, the drive to control lower-class morals dominated the Norwegian scene, as it did in India. The Salvation Army, and the Home and Seamen's Missions where Storjohann was active, demanded higher standards of believers, in terms of abstention from sin. Alcohol became more sinful by the 1890s than it was in the 1870s. Skrefsrud's and Börresen's simple faith was caught in the new developments. Börresen now left more and more work to Skrefsrud; but the latter changed—the timing fits Storjohann's visit to Ebenezer and Skrefsrud's visit to America—towards more exacting moral standards and new expectations of spirituality in the converts. Skrefsrud moved with the times: but it may have been too much to expect the Santals to move along with him.

## NOTES

1. Lunde to Hertel, 03.03.1880, cited by Nyhagen, 1990, II: 23.
2. Lunde to Hertel, 25.08.1882.
3. Skrefsrud to Hertel 20.08.1877, cited by Nyhagen, 1990, II: 23 and notes.
4. Skrefsrud to N.B. Aasen, 14.06.1879, *Oplandenes Avis* (the journal of O. Arvesen), 10.09.1879.
5. Skrefsrud to Hertel, 30.08.1879, cited by Nyhagen, 1990, II: 24.
6. Report to the NMS from C. Amble, 20.05.1880.
7. *Misjonstidende* 1880: 457-9.
8. *Fädrelandet*, 02.02.1881.
9. Skrefsrud to Hertel, 05.05.1879.
10. *Östlandsk Tidende*, 10.08.1881.
11. *Santalen*, 1883: 75-6; Nyhagen, II: 31.
12. These men wrote 'the four great classics' of Norwegian literature.
13. Kielland's bitterly critical novels, inspired by Zola, introduced naturalism to Norwegian literature.
14. Letter to H.L. Bräkstad, 29.04.1883.
15. Untill 1900, the vote was restricted by property and taxation. For Lunde's views, see Nyhagen, II, 1990: 227.
16. 'Progress'.
17. *Gudbrandsdölen*—Lunde had apparently put up the money, and supported the new journal with generous advertisements. Björnson, also on the founding committee, wrote the introductory article for the first number and contributed steadily thereafter (Ramberg 1994: 153-4).
18. 'The League of Youth' was seen as an attack on Sverdrup, though Ibsen, in general was a man of the left.
19. Often descended from farmers. They benefited from banishing the monopolies of Chartered towns, a reform introduced by the Agrarians.
20. He was well known abroad, especially in Germany. Thomas Mann was to cite him as a main inspiration.
21. Pahle to K.M. Eckhoff, 22.06.1884.

22. 18.02.1885.
23. Pahle to Eckhoff, 10.03 and 19.07.1884.
24. In the weekly *Göteborgs Weckotidning* 07.02.1884.
25. The letter has not been found, but one tends to interpret Kullgren's words in terms of the events that follow.
26. Pahle did not send it untill January 1885, but Nyhagen takes it to have been written in September 1884.
27. *Dahkwala*, no. 2, February 1885.
28. In America, the priest Erik Petersen alluded to the accusations in *Budstikken*, an influential journal there.
29. Hodne (1966: 59-60) and Nyhagen (1990, II, 115) accept this.
30. Paulsen to Hertel, 05.05.1883.
31. No. 2, 1885.
32. 1885: 27.
33. Letters of 15.12.1884; 12.1.1885.
34. Krüger to Skrefsrud, 03.02.1877.
35. Börresen to Birkedal, 07.04.1885.
36. *Almindelig Kirketidende*, 1885: 175.
37. Lunde to Hertel, 17.11.1885.
38. Letter to Hertel 09.03.1886.
39. Letter to *Dahkwala*, dated 28.10.1885, not published since Skrefsrud had already had his explanation published in the journal.
40. Her criticism is clear from several letters. Her letter to *Santalen* remained unpublished.
41. *Budbäreren*, 15.4.1885.
42. 'You do not, cannot, understand the Free Church controversy' wrote Hastie in answer to a letter of which he thought Banerjee was the author, 'no mere native Christian can'.
43. By 'a member of St. Andrew's Kirk' who was probably Hastie himself.
44. To the allegation that Miss Pigot and Professor Wilson had been 'in continuous contact', Wilson explained that everyone was sitting under a banyan, supporting each other by sitting back to back. Banerjee denied any physical contact. Then the judge found that Miss Pigot had tried to peep at the reporter's notes. He put her to a cross-examination of 333 questions in two hours; she broke down, and the case was lost.
45. She was also a friend of Keshub Chandra Sen.
46. Note that the case was tried in the wake of the debate on the Ilbert Bill.
47. Hastie went too, but was imprisoned for having failed to pay his dues, amounting to twelve thousand rupees. Having deposited three thousand secretly with his mother and sisters, he was declared insolvent, and was let off.
48. 1886: 136-8.
49. Letter to Hertel 15.05. 1886.

50. Björnson published an article where he claims to have 'converted' a certain person, often thought to be Nissen.
51. Pauss to Hertel , 07.05.1893.
52. *Twenty-third Annual Report*, Danish translation by L. Hertel, Copenhagen, 1890.
53. *Twenty-third Annual Report*: 3-4.
54. Ibid.
55. Ibid.: 10.
56. Börresen to Rudin, 18.11.1885.
57. Letter to Nissen 2.2.1885, cited by Nyhagen, op. cit., 183.
58. Letter Skrefsrud to Nissen 7.4.1885, cited by Nyhagen, op. cit., 183.
59. *Friend of the Santals.*
60. *Dahkwala*, 1890: 125.
61. Skrefsrud to Hertel, 06.05.1880.
62. Such government aid had been a feature of Evangelical administrations, such as that of George Campbell.
63. K. Fagstad to L. Hertel, 04.11.1891.
64. Ibid., 08.10.1892.
65. H.P. Börresen to L. Hertel, 18.01.1892.
66. Skrefsrud to O. Berg, 24.01.1894.
67. Skrefsrud to Reedtz-Thott, 04.10.1892.
68. The 11th Wisconsin.
69. Janson had been a teacher at Vonheim, Bruun's school at Lillehammer, and an active Grundtvigian before going to America, where he broke with Lutheranism and tried in vain to win Norwegians for Unitarianism.
70. Sometimes translating articles from *Oplandenes Avis*.
71. The 'little' home mission differed from the older home mission in accepting lay preachers.
72. Mainly drawn from Traasdahl's earlier book, itself largely a copy of Hertel's.
73. Falk Giertsen, then at Racine, objected strongly to Thrane's efforts at 'enlightenment' among Norwegian-Americans: he declared 'that political education hurt the people and that the only enlightenment people need is Christianity' (Leiren 1987: 43).
74. Falk Gjertsen was asked to resign in 1900, because of a letter allegedly sent by him to a young, married woman, Esther Paulsen, in Oslo. He spent about a year and a half in Norway, and succeeded in clearing himself.
75. A.J. Hulteng who led the American support committee from 1902 to 1938, and the carpenter Kristensen, who helped Skrefsrud recover from jail. His brother and nephew died in an accident just before he left America.

76. Preus was consistently conservative. As a leader of the Norwegian Synod, he wrote 'a warning to all Christians against Marcus Thrane's 'Norske Amerikaner', published in the synod's organ *Kirkelig Maanedstidende* and the more widely distributed *Emigranten*, when the old socialist leader started publishing his newspaper in Chicago in 1866 (Leiren 1987: 48-9).
77. Among German-Americans, the main split was between the General Synod and the orthodox Missouri Synod.
78. Here the Norwegian-Americans can be much clearer than their Norwegian brethren, since they are freed from the ambiguities of the State Church.
79. 'There is a higher logic than the Aristotelian', the Augsburg professors stated in their 1874 Programme, 'a higher truth than the reasonable 'pure doctrine', namely, a conviction of faith that cannot be demonstrated and does not fit at all in the usual thought forms and logical categories . . . Dogmatics is not scientific knowledge but something higher' (Hamre 1986: 48-9).
80. 'Humanism in its pure and finished form', wrote Sverdrup, 'starts from the idea that what is truly human is something quite different from that which is Christian. The truly human is found in its purity only where Christianity has not had any influence—among the pagan people who lived, thought, and wrote before Christianity came into the world' (Hamre 1986: 117-18).
81. *Santalmissionaeren.*
82. *Santalen*, 1892: 18.
83. *Dahkwala*, 1893: 116.
84. 1896, pp. 17-21.
85. *Santalen*, 1897: 188.
86. Bodding to Pauss, 19.06.1894.
87. Skrefsrud to H. Hansen, 18.05.1904.
88. Smiles 1860: 293, cited by Bebbington 1989: 166.
89. Max Weber was among the intellectuals active in this work from the 1890s.
90. Memo from Ilbert 04.09.1882, cited by Metcalf 1995: 205.
91. Nine out of ten civilians were against the Bill, says Mason (1985: 285).
92. It is typical of Kipling that he had considerable respect for Booth and his Salvation Army (1938: 93-5).
93. It is striking how this last line from 'The Ballad of East and West' has been ignored, as compared to the first lines 'Oh, East is East and West is West / and never the Twain shall meet'.

# 9

# Tradition and its Reinvention

## SANTAL ORAL LITERATURE

To be politically effective, myth must promise a better future. Santal narratives imagine the degraded homeland landscape as a once luxurious forest, sheltering the lost kingdom. The time since rebellion is the Kaliyuga, when the rule of the Sahib prevails, when the forest is lost and the landscape disfigured by industrialization. Santals often feel their history starts with the Hul, which marks a break in Santal thought since they came to feel the need to understand their own place in history. In the Santal texts describing the Hul, we find criticism of the chiefs, accused of being despotic and greedy. Despite the lack of coherence in their strategy, Sidhu and Kanhu wrapped the dream of autonomy in the imagery of a Santal *raj*, to chase the *diku* and build a new Santal identity. We see here, the reflexive nature of Santal memory.

The missionaries pursued their own utopia, inventing Santalistan, a Santal territory centered on the Mission headquarters in Dumka, where heathens surrounded the Christianized Nankar district. The utopia of the missionaries was based on the figure of the noble savage and contributed to strengthen Santal identity. But the missionaries did not base this identity in the historical locus of the Hul, nor in the various traditions of migration that pervade Santal myth. When they tried to provide the Santals with a history, we find Christian textbooks conveying notions of Greek antiquity to Santal children. Rome and Athens, as heathen countries, are opposed to the Holy Land. Periodicals such as *Hor Pera* speak of Scandinavian revival centered on Hauge and throw the Santal straight into Lutheran religious debate. The missionaries want to store tribal knowledge by transforming heathen beliefs and ritual into a folklore of the past that children may learn at school, desacralizing the bongas so Santals would gradually forget them and embrace Christianity. By the same token, pre-colonial history becomes prehistory.

The national identity that the missionaries sought to identify was, above all, a matter of language. The richness of language makes up, in a way, for the poverty of history in granting a real culture to the Santals in the missionary mind. The Santals are fond of their language and love to play with words. This clearly impressed Skrefsrud and Bodding. Formal language is particularly rich, though everybody does not master ritual discourse or political oratory. The knowledge of riddles, proverbs and prohibitions is unequally shared (Keesing 1981, 1992; Barth 1975, 2002). The latter have their roots in everyday life but their elaboration depends on tradition known to chiefs, priests, and elders but beyond common knowledge. Still, ritual discourse allows us to explore the semantic universe of the Santals.

When Skrefsrud proved able 'to speak like a *pargana*' he was accorded the title, as other chiefs recognized his oratory art. Though his discourse aimed at converting them, he used Santal similes, casting abstract and moral notions into images. Some were derogatory and identified the heathens with the jungle, an image the Santals used during the rebellion petitioning as 'we jungly Santals'. They had interiorized this stigma.[1] During the rebellion they realized their inability to write, and had to ask Hindu sympathizers to do so on their behalf (Guha 1983). Thakur, we recall, appeared to Sidhu and Kanhu brandishing a book, perhaps the Bible. Curiously, one text from the Santal archives tells us the brothers were taught reading and writing by a brahmin, as their stepfather Bhogon Manjhi was rich. On the way to school, they had a vision of a *sadhu* or *yogi* who blessed them, and told them to petition the government about the heavy rent. 'If the raj does not listen to you, you make yourselves kings. I shall help you'. He warns them not to be greedy and to stay pure. Anxiously, the two boys answer: 'how we can make ourselves kings? We do not know how to read and write'. They ask the apparition to teach them. The narrator continues: 'Somehow they wrote a letter'. The fascination with writing is clear (Andersen, forthcoming). But the story also shows a consciousness of knowledge as a relation: one has to learn from somebody. Writing comes from without, whether its origin is colonial or supernatural. One parallel would be the supernatural origin of goods in the cargo cults. In both cases, introducing a supernatural agent to found knowledge otherwise colonial, effectively constitutes a counter-cultural claim. These observations also apply to the several later inventions, based on revelation, of a specifically Santal script (Carrin 2002).

We see how narrator of the 1890s links the charismatic power of the brothers to their control of writing—of which he is nevertheless not sure. The text asserts a craving for knowledge: 'without knowledge we cannot govern a country'. The realization of the use of knowledge, here, precedes knowledge itself.[2] Writing is becoming essential to the exercise of power, while possession is false: 'they pretended to be mad. They began to make some sacrificial offerings and called themselves Subah Thakur and the villagers gathered around them'. The criticism of possession reflects Christian influence while the stress on writing shows an understanding of the colonial system: Sidhu and Kanhu write a petition. The fetishization of writing has pervaded Santal culture ever since, aiding the progress of education and inducing the Santals to redefine their own culture.

The missionary colonization of the Santal mind advanced on two fronts. First, Santals were exposed to preaching aimed at conversion. Second, the missionaries induced them to produce an inventory of their knowledge, a reflexive process which changed the knowledge itself. We cannot judge, from the texts, how the preaching was received, but we have Sona's and Anpi's testimonies of how it might fascinate children. In both cases, their parents were more reluctant. In some of the archive texts, we perceive the effects of Christian teaching in various ways. The authors seem to store knowledge of their own culture so as to evaluate the changes they have undergone since the rebellion. They may have resented, sometimes, the missionary demand of writing down their tradition, at a time when its practice was banned. One writer tells how he feels his description of ritual may be incomplete: he will try to find somebody else who knows better, in order to complete his account. When one of them notes, at the end of a story, 'Today I am tired. I do not want to go to Church', we get a glimpse of this difficult process. Another, Sagram, goes on 'strike', and leaves the work, preferring to remain a postman. Even today, some ojhas feel that writing down secret knowledge is dangerous, and that it should remain safe from missionaries. The bongas, too, might read the secret formulas.[3] The writing down of tribal knowledge may have been viewed as dispossession.

These messages to Bodding in between the stories are, as Soren puts it, 'the only windows left through which one can peek into the background scenario of the writers' (1999: 9). A narrator wonders why informants give different versions of a story, or express different opinions. The understanding of culture as a process of communication emerges slowly from the conclusions. Thus a narrator concludes a story dealing with love between humans and bongas[4]:

> Now the story comes to an end, and the boy who was with the female bonga still exists. And this boy, who was from Jomkandor, still lives. And other people who are dead have left their story. And we know three or four stories of that sort. But we do not write all the versions. And the stories sometimes join and sometimes get divided. Therefore, I did not write everything. And thus people know about the female bonga as they are seductive and come quickly to the point. It is for this reason that the boy had played the flute to call the bonga. As a matter of fact, Santal women are like that.

This return to generalization at the end of the story seems to show an acute sense of why such stories are important; more than simply narratives, they are meant to reveal Santal 'culture'. Implicit is the idea of culture as an object, but this reifying process is clearly something with which the writers struggle, perhaps feeling rather vaguely the objections that later generations of anthropologists were to make in this regard. Missionaries, too, were probably ambiguous as to what they wanted to show: on the one hand, there was the idea of a national spirit—in Herder's sense—on the other hand, the collection of individual cultural traits that characterized diffusionist ethnology in the pre-functionalist period.

Another remark shows these various influences but borrows the missionaries' common sense when he warns the reader: 'Everybody plays violin, sings love songs, and dances. And at that time, humans and bongas are charmed by tying their hair with pins. But, by making merry and playing instruments and by dancing, one does not earn one's life. Those who are unable to understand this are peculiar people, these people have no discipline. And thus, this story comes to an end' (Bodding 1924).

## AN INDIGENOUS INVENTORY

The archives offer another challenge: different voices speak through the narrators. Chiefs and priests, men and women, people of different clans and subclans, have seen the events from various villages. There is diachronic as well as spatial diversity: the collection of texts lasted some forty years and involved three generations. Some informants had experienced the *Hul* during their youth, while others had been living in tea gardens. Unhappily, the stories are not dated, so their date must be inferred from their content.

The archives contain several types of texts, but prominent among them are folk tales. Sagram Murmu must have started to write them before 1893. Besides myths and tales, there are descriptions of ritual, for birth and purification, marriage and death. There are stories concerning the clans, the bongas and the festivals. Other genres such as omens, riddles, songs, prayers, witchcraft incantations, and songs are also represented. Some stories deal with events such as the Santal rebellion while others describe the different kind of ritual specialists.

One may group the texts in three categories. First, myths of creation, exodus, and dispersion of the clans reflect a Santal historicity, legitimating identity by a mythical past. Some myths evoke Santal society at the time of the Champa kingdom, presenting clans tied to complementary functions such as soldiers, musicians, or agriculturists. They describe the loss of the kingdom, explained by the dispersal of the ancestors, wars, and being dispossessed of their territory. Migrations are the *leitmotif* of myths explaining the origin of sub-clans, where some ancestors fulfil their duty with difficulty while others neglect taboos. The first become elders and the latter juniors or inferiors.[5] In creating a ranked order, these myths effect an important transformation, expressing the disenchantment that follows the golden age.

Other texts concentrate on the pleasure of playing with words, such as riddles, which also transmit knowledge when told to children by their grandparents.[6] The semantic logic of riddles is rooted in landscape imagery and they use metaphor to link village life to nature. When they take cattle for grazing, children play games and amuse themselves with riddles. Some riddles are used to avoid naming the unpleasant, like disease or death. If an old person is seen losing his teeth one may say 'the white pebbles are falling'. When someone dies, 'he has taken the crocodiles to graze', an allusion to the mourner who stands in the Damodar River to immerge the bones of the deceased. It is impolite to say a girl is pregnant: 'she is carrying a bundle'. When hunting, the Santal avoid naming their prey, calling the leopard a wild cat, the snake a fibre, and so on. It is inauspicious to evoke bongas literally and Santals prefer euphemisms. Metaphor is also used for social roles: a husband is 'the umbrella shadow' for women,[7] while husbands call their wife a 'basket bonga',[8] alluding to her reproductive powers but also to witchcraft. Children are likened to paddy ears seen as wealth.

By learning the art of riddles children understand the rules of social exchange. At marriage the spouses' parents compete at making riddles. None should know better riddles than the other, since they are equal, and the exchange stresses the reciprocity of in-laws likened to two pairs of buffalos yoked together. The bride is a wild deer, becoming a cow in the stable. An old woman is a niche in the wall, an old broom, or a slow fire in the hearth. Ojhas too exchange riddles alluding to bongas which convey secret knowledge. Riddles induce a sense of poetry, help to understand love songs, and to master the enigmas of ritual discourse. They link daily life with religious symbolism, uniting them by striking metaphors.

Riddles may convey ethnic stereotypes such as, for example, 'From each side of the head, one ear does not hear the other'. Here, the Mundas are one ear and the Santals the other; the implicit reference to the head evokes the dominant Hindus. The riddle alludes to manipulation by the dominant. The tribes are like ears listening to orders from the Hindu head, but, said one informant, nowadays the Santals and Mundas have got a voice.

Proverbs are central to Santals, 'Gossip stings like cold water'. Some, known to all, express experience with the *diku*: 'a *diku* cat, a bush of thorns'. Some are satirical: men say that 'women's speech irritates like an insect's bite'. Others express the need for the other sex: 'every leopard should have his goat'. The lazy daughter-in-law, the lascivious wife, the potential witch, and the lazy husband are caricatured by proverbs.

Communication also rests on gestures such as formal salutations, rare today but still common in Skrefsrud's time, and banned by the missionaries.[9] Boys and girls learnt to respect elders and greet their kin. When a son meets his father, he should bow low, touch his right elbow with his left hand, and raise his right fist to the level of his forehead. The father reciprocates by touching his right arm loosely with his left hand and opening it. Specific salutations are used for different kin and convey the content of the relationship. Thus, parents-in-law of the same sex catch each other's arms a certain number of times, expressing their solidarity. Mutual respect is also expressed through language: one has to use the correct term of address. When people quarrel, they abuse each other, but should avoid implying bestiality, impotence or sexuality. Still, disputes often start by remarks such as 'I will fuck your mother'. Common insults involve the threat to kill the opponent, or he is a bastard, an outcaste, a thief, or incestuous kin. During exorcism, ojhas accuse malevolent deities of incest or promiscuity. To insult a woman, one alludes to her tongue, or to her uterus as 'an old pot in which too much rice-beer has been brewed'. Boys insult girls by referring to urine, which also alludes to sperm. Insults are strongly gendered. A man can say to another 'I shall eye you', but a woman will never do so as she would be accused of witchcraft: eye for a woman implies the evil eye.

Santal prohibitions are numerous. While some concern the community, others are specific to men or women, or particular categories of people. No one may plough in the sacred grove or cut its trees. Women must not cut branches there nor climb its trees. Bongas sit in trees and dwell on roofs, so women should avoid climbing a roof or a tree. Perhaps significantly, Bodding tells us Sona loved to rest on the roof of the bungalow, watching the others. Did she break the taboo since she was conscious of not being in the bonga's eyes?

Menstruating women must not enter the sacred grove or touch a bow and arrow. Priests fast and abstain from sex on the eve of agricultural rituals. Clans and sub-clans have prohibitions which follow a 'totemic logic' of analogies between humans and natural species, established by myth. Santals often say it is hard to remember these prohibitions, some of which are tacit. A prohibition is often realized only when infringed, when suffering the consequences. Stories of bongas allude to ritual mistakes or offences, as they are eager to trap humans who forget prohibitions such as 'resting under a cotton tree in the early afternoon'.

To exchange riddles, tell proverbs, insult, or joke defines everyday rhetoric. The Santals made fun of Skrefsrud, since the Biblical stories seemed excessive to them.

## TELLING FOLK TALES

Santal folk tales often humorously evocate their peripheral position, exploited by the *diku* but able, as we shall see, to answer back. One tale opposes a Hindu moneylender to a Santal farmer and the story turns on debt.[10] We are at the end of January, when the interest rate is high,[11] and villagers must pay their debts. The hero, unable to pay, goes away leaving his wife at home. When the moneylender comes, the wife says her husband has gone to play a game called 'backward and forward' in the field. Playing, of course, is the privilege of those who don't work, showing the Santal's careless attitude, but the moneylender is looking at the ripe beans in the garden. Making a slip of tongue he says he would like some of these *sim*—the Santal name for chicken—as a token payment. Here, language becomes a weapon when a lapse of the usurer reveals his hidden intentions which always leads to exorbitant claims.

He tries to take some beans but the woman chases him with a stick, till the moneylender finds his debtor warming himself near an open fire in the field. Exasperated, he asks the farmer how he spends his days. The Santal maliciously tells him he enjoys himself tremendously playing the famous game. The Hindu proposes to reward him for teaching him the game but the Santal just wants to be released from his debt. The moneylender accepts: he calls a witness and promises to cancel the debt when he has played the game. Next day, the Santal takes the moneylender and his witness to the fire and starts to undress, asking his companions to do the same. When they have warmed themselves a while, the moneylender gets impatient and asks about the game which he clearly associates with some erotic pastime. The Santal throws a bundle of straw into the fire and the flames make the moneylender move back. When the latter asks again when he will get to play, the Santal says 'we are already playing: you were forward, now you came backward. Try to concentrate', adds the Santal, 'and you will see that you are learning!' The moneylender gets angry and declares he won't release the Santal from his debt for this game. But bound by his promise, he is trapped by the erotic associations that the *diku* apply to the Santal. He probably thinks he will be given a girl,[12] as Santals indulge in pleasure, drinking and debauchery. For the Santals, the text shows how *diku* understand nothing of the conviviality friends share, drinking and exchanging jokes that are the salt of speech. The story shows how nudity annuls social inequality. Nudity is more natural to the Santal's muscular body, trained by manual work than to the obese usurer. The evocation of Santal promiscuity is sustained by the pun on forward and backward which the moneylender reads as a crude description of coitus.

Another story stages a *diku* moneylender, who denies having received any money and asks his debtor to produce witnesses. The Santal farmer, no poor man as he has 'five ploughs' of land, cannot do so. They go to Court where the moneylender produces three witnesses swearing they have seen the Santal receive money.

Meanwhile, the Santal hangs around and meets a Hindu who says: 'If you do not have any witness, give me two rupees and make me your witness.' The Santal accepts and tells his witness that he works 'five ploughs'. Anxious, the moneylender orders his witnesses to answer only to the British Judge. The Judge asks the witness what he knows about the affair (*hal*), a term which means either an affair, a case, or a plough. The witness says the farmer is ploughing with five ploughs at a time, made of different woods, and the judge feels he is mad. He tells the other witnesses in Bengali to swear to tell the truth, and they repeat: 'tell the truth, tell the truth'. The Judge is offended and asks his chaprasi to turn them out. But they point to the Judge and tell the chaprasi to turn him out! The stupid witnesses just repeat what they have heard. The audience bursts into laughter. The Magistrate acquits the Santal as he no longer takes the moneylender's complaint seriously (Bodding 1925-9, 11: 208-15).

## NARRATIVE AS A MIRROR OF CONFLICTING IDEOLOGIES

Santal discourse on identity is not of a single voice. Writing for the missionaries, the Santals want to prove their belief in the bongas as more than mere superstition. They insist on the value of knowledge of Hindu gods, 'for it is useful to know about the beliefs of our neighbours'. Though they complain about their own deities, never content with their sacrifices, they also criticise Christianity.

Still, missionary presence resulted in thousands of pages of narrative where Santals recast their traditions as knowledge, institutions, and laws, a way of life constructing the Santal as a *samaj*—a community. The patterns of domination are reflected in the texts: that of the foreigner, but also that of the inner *diku,* who usurp power or manipulate the bongas to take advantage of their Santal brothers. We are told of an ojha who wants supernatural powers to influence others, or of villagers following bongas who, like thieves, steal to make their own devotees rich. These themes relate to the evil eye, which characterizes anti-social elements. Hunts for such elements seems to coincide with crisis, as when the zamindars of the Jungle Mahals lose their power, or during the Santal rebellion. Sidhu and Kanhu submitted women suspected of witchcraft, or thought to have had sexual relations with the *diku*, to ordeals. This was clearly to strenghten tribal cohesion and the ethnic boundary.

The strong egalitarian ethos serves as reference for reinventing tradition, and allows for class consciousness. The concept of the foreigner as moneylender, contractor, or excise officer is applied to Hindus acting for the colonial system while seeking their own advantage, while the artisan castes who lived with the Santals were *hurin diku*, small foreigners, a term without pejorative value (Carrin-Bouez 1991a). Class consciousness did not conflict with Santal ethnicity.

Santals ambiguously include Christianity in their world: some see the benefit of education while for others the new religion does not fit Santal ideas. In the texts we see how the coming of the Sahebs, the introduction of money and the market, were assimilated to the land of death. Colonial labour is cast in the metaphor of human sacrifice, while death is likened to a colonial work camp. We are in the Kali age, as the golden age is lost, and natural procreation no longer exists (Carrin-Bouez 1993).

The narratives express the coercive character of colonial rule but show the Santals reinventing their tradition, to prevent the memocide (Samaddar 1998) that might otherwise have followed pauperization and migration. Narratives of conversion, even when describing resistance, show the emergence of a Santal individual defining himself through writing.

## BODDING'S LITERARY WORK

None of the missionaries have tried to enter into the Santal world more fully than Bodding. Skrefsrud had soon realized his potential for studies of language and culture. After some ten months at Benagaria, Bodding was put in charge of a small station, Mohulpahari, to give him time for literary work. There, 'the only ones to talk to, if I was to talk at all, were Santals; and the only means of communication was Santali' (1915: 6).

Bodding regretted the lack of Christian literature in Santali when he came out. Skrefsrud's Bible translation was not finished, and Cole's suffered 'from such serious shortcomings that we here have never found it possible to use it' (1915: 4). Skrefsrud got malaria in 1890, and Heuman took him to Darjeeling to convalesce. On his return, Skrefsrud again started to translate the New Testament, urged by Bodding (Nyhagen 1990, II: 189) who never saw the first attempt. Skrefsrud felt the work would be easy, once the dictionary was done, but Bodding wanted him to do the New Testament first. In the end he gave in, and the first three gospels were printed when he went to America. The Book of John was translated, but not revised. The translation was passed to Heuman for comment, then to Bodding, who returned it to Skrefsrud for final revision.

Then Bodding took over, aided by Biram, who 'had an excellent knowledge of his own language, as he had likewise unusual capabilities for a Santal in several fields; he was even-tempered and thoughtful, was not too impressed by Europeans and did not agree to anything when he felt the use of language was not correct'. Heuman and Bodding went through Skrefsrud's translation of John together, while Bodding and Biram prepared it for the press (Bodding 1915: 4-5). Plans for finance by the Scandinavian Bible Societies came to naught, nor did the Calcutta Auxiliary Bible Society help, but in 1895 the gospels were printed at the Mission's own press (Nyhagen 1990, II: 189). Bodding says the first three Gospels are better than the Gospel according to John, due to Skrefsrud's presence. They translated from the Greek and Hebrew originals but also used a Norwegian translation, and the revised English version of 1880, as well as a German translation by Kautch, a Swedish one for poetic and prophetic language and finally the vulgate. When Skrefsrud came back from America he translated much of the Acts.

## ON THE SANTALI LANGUAGE

Bodding comments on translating into a largely unwritten language, as Santali still was. All writing then had been done by missionaries. In transcription, Skrefsrud was well ahead of his colleagues, yet there was 'a deplorable Thirty Years' War about some letters'—mainly the half-consonants—between the Scandinavians and their British colleagues (1915: 10). In 1899, Skrefsrud and Bodding called a Conference at Benegaria, with the Scots, the CMS, and themselves. They agreed on the transcription to be used in the Old Testament.

Skrefsrud understood from the start the nature of the half-consonants and invented diacritical marks for them. Others did not see the use, and Bodding feels their imprecise transcription make other missionaries uncertain of their pronunciation, while 'our Santals have taken to our system quite naturally . . . as soon as a Santal learns how to write, he finds it easy. . . . We do not have the many difficulties that we have in Norway to learn how to spell correctly, not to mention the hopeless situation which exists in English'. They agreed to use Skrefsrud's alphabet and to mark open vowels except in verbal suffixes and personal pronouns. Skrefsrud and Bodding found this illogical, but complied. Bodding was asked to read from the translation. They liked it, but someone felt 'it was just as the people were speaking, while he held that in written language one should keep a slightly different sequence of words' (1915: 9). Bodding and Skrefsrud disagreed. For Bodding, it was instead an advantage that no choice had to be made between literary and oral language. 'It is the living language of the people . . . as it is used by everyone . . . a language, which is felt as their own, such a language it is, that is needed'. The Bible Society decided to pay for printing the Old Testament, using the Benagaria version as revised by Campbell and Cole. It finally appeared in 1914.

The lack of a literary tradition meant, however, that words and expressions were lacking, and they wanted to avoid 'the mode of expression of one's own language . . . whereby is attained what is called Saheb-Santali' (1915: 16). This recalls the language struggle in Norway, which still continues. The nation was born with Danish as a written language, and a host of oral dialects. The new, written language Ivar Aasen created from 1853[13] was seen as a major democratization, and Skrefsrud, who kept his dialect to the last, sympathized with the Neo-Norwegian movement. Norwegians tend to see oral language as the norm, to which any written form is but an approximation. This ideology is clearly present in our missionaries' approach to writing Santali.

Bodding found his voyage to the Holy Land useful, as the concreteness of Santali expressions required knowledge of how things were done in Palestine. Thus, the verb 'to carry' in Norwegian or English assimilates several actions specified in Santali: 'one may carry on the head, on the shoulder, on the arm, in the lap, in the hand, at the hips, under the arm, stuck behind the ear, and so on. One must find the right word' (1915: 29-32). For the verb *see*, there are several words in Santali, one more general than the others, since it does not specify whether one looks up, down, or whatever. Used in one way it means 'looking in an unfriendly manner' (1915: 36-7).

For the verb 'to honour', Skrefsrud used *manao,* a Hindi loan word which means honour, respect, or worship a deity. But one day an old man asked Biram if Christians sacrificed to their ancestors.

Certainly not, said Biram, but, said the other, the fourth Commandment says: 'Thou shalt honour *(mane)* Thy father. . .'. But 'this is precisely what the heathens do; they show *manao* by sacrificing to them'. Biram went to Skrefsrud, and the word was changed (1915: 35).

Complicated, too, is the system of pronouns: the English *we* may be rendered by six terms. Two of them are easy. But dual and plural forms, with inclusive and exclusive, create four alternatives: Thou and I; He and I; You (pl.) and I; They and I. 'When Peter on the mountain said to the Lord, 'It is well that we are here', or when the disciples cried, during the tempest, 'Save us, we are perishing' — was the Lord included or not ? The problem here lies not in Santali, but in Hebrew and Greek (Bodding 1915: 33-4).

Santali is an agglutinative language, rich on the concrete and specific level, but 'poor in general and abstract expressions, where Greek is so highly developed'. But the catch is that our words are polysemic, from the point of view of a Santal. The nature of Santali rebels against polysemy, 'perhaps one of the reasons for the truthfulness that has characterized the Santal people. They do not easily take the middle road; they must speak truth or lie' (1915: 32). Concreteness is a problem in terms like 'longing for'. Santali has a beautiful expression for longing, but it applies only to objects already seen or known. When speaking of longing for our home in heaven, a different expression must be found.

Loan words may take on a new sense in the new language. Bodding mentions the word *asis,* loaned from Hindi and Sanskrit, where it means a benediction. In Santali it has come to mean a malediction. 'Perhaps it has . . . to do with what we learn out here, and which is a trait of character with at least the Santals, to judge from what is done, not what is said' (1915: 34-5). Implicitly, Santals find the *dikus* saying one thing and doing another.

Sometimes, there simply is no word in Santali, mainly for abstract concepts. The missionaries avoided loan words, though they did simplify Hindi, Bengali, or even Hebrew terms to render pronunciation easy. They never used English words, but tried to create new Santali words from existing roots. For a term like conscience, the problem was to convey a new, Christian content, not to explore existing semantics. At first they used terms such as 'the inner witness' or 'the inner voice'. But for an expression like 'to cleanse conscience from dead acts', this would not work. Bodding finally decided to form a new word in the same way as the Greek word for conscience, with an active elementary mode.[14] They used it for sometime, 'but it did not and could not stand the test, until we realized the point about the active mode. I remember how glad we were, when we found the word able to stand any test . . . Skrefsrud and I and Biram sat trying it till far into the night' (1915: 39-40).

Finally, Santali 'absolutely protests' against many a metaphor. Campbell had translated a verse in Matthew, 'The Lord having opened his mouth to gape wide open, taught them. . .'. 'Apart from the ugly expression' says Bodding, 'one can of course not speak with the mouth wide open'. If one says 'lifting his eyes' in Santali, a Santal will ask: 'How did he do it ? Did he take them out and lift them in his hand?' Bodding wishes 'that we were equally precise, which would save us an immense amount of sheer nonsense' (1915: 37-8).

Bodding is acutely aware of the cultural embeddedness of language. 'A language shows the mode of thinking and the thoughts of a people' (1915: 31). Thus he went to a Jewish cemetery in Jerusalem and found inscriptions stating that 'he who lay here, had been a man beyond reproach and straight in all his dealings, the very words describing Job and what is said of Zacharias . . .' (1915: 30). A phrase which troubled Bible translators was little more than a graveyard convention—this, paradoxically, 'made everything come alive'. The real dead made the dead language real.

Bodding explains to his readers how a word may change its meaning over time, how the circumstances that accompany an action change, too, so the word may end by referring to these, rather than the action itself. The linguist and the ethnologist, then, are one, and we see why he should spend much of his life perfecting an extraordinary dictionary.

## SANTAL COLLABORATORS

Among the Santals, there were as yet nobody capable of such translation. Curiously, says Bodding, no such work has been successful in India even among 'more advanced races': it suffers from clumsiness and tendentious language. So he needed Santal teachers, who, in the logic of the situation, became his assistants. He explains their role as 'living lexica'. Yet 'they are not easy to consult. They are not ordered alphabetically, nor systematically, and their content can be rather irregular. To get the right people for such work is extremely difficult' (1915: 8). Still, some were better than others; and best were those who had taken an active part in public life, such as chiefs and ojhas. And Santals are not prone to 'the terrible splitting of hairs for which the Bengalis have such a great flair'. Santals have 'what the English call common sense' (ibid.). Bodding realized that the work was as tiresome to the 'living lexica' as to the one consulting them. He cites Biram, who told a man wanting to be taken on that 'the work was to be like a tied-up monkey'. Humour or resistance? Santals were used to freedom, and to Bodding the worst were those who answered to please when they were tired. Biram always stood his ground: 'You are a Saheb', he might say, 'and I cannot stop you from writing what you want—but we do not say it like that' (ibid.: 20). But the 'live lexica' are resolutely concrete: 'They may say, for example, that such and such is, when one does this or that . . . one does get the concrete usage and gets a chance to understand by oneself' (1915: 18-19).

When Skrefsrud left for America Heuman and Bodding worked as equals, but Biram was placed at Bodding's side for the final revision. Skrefsrud had confidence in Biram, whom he called his guru. When Khudu died in 1877, Biram became Skrefsrud's main Santali teacher. 'I have yet to meet (another) Santal', he says, 'who can define the true meaning of a word with such certainty and such a clear demarcation. He has a thoughtfulness and a judgment which is quite astonishing' (Dahkwala 1891: 145). Skrefsrud wrote that no Santal had ever been so close to him. Biram was also Bodding's first teacher of Santali.

Biram was born in Bhalka close to the Mor River, though his father came from farther west. Later they moved to Benagaria, where they lived during the rebellion. In 1866, a famine year, they came to Suri: in spite of Johnson's efforts the father died. Biram later served the chief at Benagaria, and was baptized there in 1874. He taught himself to read and write. Later, he wrote his autobiography, translated and printed in *Dahkwala*.[15] Humble and just, he was a support for the Christians of his village. He died in 1897, and in his obituary Skrefsrud describes him as the soul of everything they have written in Santali the last 21 years.

Phagu was the first of Bodding's teachers at Mohulpahari. He was a guru,[16] and 'had a bottomless treasure of knowledge about Santal traditions and other matters'. From him Skrefsrud got the old songs included in the *Mare Hapram ko*. Bodding learnt much about Santal custom from him. But he died a year later. His son had gone to a tea garden, and the father went to find him. On the way he caught cholera, and was left dead by his companions (1915: 20).

Next Bodding was helped by an old man, Mongol, from a family of lepers at Mohulpahari. 'It was of course not so nice to have a leper so close', says Bodding, 'and we arranged it so that the man could sit outside'. He was 'completely unlearned', but his knowledge of santali was 'in some ways even richer than I was to find with anyone else'. Bodding got several thousand words from him. Mongol is described as a 'peaceful, balanced and humble Christian, purified by suffering'. One evening, Mongol was kneeling in prayer when a venomous snake crept across his body. He did not move till the prayer was over, and the snake did not bite. Bodding wonders 'if anyone else could have done this' (1915: 21).

Mongol was not his only illiterate assistant: Bodding wanted to have one around, to test his translations, and make sure that 'the common man will understand it'. But they could only supplement more learned assistants (1915: 22). So when Phagu died, there was the need to replace him by somebody in addition to Mongol .

Then one day a man walked in, asking Skrefsrud for work. Sagram Murmu came from Godda, in the northern part of Santal Parganas, where he had been to the CMS school. Skrefsrud had noticed the man's language, and sent him to Mohulpahari, where he married and settled, becoming schoolmaster and postmaster in turn. Sagram, still farming at Mohulpahari as Bodding writes, 'has a great knowledge of his language and its oral literature. In addition, he has a quite special ability to write his own language fluently and lightly'. He therefore used him to write folk tales. 'He first wrote down everything he knew, and whenever I heard of new [tales] I sent the story-teller to him, and he then reproduced the tale in writing.' Thus, Sagram was the main author of the three volumes published by Bodding. He admits as much: 'I now have an enormous collection of Santal Folk Tales written in a superb language, which has not been tainted by passing through a European brain'. And, perhaps to put his readers at ease, he says that while they are mainly meant for students of folklore, they have helped him 'find a suitable form for the stories of the Bible' (1915: 23). In the published work, the first but laconic footnote in the second volume states, 'All tales are as told by Sagram Murmu of Mohulpahari when no other name is given' (Bodding 1925-9, II: 2n.). But then, Bodding had quite a few difficulties with Sagram, describing him as a 'combination of bully and coward'. But he knew how to write, and Bodding kept his letters as language samples. He worked for Bodding more than twenty years, with some breaks.

Once when he left in anger, Bodding was assisted by Biram's son Suna, who later became a Sirdar of Nankar. But he left when Bodding went to Europe in 1900. When Bodding returned, he again tried to work with Sagram, but the latter 'went on strike'. Partly, he wanted a pay increase. But he was also unable 'to do two different kinds of work at the same time'. So he stopped writing folk tales, and continued as postmaster, while Bodding asks us not to take his criticism of Sagram more seriously than intended (1915: 24). Everyday resistance, perhaps, in the sense of Scott? (1987, 1990)

Bodding discussed possible replacements with Skrefsrud, then mentioned the chief, Sido Desmanjhi. Though a heathen, he 'had many of the qualities we were looking for'. Sido was willing to help, and the religious problem was solved later, when he converted. He was

> probably the most outstanding Santal we have ever had in the Mission . . . . He has considerable ability in several fields and is interested in everything that is human. If there is a party, it is as nothing to him to make a song for the occasion. He has been a social leader; he has been a judge in the villages; he has been an Honorary Magistrate. At the moment he is a Sirdar;[17] they asked to have him. Sido was with me till the translation work had been done; later we sat together two years working on the dictionary; and he has accompanied me on many tours. It has been a pleasure to have him as an assistant; sometimes he drops in, and sometimes I send for him, when I want to have his help. And if I should really have a need for him, I think he would surely give up his present post to come'. And then, a little lamely, 'There is some kind of contact between us'. (ibid. 1915: 25)

## THE MUNDA REBELLION

Meanwhile, resistance continued in the tribal areas. Like the Santals, the Mundas and Oraons were during 1875-1905 raising their voices against the *diku* landlords, the British, and the missionaries. The Sardar Larai was linked to several Munda rebellions, seven from 1789 to 1832, but chiefly in 1811 and in 1832. The movement aimed at restoring land to the tribal peasants and refused forced labour. The landlords increased rents, destroying the resisting peasants' crops and houses. After 1857 Mundas had turned in numbers to the Lutheran Mission in Chotanagpur, which promised to back their vindication. But the Mundas soon crossed the limits of legal resistance, and the mission could not follow. The Mundas felt betrayed. A Belgian Jesuit, C. Lievens, started another mass conversion in 1885-6, promising his help to regain Munda lands. When he returned, worn out, to die in Belgium seven years later, the Mundas were still expecting a charismatic leader to end the oppression.

In 1895 such a man was found. Birsa Munda's birth, 15 November 1875, was marked by supernatural events: a comet and a flag floating in the skies. In 1886 he was confirmed by the Gossnerians, and went to their school from 1886 to 1894. His parents worked for minor landholders. The Sardars, who opposed the missionaries, incited Birsa's father, who had become anti-Christian, to withdraw his son from school. Birsa worked as a farm labourer for a Munda village chief, and realized that it was the converts who better resisted landlord oppression. But in 1890, he met Anand Panre, who worked for Jagmohan Singh, the Vaishnava zamindar of Badgaon. Anand's anticaste views influenced Birsa. He married several wives, inviting missionary criticism. He interested himself in a move by the government to protect the rights of the forest tribes of Singhbhum. In 1894, petitions were sent by the chiefs of eight parganas and fourteen thousand Christians to the Commissioner of Chotanagpur. Birsa was identified by the police as the instigator of a protest march ( Zide and Munda 1969: 39).

In 1895 a strange incident estranged Birsa from his community. Hearing that a woman dead in childbirth has just been buried, as was the custom, with her ornaments, Birsa robbed the grave and tried to sell the jewellery. He wanted to help his family suffering from famine, but was discovered, and his parents refused the money. Birsa was cast out from Munda society. Yet the sacrilegious act conferred a certain power on him.[18]

Birsa dreamt he was confronting three symbols of authority: a king, a zamindar, and Sing Bonga, the god of creation. Each tried to plant a twig in the soil, like the old chiefs used to do, and failed, but Birsa succeeded. Next day he declared he had been invested with the power to lead the Mundas towards a better future. He criticized the *deonra*,[19] the diviners, for extorting money from villagers, echoing missionary critics. One day, as Birsa walked through the forest, a lightning lit his face, as is held to have happened to Luther (Hoffman and van Emelen 1950: 567). Soon Birsa cured people and is said to have brought a Muslim child back to life. He began to preach, clad in a saffron dhoti and wearing wooden sandals.[20] He wrote a book containing his 'commandments', giving it to his twelve disciples. He started evening classes to teach his new faith, which evoked Munda tradition and included pilgrimages to the sacred sites of the tribe.

The Birsaite movement *(ulgulan)* of 1895 was agrarian and anti-colonial. Like Sidhu, Kanhu, and Bhagrit, Birsa wanted to recover the lost kingdom. The new *raj* was to be preceded by a rain of fire to mark the birth of a new age. Birsa, shining like gold, feared neither fire nor water. He declared he would save the Mundas from the next deluge, and staged a third creation marked by the coming of the Munda *raj*. He would get rid of the European and Hindu exploiters, then march on Calcutta to assume power. He revolted against the Protestants and government, but was in touch with the more liberal Catholic missionaries. The Munda *raj* was to unite all speakers of Munda languages in Chotanagpur, prefiguring the claims of the modern Jharkhand Party. His charismatic authority, said to stem directly from God, countered that of the traditional chiefs. Like Sidhu and Kanhu, Birsa gave orders while possessed. His figure recalls Christ: it is said that a cross was inscribed on his palms (Singh 1983: 38). He performed miracles, e.g. creating a whole store of rice from a few grains. Birsa addressed himself to the entire Munda community. He had come to free humanity but only his followers would be saved. Long after his death, his followers believe he will return, like Jesus, to his disciples.

The first months of the movement were dominated by the religious aspect, then it exploded. Birsa's followers attacked the Christians in Ranchi with bows and arrows on Christmas eve, 1894. The missionaries escaped, but the church was pillaged. Anti-colonial feelings and agrarian claims inspired Birsaite songs as well as the speeches of their leader (Singh 1983: 99–147). Birsa declared the Sahibs and the missionaries the enemies of the Mundas, though he spared the converts. 25 August 1895 was the day of the coming of the Munda *raj*. On the 22nd, Birsa was arrested. It is told that a wall crumbled as he entered the prison yard. But the promised fire rain did not come. In court, the Mundas were defended by a lawyer, K. Mukherjee, who knew their language.[21] They were declared not guilty and Birsa was freed after two months.

The famines of 1896-7 and 1899-1900 allowed Birsa and the Sardars to reopen the conflict. Birsa, imprisoned, was again freed on 30 November 1897. Some days later, lightning struck his plough but he was unhurt. The missionaries excommunicated his followers. Birsa went to Puri and said the waters of Jagannath's well inspired him to fight inequality and exploitation. He organized processions to revive the old sacred sites. In February 1898, the Mundas assembled for Holi at Dombar. Birsa wanted to end the kingdom of Ravana—the British *raj*. At a hilltop meeting, he set fire to the Union Jack and planted a red flag—possibly a borrowing from the socialists—to mark the end of exploitation. Later, an effigy of Queen Victoria was burnt and the destruction of British rule symbolized by the felling of a plantain. Birsa hesitated to use violence, but the Sardars put pressure on him (Singh 1983: 79-98). In 1900, the Birsaites, trapped at Sael Rakab, refused to surrender. The British attacked and took many prisoners. Birsa is said to have appeared on the hilltop, exposing himself with immunity to British fire. He escaped towards Singhbhum, while survivors claimed that those who fell were lacking faith in Birsa. He again gathered his adepts at Rogoto hill, but was captured by Munda collaborators and handed over to the British. Birsa, then, like Kanhu, was betrayed by his own. The movement ended in a brutal massacre. Nearly 350 Mundas were hanged and 44 transported for life. On 9 June 1900 Birsa died in prison, allegedly from cholera. Many Mundas died in jail.

When Birsa was arrested, the local authorities tried to prevent the rebellion from spreading to the Kol. There was solidarity not only between tribals but also with low castes living close to them, such as artisans, potters, blacksmiths, and herdsmen, implying a degree of class consciousness (Samaddar 1998). The agrarian base of Birsa's movement, a recurrent element in the history of the area, spawned other forms of resistance based on ethnic solidarity. The social and moral order aimed at was later expressed in the Jharkhand movement. Ethnicity became a platform for political and economic demands and an instrument to organize resistance against the colonizer and his Hindu representative.

Resistance continued. The Santals of Rampurhat rose against zamindars and moneylenders in 1906-7. They fought for their lost lands but also against Christianization by the Santal Mission. Durga Manjhi, the pargana of Rampurhat, was educated, and the power of his oratory made him the undisputed leader of the Santal. In

December 1906, he wrote a petition to the Lieutenant-Governor, repeated in 1907, demanding the rights that the Santals enjoyed in Santal Parganas. But discrimination persisted, with increasing discontent among the Santals.

Another revivalist movement, the Tana Bhagat, took place among the Oraons from 1914 to 1919. It was led by Jatra Oraon, who claimed to be inspired by the god Dharmesh.[22] He, too, aimed at reviving a lost kingdom, and like the Kherwar, he wanted to purify the Oraon. They had lost more land than their neighbours and had to pay much more rent than the Munda (Ekka 1972). Jatra urged his followers to stop ploughing the landowners' fields. He mobilized 26,000 men, and the movement spread to the Oraon of Ranchi, Palamau, and Hazaribagh. It was joined by some Mundas and Kharias. Jatra was arrested in April 1914 and imprisoned for a year. Later, he came in with Gandhi and, unlike most tribal groups, the Oraons joined the non-cooperation movement (Ghosh 1998: 30).

## ETHNICITY AND CLASS CONSCIOUSNESS

The Santal rebellion, too, had a strong ethnic overtone. The leaders promised to recover the Santal kingdom, whose revival was legitimized by royal symbols granted by Thakur to Sidhu and Kanhu in their visions. Legitimizing the brothers, Thakur symbolized the power of the *diku* which they were appropriating. But above all, resistance and common suffering forged a new Santal identity.

Did Lutheran missionaries construct a tribal stereotype? Inspired by an image of the noble savage they acted to reinforce Santal identity, especially through literary activity. They provoked a reinvention of Santal tradition, but there was no need to invent it, as is clear from the rich content of what the Santals wrote when urged to put their lore in writing. Yet the missionaries concentrated on language, semantics, and folk tales, and left unpublished narratives of such events as the Santal rebellion, Kherwar movement, famine, accusations of human sacrifice, or relationships with Hindu castes. When reading these unpublished texts today, we see how they constitute an attempt by the Santals to reorder their experience of the colonial impact.

The recorded narratives rebel against hierarchy. In folk tales Brahmans are derided as unable to distinguish real values from the pretentions of the newly rich or religious hypocrites. We recall the story of the prince Mandho Singh, born of a Santal mother and a

Hindu father, who tried to establish a kingdom in Chotanagpur. Some Santals, refusing to follow him, hung cowhides at their village gates. Mandho Singh understood that they refused Hinduism and left, followed by some Santals who are seen as traitors, and their king the petty vassal of a hinduized Munda raja in Chotanagpur. Such criticism is shared by the Mundas whose raja in the nineteenth century gave villages to brahmins and merchants, to pay for luxury goods. The Santal narrators are also sarcastic towards the Saph hor, the Kherwar reformist sect.

Mandho Singh who dreamt of civilizing the Santals reminds us of the Hindu kings of north Orissa who received the *tika*[23] from the hands of a tribal chief, and paid homage to a tribal goddess in a forest shrine (Kulke 1976; Carrin-Bouez 1978b). The king's ambiguity is shown by his vindication of tribal ancestry, while the man who put the *tika* was often sacrificed to become the king's chosen deity (*ishta deva*) on the king's death. In the Mandho Singh story, the Santals refused alliance with the prince (Carrin-Bouez 1991).

Wildness (Skaria 1999) may find its validation in the recruitment of tribal groups for the armies of Hindu kings (Mahapatra 1978). But like the wilderness itself it may also symbolize cultural resistance for indigenous peoples who evoke past landscapes to situate a glorious past, allowing them to reinvent tradition (Ranger 1994). In Chotanagpur as in southern Bengal and Northern Orissa, modern resistance is rooted in this remembered landscape.

In many stories, the Santals emphasize their egalitarian values, which may explain their scepticism towards Sidhu and Kanhu, viewed as usurpers in some *Hul* narratives.[24] They are accused of having taken the best part of the loot, and the most attractive women. Traditionally, the prerogatives of chiefs and priests are controlled by the judgement of the burnt forest, during the ritual hunt. Here anyone may ask for justice before the *pargana* and *desh manjhi*, chiefs elected for a certain period, who are considered as *primus inter pares*. The Santals like to be able to control their chiefs.

## THE *ADIVASI* CONCEPT AND THE JHARKHAND MOVEMENT

Changes in the chiefs' position date from at least the Permanent Settlement, which enriched those tribal headmen who acted as revenue collectors (Guha 1983). Later, encroachment on tribal territory intensified, as Hindu migrants came to exploit new markets, when the State started exploiting the forest.

From the late nineteenth century, a number of social reform associations led by Christian missionaries and their students emerged in Chotanagpur. They stressed the egalitarian ideas among Munda groups and wanted to improve their condition. They fought witchcraft and worked for solidarity among those oppressed by zamindars and mahajans. In 1898, the Christian Association was formed by Lutheran graduates to promote education. It was renamed the Christian College Union in 1918 (Ghosh 1998: 37). The Roman Catholic Cooperative Society, formed in 1906, attempted to raise the tribal standard of living. Then, the Chotanagpur Charitable Association was formed in 1912 by Christian and non-Christian tribals. It aimed at uniting different sections of the people. The first really efficient organization, the Chotanagpur Unnati Samaj, formed in 1915, was led by J. Bartholomew, a student. It was apolitical but held regular meetings and opened its doors to non-Christian tribal people. Urban-based, it had little influence in the villages but helped the students find jobs. Its leadership was in the hands of the Oraon elite and they kept the Mundas and Santals away.

Christian education developed considerably between 1905 and 1920, offering a way to climb socially. The Christian ideal of justice partly filled the gap left when adivasis lost their ancestral values and their respect for the chiefs. Mission schools allowed Christian elites to form among the Santal, Munda, Ho, and Oraon communities. In Ranchi during the 1920s, students from these circles forged the term '*adivasi*' to label the original inhabitants. The Munda and Oraon activists who developed the concept saw Adivasis as entitled to special rights, perceived as compensation for the spoliation they had suffered from caste society.

From 1920 to 1938 a partly westernized class emerged, led by catechists and teachers. By this time, teachers and peasants were inventing new scripts and staging folk theatre in order to renew tribal culture by placing it in the perspective of colonial oppression. The tribal leaders of the 1930s wanted the Adivasis to be equal, without acknowledging their own prestige position. The Christian elite was conscious that major and minor tribes existed and wanted to level the differences, which proved impossible.

In 1928, some members of the Simon Commission submitted a memorandum demanding special treatment for tribes. Several organizations like the Kisan Sabha[25] (1931) and the Catholic Sabha (1936) tried to promote tribal rights. With the introduction of provincial autonomy by the Government of India Act, 1935, Chotanagpur and the Santal Parganas were put under the special responsibility of the governor. But tribal leaders won few seats in the 1937 elections, as the Congress swept the polls. Still, from 1938 there was a determined attempt at building a political platform to redress tribal grievances. Different organizations tried to bridge the gap between Christians and non-Christians. The result was the formation of the Adivasi Mahasabha in 1938, in which the different organizations merged. This Mahasabha successfully maintained a balance between the three Christian groups: Anglicans, Lutherans, and Catholics. It generally chose a Lutheran, or a Catholic as secretary under an Anglican President.

Since 1951, the Indian government has instituted a series of rehabilitation measures such as the reservation of a percentage of posts in the administration and places in universities for the 'Scheduled Tribes'. The reservation policy has helped build tribal elites.

But such measures can hardly solve the problem of caste prejudice in India. Among the Munda groups, the term *Adivasi* seems to have been seen as a stigma. Though enjoying special status, *Adivasis* are associated with untouchables and placed with the lowest in society. To the state, these are backward communities educationally, economically, and socially. In the early years, reservation did not necessarily have the negative overtone it has now, as those who implement *adivasi* programmes are becoming less and less secular.[26]

The Adivasi Mahasabha demanded the separation of the tribal districts from Bihar, but in 1947 the Congress rejected the demand. From then to 1960 government reports dealing with the 'tribal problem' tended to consider the Jharkhand as an irrational answer to the progressive policies of independent India. It was assumed that the idea of a separate state had been provoked by the isolationist tribal policies of the colonial government and by missionary activity. Some government officers felt the word Jharkhand was used by individuals and groups in their own interest at the expense of the tribal community (Corbridge 1988).

The Adivasi Mahasabha was led by educated leaders like Jaipal Singh, a Munda who returned from Oxford to lead the Indian hockey team to victory in the 1928 Olympic games. In 1950, he became the leader of the Jharkhand Party formed on 5 March 1949, at a Conference of the Adivasi Mahasabha in Ranchi. But the Santals did not identify with the party in its early years; the members were mostly Munda and Oraon. Organizations such as the Sarna Dhorom Samlet, launched in the north of Orissa by Ragunath Murmu, tried to assert Santal identity, rejecting Christianization.

Meanwhile, the proletarization of *Adivasis* and the scarcity of land gradually induced the Santals to join the Jharkhand movement, led among others by Satrughna Besra, an MLA from Jamtara who launched an agrarian movement in the Santal Parganas, lasting from 1955 to 1961. Since then, the role of the Santals in the Jharkhand movement has always been central while reflecting Santal specificity. After the rebellion, the vindication of the Santals retained a religious overtone. Since they have joined the Jharkhand party, the quest for a Santal *raj* has taken the form of demand for a Jharkhand state. From 1952 to 1957 the Jharkhand, demanding a separate state, won a considerable number of votes, especially in Chotanagpur and in the Santal Parganas. But the party had no agrarian programme—its urban elite had lost contact with the village economy.

In the 1960s Adivasi organizations multiplied.[27] In 1968, the Hos and Mundas created the All India Jharkhand Party which organized the Ranchi bandh in 1978. From this experience stem the first Adivasi conferences at Jamshedpur, as well as the socialist Jharkhand Mukti Morcha, led by the Santals. Their politics were marked by cultural organizations engaged in the reinvention of Santal tradition. In the 1960s forgotten ritual was revived, like the cult of the sacred grove and of the village founders. This cultural strain stressed education and economic co-operation.

From 1978, the Jharkhand stir expanded, in the wake of the ecological movement[28] in Singhbhum. In 1980, it allied itself to non-Adivasi groups but the alliance was beaten in 1984. Then, in 1987, the president of the JMM was murdered at Jamshedpur, and ethnicity became a main issue. The Jharkhand revival was marked by mass meetings in Ranchi in 1987 and Calcutta in 1989. A parallel government was established, which organized a series of strikes uniting the JMM, led by Sibu Soren, with the All Jharkhand Union under B.B. Mahato. In the 1990 elections, the JMM supported the BJP, accepting to confine their demands for Jharkhand to Chotanagpur and the Santal Parganas. That year, the central government proposed an autonomous council for these districts, which the

JMM accepted. The council—created in 1995—had limited powers, but did represent a step towards Jharkhand, even if half the nominated members refused their seats. The All Jharkhand Union and JMM together sent an ultimatum to the government, demanding the creation of a state including the twenty-two districts[29] of their original demand. The Jharkhand leaders now saw these regions as internal colonies of India. The 1996 Lok Sabha election showed widespread deception with the Jharkhand, which won only one seat in the Assembly. But in 2000, the project of a separate state was finally realized. At the moment of writing, the main problem from a tribal point of view is to gain a political majority in the new Jharkhand state, where tribal people form some 27 per cent of the population.

How does it feel to be a Santal, and how is this consciousness affected by being a Santal *and* a member of a scheduled tribe, being a Santal *and* an adivasi, being a Santal *and* a Jharkhandi, being a Santal *and* an Indian citizen? These oppositions imply others, such as between Christians and non-Christians, or between the elite and the masses. They know that they have a different language and share much with the Mundas. Their leaders stress that the Santals have maintained a specific way of life. They often insist on the present degradation of Santal society, which they attribute to Hinduization or Christianization.

Munda speakers see themselves as original inhabitants of their regions. Their migrations do not reduce their 'indigenousness' in their view, since common experience of exploitation has forged a consciousness of 'difference' rooted in a realization of being subaltern. This shared experience does not preclude disagreement. Differences between religious congregations have split several of the pan-tribalist efforts since the creation of the Adivasi Mahasabha in 1938. In 1943-4 some members of the Hinduized Saph Hor played an important role in the Freedom Movement. After Independence, other Hinduized movements such as Birsaites or Sarnites[30] became sects, and did not make political claims. But simultaneously, a return to tribal religion took place.

A majority of Santals consider they are Jharkhandis, a term which labels their political involvement in the Jharkhand party. As Jharkhandis, Santals share interests with other Munda groups, though they may belong to different factions of the tribal party. They also welcome as Jharkhandi non-adivasi people, such as the agricultural castes who have been sharing the same life conditions during the last one or two centuries.

To what extent can we define an autonomous sphere of subaltern action and thought, outside the reach of the dominant class? Is there a specific tribal way to define a sphere of subaltern action? The exploited in India have long been seen as passive, but this image is largely constructed by administrators and social workers manipulated by what is at best a paternalistic elite. Only recently has the image been challenged, notably by the subalternist historians. Yet, 'in challenging older stereotypes of passivity and aquiescence to elite manipulation, the subalternists at first focused largely on moments in Indian history when subordinate groups engaged in direct violent, often very conscious, challenges to colonial or elite power' (Haynes and Prakash 1991: 7). Everyday resistance, less spectacular, was still largely ignored, as Scott (1987) points out.

In the history of tribal resistance, the missionary influence must not be underestimated. Certainly, Christians are and were a small minority among tribals. But the role of missionary education in creating a tribal elite has been important, and missionaries did not accept the hierarchical subordination of tribes to Hindus. The role of missionary influence in forging an egalitarian counter-culture among Adivasis has been crucial in resisting the pressure of the cultural imperialism of high-caste Hindus.

## SKREFSRUD AS A NATIONAL HERO

While the Santal *raj* was still a dream, Norway was becoming a nation, needing heroic figures to metonymize asserted national qualities. That Skrefsrud should become a national hero, is paradoxical in view of his scathing remarks about his countrymen. But his numerous biographies are popular hagiographies.[31] He certainly figures as the 'apostle' to the Santals,[32] in a teleological perspective where the goal is an evangelized world, but his hagiography is dominated by the national hero, taking his place in a statuary of great men. In Norwegian myth, the missionary recedes into the background, as his story becomes a building-block in the construction of the nation.

Typical is Saeter's biography (1940)[33] opening with Björnson's poem to Skrefsrud, thus linking two key figures of Norwegian national pride. Then: 'Lars Olsen Skrefsrud, the tenant farmer's boy . . . is now recognized by all as one of the great spiritual figures of our country'. 'With pleasure and patriotic pride' he concludes, Skrefsrud 'may be placed among the first and the greatest in our recent history' (Saeter 1940: 9-10). Döhl (1944) is even more eloquent. Skrefsrud's name, he begins, 'is written into Norwegian cultural history in capital letters. His life and work is a glittering adventure from everyday life' (1944: 7). Then comes Björnson's poem. Throughout Döhl's book, the accent is on the national hero.

Saeter opens by describing the little tenant farm of Skrefsrud: the splendid view from the cottage, high above lake Mjösa and the town of Lillehammer. The proximity of the river, where Skrefsrud is said to have gone fishing and built dams and mills dreaming of becoming a great engineer, is stressed as is the forest, where the boy was hunting for birds. The river and forest, here, are phrased to fit into the cult of nature which had become central to Norwegian national feeling. Rather a pity, then, that Döhl corrects a detail: Skrefsrud's childhood was not spent at Skrefsrud. The family moved there when Lars was twelve years old (1944: 8-9).

Surprisingly, Saeter does not stress the boy's religious character. Rather, his boyhood is drawn on the lines of other great men: unusual initiatives, uncommon intelligence and a consciousness of being different, mixed with suffering since his mates cannot understand him. The father's alcoholism is left in the background (Saeter 1940: 11-14). Döhl does not deal with images of nature, until we get to India. Instead, the poverty of the family and the father's drinking is in focus (1944: 8).[34]

Saeter describes Lars' first churchgoing on a Christmas day: 'the candles, the host of people, the vicar with a gold cross on his back, the singing and the mighty roar of the organ! The boy's shiny eyes sparkled under his locks, and the boy's senses became excitedly active' (1940: 17). This, we note, is church, not chapel. Döhl does not mention the religious influences on Skrefsrud's childhood at all.

Learning enters Lars' life by way of the school.[35] 'The schoolmaster, seen as a learned man in his own circles, often had to put him right, saying it was a sin to be so curious' (Saeter 1940: 17-18). Döhl only notes Lars' interest and aptitude for learning (1944: 9). Saeter constructs the boy's confirmation[36] as an encounter with erudition. Lars did not know what erudition meant, but if only he did well, 'he would become erudite himself – collect many books and write books himself' (1940: 18-19). Indeed, he was the first to be examined (says Saeter), uncommon honour for a tenant's son since it meant he was held to be the best.

The town of Lillehammer is described as an antidote to nature and the countryside. In Saeter's description, we forget how small the town then was: 'there was a continuously changing traffic . . . people from all over the place. Boys and girls went arm in arm in the streets, and from the dance halls the tune of fiddles was ringing. There were sleighs in the courtyards—and the trade in horses was going full swing . . . One heard many an indecent joke, and the laughter rolled like waves all over the town. Here, it seemed, nobody was sad, and life seemed like pure joy' (Saeter, op. cit.: 19-20).

Throughout, Saeter aims at a particular figure, dear to Norwegian imagination: the village genius, the sudden flowering of intelligence among the people, which affirms a 'natural', individualistic equality[37] between people and elite, between peripheral Norway and the centres of European culture. But the problem of the clever youth from simple surroundings is that the milieu cannot discern genius from madness. Here, Saeter tacks on to themes common in Norwegian—and American—biographies: the country boy must get out in the world to realize himself. Saeter's Skrefsrud is a Samuel Smiles figure.

As the boy and his mother go to settle him with the master craftsman Erik Bu, Saeter invents a meeting with the rich farmer David Onsum, and his daughter, Anne. The romantic account is very different from the sober way in which Hodne (1966) describes an unhappy but, for Skrefsrud, useful alliance (1940: 23). The seamstress Oline, whom Hodne sees as Skrefsrud's real love,[38] is mentioned by Saeter, but only as one among several acquaintances. He may have found this premarital affair unsuited to the construction of his hero. Döhl speaks of Oline, but does not mention her name. Lars got engaged the winter, he notes, when 'things small and large disappeared—many were those who realized they had had uninvited guests' (1944: 10). But then he was caught.

Saeter's Lars is intrigued by the smithy. Bu was a mechanic, too. Lars, the author tells us, wants to become a 'coppersmith, an engineer or a mechanical inventor—as famous as Erik Bu himself!' (ibid.: 25). Bu is taken in: 'There is an engineer hidden in you, boy', he says. Saeter makes much of Bu as a follower of Thrane, the socialist leader,[39] who had a private school at Lillehammer some years earlier (1940: 26). He even lets Lars propose a working man's society in the spirit of Thrane. Nyhagen does in fact state that Skrefsrud was 'taken in' by Thrane's ideas (1990, I: 92). Hodne (1966), however, stresses the lack of any links to the socialist movement, in spite of its presence at Lillehammer when Skrefsrud was young.

But to be a man also implies drink, cards, fights, and girls. One night, Saeter tells us, Lars returns in the early morning, to find his mother has died. At night he sees his mother in his dreams, entreating him to stop drinking and feasting (Saeter 1940: 26-30). Yet he continues. 'Two powers were fighting to control him', says Saeter, 'one dark, one luminous' (ibid.: 33). This manichaean strain may be seen as part of the toolbox of the popular biographer: yet Skrefsrud uses the same tools later, not least in describing the Santals.

Saeter does not spill much ink on the burglary at Fagstad's shop. People thought he was the more innocent party to the crime. Yet he refused to name anybody else. We are made to feel that Lars wanted to accept the punishment. Then Saeter lets him note his father's presence in court. The father breaks down, telling what a bad father he has been: he wants to be jailed with his son. 'As in a vision (Lars) sees in his father the symbol of the suffering and degradation of the working class as well as his own' (ibid.: 38-45).

On the train to jail in Christiania Saeter makes Lars lecture the *lensmann*[40] on the technology of railways. On his return, he and Erik Bu should 'go to Armstrong in England to get money for factories along the Mesna River—great works to cast cannon and produce power for turbines and engines' (ibid.: 45-6).

In jail, Saeter lets Lars' thoughts dwell on Anne. Anne believes in him, and one day, she comes to visit (ibid.: 59). The romanced account, here, may be closer to truth than much else in Saeter's book, since it seems that the visit was a major event leading to their marriage. Anne's devotion rings true; it is less clear what Skrefsrud felt.[41] Döhl deals with Anne's letters: she is said to have heard of Skrefsrud when working as a maid for his jailor. Her first letters, then, are examples of Christian social work. But, impressed by his conversion and his plans to be a missionary, she falls in love. She takes the first step: Lars 'never dared to aim that high'. It is she who makes her parents accept the marriage (1944: 13-15).

Saeter writes of Lars' demand for books, and of his religious crisis. But he says little about the books Skrefsrud read, though he mentions Fjeldstedt, the Swedish missionary from a peasant background. He constructs a discussion with the jail priest, where the latter mentions 'as a terrifying example . . . of religiously romantic fervour', the sentences against the Laestadians[42] of Finnmark. Five of their leaders were beheaded. 'Christ's first disciples were killed, too', says Lars, shocking the vicar (1940: 47-54). Döhl's account is less romantic. He mentions no vision or mystical experience, though he lets Skrefsrud ponder his salvation. In his view, it is the reading of E. Mann's book *Kristelig Samler*[43] which puts Lars on to his future calling. He cites only works fitting for a would-be missionary, omitting Swedenberg and other 'dubious' authors.

Skrefsrud finds himself marked by his sentence. Lillehammer people are sceptical. He finds support, however, with some who knew him before his fall. 'You were dumb', says Bu, 'you should have named your collaborators . . . but I take it you wanted to be some kind of hero, as always'. He is too good for such a hole as Lillehammer. Then the smith enters a long tirade on the damned society that makes slaves out of men (Saeter 1940: 63-5). Saeter even invents a meeting with Thrane. He stresses what they have in common: both have been to jail, and Thrane, too, lived some years at Lillehammer. Thrane talks of the day of judgement, when 'black hands' will strike at the 'white hands of silk'. They talk of raising the downtrodden: but while Skrefsrud refers to sin, Thrane's mind is on the material. They cannot agree, and part, sad not to get closer. Lars returns to the Pietists (ibid.: 76-9). When Saeter wrote in 1924, socialism had become a real force,[44] rivalizing with the Inner Mission for working class support. This attempt at reconciliation, then, goes with Saeter's stress on Skrefsrud as a major figure, integrating the nation. Its importance would have been even greater later. Since the Labour party came to power in 1934, social democracy became, for a long time, part of the national identity, and the 'poor country without poor people' a main source of national pride.

In Christiania, Lars goes to Nylands Verksted. According to Saeter, he asks straight for the Director, when suddenly the great man himself arrives to ask what he wants. Against all odds, he immediately engages the coppersmith straight from jail. The story recalls a series of other Norwegian myths, where the courage to go 'straight to the top' is the secret of success. This, too, has become a kind of self-assigned ethnic marker.

Saeter says Skrefsrud became well known among students in Christiania, as among poets, painters and actors. He knew Björnson, Ibsen, Vinje among the authors, and Thrane and Fjörtoft among the ultra-radicals (ibid.: 69-75). No other source makes such claims. The city was small, and most of these men knew each other. Like the cities Hannerz (1992) deals with,[45] Christiania was fermenting with cultural activity and men such as Ibsen were not the distant celebrities they became later. Still, the main implicit point here is, clearly, to integrate several national heroes into a coherent pantheon.

There is little about the Berlin period that concerns us here. But Döhl tells us that Skrefsrud returned in triumph to Norway: several newspapers wrote about him. Nobody else mentions this. Döhl is eager, here, to show that Norway had already accepted its future hero: that the usual picture, of his leaving Norway bitter and deceived, is false (1944: 18).

When Skrefsrud and his German colleague find their mission station unfinished, Krüger, Döhl says, wants to give up and return to Europe. But Skrefsrud 'supposes they came here to do some work'. Certainly not carpenter's work, Krüger answers. 'One kind of work is as good as another', says the Norwegian, 'and my father was a carpenter' (Döhl 1944: 20). Then Skrefsrud goes to the mine in the jungle to get doors—and comes down with fever. We are in a favourite ethnic mytheme: the Norwegian, unafraid of work, outshines the cultivated but pusillanimous German. Krüger here parallels the brahmin in many Santal stories. The myth of Skrefsrud takes its place in the defence of the periphery, the subaltern strategy of opposing human qualities to institutionalized power and culture.

## EPILOGUE

This book deals with a meeting of cultures. Culture, however, is a contested term that begs definition. We see it as semantic space, in which humans construct and represent themselves and others. It contains polyvalent messages and actions, and the degree to which they form wholes is problematic. Frontiers between cultures are necessarily fuzzy, yet our missionaries and their Santal interlocutors are very differently situated in cultural space. The distance between their respective starting points is considerable, and is not simply annihilated by physical proximity.

Yet Skrefsrud's tenant background is not that different from many a Santal peasant's. Both are subalterns, and both oppose high culture.

Skrefsrud's attitude to 'his' chosen people recalls that of a mafia leader: he is a man of the people, but one that has made good.

What happens in Europe affects the Santals, and what happens in India affects Europe. Santals, like the several European peoples, live in various semantic spaces, in different micro-worlds. But these are all parts of the same, contemporary, world. There is no 'evolutionary gap': Santals see their first trains at the same time that Norwegians do. Their differing relations to the new technological and social innovations of the nineteenth century result, not from displacement of time, but from their positioning in their respective power systems. Norwegians will soon replace the British engineers: Santals will not—till very much later.

Our idea of semantic space implies the need to contextualize the fragile worlds framed by individual projects, which expand to become social, political, and ideological, as our missionaries try to cast the Santals into images contrasting with themselves. The encounter unites these fragile worlds, creating a space for specific projects: education, sanitation, economics, and, above all, faith. The missionaries want to base faith in a national character: but this character is as much their own construction as that of the Santals. They are unable to give equal status to Santal knowledge. Though they may speak in terms of two cultures, they cannot recognize two histories. Briefly, the Santals have a culture and myths, but no history. In spite of efforts to recognize Santal culture, the missionary discourse is ethnocentric.

But there is a Santal answer, which we find mainly in the Oslo archive texts. There, the writers certainly try to satisfy missionary demands for knowledge about Santal culture. But they are doing more than that. They also try to evoke their own forgotten past, struggling against the threat of memocide that conversion implies. Though willing to stop propitiating bongas, they do not want to forget them. They want to avoid a monolithic view of Santal culture. Outsiders may see it as an undifferentiated whole, but the writers are aware of the reality of discourse; differing opinions, regional differences, and changes over time. 'There are those who think this, and others think that', say the writers time and again. Nowhere in the texts do the Santals seem to fear ethnocide: they know they have suffered greatly, but also that they are still present in strength. Humour and the pleasures of life become strategies in their struggle to keep their identity when fighting exploiters, moneylenders, and missionaries. If there is one matter for which they are grateful to the missionaries, it is the gift of writing, which, contrary to much the missionaries claim to be doing for them, is a lasting acquisition. It is the idea present in Sidhu's and Kanhu's visions, that writing is necessary to deal with the colonial power and oppose it. It is used, in the encounter itself, as a way to record it.

Cultural encounter is always dialectic, but this is not always reflected in the records. Here, we have tried to draw upon Santal writing to reconstitute at least some of its dialectic character. As the Comaroffs put it, all local worlds have their own historicity (1992: 24). The problem, then, is the memocide (Samaddar 1998) that characterizes peoples who did not write their history themselves. To recover the unwritten history, then, is to recover the subject.

The Santals' own efforts'—as they emerge from the archives—seem to be characterized by three discernible trends. The first is a tendency to put history in a nutshell, bounded by the image of the lost kingdom. The king is symbolized as a kind of semi-divine agency, but there is a contradiction here, as he is criticised and abandoned. Rebellion is central to the image, but this in turn depends on the king. The second tendency is a desperate recognition of deculturation, implying progressive destruction of culture, which projects into three alternatives: future assimilation as a low caste, or withdrawal to the wilderness, as if one could exit from history, or the challenge of Christianity, with education as a strategy for a better future. Some Christian Sanṭals feel that missionary criticism of their traditional society is just, and the future lies in getting rid of such negative markers as witchcraft or alcoholism.

The third trend is towards resistance. It is not easy to determine what constitutes resistance, as B.P. Karlsson (2000) underlines. Scott's concept of everyday resistance (1987, 1990) is obviously useful here. But the question of when and how resistance becomes openly and consciously political, must be judged by the information available, set into a contextual interpretation linked to the scale of the system considered. This question will obviously be judged differently by the subalterns themselves, by the dominant, or by the anthropologist in search of comparative understanding.

Writing allows an evaluation of identity, strengthening the salience of ethnicity. Yet the creation of a literate elite affects solidarity, as upward mobility threatens to split the group. Egalitarianism becomes both a problem and a strength here. Emerging leadership has difficulty in attaining credibility, for the leaders are 'no longer like us'. The leader may then be cast in the mould of the king against whom real Santals rebel. The new charismatic leader is not a chief or king, however, and successive efforts at leadership consciously try to avoid the royal parallel, with more or less success. Success, one may think, will accrue to a leader capable of charismatic inspiration while avoiding hierarchical overtones. He must be seen as dedicated, but not greedy or interested. He must have authority without exercising power.

Yet egalitarianism also has its advantages. Solidarity is potentially present whenever people unite against exploitation or domination. The strong Santal support for Naxalism and other Maoist movements is a case in point (Duyker 1987). Egalitarianism underpins the old Santal values of aestheticism and love of pleasure, which imply collective activity and act as a restraint against the rational individualism that the missionaries, steeped in liberal economic thought, want them to adopt.

One fascinating aspect of missionary history is the contrast between the modest origins of many actors and their subsequent displacement across the world. Our main figures are probably extreme, since they do not move in a pre-established support network but have to create one of their own. Yet contrasting elements of parochialism and cosmopolitanism seem to be a feature of many personalities in mission history—one need only think of Carey the shoemaker who ends up translating the Bible into a large number of languages while remaining, for most of his time in India, in a single place. The Comaroffs have shown conclusively how the Evangelical missionaries to South Africa in the early part of the century came from 'laboring, peasant and artisan backgrounds' (1992: 194-7).[46] To be sure there are also gentleman missionaries—James Long of the *Nil Darpan* affair is one example—and yet when meeting as fellow Evangelicals, differences of class origin seem to have taken a back seat in spite of their importance in the larger society during the second half of the nineteenth century. Evangelicals tended to be sensitive to human suffering: Long, who was of middle-class origins, still came from a declining industrial town where unemployment was conspicuous, in an Ireland where rural poverty was legion (Oddie 1999: 17). Börresen and Skrefsrud had themselves been poor, and were concerned, from the start, with the suffering of the Santals.

In this, they were probably more typical than Long: like many others, they were not radicals but they were men of the people.

The missionaries represent a particular class and ideological standpoint within the total colonial system. On an objective level, they may be seen as agents of colonialism. But this view is culturally superficial and to some extent ahistorical. The Comaroffs analyse their missionaries as 'the conscience of British colonialism' (1992: 184). This rings true for many British missionaries in Bengal, and Long's role in the indigo controversy is a case in point. But in our case, the situation is more complicated. The term 'conscience' implies that colonialism has a conscious agent. But was the British Empire a conscious creation? It grew by fits and starts, as often in reaction to what seemed like foreign threats as due to a will to conquer or subdue. Yet, skipping this issue, we must ask: were our missionaries conscious of being part of this agency? They were quite conscious of not being British. To them, as to most non-British, the Empire was simply there, part of a world order in which they were free to create their own projects. The Empire really was a World Empire then, open to all who conformed to its laws. The Scandinavian missionaries were as much or as little part of the imperial agency as were artisans or prostitutes from various nations. Both were part of colonial dynamics, but not of the colonial project. They were there to realize their own.

Skrefsrud and Börresen see their moral duty not in terms of colonialism, but of the missionary enterprise, an international evangelizing project. It is not materially affected by the refusal from the Norwegian Missionary Society, by joining or leaving the German Gossner Mission, being helped by Bengali Baptists, or taken on by the British BMS. This itinerary may strengthen their independence from national sentiment or links; but it does not create it. Friends and allies are defined by Evangelical solidarity. Yet Skrefsrud and Börresen are vain; they are flattered by attention from colonial authorities—as they are by the support they receive from Danish aristocracy or the Scandinavian intelligentsia.

As soon as they can, they shake off their links to the BMS and thus to an institutional link with the colonial project. What they try to realize is an independence supported by their community of converts, hoping that the moral message of conversion will attract the funds they need. The project fails, but for some years they are effectively their own masters, carving out their own space within the colonial setting. The loss of this hard-won independence is contingent on changes in the colonial system: not only is the Santal country more and more taken in hand by the colonial administration—the government take-over of their schools is important here—but their Scandinavian supporters come to see their work more and more in a colonial idiom, a religious colonization albeit in a territory belonging to another state.

The congregationalist structure they envisage for the Santal church echoes the debate on church and Christian community since Protestantism began—and Skrefsrud later finds his ideal realized, better than anywhere else, among Lutheran friends in Minnesota. When, paradoxically, he feels that the congregationalist church must have a bishop this is refuted by his Norwegian and Swedish associates, who defy the authority of their own bishops. Thus, ideas of church, nation, Christian community, and democracy are banded back and forth across the oceans, acting through individuals as much as enacted by them. Agency, then, dwells in networks and exchanges, acting through a semantic space that extends beyond the consciousness of any individual. This space is not unitary, but constructed from the multiple representations that differentially positioned actors produce, each in their own situated experience of the world.

The Santal mission received support from very different groups and countries at different times in its history: but at no time did it represent an official church organization. Organizationally independent, the Santal missionaries had to appeal to a number of different groups in order to raise the necessary funds and support. They did not mind receiving support from members of the Danish royal family and aristocracy, as well as from low-class activists in the Home Mission.

Our missionaries were deeply marked by the romanticism of the mid-century, and in this they differed from the Methodists and other missionaries inspired by the Enlightenment. Typical of our missionaries was a sympathy with the tribal or low caste populations among whom they worked, which tended to remain constant whether it led them to support or to oppose official measures. Unlike the missionaries to Southern Africa (Comaroff and Comaroff 1992: 268-9) it cannot be said of Skrefsrud and Börresen that they saw the country as 'empty' in cultural terms. They take for granted that Santals are a people with a culture, a 'nation' in their terms, and see their task as cleansing Santal culture of its 'superstitious' elements and replace them with 'real' religion. This particular way of 'colonizing consciousness' thus implied a radical separation between culture and religion, which had served its purpose in the missionaries' own world by isolating the spiritual from worldly concerns, but which ultimately made little sense in the Santal context. Their ideal of the democratically constituted Christian community was strong, and led them to adapt traditional Santal institutions such as the Kulhi Durup'—the meeting of villagers where all men had the right to speak. What they wanted was to create a Church founded on such democratic institutions with little need for outside authority. The only element which could not fit this structure was the position of the missionaries themselves, outside and above the community of converts.

One of the fundamental contradictions of our story, then, is this. The evangelical utopia of the mission's founders fits rather well the egalitarian and fundamentally democratic values of Santal culture. But the authority needed to keep to the narrow path could incarnate only in the foreign missionary, who could never become the *primus inter pares* in the community that the emissary or elder could be at home. Skrefsrud tried to bridge this gap by converting the chiefs. But the Santal chief's authority remained fluid and uncertain even compared to their Tswana counterparts (Comaroff and Comaroff 1991).

Thus the cultural implicits that Skrefsrud and Börresen brought to the mission field were not the same as those of the men who ruled India. They were foreigners, and they came from a low class background. But most of all, they were adventurers—individuals who carved out a niche for themselves within the colonial set-up. As such, they were far more concerned with defending this niche, and their own relative independence, than with overall imperial designs. Rather than loyal subjects of British India, they tried to negotiate concessions for the services they could render to government.

The missionaries create, from personal history, their own myth: the Santals try to forge history from theirs. The latter are able to use the main gift of the missionary enterprise – writing—to build a future: writing the myth of a missionary helps the Norwegians reinvent their past. From such myths modernity was forged. It was not the product of a single place or culture, but has a global history (van der Veer 2001: 160). Its genesis is linked to the exchange of ideas. Seldom equitable, often determined by power, ideas do not remain bound by the intentions and strategies that move them. The encounter we have described is but a minor episode in history. But the ways in which ideas travel, knowledge is created and recast, myth turned to history and *vice versa,* is, we think, significant beyond the limits of our story.

## NOTES

1. The term 'jungly' certainly has a stigmatizing tone today. Skaria (1999) may be right, however, in affirming that wildness was not necessarily stigmatic in a precolonial setting.
2. Barth (2002: 3) similarly speaks of the validity of knowledge, though he does not explicitly treat the possibility that the validity precedes the knowledge.
3. Red ink cannot be read by the bongas but the texts were not written in red ink. Ojhas told Carrin she should note mantras in red ink (or in French, which bongas do not read). Elsewhere in India messages from Hindu goddesses are sometimes written in red ink.
4. Bonga bapla Reak' Katha (Tales of Santals who have married bongas). Bodding 1924; Andersen, Carrin and Soren (forthcoming).
5. As Pfeffer (1997) notes, this division and its explanation is a common trait among Middle Indian tribes.
6. Santal riddles deal with plants and animals, and construe a semantic of bodily functions—how people eat, digest, excrete, and reproduce themselves (Carrin-Bouez 1985).
7. On the pretext of protecting the wife, like an umbrella, the husband is ever present, mingling in his wife's affairs.
8. The bride is ceremonially brought in a huge basket during the marriage ceremony.
9. It is not clear whether these gestures were banned because missionaries suspected hidden heathen overtones or simply because they were thought irrational.
10. 'A moneylender and his debtor' (Bodding 1925-29, II: 263-75).
11. More than 30 per cent.
12. The story recalls the complicity of a Santal pimp and his customer in a modern context, like the situation Freeman (1979) describes for the Bauri of Orissa.
13. This was the year of Aasen's first systematic attempt at creating a new Norwegian language. In 1885 the language based on his work became legally the second, national language. At the same time, the other language gradually became more Norwegian, adapting grammar and vocabulary from the colloquial.

14. By active mode here Bodding refers to a noun derived from a verb: 'thinking' is thus active; 'thought' is passive.
15. *Dahkwala* 1893: 48-50, 81-5, 93-101, 113-15, 126-31. Santalen 1897: 179-80, *Annual Report 1897-98*: 34.
16. By this term, Bodding usually means an *ojha*.
17. A Sirdar was effectively in charge of local police duties.
18. According to tantric ideas, those who deal with death—at graveyards or cremation grounds—gain supernatural powers.
19. Among the Munda, the *deonra* is a diviner who cures maladies. He is sometimes suspected of manipulating his clients to extort substantial sums.
20. Thus he was clad like a Vaishnava ascetic.
21. Even at this time, then, some Hindus sided with the tribes. This was not a monopoly of the missionaries.
22. Dharmesh is rather similar to Dharmo Thakur, another low-caste deity of Shaivite inspiration whose followers, like many Vaishnava sects, oppose the caste system (see Carrin 1997).
23. A mark of blood put on the king's forehead at his installation.
24. *Hul Reak' Katha*, Santal Manuscripts 1448 O.
25. As Ghosh notes (1998: 30) the Kisan Sabha programme, suitable for Gangetic Bihar, was unsuited to Chhotanagpur and Santal Parganas which were regulated by special tenancy Acts.
26. As in the case of discrimination against Muslims in Uttar Pradesh (Jeffery and Basu 1998).
27. The *Santal Samaj Sudha Baisi*, allied to the Jan Sangh, was founded in 1963. Recruiting in the villages, it opposed Christian missions. The *Sidhu Kanhu Baisi*, immortalizing the heroes of the rebellion, followed in 1966. Among the Mundas, the Birsa Seva Dal of 1967 is socialist, even Naxalite, opposing moneylenders.
28. *Jangal Andolan*.
29. These districts were divided between Bihar, Bengal, Orissa and Madhya Pradesh.
30. From *sarna*, 'sacred grove'. This revivalist movement aims at asserting tribal values (Carrin 2002).
31. The only exception is Hodne (1966).
32. Like Hans Egede, 'the apostle to Greenland', Thomas von Westen, 'the apostle to the Lapps' or even Ansgar, the 'apostle' to the Nordic countries.
33. Saeter stresses his book is mixture of history and fiction. He had written similarly about the lives of other great men. We use the 5th edn. of 1940, appearing on the hundred years' jubilee of Skrefsrud's birth.
34. He adds that Skrefsrud's father was known to steal from places where he worked.
35. Norway's advance in literacy and elementary schooling was bought at the cost of quality. There were no school buildings in the countryside:

farmers took turns to accommodate the classes. This ambulatory system aimed mainly at the three R's and religion.

36. The initiation to adulthood in the Lutheran churches, implying a brief and public oral examination in Church.
37. 'Natural' egalitarianism in Jayawardena's sense (1968). For the Norwegian variant, see Gullestad (1992), Gosselin (1987).
38. Nyhagen, too, notes this early love affair in his history of the Santal Mission (1990, I: 105).
39. Nyhagen 1990, I: 92. Skrefsrud himself refers to Thrane's journal and ideas as well known at Lillehammer (Santalposten 1901: 103), and mention is made of Skrefsrud's participation in a branch of the Thrane movement in Norvegia Sacra, 1923: 203.
40. The police commissioner in a country district.
41. Hodne lets us understand that Oline Nubben (Udsigtsbakken) was his only real love (1966: 53), and stresses the social advantages to Skrefsrud of the marriage to Anne (1966: 55).
42. The Laestadians, named after the priest Lars Levi Laestadius of Karesuando in Swedish Lapland, is a Pietist movement which has remained important among the Sami, to the point of serving, sometimes, as an ethnic marker. It was in 1845 that Laestadius started his reform, which included several kinds of ecstatic experience. Confrontation with the Norwegian church and secular authorities led to the Kautokeino revolt in 1852 where five Sami leaders were sentenced to death, though only two were finally executed (Odner 2000: 296-7).
43. *Christian Collector*, not a book, but a Grundtvigian magazine. Döhl clearly was not acquainted with religious literature.
44. The first socialist government came to power in 1928, albeit for only a hundred days.
45. Calcutta during the Bengal Renaissance is one of Hannerz' main examples (1992: 182-92; also 199-210).
46. 'Of the 17 LMS and WMMS missionaries who began work among Southern Tswana before 1860, and for whom we have sufficient information, 12 came from Scotland or the north of England, 2 from Wales, and only 3 from southern England; 13 of them being from either the industrializing river valleys, the urban peripheries or proletarianized villages. Sixteen of the 17, moreover, fit Hobsbawm's description . . . of persons caught between rich and poor, either indeterminate in their class affiliation or struggling to cross the invisible boundary into the bourgeouisie. Five of them came from peasant stock, five were from artisan backgrounds, three had been petty clerks or traders, and three had risen directly from the ranks of the laboring poor. Many, like Moffat and Livingstone, were from displaced rural families' (Comaroff and Comaroff 1992: 196-7).

# Bibliography

## PRINTED SOURCES : BOOKS AND ARTICLES

Aareflot, A., 1967, *Norsk Kirkehistorie II*, Oslo: Lutherstiftelsen.

Allan, D., 1993, *Virtue, Learning and the Scottish Enlightenment*, Edinburgh: Edinburgh University Press.

Allanson, H.L., 1912, *Final Report of the Survey and Settlement Operations in the District of Sonthal Parganas 1898-1910*, Calcutta: Bengal Secretariat Book Depot.

Andersen, A.W., 1975, *The Norwegian-Americans*, Boston: Twayne.

Anderson, B., 1983, *Imagined Communities: Reflections on the Origin and Spread of Nationalism*, London: Verso.

Andersen, P., 1992, 'Is there a Cult for the Santal God Thakur?', in P. Bellwood (ed.), *Man and His Culture: A Resurgence*, Delhi: Books and Books: 325-33.

———, forthcoming, Literacy and the Santal Hul, in M. Carrin and H. Tambs-Lyche (eds.): *People of the Jangal. Reformulating Identities and Adaptations in Crisis*, Delhi: Manohar.

Andersen, P., M. Carrin and S.K. Soren (forthcoming), *From Fire Rain to Insurrection: Asserting Santal Identity through Narrative*, Copenhagen.

*Annual Reports*

*Fourth Annual Report of the Indian Home Mission: Auxiliary to the Baptist Mission to the Sonthals for the year 1870*. Benaras: n.p.

*Annual Reports from 1872 to 1910*, published as: *Annual Report of the Indian Home Mission to the Santals*. Some printed at Benares; some at Calcutta; some at Benagaria: n.p.

*Annual Reports from 1911 to 1930*, published as: *Report of the Santal Mission of the Northern Churches*. All printed at Benagaria: n.p.

Archer, W.G., 1945, 'Santal Rebellion Songs', *Man in India*, XXV, no. 4: 207.

———, 1974, *The Hill of Flutes: Life, Love and Poetry in Tribal India*, London: Allen and Unwin.

———, 1984, *Tribal Law and Justice: A Report on the Santal*, Delhi: Concept.

Archer, W.G. and W.J. Culshaw, 1945, 'The Santal Rebellion', *Man in India*, XXV: 29-42.

Arnold, D., 1986, 'Cholera and Colonialism in British India', *Past and Present*, no. 113 (132).

———, 1993, *Colonizing the Body: State Medicine and Epidemic Disease in Nineteenth Century India,* Delhi: Oxford University Press.

Asad, T., 1996, 'Comments on Conversion', in P. van der Veer (ed): *Conversion to Modernities: The Globalization of Christianity*, London: Routledge: 263-73.

Asbjörnsen, P. Chr. and J. Moe, 1982, *Norske Folkeeventyr, I-II*. Oslo: Den Norske Bokklubben.

Bailey, F.G., 1959, *'Tribe, Caste, and Nation'*, Manchester: Manchester University Press.

———, 1961, 'Tribe and Caste in India', *Contributions to Indian Sociology*, V: 7-19.

Bakhtin, M., 1981, 'Discourse in the Novel', in M. Holquist (ed): *The Dialogical Imagination*, Austin: University of Texas Press.

Ballhatchett, K., 1980, *Race, Sex and Class under the Raj*, London: Weidenfeld and Nicholson.

Banerjee, P., 1975, *Calcutta and its Hinterland: A Study in Economic History of India, 1833-1900*, Calcutta: Progressive Publishers.

Banerjee, S., 1989, *The Parlour and the Street: Elite and Popular Culture in Nineteenth Century Calcutta*, Calcutta: Seagull Books.

Bang, A.C., 1924, *Hans Nielsen Hauge og hans Samtid*, Christiania: Gyldendal.

Barker, T.C. and M. Robbins, 1975, *The History of London Transport,* 1, London: Allen and Unwin.

Barnes, J., 1954, 'Class and Committees in a Norwegian Island Parish', *Human Relations*, vol. 7: 39-58.

Barth, F., 1959, *Political Leadership among the Swat Pathans*, London: Athlone.

———, 1969a, 'Pathan Identity and its Maintenance', in *Barth* (ed): 117-34.

——— (ed), 1969b, *Ethnic Groups and Boundaries*, Oslo: Universitetsforlaget.

———, 1975, *Ritual and Knowledge among the Baktaman of New Guinea*, New Haven: Yale University Press.

———, 1995, *Balinese Worlds*, Chicago: University of Chicago Press.

———, 2002, 'An Anthropology of Knowledge', *Current Anthropology*, 43: 1-17.

Bates, C., 1995a, 'Lost innocents and the loss of innocence', in R.H. Barnes, A. Gray and B. Kingsbury (eds): *Indigineous Peoples of Asia*, American Association for Indian Studies, Michigan: 103-19.

———, 1995b, 'Race, Caste and Tribe in Central India: Early Origins of Indian Anthropometry', in Robb (ed): *The Concept of Race*: 219-59.

Bates, C. and M. Carter, 1993, 'Tribal and Indentured Migrants in Colonial India: Modes of Recruitment and Forms of Incorporation', in P.

Robb (ed): *Dalit Movements and the Meanings of Labour in India*: 159-85.

Bayly, S., 1995, 'Caste and Race in Colonial Ethnography', in P. Robb (ed): *The Concept of Race in South Asia*: 165-218.

———, 1999, *Caste, Society and Politics in India from the Eighteenth Century to the Modern Age*, The New Cambridge History of India, IV.3, Cambridge: Cambridge University Press.

Bebbington, D.W., 1989, *Evangelicalism in Modern Britain: A History from The 1730s to the 1980s*, London: Routledge.

Bedarida, F., 1990, *La société anglaise du milieu du XIXe siècle à nos jours*, Paris: Seuil.

Berry, C.J., 1997, *Social Theory of the Scottish Enlightenment*, Edinburgh: Edinburgh University Press.

Beteille, A., 1986, 'The Concept of Tribe with Special Reference to India', *Archives Européennes de Sociologie*, XXVII (2): 297-318.

Beyer, H., 1961, *Norsk og Fremmed*, Oslo: Aschehoug.

———, 1971, *Utsyn over norsk litteratur*, Oslo: Cappelen.

Bhowmick, P.K., 1963, *The Lodhas of West Bengal*, Calcutta: Punthi Pushtak.

Bhowmik, S., 1981, *Class Formation in the Plantation System*, Delhi: People's Publishing House.

Birkeland, K.B., 1902/1905, *En Menneskeven*: *Hans Peter Börresens Liv og Arbeide*, Minneapolis, 1902; Minnehaha Press, also (revised edition) Kristiania, 1905, Thronsen.

Biswas, P.C., 1956, *Santals of Santal Parganas*, Delhi: Bhartiya Adimjati Sewak Sangh.

Blochmann, H., 1968, *Contributions to the Geography and History of Bengal: Muhammedan Period*, Calcutta: Asiatic Society.

Bodding, P.O., 1898, 'On the Different Kinds of Salutations Used by the Santals', *Journal of the Asiatic Society of Bengal*, LXVII. pt. III, no. 1: 35-43.

———, 1910a, 'A Brief Survey of the Assam Colony from its Inception to Date', Benagaria: Indian Home Mission's Press (reprinted from the 43rd Annual Report). Also Danish translation by P. Eller, 1910.

———, 1910b, 'Et Land, der Kalder', Copenhagen: Den Danske Komité for Santhalmissionen.

———, 1915, 'Om Santalbibelens Tilblivelse', Copenhagen: Den Nordiske Santalmission.

———, 1919, *Sona: En kristen Santalkvindes liv og gjerning*, Copenhagen: Den Nordiske Santalmisjon.

———, 1921, 'The Kherwar Movement among the Santals', *Man in India* (4) 222-32.

———, 1922, 'A Santal Sect', *The Modern Review* (Calcutta), vol. 31, March: 358.

———, 1924, 'A Chapter of Santal Folklore', in *Kristiania Etnografiske Museums skrifter,* vol 3, pt 2: 44-119.

———, 1925-9, *Santal Folk-Tales*, Oslo: H. Aschehoug & Co (W. Nygard), vol. I, 1925; vol. II, 1927; vol. III, 1929.

———, 1926a, 'The Meaning of the word Buru and Bonga in Santali', *Journal of the Bihar and Orissa Research Society*, 12 (1): 63-7.

———, 1926b, 'Erindringer om Skrefsrud', *Nordmannsforbundet*, Kristiania: 54-8, 92-7.

———, 1929-30, 'Materials for a Santali Grammar', I-II, Dumka: Santal Mission of the Northern Churches.

———, 1932-6, *A Santal Dictionary*, vols. I-V, Oslo: Jacob Dybwad.

———, 1944, *A Santali Grammar for Beginners*, Benagaria: Santal Mission of the Northern Churches.

———, 1986, *Studies in Santal Medicine and Connected Folklore* (reprint of three publications dated 1925-40), Calcutta: The Asiatic Society.

Bompas, C.H., 1909, *Folklore of the Santal Parganas*, London: David Natt.

Borthwick, M., 1984, *The Changing Role of Women in Bengal, 1849-1905*, Princeton: Princeton University Press.

Bose, S., 1993, *Peasant Labour and Colonial Capital: Rural Bengal since 1770*, The New Cambridge History of India, III.2, Cambridge: Cambridge University Press.

Bouez, S., 1985, *L'Alliance chez les Ho et les Santal de l'Inde*, Paris: Société d'Ethnographie.

Bouez, S. and M. Carrin-Bouez, 1974, 'Le Mythe de Création Santal', *ASEMI* 5: 124-52.

Bradley, I., 1976, *The Call to Seriousness: The Evangelical Impact on the Victorians*, London, Cape.

Bradley-Birt, F., 1905, *Story of an Indian Upland* London 1905, Smith, Elder & Co.

Briggs, Asa, 1954, *Victorian People,* London: Odham's Press.

———, 1959, *The Age of Improvement,* London: Longmans, Green.

Brimnes, N., 1999, *The Colonial Encounter*, London: Curzon.

Broomfield, J.H., 1968, *Elite Conflict in a Plural Society,* Berkeley: University of California Press.

Brundin, G., 1926, *Ernst Heuman. Biskop av Tranquebar,* Stockholm: Svenska Kyvrkans Diakonistyrelses Bokförlag.

Buchanan, F., 1939, *An Account of the District of Bhagalpur in 1810-1811*, Patna: Rai Bahadur Radha Krishna Jalan.

Buckland, C.E., 1902, *Bengal under the Lieutenant-Governors,* vols. I-II, Calcutta: Kedarnath Bose.

Bull, E., 1985, *Arbeiderbevegelsens Historie i Norge – I: Arbeiderklassen blir til (1850-1900)*, Oslo: Tiden.

Burton, A., 1994, *Burdens of History: British Feminists, Indian Women and Imperial Culture 1865-1915*, Chapel Hill and London: The University of North Carolina Press.

———, 1998, *At the Heart of the Empire: Indians and the Colonial Encounter in Late Victorian Britain*, Delhi: Munshiram Manoharlal.

Börresen, H.P., 1884, *Famine Relief Operations in Connection with the Indian Home Mission to the Santhals,* Calcutta: the Author.

———, 1885, *Foranstaltninger under Hungersnöden i Santhalistan i Aaret 1884*, Copenhagen (n.p.).

Caisson, M., 1991, 'Lumière de Herder', *Terrain*, 17: 17-28.

Campbell, A., 1891, *Santal Folk Tales*, Pokhuria: Santal Mission Press.

———, 1894, 'Traditional Migration of the Santal Tribes', *The Indian Antiquary*, vol. 23, April: 103-4.

———, 1915a, 'Superstitions of the Santals', *Journal of the Bihar and Orissa Research Society*, 1: 2: 213-28.

———, 1915b, 'Rules of Succession and Partition of Property as observed by the Santal', *Journal of the Bihar and Orissa Research Society*, 1: 1: 21-5.

———, 1916a, 'The Traditions of the Santals', *Journal of the Bengal and Orissa Research Society*, 2: 1: 15-29.

———, 1916b, 'Santal Legends', *Journal of the Bengal and Orissa Research Society*, 2: 2: 191-200.

———, 1916c, 'Santal Marriage Customs', *Journal of the Bengal and Orissa Research Society*, 2: 3: 304-37.

———, 1916d, 'Death and Cremation Ceremonies among the Santals', *Journal of the Bengal and Orissa Research Society*, 2: 4: 449-56.

———, 1988, *Santali English Dictionary*, rpt. of 3rd edn. (1953): Firma KLM, Calcutta (Ist published 1903).

Campbell, G., 1865, 'Comparative Table of Aboriginal Words', *Journal of the Asiatic Society of Bengal*, 35, 2: 204-6.

——— (ed), 1874, *Specimens of Languages of India, including those of the Aboriginal Tribes of Bengal, the Central Provinces, and the Eastern Frontier*, Calcutta: Bengal Secretariat Press.

———, 1886, 'Ethnology of India', *Journal of the Asiatic Society of Bengal*, vol. 56, pt. 2: Special Number: *Ethnology*: 1-152.

———, 1893, *Memoirs of My Indian Career*, London: Macmillan.

Carrin, M., 1995, 'Les bonga alibi du désir: Des récits tenus pour réels', in C. Champion (ed): *Traditions Orales dans le Monde Indien, Purusartha 18*, Paris: EHESS: 367-81.

———, 1996a, 'Les tribus de l'Inde: repli identitaire et mouvements insurrectionnels', in C. Jaffrelot (ed): *l'Inde contemporaine de 1950 à nos jours*, Paris: Fayard.

———, 1996b, 'Celles qui sont sorties du regard: Histoires de sorcières en pays santal', *Cahiers de Littérature Orale*, no. 39-40: 157-74.

———, 1997, *Enfants de la déesse: dévotion et prêtrises féminines au Bengale*, Paris: Editions du CNRS et Maison des Sciences de l'Homme.

———, 2002, 'Retour au bosquet sacré: réinvention d'une culture adivasi', in M. Carrin and C. Jaffrelot (eds): *Tribus et Basses Castes, Résistance et Autonomie dans la Société Indienne*, Purusartha 23, Paris: EHESS: 245-64.

———, Forthcoming 'Santal Autonomy as a Social Ecology', in: M. Carrin and H. Tambs-Lyche, *People of the Jangal*, New Delhi: Manohar.

———, 2005, 'Le Sacrifice Humain Dans Les Royaumes de Jungle', in J-P. Albert and B. Midant-Reynes (eds.): *Le sacrifice humain en Egypte ancienne et ailleurs*, Paris: Soleb: 190-211.

———, forthcoming, *Le Parler des Dieux, Genres et Arguments du Discours Rituel Santal*, Paris: CNRS éditions.

Carrin, M. and H. Tambs-Lyche, 1998, 'Une église nationale pour les Santal: du romantisme scandinave à l'orthodoxie luthérienne', *Archives des Sciences Sociales des Religions*, 103: 99-127.

———, 2003, 'The Santals, Though Unable to Plan for Tomorrow, Should be Converted by the Santals', in R. Frykenberg (ed.): *Christians and Missionaries in India: Cross-Cultural Communication since 1500*, Grand Rapids, William B. Eerdmans: 274-94.

Carrin-Bouez, M., 1978a, L'ascension des filandres: Chants des initiés santal, *Cahiers de* littérature orale, 3: 89-138.

———, 1978b, 'Acculturation and/or Dialectics: The Relevance of the Hindu Model for the Understanding of Santal Society', in R. Moser et M. Gautam (eds.): *Aspects of Tribal Life in South Asia: Strategy and Survival*, Studia Ethnologica Bernensia, 1, Bern: Institute of Ethnology: 83-92.

———, 1985, L'inégalité bien partagée, ou l'impureté comme mythe chez les Santal, *Cahiers de Littérature Orale,* 3: 74-104.

———, 1986, *La fleur et l'os: symbolisme et rituel chez les Santal* Paris: EHESS.

———, 1987, 'La bière de riz santal: ferment et monnaie du rite', *Information sur les Sciences Sociales*, 26 (3): 611-32.

———, 1988, Le Paradis dans les jardins du thé, *l'Homme*, XXVIII (2-3): 199-212.

———, 1991a, *Inner Frontiers: Santal Responses to Acculturation,* Bergen, Chr. Michelsen Institutt.

———, 1991b, 'Un roi venu d'ailleurs', *Cahiers de Littérature Orale*, 29: 89-124.

———, 1991c, 'Puissances Occultes, Divination et Justice Chez Les Santal', in R. Verdier (ed.), *Le Serment*, vol. 1: *Signes et Fonctions*, Paris: Editions du CNRS: 67-80.

———, 1992, 'On the Semantic Structure of the Santal Ojha's Religious Discourse', in S. Mahapatra (ed): *The Realm of the Sacred*, Delhi: Oxford University Press: 146-61.

———, 1993, 'Rethinking Female Participation in Tribal Labour in Chotanagpur and Bengal', in P. Robb (ed): *Dalit Movements and the Meanings of Labour in India*, Delhi: Oxford University Press: 150-8.

Carstairs, R., 1912, *The Little World of an Indian District Officer*, London: Macmillan.

———, 1935, *Harma's Village: A Novel of Santal Life*, Pokhuria: Santal Mission Press.

Cederlöf, G., 2003, 'Social Mobilization among People Competing at the Bottom Level of Society: The Presence of Missions in Rural South India, ca. 1900-1950', in R. Frykenberg (ed.) (q.v.): 336-56.

Chakrabarty, D., 1997, 'The Difference-Deferral of a Colonial Modernity: Public Debates on Domesticity in British Bengal', in F. Cooper and A.L. Stoler (eds), *Tensions of Empire* (q.v.) : 373-405.

Chatterjee, P., 1993, *The Nation and Its Fragments: Studies in Colonial and Post Colonial Histories*, Delhi: Oxford University Press.

Chattopadhyay, K.P., 1944, 'Santal Migration', *Proceedings of the 31st Indian Science Congress, Part 3, Abstracts.* Delhi.

Chaudhuri, A.B., 1987, *The Santals: Religion and Rituals*, Delhi: Ashish Publishing House.

Chaudhuri, T., 1995, 'Missionaries among the Santals, 1857-1882: An era of Exploration and Experiment', in R.K. Roy (ed.), *Retrieving Bengal's Past: Society and Culture in the Nineteenth and Twentieth Century*, Calcutta: Rabindra Bharati University: 242-84.

Chitnis, A., 1976, *The Scottish Enlightenment: A Social History*, London: Croom Helm.

Chowdhury, B., 1975, 'The Growth of Commercial Agriculture in Bengal, 1757-1900', Calcutta: Indian Studies Past and Present.

Cohn, B., 1996, *Colonialism and its Forms of Knowledge*: *The British in India*, Princeton: Princeton University Press.

———, 1987a, 'The Census, Social Structure and Objectification in South Asia', in *An Anthropologist among the Historians and Other Essays*: 224-54.

———, 1987b, *An Anthropologist among the Historians and Other Essays*, New York: Oxford University Press.

Cole, F.T., 1874, 'Santal Ideas of the Future', *The Indian Antiquary*, no. 7: 273-4.

———, 1875a, 'Santali Folklore', *The Indian Antiquary*, no. 4: 10, 12, 257-9.

———, 1875b, 'Santali Riddles', *The Indian Antiquary*, no. 4: 164.

———, 1896, *Santali Primer*, Pokharia: Santal Mission Press.

Comaroff, J.&J., 1991, *Of Revelation and Revolution: Christianity, Colonialism and Consciousness in South Africa*, vol. 1, Chicago: University of Chicago Press.

———, 1992, *Ethnography and the Historical Imagination*, Boulder: Westview Press.

Copley, A., 1997, *Religions in Conflict: Ideology, Cultural Contact and Conversion in Late Colonial India*, Delhi: Oxford University Press.

Corbridge, S., 1988, 'The ideology of tribal economy and society', *Modern Asian Studies*, 22: 1: 1-42, republished in S. Corbridge, S. Jewitt and S. Kumar: *Jharkhand: Environment, Development, Ethnicity*, Delhi, Oxford University Press: 2004: 17-55.

———, 1993, 'Ousting Singbonga: the Struggle for India's Jharkhand', in P. Robb (ed), *Dalit Movements and the Meanings of Labour in India*, Delhi: Oxford University Press: 121-50.

Crawford, S.C., 1987, *Ram Mohan Roy: Social, Political and Religious Reform in 19th Century India*, New York: Paragon.

Culshaw, W.J., 1949, *Tribal Heritage: A Study of the Santals*, London: Lutherworth.

Datta, K., 1940, *The Santal Insurrection, 1855-1857*, Calcutta: Calcutta University Press.

Day, L.B., 1855, *Bengal Peasant Life.* Reedition 1980, New York: AMS Press.

———, 1879, *Recollections of Alexander Duff, D.D., LL.D. and of The Mission College he founded in Calcutta*, London: Nelson.

De Certeau, M., 1975, *l'Ecriture de l'Histoire*, Paris: Gallimard.

De Haan, A. (1994), 'The Jute Industry and its Workers: Changes in Stratification in Eastern India', in S. Bandyopadhyay, A. Dasgupta and W. van Schendel (eds), *Bengal: Communities Development and States*, Delhi: Manohar.

Devalle, S.B.C., 1992, *Discourses of Ethnicity: Culture and Protest in Jharkhand*, Delhi: Sage.

Dirks, N.B., 1996, 'The Conversion of Caste: Location, Translation and Appropriation', in P. van der Veer (ed.) : 115-36.

Döhl, E., 1944, *Lars Skrefsrud*, Oslo: Fonna.

Draxten, N., 1976, *Kristofer Janson in America*, Boston: Twayne.

———, 1988, *The Testing of M. Falk Gjertsen*, Northfield, Minn.: The Norwegian-American Historical Association.

Dube, S., 1995, 'Paternalism and Freedom: The Evangelical Encounter in Colonial Chhattisgarh, Central India', *Modern Asian Studies* 29, 1: 171-200.

———, 1998, *Untouchable Pasts: Religion, Identity, and Power among a Central Indian Community, 1780-1950*, Albany: State University of New York Press.

Duff, W.P., 1890, *Memorials of Alexander Duff*, D.D. London: James Nisbet.

Dumont, L., 1966, *Homo Hierarchicus*, Paris: Gallimard.

———, 1979, Peuple et nation chez Herder et Fichte, *Libre*, no. 6: 233-50 (reprinted in *Essai sur l'individualisme,* Paris, 1983: Seuil).

Dumont, L., 1991, *Homo Aequalis, II. L'Idéologie Allemande: France-Allemagne et retour*, Paris: Gallimard.

Duyker, E., 1987, *Tribal Guerrillas: The Santals of West Bengal and the Naxalite Movement,* Delhi: Oxford University Press.

Eisenstadt, S.N. and S. Rokkan (eds), 1973, *Building States and Nations*, Beverly Hills: Sage.

Ekka, P., 1972, 'Revivalist Movements among the Tribals of Chotanagpur', in K.S. Singh (ed), *The Tribal Situation in India*, Simla and Delhi: Indian Institute of Advanced Study and Motilal Banarsidass: 424-31.

———, 1982, 'Reform Movement of Rajmohini Devi', in K.S. Singh (ed): *Tribal Movements in India*, vol II, Delhi: Manohar: 209-22.

Ellegaard, A., 1957, *The Readership of the Periodical Press in Mid-Victorian Britain*, Gothenburg: Almkvist and Wiksell.

Elwin, V., 1939, *The Baiga*, London: Murray.

———, 1944, *The Aboriginals*, London: Oxford University Press.

———, 1949, *Myths of Middle India*, Bombay: Oxford University Press.

———, 1955, *The Religion of an Indian Tribe*, Bombay: Oxford University Press.

Eschmann, A., H. Kulke and G.C. Tripathi (eds), 1978, *The Cult of Jagannath and the Regional Tradition of Orissa*, Delhi: Manohar.

Fenger, F.J., 1863, *History of the Tranquebar Mission*, Tranquebar: Evangelical Lutheran Mission Press.

Fichte, J.G., 1992, *Discours à la nation allemande*, Paris: Imprimerie nationale, éd. la Salamandre (1st German edn 1807).

Forrester, D.B., 1980, *Caste and Christianity: Attitudes and Policies on Caste of Anglo-Saxon Protestant Missionaries in India*, London: Curzon.

Fox Young, R., 2003, 'Receding from Antiquity: Hindu Responses to Science and Christianity on the Margins of Empire, 1800-1850', in R. Frykenberg (ed.): (q.v.): 183-222.

Frake, C.O., 1964, 'How to Ask for a Drink in Subanun', in J. Gumperz and D. Hymes (eds): *The Ethnography of Communication,* American Anthropologist Special Publication 66 (6), pt. 2, Washington D.C.

Freeman, J.M., 1979, *Untouchable: An Indian Life History*, Stanford: Stanford University Press.

Frere, B., 1873, *Indian Missions*, London (n.p.)

Frykenberg, R. (ed), 2003, *Christians and Missionaries in India: Cross-Cultural Communication since 1500*, Grand Rapids: William B. Eerdmans.

Fuchs, S., 1965, *Rebellious Prophets: A Study of Messianic Movements in Indian Religions*, Bombay: Asia Publishing House.

Fürer-Haimendorf, C. 1985, *Tribal Populations and Cultures of the Indian Subcontinent.* Leiden: E.I. Brill.

Gausdal, J., 1922, *Fra Assamkolonien*, Kristiania: Den Nordiske Santalmission.

———, 1929. *Tre Mindekranse*, Oslo: Santalmisjonens Forlag.

———, 1937, *Santalmisjonens historie paa misjonsmarken*, Oslo: Santalmisjonens Forlag.

———, 1960, *The Santal Khuts: Contribution to Animistic Research*, Oslo: Institutt for sammenlignende kulturforskning.

Gautam, M.K., 1977, *In Search of Identity: A Case of the Santal of Northern India*, Leiden: Thesis; Rijksunivesiteit te Leiden.

Ghose, J.M., 1901, *Sanyasi and Fakir Raiders of Bengal*, Calcutta: Bengal Secretariat Book Depot.

Ghosh, A., 1998, *Jharkhand Movement: A Study in the Politics of Regionalism*, Calcutta: Minerva Associates.

Ghosh, K.C., 1999, 'A Market for Aboriginality: Primitivism and Race Classification in the Indentured Labour Market of Colonial India', in G. Bhadra, G. Prakash and S. Tharu, *Subaltern Studies X*, Delhi: Oxford University Press: 8-48.

Ghurye, G.S., 1943, *The Aboriginals so-called and their Future*, Bombay: Popular Book Depot.

Gilbert, A.D., 1976, *Religion and Society in Industrial England: Church, Chapel and Social Change, 1740-1914*, London: Longman.

Giverholt, H., 1969a, 'Sverige: Historie' in *Aschehougs Konver-sasjonsleksikon*, 18: 397-413, Oslo: Aschehoug.

———, 1969b, 'Danmark: Historie', in *Aschehougs Konversasjonsleksikon*, 4: 523-41, Oslo: Aschehoug.

Gjesing, K., 1961, *En Missionspioner, H. P. Börresens liv med saerlig henblik paa hans missionsvirksomhed*, København: G.E.C. Gad.

Gjesing-Pedersen, K., 1953, *Santalmisjonen i Fortid og Nutid,* København. Santalmisjonens Forlag.

Gluckman, M., 1940, 'Analysis of a Social Situation in Modern Zululand', *Bantu Studies*, XIV, reprinted separately 1958, Manchester: Manchester University Press for Rhodes-Livingstone Institute.

Gosselin, G., 1987, 'Sur l'individualisme norvégien', *Informations sur les Sciences Sociales*, 26, 4: 803-15.

Graham, A., 1875, *The Gospel in Santhalistan: By an Old Indian*, London: the Author.

———, 1881, *The Experence and Prospects of the Christian Colony at Goalpara in its first Year*, Edinburgh: the Author.

Gray, J., 1975, 'Bengal and Britain: Culture Contact and the Reinterpretation of Hinduism in the XIX Century', in R. van Baumer (ed), *Aspects of Bengali Economy and Society*, East Lansing: University of Michigan Press.

Guha, R., 1963, *A Rule of Property for Bengal: An Essay on the Idea of Permanent Settlement*, Paris: Mouton.

———, 1983, *Elementary Aspects of Peasant Insurgency in Colonial India,* Delhi: Oxford University Press.

———, 1998, *Dominance without Hegemony: History and Power in Colonial India*, Delhi: Oxford University Press.

Gullestad, M., 1992, *The Art of Social Relations*, Oslo: Scandinavian University Press.

Gupta, R.K., 1977, 'Agricultural Developments in a Bengal District: Birbhum, 1793-1852', *Indian Historical Review*, 4, 1 July 1977: 47-74.

Gupta, S., 1999, 'Hindu Woman, the Ritualist', in H. Tambs-Lyche (ed): *The Feminine Sacred in South Asia*, Delhi: Manohar: 88-99.

Hadders, H., 2001, *The Gift of the Eye: Mortuary Ritual Performed by the Jadopatias in the Santal Villages of Bengal and Bihar, India*, Trondheim: Trondheim Occasional Papers in Social Anthropology.

Hall, B., 1922, *Lars Skrefsud: En Folkebog*, Kristiania: Björnstad.

Hamilton, W., 1828, *The East India Gazetteer*, 2 vols, 2nd edn., London: W.H. Allen.

Hamre, J.S., 1986, *Georg Sverdrup: Educator, Theologian, Churchman*, Northfield: The Norwegian-American Historical Association.

Hannerz, U., 1992, *Cultural Complexity: Studies in the Social Organization of Meaning*, New York: Columbia University Press.

Hardiman, D., 1995, *The Coming of the Devi*, Delhi: Oxford University Press.

Haynes, D. and G. Prakash, 1991, *Contesting Power, Resistance and Everyday Social Relations in South Asia*, Delhi: Oxford University Press.

Heggtveit, H.G., 1905/1920, *Den norske Kirke i det nittende Aarhundrede*, vols I-II, Oslo: Cammermeyer.

Herder, J.G., 1964, *Une autre Philosophie de l'histoire*, Paris: Aubier (1st German edn. 1774).

Hertel, L., 1877, *Indisk Hjemmemisjon blandt Santalerne,* Kolding: Indisk Hjemmemisjon: C.A. Topp.

———, 1884, *Den nordiske Santhalmission,* Köbenhavn: Lehmann & Stage.

———, 1892, *För og nu. Guds Gjerninge i Santhalistan i 25 aar,* Copenhagen: Foreningen til Gudelige Smaaskrifters Utbredelse.

Heuman, E., 1892, 'Gramatisk studie öfver Santal-språket', in *Oversigt over det Kongelige Danske Videnskabernes Selskabs forhandlinger* . . . Copenhagen: 148-230.

Hjellestad, H., 1933, *Fana-boki*, vols. I-II, Bergen: Beyer.

Hobsbawm, E., 1964, *Labouring Men: Studies in the History of Labour*, London: Weidenfeld and Nicholson.

Hodne, O., 1950, *I gode og onde dager, Anna Onsum Skrefsrud 1838-1870,* Oslo: Santalmisjonens Forlag.

———, 1966, *L.O. Skrefsrud: Missionary and Social Reformer among the Santals of Santal Parganas,* Oslo: Land og Kirke.

———, 1992, *Santalmisjonens Historie*, III, Oslo: Santalmisjonens Forlag.

Hoffmann, J. and J. Van Emelen, 1950, *Encyclopaedia Mundarica,* 13 vols., Patna, Superintendent Government Printing; rpt. 1990, New Delhi: Gyan.

Holmquist, H. and J. Nörregaard, 1939, *Kristendommens Historie i Romantikens, Liberalismens og Realismens Tidsalder*, vols. I-II, Copenhagen: J.H. Schultz forlag.

Holsten, W., 1949, *Johannes Evangelista Gossner*, Göttingen: Vandenhoeck & Ruprecht.

Howells, G., 1927, *The Story of Serampore and its College*, Serampore: Serampore College.

Hulin, F., 1979, *Hegel et l'Orient*, Paris: Vrin.

Hunter, W.W., 1875, *Statistical Account of Bengal*, vol. XIV, London: Trübner.

———, 1894, *Bengal Manuscript Records*, a Selected list . . . with an Historical Dissertation and Analytical Index, London: W.H. Allen.

———, 1976/1877, *Statistical Account of Bengal*, vol. XVII, Original edition, London, 1877: Trübner; rpt. Delhi: Concept.

———, 1975, *The Annals of Rural Bengal* (VII edn), London, 1897, Original edition 1868; rpt., 1975, Delhi: Concept.

Inden, R.B., 1976, *Marriage and Rank in Bengali Culture*, Delhi: Vikas.

———, 1990, *Imagining India*, Oxford: Blackwell.

Ingold, T., 1986, 'Comments' to A. Beteille: 'Individualism and Equality', *Current Anthropology*, 27, 1: 129-30.

Jayawardena, C., 1968, 'Ideology and Conflict in Lower Class Communities', *Comparative Studies in Society and History,* 10: 413-46.

Jeffery, P. and A. Basu (ed), 1998, *Appropriating Gender: Women's Activism and Politicized Religion in South Asia*, London: Routledge.

Jellinghaus, T., 1878, *Das Evangelium in Santalistan*, Basel: Verlag der Missionsbuchhandlung.

Jensen, M., 1963, *Norges Historie, 1814-1905*, Oslo: Univers-itetsforlaget.

Jensen, M.C., 1888, 'Tolv Billeder fra Santhalistan med Text', Copenhagen: Lehmann & Stage.

Jha, J.C., 1964, *The Kol Insurrection of Chotanagpur*, Calcutta: Thacker, Spink.

———, 1967, *The Bhumij Revolt, 1832-33*, Delhi: Munshiram Manoharlal.

Jolly, M., 1996, 'Devils, Holy Spirits, and the Swollen God: Translation, Conversion and Colonial Power in the Marist Mission, Vanuatu, 1887-1934', in P. van der Veer (ed.): *Conversion to Modernities*.

Jörgensen, H.F., 1920, *Evangeliet blandt Santalerne: Den Nordiske Santalmissions Historie*, Copenhagen: Den Nordiske Santalmission.

Kaarsholm, P. and J. Hultin (eds), 1994, *Inventions and Boundaries: Historical and Anthropological Approaches to the Study of Ethnicity and Nationalism*, *Occasional Papers no. 11*, Roskilde: Roskilde University.

Kantorowicz, E.H., 1957, *The King's Two Bodies*, Princeton: Princeton University Press.

Karlsson, B.G., 2000, *Contested Belonging: An Indigenous People's Struggle for Forest and Identity in Sub-Himalayan Bengal*, London: Curzon.

Kaviraj, S., 1993, 'The Imaginary Institution of India', in P. Chatterjee and G. Pandey (eds), *Subaltern Studies VII*, Delhi: Oxford University Press.

———, 1994, 'Religion, Politics and Modernity', in P. Kaarsholm and J. Hultin (eds), *Inventions and Boundaries*: 163-83.

Keesing, R.M., 1981, *Cultural Anthropology*, New York: Holt, Rinehart & Winston.

———, 1992, *Custom and Confrontation: the Kwaio Struggle for Cultural Autonomy*, Chicago: University of Chicago Press.

Kent, J., 1978, *Holding the Fort: Studies in Victorian Revivalism*, London: Epworth Press.

Kipling, R., 1938, *Lidt om mig selv*, (Danish translation of *Something of Myself*), Copenhagen: Gyldendal.

Kitson Clark, G., 1967, *An Expanding Society: Britain 1830-1900,* Cambridge: Cambridge University Press.

Kling, B., 1975, 'Economic Foundations of the Bengal Renaissance', in R. van Baumer (ed), *Aspects of Bengali Economy and Society*, Honolulu: University Press of Hawaii: 26-42.

Kopf, D., 1969, *British Orientalism and the Bengal Renaissance*, Berkeley: University of California Press.

———, 1975, 'The Universal Man and the Yellow Dog: The Orientalist Legacy and the Problem of Brahmo Identity in the Bengal Renaissance', in R. van Baumer (ed): *Aspects of Bengali History and Society*, Honolulu: University Press of Hawaii: 43-81.

———, 1979, *The Brahmo Samaj and the Shaping of the Modern Indian Mind,* Princeton: Princeton University Press.

Kosambi, D.D., 1975, *An Introduction to the Study of Indian History* (revd. 2nd edn.), Bombay: Popular Prakashan.

Kramer, J., 1984, 'Norsk identitet–et produkt av underutvikling og stammetilhörighet', in A.M. Klausen (ed.), *Den norske vaeremaaten,* Oslo: Cappelen.

Kulke, H., 1976, 'Ksatriyaization and Social Change in Post-Medieval Orissa', in S.D. Pillai (ed): *Changing India: Studies in Honour of Professor G.S. Ghurye,* Bombay: Popular Prakashan.

Kullerud, D., 1996, *Hans Nielsen Hauge: Mannen som vekket Norge,* Oslo: Aschehoug.

Kuriakose, M.K., 1982, *History of Christianity in India: Source Materials,* Madras: The Christian Literature Society.

Laird, M.A., 1972, *Missionaries and Education in Bengal, 1793-1837,* Oxford: Clarendon.

Lakoff, G. and M. Johnson, 1980, *Metaphors we live by*, Chicago: University of Chicago Press.

Leiren, T.I., 1987, *Marcus Thrane: A Norwegian Radical in America*, Northfield, Minn.: The Norwegian-American Historical Association.

Lewis, C.B., 1878, *Second Memorandum on the Santal Mission,* printed MS: Calcutta: the Author.

Liebau, H., 2003, 'Country Priests, Catechists, and Schoolmasters as Cultural, Religious, and Social Middlemen in the Context of the Tranquebar Mission', in R. Frykenberg (ed:) (q.v.): 70-92.

Lokies, H., 1956, *Johannes Gossner*, Giessen n.p.

Lovett, R., 1899, *The History of the London Missionary Society, 1795-1895*, I-II, London: H. Frowde.

Ludvigsen, H.G., 1952, *All Heart: Life Story of H.P. Börresen,* Blair: Lutheran Publishing House.

Löfgren, O., 1980, Historical Perspectives on Scandinavian Peasantries, *Annual Review of Anthropology*, 9: 187-215.

Löth, J.K., 1914, *L.O. Skrefsrud: Missionär blandt Santalerne*, Copenhagen: Lehmann & Stage.

———, 1916, *Den Nordiske Santalmission i tekst og billede*, Copenhagen: Den Nordiske Santalmission.

———, 1919, *Gjennom Kamp: Santalmissionens Begyndelse*, Kristiania: Den Nordiske Santalmission.

Macphail, J.M., 1893, *Four Months on Tour: A Sequel to Three Months in Camp*, Pokhuria: Santal Mission Press.

———, 1904, *Missions of the United Free Church of Scotland: Santalia*, Edinburgh: United Free Church Publication Office.

———, 1913, 'The Cycle of Seasons in a Santal Village', *The Calcutta Review*, n.s., 159-68.

———, 1922, *The Story of the Santal with an account of the Santal Rebellion*, Calcutta: Thacker, Spink.

Macphail, R.M., 1964, *An Introduction to Santali* (3rd edn): Benagaria: The Santal Literature Board, Santalia Christian Council.

MacPherson, S.C., 1865, *Memorials of Service in India, from the Correspondence of the Late Samuel Charters MacPherson, C.B., Political Agent at Gwalior during the Mutiny and Formerly Employed in the Suppression of Human Sacrifice in Orissa*, edited by his brother, London: Murray.

Mahapatra, L.K., 1978, 'Gods, Kings and the Caste System in India', in K. David (ed): *The New Wind. Changing Identities in South Asia*, The Hague: Mouton: 159-78.

———, 1987, 'Ex-Princely States of Orissa: Mayurbhanj, Keonjhar and Bonai', in S. Sinha (ed): *Tribal Polities and State Systems in Pre-Colonial Eastern and North Eastern India*, Calcutta: K.P. Bagchi.

Majumdar, R.C., 1960, *Glimpses of Bengal in the Nineteenth Century*, Calcutta: KLM.

———, 1963, *British Paramountcy and Indian Renaissance*, Bombay: Bharatiya Itihasa Samiti.

Man, E.G., 1867, *Sonthalia and the Sonthals*, Calcutta: George Wyman.

Marriott, Mckim (ed), 1955, *Village India: Studies in the Little Community*, Chicago: University of Chicago Press.

Marshall, P.J., 1976, *East Indian Fortunes: The British in Bengal in the Eighteenth Century,* Oxford: Clarendon.

Mason, P., 1985, *The Men Who Ruled India*, London: Pan Books.

McAlpin, M.C., 1909, *Report on the Condition of the Santals*, Calcutta: Bengal Secretariat Book Depot.

McLeod, H., 1974, *Class and Religion in the Late Victorian City*, Hamdon, Conn.: Archon Press.

———, 1984, *Religion and the Working Class in Nineteenth Century Britain*, London: Macmillan.

Mcpherson, H., 1909, *Final Report on the Survey and Settlement Operations in the District of Santal Parganas, 1868-1907*, Calcutta: Bengal Secretariat Book Depot.

Metcalf, T.R., 1990, *The Aftermath of Revolt: India, 1857-1870,* 2nd edn.: Princeton and Delhi: Princeton University Press and Manohar.

———, 1995, *Ideologies of the Raj: The New Cambridge History of India,* III.4, Cambridge: Cambridge University Press.

Mill, James, 1818, *History of British India*, 2nd edn. 1972: Delhi: Associated Publishing House.

Mill, John S., 1863, *On Liberty,* Boston: Ticknow and Fields.

———, 1874, *Nature, the Utility of Religion, and Theism*, London: n.p.

Molland, E., 1951, *Fra Hans Nielsen Hauge til Eivind Berggrav*, Oslo: Gyldendal.

———, 1969a, Haugianere, in: *Aschehougs Konversasjonsleksikon,* 8: 672, Oslo: Aschehoug.

———, 1969b, Brödremenigheten, in *Aschehougs Konversasjonsleksikon,* 3: 456-7, Oslo: Aschehoug.

———, 1969c, Herrnhut, in *Aschehougs Konversasjonsleksikon,* 8: 979, Oslo: Aschehoug.

———, 1969d, 'Gossner, Johannes Evangelista', in *Aschehougs Konversasjonsleksikon,* 7: 967-8, Oslo: Aschehoug.

———, 1969 e, Sverige: Religion, in *Aschehougs Konversasjonsleksikon,* 18: 369-70, Oslo: Aschehoug.

Moltke, E., 1885, *Santhal-kolonien i Assam,* Copenhagen: Kjöbenhavns Komité for Santhalmissionen.

Moorat, M.A.C., 1925, *Alfred and Eliza Stark*, Calcutta: published privately.

Moore-Gilbert, B.J., 1986, *Kipling and Orientalism*, New York: St. Martin's Press.

———, 1997, *Postcolonial Theory: Contexts, Practices, Politics*, London: Verso.

Moorhouse, G., 1974, *Calcutta*, Harmondsworth: Penguin.

Morgenstierne, G. and O.G. Myklebust, 1958, 'Lars Skrefsrud', in *Norsk Biografisk Leksikon,* fasc. 66, Oslo: Aschehoug.

Morris, J., 1978, *Farewell the Trumpets: An Imperial Retreat*, Harmondsworth: Penguin.

Mukherjee, S.N., 1978, 'The Social Implications of the Political Thought of Raja Rammohan Roy', in R.S. Sharma and V. Jha: *Indian Society: Historical Probings*, Delhi: People's Publishing House: 356-89.

Mukherji, S., 1975, 'A Chapter on the Tribal Sources of Bengal History in the Muslim Period', *Bulletin of the Cultural Research Institute*, 11, 1-2: 20-4.

Mukhopadhyay, A.K., 1979, *The Bengali Intellectual Tradition*, Calcutta: K.P. Bagchi.

Murmu, S., 1945, *Karam ar caco chatiar,* Benagaria: Mission Press.

Murmu, C., 1938, *Chotrae Desmanjhi Reak' Katha* (in Santali), Benagaria: Mission Press, rpt. 1964.

Nuttall, G.F., 1951, *Richard Baxter and Philip Doddridge: A Study in a Tradition,* Friends of Dr. Williams Library 5th Lecture, London.

———, 1965, *Richard Baxter*, London: Nelson.

Nyhagen, J., 1990, *Santalmisjonens Historie,* vols. I-II, Oslo: Santalmisjonens Forlag.

Oddie, G.A., 1979, *Social Protest in India: British Protestant Missionaries and Social Reforms, 1850-1900*, Delhi: Manohar.

———, 1994, "Orientalism' and British Protestant Missionary Constructions of India in the Nineteenth Century', *South Asia*, XXVII, 2: 27-42.

———, 1995, *Popular Religion, Elites and Reform: Hook-Swinging and its Prohibition in Colonial India, 1800-1894*, Delhi: Manohar.

———, 1999, *Missionaries, Rebellion and Proto-Nationalism: James Long of Bengal, 1814-87*, London: Curzon.

——— (ed) 1973, *Religion in South Asia: Religions and Conversion Movements in South Asia in Medieval and Modern Times,* London: Curzon.

Odner, K., 1996, Norsk makt, likhet og moral: Eksempler fra Hedmarken, *Norsk Antropologisk Tidsskrift,* no. 2: 149-59.

———, 2000, *Tradition and Transmission: Bantu, Indo-European and Circumpolar Great Traditions,* Bergen: Norse.

O' Hanlon, R., 1988, 'Recovering the Subject: Subaltern Studies and Histories of Resistance in Colonial South Asia', *Modern Asian Studies* 22, no. I: 189-224.

O'Malley, L.S.S., 1910, *Bengal District Gazetteers, Santal Parganas,* Calcutta: Bengal Secretariat Book Depot.

———, 1911, *Bengal District Gazetteers, Midnapore*, Calcutta: Bengal Secretariat Book Depot.

Padel, F., 1995, *The Sacrifice of Human Being: British Rule and the Konds of Orissa,* Delhi: Oxford University Press.

Palit, C., 1975, *Tensions in Bengal Rural Society*, Calcutta: Progressive Publishers.

Parkin, R., 1992, *The Munda of Central India,* Delhi: Oxford University Press.

Pearson, H., 1835, *Memoirs of the Life and Correspondence of the Rev. Christian Schwartz*, London: J. Hatchard & Sons.

Pfeffer, G., 1997, 'The Scheduled Tribes of Middle India as a Unit: Problems of Internal and External Comparison, in D.K. Behera and G. Pfeffer (eds): *Contemporary Society: Tribal Studies I: Structure and Process,* Delhi: Concept: 3–27.

Phillips, J., 1852, *An Introduction to the Santal Language*, Calcutta: Calcutta School Book Society Press.

Poddar, A., 1970, *Renaissance in Bengal*, Simla: Indian Institute of Advanced Studies.

Poffenberger, M., 1995, 'The Resurgence of the Community Forest Management in the Jungle Mahals of West Bengal', in D. Arnold and R. Guha (eds), *Nature, Culture, Imperialism*, Delhi: Oxford University Press: 336-69.

Potts, E.D., 1967, *British Baptist Missionaries in India, 1793-1837,* Cambridge: Cambridge University Press.

Pouchepadass, J., 1990, *The Ecological History of the Central Western Ghats in the Modern Period: A Preliminary Survey*, Pondicherry: IFP.

Preus, A.H., 1990, *Vivacious Daughter: The Norwegian Church in America*, Northfield, Minn.: The Norwegian American Historical Association.

Puxley, E.L., 1868, *A Vocabulary of the Santali Language*, London: W.W. Watts.

Ramberg, O., 1994, *I dögnets tjeneste: Avishuset Gudbrandsdölen Lillehammer Tilskuers historie I*, Lillehammer: GLT.

Ranger, T., 1994, 'The Invention of Tradition Revisited', in P.H. Kaarsholm and J. Hultin (eds), *Inventions and Boundaries:* 9-50.

Rao, A. and B.G. Rao, 1992, *The Blue Devil: Indigo and Colonial Bengal*, Delhi: Oxford University Press.

Ray, A.K., 1982, *A Short History of Calcutta Town and Suburbs* (reprint from Census of India, 1901, vol. VII, pt.1), re-edited by N.R. Ray, Calcutta.

Ray, R., 1979, *Change in Bengal Agrarian Society*, Delhi: Manohar.

Ray, R.K., 1984, *Social Conflict and Political Unrest in Bengal, 1875-1927*, Delhi: Oxford University Press.

Ray, T., 1983, *Santal Rebellion: Documents,* Calcutta: Subarnarekha.

Renan, E., 1992, *Qu'est-ce qu'une nation? et autres essais politiques*, Paris: Presses Pocket, collection Agora.

Revel, J., 1996, *Jeux d'échelles: la micro-analyse à l'expérience*, Paris: Gallimard-Seuil.

Risley, H.H., 1891, *The Tribes and Castes of Bengal*, vol. II, Calcutta: Bengal Secretariat Press.

Robb, P., 1997, 'The Colonial State and Constructions of Indian Identity: An Example on the Northeast Frontier in the 1880s', *Modern Asian Studies,* 31, 2: 245-83.

———, 2000, 'Credit, Work and Race in 1790s Calcutta: Early Colonialism through a Contemporary European View', *The Indian Economic and Social History Review*, 37, 1, 2000: 1-25.

——— (ed), 1993, *Dalit Movements and the Meanings of Labour in India*, Delhi: Oxford University Press.

——— (ed), 1995, *The Concept of Race in South Asia,* Delhi: Oxford University Press.

Rolt, L.T.C., 1970, *Victorian Engineering*, Harmondsworth: Penguin.

Rothermund, D. and D.C. Wadhwa., 1978, *Zamindars, Mines and Peasants: Studies in the History of an Indian Coalfield and its Rural Hinterland*, Delhi: Manohar.

Rottger-Hogan, E., 1982, 'Insurrection or Ostracism: A Study of the Santal Rebellion of 1855', *Contributions to Indian Sociology*, vol. 16, no. 1, 1982: 79-96.

Roy Chaudhury, P.C., 1965, *Bihar District Gazetteers: Santal Parganas*, Patna: Secretariat Press.

Roy, Rammohun, 1945, *English Works* (ed. K. Nag and D. Burman), Calcutta: Sadharan Brahmo Samaj.

Roy, N.B., 1961, 'More light on the Santal Insurrection', in *Historical Records Commission Proceedings* (Chandigarh), vol. 36, p. 2: 61-72.

Roy, S.C., 1912, *The Munda and their Country*, Calcutta: City Book Society.

———, 1915, *The Oraons of Chota Nagpur*, Calcutta: The Brahmo Mission Press.

———, 1925, *The Birhor: A Little Known Jungle Tribe of Chota Nagpur*, Ranchi: Man in India Office.

Rönning, N.N., 1940, *Lars Skrefsrud: An Apostle to the Santals*, Minneapolis: The Santal Mission in America.

Saeter, I., 1940, *Skrefsrud*, Oslo: Gyldendal.

Sahlins, M.D., 1985, *Islands of History*, Chicago: University of Chicago Press.

Said, E., 1978, *Orientalism: Western Conceptions of the Orient*, London: Routledge & Kegan Paul.

Samaddar, R.S., 1998, *Memory, Identity, Power: Politics in the Jungle Mahals (West Bengal) 1890-1950*, Hyderabad: Sangam Books.

Schütz, A., 1962, *Collected Papers I: The Problem of Social Reality*, The Hague: Martinus Nijhoff.

Scott, J.C., 1987, *Weapons of the Weak: Everyday Forms of Peasant Resistance*, New Haven: Yale University Press.

———, 1990, *Domination and The Arts of Resistance, Hidden Transcripts*, New Haven: Yale University Press.

Sen, A.P., 1993, *Hindu Revivalism in Bengal 1872-1905*, Delhi: Oxford University Press.

Sen, J., 1968, *Community Development in Chotanagpur*, Calcutta: The Asiatic Society.

Sen, S., 1984, *The Santals of the Jungle Mahals*: Calcutta: Ratna Prakashan.

———, 1997, *The Santals: Crises of Identity and Integration*, Calcutta: Ratna Prakashan.

Sharma, J., 2003, 'Missionaries and Print Culture in Nineteenth-Century Assam: The Orunodoi Periodical of the American Baptist Mission', in R. Frykenberg (ed.) (q.v.): 256-73.

Sher, R., 1985, *Church and University in the Scottish Enlightenment*, Edinburgh: Edinburgh University Press.

Sherring, M.A., 1884, *The History of Protestant Missions in India* (2nd edn.), London: The Religious Tract Society.

Sherwill, W.S., 1851, 'Notes upon a Tour through the Rajmahal Hills', *Journal of the Asiatic Society of Bengal*, vol. 20 (7): 544-606.

Shore, J., 1795, 'On Some Extraordinary Facts, Customs and Practices of the Hindus', *Asiatick Researches*, Calcutta, vol. 4: 331-50.

Singh, K.S., 1983, *Birsa Munda and his Movement 1874-1901: A Study of a Millenarian Movement in Chotanagpur*, Delhi: Oxford University Press.

———, 1987, 'Chhotanagpur Raj: Mythology, Structure and Ramifications', in S. Sinha (ed.), *Tribal Polities and State Systems in Pre-Colonial Eastern and North Eastern India*, Calcutta: K.P. Bagchi: 51-72.

Sinha, S., 1957, 'The Media and Nature of Bhumij-Hindu Interactions', *Journal of the Asiatic Society of Bengal*, 23, 1: 23-37.

——— (ed), 1987, *Tribal Polities and State Systems in Pre-Colonial Eastern and North Eastern India*, Calcutta: K.P. Bagchi.

Sivaramakrishnan, K., 1999, *Modern Forests, Statemaking and Environmental Change in Colonial Eastern India,* Delhi: Oxford University Press.

Skard, S. 1976, *USA i Norsk Historie*, Oslo: Det Norske Samlaget.

Skaria, A., 1998, Being *jangli*: the Politics of Wildness, *Studies in History*, 14, 2, n.s.: 194-215.

———, 1999, *Hybrid Histories: Forests, Frontiers and Wilderness in Western India*, Delhi: Oxford University Press.

Skrefsrud, L.O., 1873, *A Grammar of the Santhal Language*, Benares: Medical Hall Press.

———, 1876, *What is the Correct Term for God in Santali?* Benares: Medical Hall Press.

———, 1877, *The Indian Home Mision to the Santals*, Benagaria: Mission Press.

———, 1881a, 'The Santhal Land Settlement', *Friend of India*, 3 Nov. 1881.

———, 1881b, *Tvende foredrag,* Arendal. (n.p.)

———, 1887, *Horkoren Mare Hapramko reak' Katha,* Benagaria: Mission Press.

———, 1892, *En kort beretning om santalmisjonen og dens grunnleggere*, Minneapolis: n.p.

———, 1897, Praedikener og Foredrag, I-II, Minneapolis: Ungdommens Ven's trykkeri.

———, 1903, 'Marriage amongst the Santals', *Journal of the Asiatic Society of Bengal*, 72, 3: 90.

———, 1942, *Traditions and Institutions of the Santals, Horkoren Mare Hapramko reak' Katha*, Bilingual edition translated by and with an introduction by P.O. Bodding, Oslo, 1942; rpt. 1994 by Bahamukhi Prakashan, New Delhi.

Söderblom, N., 1923, *Waldemar Rudins inre liv*, Stockholm: Bonnier.

Soren, S.K., 1999, *Santalia: Catalogue of Santali Manuscripts in Oslo*, Copenhagen: NIAS.

Spurr, D., 1993, *The Rhetoric of Empire*, Durham: Duke University Press.

Srinivas, M.N., 1952, *Religion and Society among the Coorg*, Oxford: Clarendon.

———, 1962, *Caste in Modern India and Other Essays*, Berkeley: University of California Press.

———, 1967, *Social Change in Modern India*, Berkeley: University of California Press.

Stern, H., 1986, 'Le temple d'Eklingji et le royaume du Mewar (Rajasthan)', *Purusartha* 10: 15-30.

Stock, E., 1899-1916, *History of the Church Missionary Society*, I-II, London: Church Missionary Society.

Stoler, A.L. and F. Cooper (eds.), 1997, *Tensions of Empire: Colonial Cultures in a Bourgeois World*, Berkeley: University of California Press.

Storstein, O., 1949, *Kielland paa ny*, Oslo: Gyldendal.

Sundar, N., 1997, *Subalterns and Sovereigns: An Anthropological History of Bastar 1854-1996*, Delhi: Oxford University Press.

Sundt, E., 1855/1967, *Om Giftermal i Norge,* Oslo: Universitetsforlaget.

———, 1857/1968, *Om Sedelighetstilstanden i Norge,* Oslo: Universitetsforlaget.

Tambs-Lyche, H., 1991, 'Heroes in the Hills, Power in the Plains: Patterns of Traditional Leadership in Western South Asia', in R. Grönhaug, G. Haaland and G. Henriksen (eds): *The Ecology of Choice and Symbol*, Bergen: Alma Mater: 121-38.

———, 1994, 'Ethnic Groups and Boundaries; Nordic Schools of Approach', in P. Kaarsholm and J. Hultin (eds.), *Inventions and Boundaries*: 51-73.

Thapar, R. and H.M. Siddiqi, 2003, 'Chotanagpur: the Pre-colonial and Colonial Situation', in R.D. Munda and S. Boru Mullick, *The Jharkhand Movement: Indigenous People: Struggle for Autonomy in India*. Copenhagen: IWGIA.

Thompson, E.P., 1968, *The Making of the English Working Class*, Harmondsworth: Penguin.

Thorne, S., 1997, 'The Conversion of Englishmen and the Conversion of the World Inseparable: Missionary Imperialism and the Language of Class in Early Industrial Britain', in Stoler and Cooper, 1997: 238-62.

Tinker, H., 1974, *A New System of Slavery: The Export of Indian Labour Overseas, 1830-1920*, Oxford: Oxford University Press.

Todorov, T., 1977, *Symbolisme et interprétation*, Paris: Seuil.

Tomlinson, B.R., 1993, *The Economy of Modern India, 1860-1970,* The New Cambridge History of India, III.3, Cambridge: Cambridge University Press.

Trevelyan, G.M., 1944, *English Social History,* London: Longmans, Green.

———, 1964, *Illustrated British Social History*, vol. 4, Harmondsworth: Penguin.

Van der Veer, P., 2001, *Imperial Encounters, Religion and Modernity in India and Britain*. Princeton: Princeton University.

——— (ed), 1996, *Conversion to Modernities,* London: Routledge.

Vidyarthi, L.P., 1964, *Cultural Contours of Tribal Bihar*, Calcutta: Punthi Pustak.

Viswanathan Peterson, I., 2003, 'Tanjore, Tranquebar, and Halle: European Science and German Missionary Education in the Lives of Two

Indian Intellectuals in the Early Nineteenth Century', in R. Frykenberg (ed.): (q.v.): 93-126.

Vitebsky, P., 1993, *Dialogues with the Dead*, Cambridge: Cambridge University Press.

Waddell, L.A., 1893, 'The Traditional Migration of the Santal Tribe', *The Indian Antiquary*, 22, Oct: 294-96.

Weber, M., 1930, *The Protestant Ethic and the Spirit of Capitalism*, London: Allen and Unwin.

Wenger, E.S., 1908, *The Story of the Lall Bazar Baptist Church*, Calcutta: Edinburgh Press.

White, Hayden., 1978, *Tropics of Discourse: Essays in Cultural Criticism*, Baltimore: The Johns Hopkins Press.

Wislöff, C.F., 1971, *Norsk Kirkehistorie,* III, Oslo: Lutherstiftelsen.

Young, G.M., 1936, *Victorian England: Portrait of an Age*, London: Oxford University Press.

Yule, G., 1858a, 'Report on the Sonthal Pergunnahs for 1858', in *Man* 1867, Appendix: 22-7.

Zastoupil, L. and M. Moir, 1999, Introduction, in *The Great Indian Education Debate*, London: Curzon.

Zide, N., (ed) 1966, *Studies in Comparative Austro-Asiatic Linguistics*, The Hague: Mouton.

Zide, N. and R. Munda, 1969, 'Revolutionary Birsa and the Songs Related to Him', *Journal of Social Research* (Ranchi), 2, 37-60.

## PERIODICALS

*Dahkwala, Tidsskrift for indisk hjemmemisjon blandt Santhalerne*, Div. no., 1880-97.

## LETTERS, MANUSCRIPTS AND OTHER UNPUBLISHED SOURCES

Bidwell, A.C., 1855, *Letter to the Secretary, Government of Bengal (February 10th)*, British Library, India Office Collections.

———, 1856, *Letter to M. Grey, Secretary, Government of Bengal (February 14th)*, British Library, India Office Collections.

Croft, R., 1881, *General Report of the Director of Public Instruction, Bengal, for the year 1880-81*, British Library, India Office Collection.

Kullgren, A.L., *Gången af mitt lif I-III*, Autobiographical Journal covering the years 1845-93, Gothenburg, University Library.

Letters From Missionaries—the following collections have been consulted: Hertel collections, City Library, Aarhus; letters from Skrefsrud,

Oslo University Library; Letters to Kullgren, Gothenburg City Library; Letters to Rudin, Uppsala University Library.

Malme, A. (n.d.), 'The Pioneer Era of the Santal Mission of the Northern Churches, 1867-1910', 3 vols., unpublished Ph.D. thesis.

Santal Manuscripts, collection Santalia, University Library, Oslo: MS 1469, Santalia 2467, *Hul Pahil Reak' Katha*, Santalia 1969, *Hul Reak' Katha*, MS 1448D, Santalia 0684, *Babajiu ko Reak' Katha*, MS 1886, part 5, *Hul Reak' Katha.*

Skrefsrud, L.O., 1877, *Answers to the Ethnological Questionary of H.H. Risley*, Ebenezer, manuscript.

Yule, G., 1856, *Sonthal Police Rules*, Brochure, India Office.

———, 1858b, *Rules for Civil Procedure*, Brochure, India Office.

# Index